Getting "Saved"

THE WHOLE STORY OF SALVATION
IN THE NEW TESTAMENT

Charles H. Talbert and Jason A. Whitlark

with other contributions by

A. E. Arterbury
C. A. Barbarick
S. J. Hafemann
M. W. Martin

WILLIAM B. EERDMANS PUBLISHING COMPANY
GRAND RAPIDS, MICHIGAN / CAMBRIDGE, U.K.

Published 2011 by
Wm. B. Eerdmans Publishing Co.
2140 Oak Industrial Drive N.E., Grand Rapids, Michigan 49505 /
P.O. Box 163, Cambridge CB3 9PU U.K.

Printed in the United States of America

17 16 15 14 13 12 11   7 6 5 4 3 2 1

Library of Congress Cataloging-in-Publication Data

Talbert, Charles H.
    Getting "saved": the whole story of salvation in the New Testament /
    Charles H. Talbert and Jason A. Whitlark ; with other contributions
    by A.E. Arterbury ... [et al.].
        p.   cm.
    Includes bibliographical references and index.
    ISBN 978-0-8028-6648-6 (pbk.: alk. paper)
    1. Salvation — Biblical teaching.   2. Bible. N.T. — Theology.
    I. Whitlark, Jason A.   II. Arterbury, Andrew E.   III. Title.

    BS2545.S25T35   2011
    234 — dc22

                                                    2011008321

www.eerdmans.com

Contents

Contents

PART II. GOSPELS

PART III. CATHOLIC EPISTLES

PART IV. REVELATION

Acknowledgments

Many of the essays in this volume have appeared elsewhere and are used with permission here. "Enabling Χάρις: Transformation of the Convention of Reciprocity by Philo and in Ephesians" by Jason Whitlark is a revision of an article that appeared originally in *Perspectives in Religious Studies* 30 (2003): 325-58. "Ἔμφυτος Λόγος: A New Covenant Motif in the Letter of James" by Jason Whitlark appeared as an article in the Brill journal *Horizons in Biblical Theology* 32 (2010): 144-65. "Fidelity and New Covenant Enablement in Hebrews" by Jason Whitlark is a revision of chapter 4 in *Enabling Fidelity to God: Perseverance in Hebrews in Light of Reciprocity Systems in the Ancient Mediterranean World* published by Paternoster Press, 2008. "Paul, Judaism, and the Revisionists" by Charles Talbert appeared as an article in *Catholic Biblical Quarterly* 63 (2001): 1-22. "Indicative and Imperative in Matthean Soteriology" by Charles Talbert appeared as an article in *Biblica* 82 (2001): 515-38. "Divine Assistance and Enablement of Human Faithfulness in the Revelation to John Viewed within Its Apocalyptic Context" by Charles Talbert appeared as a chapter in *Il Verbo di Dio é Vivo* (ed. Jose Enrique Aguilar Chiu et al.; Analecta Biblica 165; Roma: Editrice Pontificio Istituto Biblico, 2007), 551-67. "The Fourth Gospel's Soteriology between New Birth and Resurrection" by Charles Talbert appeared as an article in *Perspectives in Religious Studies* 37 (2010): 133-45.

We would like to thank those who helped to bring this project to completion. Tim Brookins did the initial editing of all the manuscripts and compilation of the bibliography. Peter Rice put together the primary source index. We wish to thank Jenny Hoffman at Eerdmans for her assistance in securing permissions. Special thanks go to Michael Thomson at Eerdmans, whose patient oversight of the project from its original inception brought it to safe harbors.

Finally, the project that this volume represents would never have materialized if not for Charles Talbert's conception of it years ago. At that time he began to steadily chip away at this project, researching and publishing on the central question of this volume. Charles, however, found along the way students and colleagues eager to join him in his ongoing examination of new covenant piety in the New Testament. We hope that this volume proves a worthy contribution to his grand vision for this project.

Abbreviations

Unless otherwise indicated below, the abbreviations in this book for biblical texts, the OT and NT Apocrypha, the OT Pseudepigrapha, Dead Sea Scrolls, and other ancient sources as well as modern journals, series, and technical abbreviations follow *The SBL Handbook of Style for Ancient, Near Eastern, Biblical, and Early Christian Studies* (Peabody, MA: Hendrickson, 1999).

BECNT   Baker Exegetical Commentary on the New Testament
LNTS   Library of New Testament Studies
SFSHJ   South Florida Studies in the History of Judaism
THNTC   Two Horizons New Testament Commentary

Contributors

Andrew E. Arterbury
Associate Professor of Christian Scriptures
George W. Truett Seminary at Baylor University

Clifford A. Barbarick
Visiting Instructor of Religion
Pepperdine University

Scott J. Hafemann
Reader in New Testament
St Mary's College, University of St Andrews

Michael W. Martin
Associate Professor of New Testament
Lubbock Christian University

Charles H. Talbert
Distinguished Professor, Biblical Studies/New Testament
Baylor University

Jason A. Whitlark
Assistant Professor
Baylor Interdisciplinary Core

Introduction

Jason A. Whitlark

This volume of essays is concerned with soteriology. How does one gain a covenant relationship with God and remain in that relationship so as to experience final salvation? These questions, at the heart of the study of soteriology, have received renewed impetus in current scholarly debates in Pauline and ancient Jewish studies. Considering the broad contours of this conversation will enable us to set out the unique focus of this volume on soteriology that deals with post-conversion faithfulness of the believer.

In 1977, E. P. Sanders published *Paul and Palestinian Judaism,* which would prove to be a major force in reshaping Pauline studies in particular and modern scholarly understanding of ancient Judaism more generally. Sanders set out to discern a pattern of religion in Palestinian Judaism from Jewish texts between 200 B.C.E. and 200 C.E. For Sanders, describing the pattern of religion involved understanding how a religion gains and retains its members. Thus Sanders's two programmatic questions he put to every Jewish text he considered were *"how getting and staying in are understood."*[1] Sanders believed he could discern a unity in the pattern of religion for Palestinian Judaism that informed most of the Jewish texts he considered. He called this pattern covenantal nomism. Covenantal nomism as Sanders describes it is this:

1. E. P. Sanders, *Paul and Palestinian Judaism: A Comparison of Patterns of Religion* (Philadelphia: Fortress Press, 1977), 17, 424.

1

(1) God has chosen Israel and (2) given the law. The law implies both (3) God's promise to maintain the election and (4) the requirement to obey. (5) God rewards obedience and punishes transgression. (6) The law provides for means of atonement, and atonement results in (7) maintenance or re-establishment of the covenantal relationship. (8) All those who are maintained in the covenant by obedience, atonement and God's mercy belong to the group which will be saved.[2]

Sanders is concerned to emphasize that with covenantal nomism *"obedience maintains one's position in the covenant, but it does not earn God's grace as such."*[3] Moreover, gratitude is the primary impetus for obedience. While Sanders's monolithic description of Palestinian Judaism has not gone without critique,[4] his two programmatic questions applied to the Jewish texts he considered prove helpful when thinking about the structure of salvation for the NT documents as well.

Sanders's soteriological examination focused on entrance into the covenant relationship/community and maintenance of the relationship once entered. Timo Eskola furthered the examination of the soteriological structure of ancient Judaism and Paul in particular by considering the eschatological goal of the relationship. With regard to eschatology, the goal of "staying in" the covenant relationship was to "get in" the age-to-come. Eskola reasons that if legalism means that keeping the law effects eschatological salvation then covenantal nomism is legalistic nomism, since for covenantal nomism ongoing obedience to the law maintains the covenant relationship. In other words, once covenantal nomism is set in an eschatological context it becomes legalistic nomism.[5] Consequently, if we give due attention to salvation as not just entrance into God's covenant but also the eschatological goal of the covenant relationship, then a fuller description of the structure of salvation involves three essential considerations: How does one (1) get into the covenant relationship and (2) stay in the covenant relationship in order to (3) get into the age-to-come?

There is one final consideration when thinking about the structure of

2. Sanders, *Paul and Palestinian Judaism*, 422.
3. Sanders, *Paul and Palestinian Judaism*, 420.
4. E.g., D. A. Carson, Peter T. O'Brien, and Mark A. Seifrid, eds., *Justification and Variegated Nomism: Volume 1, The Complexities of Second Temple Judaism* (WUNT 2.140; Tübingen: Mohr Siebeck, 2001).
5. Timo Eskola, *Theodicy and Predestination in Pauline Soteriology* (WUNT 2.100; Tübingen: Mohr Siebeck, 1998), 52-60.

salvation in these terms. Timo Laato has demonstrated that such soteriological questions are accompanied by an anthropological assumption concerning intrinsic human ability to get in or stay in.[6] For instance, Laato concluded that the Judaism represented by covenantal nomism was more anthropologically optimistic and therefore synergistic. Paul, on the other hand, represented a pessimistic orientation. Such pessimism required a different soteriological paradigm or pattern of religion than covenantal nomism.[7] Laato then alerts us to the fact that, when discerning the structure of salvation, one must give careful consideration, when possible, to the anthropological assumptions of any text.[8]

While the above studies have been exclusively focused on Pauline studies and the examination of ancient Judaism, the fruits of these studies have provided programmatic questions for the examination of soteriology in the NT more broadly. What this volume presents based on these considerations above is one dimension of the soteriological patterns represented in the NT, namely, the period between getting in (entrance into the elect community) and getting in (entrance into the age-to-come).[9] The fundamental questions asked here are: (1) How is post-conversion faithfulness or "staying in" the covenant relationship so as to experience eschatological salvation understood by the various NT texts? And (2) do these Christian texts move beyond covenantal nomism (reciprocity) to a new covenant piety (divine enablement) for staying in the covenant relationship?

At this point, we ought to define what we mean by new covenant piety. The concept of new covenant piety is taken from God's promise of a new covenant with his people prophesied by Jeremiah. In that covenant, God promises to restore the relationship with Israel and Judah by "remembering their sins no more" and to remedy their serial infidelity by enabling their faithfulness to the covenant by "writing the law on their hearts." Thus, both

---

6. Timo Laato, *Paul and Judaism: An Anthropological Approach*, trans. T. McElwain (SFSHJ 115; Atlanta: Scholars Press, 1995).

7. Laato, *Paul and Judaism*, 146.

8. Recently, the relationship between divine and human agency in Paul has been taken up in John Barclay and Simon Gathercole, eds., *Divine and Human Agency in Paul and His Cultural Environment* (LNTS 335; London: T. & T. Clark, 2006).

9. There has been another recent volume that has attempted to look at the soteriologies of the NT: Jan G. van der Watt, *Salvation in the New Testament: Perspectives on Soteriology* (NovTSup 121; Atlanta: SBL, 2005). This volume, however, focuses on the language of salvation in the various NT documents that typically results in an emphasis on conversion or entrance into the Christian life and community.

getting in and staying in under the new covenant are contingent upon God's initiative to forgive sins and his empowerment of human faithfulness. New covenant piety then conveys the notion that post-conversion faithfulness or obedience is grounded in God's prior and ongoing empowerment of that faithfulness or obedience. Jeremiah's prophecy of this promised new covenant became integral to early Christian identity.[10] But was the hope for God-enabled faithfulness proclaimed in the new covenant prophecy an essential aspect of this new covenant identity among the earliest Christians? Will we find it to be a consistent feature in the NT documents? This volume attempts to shed light on this question.

In this volume, there are twelve essays by six authors representative of the NT corpus. The essays are arranged according to their canonical collections. The Pauline corpus will be considered first, both genuine Pauline letters and deutero-Pauline letters. Hebrews is also included here since it was a document traditionally linked with Paul and his mission. Next, we will consider the four Gospels, and then the Catholic Epistles followed by Revelation.

Pauline Corpus

The lead essay of the Pauline corpus and this volume is by Charles Talbert, who lays out the parameters of this volume's project by addressing the New Perspective on Paul that has been yoked with Sanders's covenantal nomism. According to Talbert's analysis of early Jewish texts, there are three distinctive soteriological patterns in Middle Judaism: legalism, covenantal nomism, and *sola gratia*. Talbert argues that Paul moves beyond the legalistic and synergistic soteriological streams in Middle Judaism and sets forth a divinely enabled obedience of the Christian life that is demonstrated among other things by Paul's use of the language of being "clothed in" or "putting on."

Jason Whitlark then takes up the deutero-Pauline letter of Ephesians. In Ephesians χάρις is a central motif in the letter's language of salvation. The language is most nearly defined by the reciprocity conventions of benefaction and patronage in the ancient Mediterranean world. Whitlark demonstrates, however, that both Philo and the author of Ephesians reject the reciprocity dynamic inherent in ancient Mediterranean benefaction or patronage (as well as in covenantal nomism). For the author of Ephesians,

---

10. Cf. Petrus J. Gräbe, *Der Neue Bund in der frühchristlichen Literatur* (FB 96; Würzburg: Echter Verlag, 2001).

ongoing obedience is not grounded in the feeling of indebted gratitude for prior benefits that is characteristic of the reciprocity rationale or χάρις-convention of ancient benefaction but in God's continual χάρις to sustain the Christian life as Ephesians relates it.

Next, Charles Talbert examines the Pastorals and their portrayal of divine enablement of Christian faithfulness between the two epiphanies of Jesus Christ (i.e., his incarnation and parousia). Talbert concludes that among the Pastorals ongoing enablement of faithfulness is conceived along two trajectories. First, through Paul's own apostolic example, enablement is brought about by visionary transformation. This motif was common among the moral philosophers. Second, the Pastorals contain distinctively Christian experiences of enablement expressed in statements about the Holy Spirit's presence, the Lord being with the believer, and the Lord's power, gift of understanding, and rescue.

Jason Whitlark concludes the examination of the Pauline corpus with an essay on Hebrews. The soteriological pattern in Hebrews has been described as covenantal nomistic by some scholars — that is, God's forgiveness and saving initiative stands at the beginning of the Christian pilgrimage but the completion of that pilgrimage depends on the believer's own faithfulness. Whitlark shows, however, that perseverance in Hebrews is not grounded in the synergism of covenantal nomism but in Jesus' high priestly ministry, which mediates the new-covenant blessing of ongoing faithfulness. More specifically, through Jesus' ongoing purification of the believer's conscience, the believer is transformed and empowered to continually come into God's presence where he or she is enabled to persevere and live faithfully in a restored covenant relationship with God.

The Gospels

When we turn to the Gospels, Charles Talbert in his essay on the Gospel of Matthew refutes those who claim that Matthew's soteriology is legalistic. While notions of empowerment for mission are clearly present in Matthew, the idea of ongoing enablement of the disciples' faithfulness is most clearly found in what Talbert calls transformation by vision. Talbert has already explored this motif in the Pastorals and applies it here to Matthew. According to this way of thinking found among the moral philosophers of the ancient Mediterranean world, being near and seeing the teacher live out his philosophy was transformative and empowering to his students, who likewise attempted to follow his example. The disciples' vision of Jesus' life both during his earthly ministry and later mediated via Matthew's Gospel empowered them to live out Jesus' vision of the kingdom.

Next, Michael Martin examines what the Isaianic new exodus motif in the Gospel of Mark contributes to our understanding of the necessity of God's empowerment for "staying in." Martin argues that Jesus in the Gospel of Mark, as the Isaianic divine warrior who leads God's people on a new exodus, is the liberator, shepherd, and covenant-maker for his disciples. According to Martin, these distinctive roles in Isaiah and Mark emphasize respectively God's ongoing deliverance, sustenance, and covenant that preserve his people on their new exodus into his eternal kingdom. Moreover, from the perspective of both Isaiah and Mark, this ongoing empowerment by God is necessary due to humanity's inherent weakness to live faithfully before God.

Andrew Arterbury takes up the soteriological question of this volume in the Gospel of Luke by comparing the denials of Jesus by Judas and Peter in Jesus' final hours. Arterbury demonstrates that, for Luke, Satan is behind both Judas's and Peter's denials and that Jesus' disciples are not sufficient in themselves to overcome their supernatural adversary. They need a more powerful advocate as Jesus proves to be in his intercession for and reclamation of Peter. Arterbury concludes that through Jesus' intercession, God was at work "behind the scenes" to restore Peter and empower his ongoing discipleship with Jesus.

Charles Talbert concludes the section on the Gospels with his essay on the Gospel of John. The "abiding in" language of John 15 has often been interpreted along the lines of reciprocity or mutuality — Jesus abides in the disciple who then is able to bear fruit, but the disciple must also abide in Jesus to experience Jesus' fruit-bearing power. From the examination of the Greco-Roman and Jewish texts, Talbert demonstrates that for Jesus to abide in the disciple means for Jesus to empower the Christian life of his disciple. Likewise, for the disciple to abide in Jesus means for the disciple to put his or her trust in Jesus to empower him or her. John's language of "abiding in" then is not the language of reciprocity and mutuality but of divine empowerment and human dependence upon God.

Catholic Epistles

Three essays are featured in this section on the Catholic Epistles. Taking up the "strawy" Epistle of James, Jason Whitlark explores the implanted word motif in James 1:21. While some interpreters have taken this motif to refer to innate human ability or reason, Whitlark shows that among pagan, Jewish, and Christian texts this language was also used to convey the idea of divine enablement. Furthermore, Christians found this language apt when discussing the inward transformation and empowerment promised in Jeremiah's new covenant. Thus, coupled with a pessimistic anthropology found in James, the implanted word in James functions as a new covenant motif of divine enablement of the imperatives for Christian living that the author of James sets forth in the rest of his letter.

Clifford Barbarick examines the word-milk metaphor in 1 Peter 2:2 as the motif of divine enablement that nourishes and grows the believer in the time between the two revelations of Jesus (his death and resurrection and his second coming). Barbarick argues that the word or gospel provides this life-sustaining and transformative milk. The gospel is understood both as the message that mediates the saving event of Jesus' death and resurrection and the power that brings about God's ongoing transformative activity in the life of the believer. Specifically, the example of Jesus as set forth in the gospel message mediates this divine empowerment. From the perspective of the moral philosophers in the ancient Mediterranean world, *exempla* not only provided patterns of life to imitate, but also beholding their lives had transformative power for the follower, as we have already seen in Talbert's essays on the Pastorals and Matthew. Thus the example of Jesus as depicted in the gospel message of his death and resurrection looms large in the exhortations in 1 Peter. It becomes the ongoing enabling power for the faithfulness of the believer in between the two revelations of Jesus.

Scott Hafemann addresses the soteriological concerns of this volume in 2 Peter. He examines 1:3-11, giving focused attention to the theological logic of 1:8-10a. Hafemann argues that the post-conversion life of virtue outlined in 1:5-7 and necessary for final salvation is not grounded in the motivation of gratitude for God's past benefits nor does it depend on the believer's own efforts to be ever increasing in the virtues listed. Through a careful, syntactical examination of 2 Peter 1:3-11, Hafemann demonstrates that God's provision and promises are determinative for the believer's ongoing life of godliness.

Revelation

Charles Talbert concludes this volume's soteriological exploration of the NT by looking at Revelation. Talbert demonstrates that the central motif of divine enablement in Revelation concerns its vision of the future. Through the vision or knowledge of God's imminent future actions and final victory, the believer is enabled in his or her unique knowledge and hope to live faithfully in his or her present struggles and to resist the pressures of assimilation arising from the imperial culture. Talbert also shows that Revelation has additional motifs of preservation and enablement of Christian faithfulness — the book of life, sealing and measuring, and clothing. These additional motifs in Revelation assume a more pessimistic anthropological perspective and, joined with Revelation's empowering vision of the future, argue for a pervading new covenant piety in this Christian apocalypse.

At this point we leave to the reader of these essays to determine if a sufficient case has been made for seeing new covenant piety as a ubiquitous element of the NT corpus. In any case, we hope that further studies beyond the beginning made here will continue to advance our understanding of the multifarious articulation in the NT of the experience of God's ongoing saving activity in the lives of believers.

PART I

Pauline Corpus

Paul, Judaism, and the Revisionists

Charles H. Talbert

Within the context of both non-Christian Jews and Christian messianists who held a variety of soteriologies (legalism, covenantal nomistic legalism, and *sola gratia*), Paul engaged both in an intra-Jewish and an intra-Christian messianist dialogue. In each he critiqued both legalism and covenantal nomistic legalism in the name of a *sola gratia* soteriology.

●   ●

There are varieties of ways that Paul's relation to non-messianic Judaism has been understood. (1) Judaism was legalistic; Paul was right in recognizing and opposing it (so the Protestant Reformers and many of their heirs).[1] (2) Judaism was not legalistic; Paul or his interpreters got it wrong; the apostle either did not oppose Jewish legalism because it did not exist[2] or, if he did, he was misrepresenting ancient Judaism[3] (so modern revisionists). (3) Palestinian Judaism was not legalistic, but some Hellenistic Jewish adherents got it wrong and were legalists; Paul rightly recognized and op-

---

1. Rudolf Bultmann, *Theology of the New Testament* (New York: Scribner's, 1951-1955); Ernst Käsemann, *Commentary on Romans* (Grand Rapids: Eerdmans, 1980).

2. E. P. Sanders, *Paul and Palestinian Judaism* (Philadelphia: Fortress, 1977); *Paul, the Law, and the Jewish People* (Philadelphia: Fortress, 1983).

3. Marvin R. Wilson, *Our Father Abraham* (Grand Rapids: Eerdmans, 1989), 20-21, describes the Reformers' view of the Judaism Paul opposed as a caricature, a misrepresentation, and a bearing of false witness.

posed the latter group.[4] (4) Middle Judaism was diverse. (a) Some were legalistic (e.g., Gentiles had to be circumcised in order to become Jews = part of God's people). (b) Many were synergistic. They advocated a legalistic covenantal nomism. A Jew got into the covenant by God's grace but remained in the covenant, and got into the age-to-come, by works of the Law. (c) Some held to *sola gratia* (by grace alone) insofar as both Gentile and Jew were concerned.[5] This type of piety held that one not only got in by grace but also remained in the people of God by grace and ultimately got into the age-to-come by grace. It will be the contention of this paper that the fourth alternative is the most accurate of the lot. Viewed in terms of this schema, Paul critiques (a) and (b) in the name of (c). His critique was first of all an intra-Jewish argument. There was one genus: Judaism. Within that genus, a number of species were in tension with one another over who represented

---

4. C. G. Montefiore, *Judaism and St. Paul: Two Essays* (New York: E. P. Dutton, 1915); Samuel Sandmel, *The Genius of Paul* (New York: Farrar, Straus & Cudahy, 1958); H. J. Schoeps, *Paul: The Theology of the Apostle in the Light of Jewish Religious History* (Philadelphia: Westminster, 1961), 213. Colin G. Kruse, *Paul, the Law, and Justification* (Peabody, MA: Hendrickson, 1997), says Judaism was not *in principle* legalistic, but *in practice* some of its adherents got it wrong. These Paul opposed.

5. *Sola gratia* was characteristic of some Christian messianic Judaism. Acts 11:20, confirmed by Gal 2:11-14, indicates a pre-Pauline Gentile church at Antioch that was law-free. Galatians 2:15-16, if addressed to Peter in the context of 2:11-14, indicates that Paul and Peter were in agreement on soteriology. This confirms the claim of Acts 15:7-11 that Peter supported the soteriology of Paul. The Johannine circle, whose origins are obscure but undoubtedly ancient, not only knows a law-free gospel but also shares the radical *sola gratia* of Paul (John 15:16, 1-5). So *sola gratia* was not limited to Paul among Christian messianists. Can it be found outside messianic Judaism? Yes. (1) The new covenant of MT Jer 31:31-34/ LXX Jer 38:31-34 begins and continues on the basis of grace. (2) The *Apocalypse of Abraham*, written between A.D. 70 and the early second century with no direct relation to the NT, tells of the Gentile Abraham's reasoning from the world to God (chs. 1–7). Then God reveals Himself to Abraham (chs. 8–9) and sends the angel Iaoel, in whom God's name dwells (10:8), to assist him (ch. 10). Abraham is told he has been chosen by God (14:2) and needs to offer a sacrifice to God (9:8; 10:16). The sacrificial animals are provided by God (12:6). Instructions for the sacrifice are given by the angel (12:8-9). Abraham is then carried up into God's presence (ch. 16). The angel kneels down and worships (17:2) and tells Abraham to do the same (17:4-5). This involves reciting the song the angel taught him (17:7-21). In the midst of the song (17:20), Abraham says: "(accept) also the sacrifice which you yourself made to yourself through me." The similarity with Paul is striking. Did such a view exist as early as Paul? Since the view apparently arose independent of Christian influences, there is no reason it could not have existed early. (3) The eschatological inclusion of the Gentiles will be an act of sheer grace (Isa 2:1-4; Tob 14:6-7). *Sola gratia* was, then, one of a number of competing Jewish soteriologies outside of as well as within Christian messianic Judaism.

the true tradition with reference to the scriptures of Israel.[6] Paul was an example of one of those species of Middle Judaism. His critique was secondly also an intra-messianist argument. The diversity of non-Christian Judaism about the role of the Law was reflected in early Christian Judaism as well. Paul, then, it will be argued, was also a critic of messianists who fell into categories (a) and (b). To ascertain just exactly how this works out is this paper's purpose.

The argument is organized around three questions. (1) When Paul polemicized against "works of the law," was he accurately addressing a real situation? (2) If so, what did Paul find wrong with "works of law"? (3) How did Paul avoid the pitfalls of the very positions that he critiqued? How did he understand divine enablement (= grace), after getting into the people of God, to work? The paper will take up each question in order.

Did Paul Accurately Address a Real Situation?

Three readings of Paul and ancient Judaism set the stage for our search for an answer to question one. (1) The foil for scholars of Pauline theology at the end of the last century was the reading offered by the Protestant Reformers and their heirs. According to the Reformers, Judaism of Paul's time was a religion of works righteousness within which God had given humans the law so that we might earn salvation by fulfilling it. Paul, in this reading, attacks the claim that salvation can be earned by acts of obedience to the law. Critics of this view contend that such an approach results in a distorted view both of Paul and of Judaism.[7]

(2) The "new perspective on Paul,"[8] initiated above all by E. P. Sanders, starts with a revised view of ancient Judaism.[9] Palestinian Judaism, says

6. The view of ancient Judaism assumed here is that reflected by Gabriele Boccaccini, *Middle Judaism* (Minneapolis: Fortress, 1991), 7-25, and by Alan F. Segal, *Rebecca's Children: Judaism and Christianity in the Roman World* (Cambridge, MA: Harvard University Press, 1986), and *Paul the Convert* (New Haven: Yale University Press, 1990).

7. For a detailed description of this position, see Francis Watson, *Paul, Judaism, and the Gentiles* (SNTSMS 56; Cambridge: Cambridge University Press, 1986), ch. 1.

8. The expression comes from James D. G. Dunn's article, "The New Perspective on Paul," *BJRL* 65 (1982-1983): 95-122.

9. Sanders's claim to be comparing patterns of religion, Palestinian Judaism and Paul, was critiqued by Jacob Neusner. J. Neusner, *Judaic Law from Jesus to the Mishnah: A Systematic Reply to Professor E. P. Sanders* (SFSHJ 84; Atlanta: Scholars, 1993), 231-46, deals with *Paul and Palestinian Judaism*. Sanders, he says, brings to the rabbinic sources the issues of

Sanders, was not legalistic. It was characterized by covenantal nomism. In this structure one "gets in" the people of God by grace and "stays in" by obedience to the law (which includes repentance and atonement). Paul, then, could not have been opposing Palestinian Judaism's legalistic soteriology because it was not legalistic! Paul's sole critique of Judaism, according to Sanders, was that salvation is in Christ alone and thus could not be by the law. As a result of Sanders's work on Paul and ancient Judaism there has been a paradigm shift in the way the apostle is read.[10] After Sanders, most scholars would accept covenantal nomism as an accurate description of the Judaism Paul knew. The new perspective, however, is now being challenged by yet another reading.

(3) Timo Eskola may serve as a representative of scholars who argue that the depiction of ancient Judaism offered by Sanders is itself skewed. The soteriology of ancient Judaism, so the post–new perspective reading goes, was synergistic. Once covenantal nomism is set in an eschatological context, it becomes legalistic nomism. How so? One may be a part of God's people by grace, but in order to stay in the people and in order to enter into the age-to-come, one must obey the law. Obedience is the condition for eschatological salvation. If legalism means that keeping the law is the way to gain eschatological salvation, then in an eschatological framework covenantal nomism becomes legalistic nomism. So the soteriology is synergistic. By God's grace one gets in the people but by human effort/obedience one gets into the Eschatological Age beyond the last judgment. It is this synergistic, legalistic covenantal nomism against which Paul fights.[11] At the moment when many

---

Pauline scholarship. All he wants to know is what addresses questions of interest to Paul. If Paul and the rabbis are not talking about the same thing, then what is it that we have to compare? In response, one might say that if what one is interested in is Pauline theology, then Sanders's method of comparing soteriologies as wholes is better than a focus on isolated parallels. The question in this paper is whether or not Sanders accurately described the soteriology of the Judaisms of Paul's time.

10. Terence L. Donaldson, *Paul and the Gentiles: Remapping the Apostle's Convictional World* (Minneapolis: Fortress, 1997), titles his first chapter "A New Paradigm and a New Problem."

11. Timo Eskola, "Paul, Predestination and Covenantal Nomism — Re-assessing Paul and Palestinian Judaism," *JSJ* 28 (1997): 390-412; *Theodicy and Predestination in Pauline Soteriology* (WUNT 2/100; Tübingen: Mohr-Siebeck, 1998). Others of the same persuasion include: Robert H. Gundry, "Grace, Works, and Staying Saved in Paul," *Bib* 66 (1985): 1-38; Timo Laato, *Paul and Judaism: An Anthropological Approach* (SFSHJ 115; Atlanta: Scholars, 1995); Charles H. Talbert, "Freedom and Law in Galatians," *Ex Auditu* 11 (1995): 17-28. Mark A. Seifrid, "The 'New Perspective on Paul' and Its Problems," *Them* 25 (2000): 4-18,

Pauline scholars are celebrating the paradigm shift associated with Sanders's work, yet another shift of equal import seems to be occurring.

At this point one must ask once again: What do the available sources say about getting into the people of God and/or the age-to-come in ancient non-Christian Judaism? We will begin with the question of the admission of Gentiles. In ancient Judaism there were basically two avenues by which Gentiles could facilitate their entrance into God's people and/or the age-to-come.[12] The first was by becoming a proselyte. Sanders claims that "the formal definition of a true proselyte and a faithful native-born Israelite is the same: a man is properly in Israel who accepts the covenant, intends to obey its commandments, performs them to the best of his ability and the like."[13] Sanders is also aware, however, that there is substantive difference between the two. In the case of the native-born Israelites, circumcision is a response to the grace of election. They are "in" unless they give evidence of being apostate. In the case of the latter, proselytes must bear the burden of proof to show that they accept the covenant and intend to keep the law. That is, they must take a human initiative to align themselves with the elect people — by works of the law.[14] Ancient sources reflect this.

Josephus says that many Greeks "have agreed to adopt our laws" (Josephus, *Ag. Ap.* 2.123 [Thackeray, LCL]). He also says that Moses took measures regarding Jewish customs "to throw them open ungrudgingly to any who elect to share them. To all who desire to come and live under the same laws with us, he gives a gracious welcome, holding that it is not family ties alone which constitute relationship, but agreement in principles of conduct" (*Ag. Ap.* 2.209-10 [Thackeray, LCL]). The ethical emphasis in what is said here is obvious. A Gentile's ethical convictions relate him/her to the Jews and apparently have the same importance as racial origin.[15] In yet another place, Josephus reiterates: "We . . . gladly welcome any who wish to share our own (customs/laws)" (*Ag. Ap.* 2.261 [Thackeray, LCL]). Precisely what the ritual was by which one became a proselyte in the first century cannot be exactly known. What seems clear from Josephus's statements, however, is that a Gentile "got in" the people of God by works of the law.

---

seems to want to move in this direction as well. The effect of the work of Friedrich Avemarie is also to buttress the case of this group of scholars (see n. 26).

12. The eschatological inclusion of the Gentiles, however, was a matter of sheer grace. Joachim Jeremias, *Jesus' Promise to the Nations* (SBT 24; Naperville, IL: Allenson, 1958).

13. Sanders, *Paul and Palestinian Judaism*, 206.

14. Sanders, *Paul and Palestinian Judaism*, 206-7.

15. N. J. McEleny, "Conversion, Circumcision and the Law," *NTS* 20 (1974): 324.

Justin's *Dialogue with Trypho* offers further, if later, evidence. In chapter 8, after Justin has told Trypho of his conversion to Christ, his Jewish dialogue partner tells Justin that his profession is empty. Trypho then gives his prescription for salvation to Justin. "If, then, you are willing to listen to me . . . , first be circumcised, then observe what ordinances have been enacted with respect to the Sabbath, and the feasts, and the new moons of God; and, in a word, do all things which have been written in the law: and then perhaps you shall obtain mercy from God."[16] Here a Jew addresses a philosopher (1) who has been converted to Christ (3-8). Trypho seems to be calling for Justin to become a proselyte. This would be accomplished by works of the law. This sounds very much like what has traditionally been called legalism. One "gets in" by works of the law.

The case of Izates makes concrete what the previous statements have said in general terms. In *Jewish Antiquities* 20.17-41, Josephus tells of the conversion to Judaism of Izates of Adiabene through the witness of a Jewish merchant named Ananias. This Ananias told Izates that circumcision was unnecessary for him to be a Jewish convert. Later, in 20.42-48, another Jew named Eleazar came from Galilee and told Izates that, according to the law, circumcision was necessary. Izates thereupon complied and was circumcised. In the case of Eleazar, in order for a proselyte to "get in" the people who would get into the age-to-come, he had to be circumcised.[17] This is what is normally called legalism.

The second avenue by which a Gentile might enter the age-to-come was by being a "righteous Gentile," that is, a Gentile who keeps the law. (1) In Rom 2:10, 14-15, in the context of an argument that operates with a non-messianic Jewish logic, Paul speaks of Gentiles who do by nature what the law requires and who receive glory, honor, and peace from God at the last judgment. The initiative of these righteous Gentiles receives approval from God in the last judgment. This sounds like legalism. From the period before A.D. 70, two Hellenistic non-messianic Jewish documents speak the same way. (2) The *Testament of Abraham,* written in Greek probably in Egypt in the first century, makes no distinction between Jew and Gentile. The sins mentioned are not specifically Jewish. Everyone is judged by the same standard — whether the majority of his/her deeds are good or evil. Both Jew and

---

16. *ANF* 1:198-99.

17. This difference of opinion about the necessity of circumcision for a proselyte is echoed in *b. Yebam.* 46a, where Rabbi Joshua and Rabbi Eliezer reflect the positions of Ananias and Eleazar.

Gentile get into heaven by having a majority of their deeds be righteous. This is what has traditionally been called legalism.[18] (3) The *Apocalypse of Zephaniah*, written probably before A.D. 70 outside of Palestine, makes no mention of covenant or election. All people, Jew and Gentile, are judged on the basis of their deeds, which are written down by angels throughout their lives. The good and the evil are then weighed in balance at the judgment. Only repentance, which can come at any point before the last judgment, effects atonement. Again, this soteriology is what has normally been called legalism. (4) After A.D. 70, the Palestinian Jewish *4 Ezra* 3:36 brings to completion one complaint Ezra makes to God about the fate of God's people. What other nation has been as mindful of the commandments as Zion? God may find individual Gentiles who have kept God's commandments, but he will not find any nations besides Israel. (5) In the Tosefta,[19] *Sanhedrin* 13:2, there is a debate between Rabbi Joshua and Rabbi Eliezer. Eliezer contends that "none of the Gentiles has a portion in the world to come." To which Joshua responds: "If it had been written, 'The wicked shall return to Sheol — all the Gentiles' and then said nothing further, I should have maintained as you do. Now that it is in fact written, 'All the Gentiles who forget God,' it indicates that there also are righteous people among the nations of the world, who do have a portion in the world to come." (6) In *Sifra*, Parashat Ahare Mot, Pereq 13.15,[20] Rabbi Jeremiah[21] asks: "How do I know that even a Gentile who keeps the Torah, lo, he is like the high priest?" The argument unfolds: the Torah is given to humans and its promises are to humans; the righteous nation enters; it is the righteous who shall enter it. The conclusion is reached: even a Gentile who keeps the Torah. . . . (7) In *Sifre*, Piska 307,[22] Rabbi Judah the Prince speaks about a righteous Gentile. This philosopher protested to the prefect about the official's burning a copy of the Torah. The prefect replied: "Tomorrow your fate will be the same as theirs (the Jews)." Whereupon the philosopher replied: "You have conveyed good tidings to me, that tomorrow my portion will be with them in the world to come."[23] In all of these tradi-

---

18. In James H. Charlesworth's *OTP* (vol. 2; Garden City, NY: Doubleday, 1983), 871-902, the editor-translator of the *Testament of Abraham* is E. P. Sanders.

19. *The Tosefta* (vol. 4; trans. J. Neusner; New York: Ktav, 1981), 238.

20. *Sifra: An Analytical Translation* (vol. 3; trans. J. Neusner; Atlanta: Scholars, 1988), 80.

21. In *b. Bava Qamma* 38a, the same tradition is attributed to Rabbi Meir.

22. *Sifre: A Tannaitic Commentary on the Book of Deuteronomy* (trans. Reuven Hammer; New Haven: Yale University Press, 1986), 312.

23. Other stories of a similar type can be found in *b. Avodah Zarah* 18a (the execu-

tions about the righteous Gentiles, it seems that such people get into the age-to-come by means of their works. This does not sound like covenantal nomism. In the case of both proselytes and righteous Gentiles, the soteriology sounds more like what has traditionally been called legalism than anything else.

What about the *native-born Jew?* How does such a one "get in" the age-to-come? Without trying to be exhaustive, let us look first at selected Hellenistic Jewish sources before turning to selected Palestinian Jewish materials. When one moves out from Palestinian Judaism to the Hellenistic Jewish world, the two pre-A.D. 70 sources previously mentioned come into play: the *Testament of Abraham* and the *Apocalypse of Zephaniah.*[24]

First, in the *Testament of Abraham* the soteriology for Jews is the same as it is for Gentiles. Everyone is judged by the same standard — whether the majority of his/her deeds are good or evil. The Jews, as well as the Gentiles, get into heaven by having a majority of their deeds be righteous. Second, in the *Apocalypse of Zephaniah* there is no mention of covenant or election. The patriarchs are mentioned but only as examples of pious men. Angels write down the good deeds of the righteous and the evil deeds of the wicked. At the judgment the good and evil are weighed in balance. Every person is judged on the basis of earthly deeds. In both of these sources, "getting in" the age-to-come is a matter of righteous behavior, not election. This is what has traditionally been called legalism.

Turning now to Palestinian Judaism, we may begin with rabbinic Judaism.[25] There are two foci in rabbinic soteriology: election and obedience.[26] Sanders says they are to be understood sequentially: "getting in" by election and "staying in" by obedience. Friedrich Avemarie, however, argues that the

---

tioner of Rabbi Hanina ben Teradion) and *b. Ta'anit* 29a (Rabbi Gamaliel and a Roman officer who saved his life).

24. I am indebted for these references to Frank Thielman, "Paul as Jewish Christian Theologian: The Theology of Paul in the Magnum Opus of James D. G. Dunn," *PRSt* 25 (1998): 381-87.

25. The difficulties in comparing rabbinic Judaism with Paul are legion. Sanders, *Paul and Palestinian Judaism*, 60, says: "I do not suppose that it [Tanaaitic source material] provides an accurate picture of Judaism or even of Pharisaism in the time of Jesus and Paul." Since, however, Sanders included the rabbis in his description of Palestinian Judaism, we will also.

26. Friedrich Avemarie, "Erwählung und Vergeltung zur optionalen Struktur Rabbinischer Soteriologie," *NTS* 45 (1999): 108-26; and *Tora und Leben: Untersuchungen zur Heilsbedeutung der Tora in der frühen rabbinischen Literatur* (TSAJ 55; Tübingen: Mohr-Siebeck, 1996).

two foci represent two models instead of two stages. Some sources place the emphasis on election, others on obedience. Sanders's favorite text is found in the Mishnah, *Sanhedrin* 10:1. "All Israelites have a share in the world to come, for it is written, 'Thy people also shall be all righteous, they shall inherit the land for ever; the branch of my planting, the work of my hands that I may be glorified.'" Here the emphasis is on election, Sanders claims. The initial assertion ("All Israelites have a share in the world to come"), however, is qualified by its supporting scripture citation ("Thy people shall be all righteous"). Furthermore, what follows qualifies "all Israelites." There are some who have no share in the world to come: for example, those who deny the resurrection; those who deny the law's heavenly origin, and others. Indeed, in 10:1-4 a long list of exceptions to "all" is found. These presumably are those whose behavior constitutes apostasy. Even with the exceptions, however, the focus is still probably on election. Nevertheless, there is even here no entry into the age-to-come apart from one's obedience to the law. This is soteriological synergism, legalistic covenantal nomism.

Other evidence points more toward a focus on obedience in the soteriology of Palestinian Judaism. (1) Mark 1:4 and Luke 3:3 say John preached "a baptism of repentance for the forgiveness of sins." Taken alone, this sounds like a call for an atoning activity done within a covenantal nomistic context so as to "stay in" the people of God who would survive the last judgment. Matthew 3:8-10 and Luke 3:8-9, however, say John told his Jewish auditors to bear fruit that befits repentance, not to presume on their ethnicity/election, and that without this fruit their election would not enable them to survive the fire of the last judgment. Here Jews must do more than avoid apostasy. They must actively seek the atonement of repentance and then act obediently. In John's preaching one "gets in" the age-to-come only if he/she has acted obediently. Descent from Abraham, taken alone, is soteriologically ineffective. This is a synergistic, legalistic covenantal nomism.

(2) The *Community Rule* at Qumran (1QS) starts with the assumption that obedience to what God commanded through Moses and the Prophets has not been actualized by most of those born Jews (I, 2-3). The community that will carry out all that God commands (I, 16-17) will be made up of Jews who "freely volunteer to carry out God's decrees" (I, 7; V, 1, 22; VI, 13). These are those selected by God for an everlasting covenant (IV, 22). Those who enter the community swear with a binding oath to revert to the law of Moses with all that it decrees (V, 8). "When someone enters the covenant to behave in compliance with all these decrees . . . , they shall test their spirits in

the Community . . . in respect of . . . his deeds in the law. . . . And their spirit and their deeds must be tested, year after year" (V, 20-24).[27] For example, when such a person has completed a year within the community, he will once again be questioned about his "deeds in connection with the law" (VI, 18). Here again, ethnicity/election (God's grace) is soteriologically ineffective. An ethnic Jew must choose to enter the community that will carry out the obedience to the law of Moses that God expects. Only these will "get in" the age-to-come. Here again, one encounters a synergistic, legalistic covenantal nomism.[28]

(3) In *4 Ezra* we find a Palestinian Jewish document that Sanders calls legalistic and that he incorrectly claims is out of step with the rest of ancient Judaism. "[I]n IV Ezra one sees how Judaism works when it actually does become a religion of individual self-righteousness. In IV Ezra, in short, we see an instance in which covenantal nomism has collapsed. All that is left is legalistic perfectionism."[29] In *4 Ezra* the covenants no longer exist (4:23). Humans have scorned God's law and denied his covenants and have not performed his works (7:24). Humans are so full of sin (7:68; 8:35) that they will have nothing to say in the judgment (7:73). This judgment of God is drawing near (8:61). Those who will be saved will be able "to escape on account of [their] works" (9:7), while those who have received the law and have sinned will perish (9:36). Here human sin has nullified the covenant (= election has been canceled). Henceforth judgment will be strictly according to one's works. Only a very few will be saved. In this structure, a Jew enters the age-to-come on the basis of works of law. This is, indeed, what has traditionally been called legalism. Since the same soteriology is found elsewhere prior to A.D. 70, Sanders's claim that it is the post-70 situation that is a catalyst for IV Ezra's legalistic soteriology is unconvincing.

(4) *2 Baruch* 41 speaks both about some of God's people's rejecting the covenant and law and about some who have fled for refuge beneath

27. Translations are from Florentino García Martínez, *The Dead Sea Scrolls Translated* (2d ed.; Grand Rapids: Eerdmans, 1996).

28. M. G. Abegg, "4QMMT C 27,31 and Works Righteousness," *DSD* 6 (1999) 139-47, contends that Paul was responding to a position like that in 4QMMT where Judaism saw in the law its distinctiveness before God, not its way to earn final salvation. This reading is suspect. 4Q398 [4QpapMMT e], frg. 2 col. II (= 4QMMT 111-18) is clear. This text uses the expression "works of the law." It sees such observance as paying off at the end of time. This payoff is described as "it shall be reckoned to you as in justice when you do what is upright and good before him" (Martinez, 84-85). At best this is legalistic covenantal nomism.

29. Sanders, *Paul and Palestinian Judaism*, 409.

God's wings (vv. 3-4). In chapter 42, God says that those who have embraced the covenant will receive the good things while those who have abandoned it will receive the reverse (vv. 2-3). Verse 5 seems to imply that Gentiles who proselytize to Judaism will gain the benefits of the New World while verse 4 indicates that Jews who go off and mingle with foreigners will not. Here it is not one's position in the covenant people conveyed by birth that yields life in the New World but obedience to the law. *2 Baruch* 51 speaks of those who at the last judgment have been "justified through their obedience to my law" (v. 3). These will be transformed so that they will look like the angels (v. 5). "Those who have been saved by their works, whose hope has been in the law" (v. 7) shall see marvels. They shall be made like the angels (v. 10) and will experience Paradise (v. 11). Here one enters the New World by works of law. Those whose obedience to the law is real will be justified.[30] Again, in *2 Baruch* we see operative a synergistic, legalistic covenantal nomism.

From our survey so far two conclusions stand out. First, there were some non-messianic streams of Middle Judaism that were legalistic; most others were synergistic. Second, these streams of ancient Judaism sometimes treated Jew and Gentile just alike. A soteriology of works did not of necessity exclude Gentiles. Sometimes it gave them near egalitarian access to the age-to-come.

It is now necessary to note that there were also Christian messianist Jews who demanded that Gentiles become proselytes in order to become fully children of Abraham. The narrative of Acts 15:1 refers to some from Judea who told Gentiles: "Unless you are circumcised according to the custom of Moses, you cannot be saved." Verse 5 identifies them as believers who belonged to the party of the Pharisees. They said: "It is necessary to circumcise them, and to charge them to keep the law of Moses." Paul's letter to the Galatians confirms the existence of such believers at the early period. In three references reflecting three subsequent time periods the apostle mentions law-observant believers who held that such observance was required for Gentiles. The first, Gal 2:3-5, in speaking about Paul's visit with the pillars

---

30. Brendan Byrne, *Sons of God, Seed of Abraham: A Study of the Idea of the Sonship of God of All Christians in Paul against the Jewish Background* (AnBib 83; Rome: Biblical Institute Press, 1979), 227-33, gives a review of Sanders's *Paul and Palestinian Judaism*. He notes that Sanders omits *2 Baruch*, which together with Pss 13 and 14 of the *Psalms of Solomon* and the *Thanksgiving Hymns* of Qumran, represents the Judaism that Paul has in mind in his polemic. *Psalms of Solomon* 14, a pre-70 Palestinian composition, certainly fits the legalistic covenantal nomistic pattern.

in Jerusalem, says that Paul did not permit the Gentile, Titus, to be circumcised as some demanded. The second, Gal 2:11-16, tells of an incident at Antioch prompted by the circumcision party whose behavior seems to have demanded that Gentiles become proselytes. The third, Gal 3:1-5; 5:1-2; 6:12, reflects the situation in Galatia when the letter was written. Apparently a law-observant mission had come to Galatia and had told Paul's converts that they needed to be circumcised and keep the law in order to complete/perfect their Abrahamic sonship in Christ.[31] So, we may conclude that there was a Christian messianist stream of Middle Judaism that was legalistic and/or synergistic just as non-Christian streams were.

If one evaluates the three different readings of Paul's struggles with the Judaism of his time — the Protestant Reformers and their heirs, the new perspective revisionists, and the post–new perspective interpreters — in light of the survey just made, it is obvious that no one of them is absolutely on target. The one that is farthest from what our survey indicates, however, is the second: the new perspective on Paul. The third is correct in seeing Palestinian Judaism as essentially a synergistic soteriological system. It is incomplete, however, due to its failure to recognize that some streams of ancient Judaism, Palestinian and Hellenistic, both non-messianic and messianic, were legalistic in their soteriology. This correction, of course, is found in the first option: the traditional Reformation reading. If this survey has yielded tenable results, then ancient Judaism's soteriology included both synergistic and legalistic tendencies.

This survey has yielded results that dovetail remarkably well with what one finds in the genuine Pauline letters. Dare we make a claim for the reliability of the Pauline evidence for a knowledge of ancient Judaism? Alan Segal does![32] He says: "Paul should be treated as a major source in the study of first-century Judaism."[33] He gives "us the only witness to a world of everyday Hellenistic Judaism now vanished."[34] "Paul is . . . our best witness to the issues that affected first-century Jews. . . . Paul is . . . one of the most fruitful and reliable sources for first-century Jewish religious life."[35] "Indeed, Paul's letters may be more important to the history of Judaism than the rabbinic

---

31. J. Louis Martyn, "A Law-Observant Mission to Gentiles," in *Theological Issues in the Letters of Paul* (Nashville: Abingdon, 1997), 7-25; *Galatians: A New Translation with Introduction and Commentary* (AnBib 33A; New York: Doubleday, 1997), 302-6.

32. Segal, *Paul the Convert*.

33. Segal, *Paul the Convert*, xi.

34. Segal, *Paul the Convert*, xiii.

35. Segal, *Paul the Convert*, xvi.

texts are to the interpretation of the Christian scriptures."[36] I concur. If one operates out of such an assumption about the evidence supplied by the Pauline letters, then to have mid-first-century confirmation of what our survey has otherwise yielded is significant indeed.

Paul's struggle would have been both against non-Christian Jewish legalism and synergism on the one hand and against Christian messianists of the same stripe on the other. As J. A. Fitzmyer says: "Paul knew whereof he was speaking when he took issue with contemporary Judaism and its attitude to legal regulations."[37] At this point we have arrived at an answer to the first question: Was Paul accurately addressing a real issue when he polemicized against "works righteousness"? My answer is: Yes. If so, then a paradigm shift beyond the "new perspective" on Paul seems not only justified but required.[38]

What Did Paul Find Wrong with Works of Law?

Again, finding an answer to a question is easier if our quest is set in the context of three different readings of Paul. (1) A major tenet of the Protestant Reformers and their heirs is that "works of law" refers to moral activity in general aimed at procuring salvation by one's own strength. This is seen as idolatry, a violation of the first commandment.[39] Jewish striving is one cultural expression of a specifically human striving, something common to all people. Käsemann says:

> Religion always provides man with his most thorough-going possibility of confusing an illusion with God. Paul sees this possibility realized in the devout Jew: inasmuch as the announcement of God's will in the law is here misunderstood as a summons to human achievement and therefore as a means to a righteousness of one's own. But that is for him the

---

36. Segal, *Paul the Convert*, 48.

37. Joseph A. Fitzmyer, S.J., *Romans* (AnBib 33; New York: Doubleday, 1993), 338-39 (albeit in the context of Qumran evidence only).

38. Dieter Georgi, *Theocracy in Paul's Praxis and Theology* (Minneapolis: Fortress, 1991), 79, says: "In none of Paul's extant letters does he take issue with a form of Judaism resembling that which one encounters in the rabbinic literature based on the tradition of the Pharisees." In light of our survey, this statement seems in need of radical revision.

39. Bultmann, *Theology of the New Testament*, 1:263-64; Ernst Käsemann, "Paul and Israel," in *New Testament Questions of Today* (Philadelphia: Fortress, 1969), 183-87.

root sin . . . ; man, in despairing presumption, erects his own work into the criterion of the universal judgment and God becomes an approving spectator of our doings.[40]

In this dominant view among the Reformers' heirs, to attempt to achieve salvation by law is already sin. A minor chord within this general reading tradition is voiced by Ulrich Wilckens.[41] Striving to fulfill the law, he says, is not in itself an act of idolatry. Rather works of the law are to be avoided because of the impossibility of their fulfillment. The heirs of the Protestant Reformers, then, offer two reasons for Paul's hostility to works of law: first, the idolatrous nature of works (legalism) and second, the impossibility of fulfilling the law by such works. For anyone persuaded by the new perspective on Paul, this reading makes no sense at all. For such a reader, Judaism was not legalistic and Judaism believed the law could be obeyed.

(2) The new perspective on Paul offers its own alternative reading. Sanders provides two explanations for why Paul opposed works of law. "When he criticizes Judaism, he does so in a sweeping manner, and the criticism has two focuses: the lack of faith in Christ and the lack of equality for the Gentiles."[42] First, for Paul, salvation is in Christ alone. Therefore, it cannot be by the law.[43] Second, works of the law are signs of Jewish privilege and, therefore, nationalistic and exclusive.[44] Paul, however, believed that one need not be Jewish to be righteous.[45] The second of these reasons for Paul's critique of works of law has been taken up with a vengeance by James D. G. Dunn.[46] By works of law Paul referred to ethnic boundary markers like circumcision, sabbath observance, and food laws that distinguish Jews from Gentiles. So Paul's polemic is against Jewish exclusiveness towards Gentiles. It is not an argument against the role of human effort in salvation. The gist of the new perspective's argument is to move the focus of Paul's theology

40. Käsemann, "Paul and Israel," 184-85.

41. Ulrich Wilckens, "Was heisst bei Paulus: 'Aus Werken des Gesetzes wird kein Mensch gerecht'?" in *Rechtfertigung als Freiheit* (Neukirchen: Neukirchener Verlag, 1974), 94.

42. E. P. Sanders, *Paul, the Law, and the Jewish People* (Philadelphia: Fortress, 1983), 154-55.

43. Sanders, *Paul, the Law, and the Jewish People*, 27.

44. Sanders, *Paul* (Oxford: Oxford University Press, 1991), 122.

45. Sanders, *Paul, the Law, and the Jewish People*, 46-47, 113-14, 159.

46. James D. G. Dunn, "The New Perspective on Paul," 95-122; "Works of the Law and the Curse of the Law (Gal 3:10-14)," *NTS* 31 (1985): 523-42; *Romans* (AnBib 38A; Dallas: Word, 1988), 154-55; "4QMMT and Galatians," *NTS* 43 (1997): 147-53; *The Theology of Paul the Apostle* (Grand Rapids: Eerdmans, 1998), 353-71.

from grace (divine initiative) versus legalism (human initiative/self-sufficiency) to universalism (inclusiveness) versus ethnic particularism (exclusiveness).

Although this revisionist reading has become critical orthodoxy, it has not been without its critics. Three examples are representative. First, R. H. Gundry contends that "Paul is not criticizing the Jews' unbelief in Christ instead of their attempt to perform the law, but he is criticizing their unbelief as caused by an attempt to perform the law."[47] Philippians 3:2-11, he says, starts with Jewish status symbols but it climaxes with confidence in personal accomplishments. The latter points to the attitudinal sin of self-righteousness alongside the mistake of missing Christ. In Rom 9:30–10:13 lack of faith does not displace but rather complements wrong dependence on one's own works. So Paul rejected non-messianic Judaism and Judaistic Christianity not only because of a conviction that God had revealed His Son to him but also because of his belief that works righteousness lay at the heart of both.[48] Second, C. E. B. Cranfield rejects the claim that works of law can be reduced to ethnic boundary markers. Works of law in Paul, he contends, refers to obedience to the law generally.[49] His exegetical examination of all the references in Romans is compelling. Moreover, works of law as obedience to the commandments generally is the way Paul's earliest interpreters understood his argument (Eph 2:8-19; 2 Tim 1:9; Titus 3:4-5). Paul's opponents also apparently understood his position, at least as they knew it, in the same way (Jas 2:14-26; Jude 4). Works of the law, then, cannot be reduced to ethnic identity markers, although such Jewish distinctives are included in the broader category.[50] This leads Frank Thielman to conclude that Paul uses works of law sometimes in connection with nationalism (Rom 2:17-20; 3:27-30; Gal 2:11-21), sometimes associated with human effort (Rom 3:9-20; 4:4-5; 9:30–10:13; 11:6; Gal 3:18; Phil 3:9), and sometimes with both (Rom 9:10-13; Gal 3:10-14).[51] Third, Jacob Neusner contends that, in ancient rab-

---

47. R. H. Gundry, "Grace, Works, and Staying Saved in Paul," *Bib* 66 (1985): 19.

48. This conclusion is supported by Timo Laato, *Paul and Judaism*, 209.

49. C. E. B. Cranfield, "The Works of the Law in the Epistle to the Romans," in *On Romans and Other New Testament Essays* (Edinburgh: T. & T. Clark, 1998), 1-14. Cf. T. R. Schreiner, "Works of Law in Paul," *NovT* 33 (1991): 217-44, who surveys Romans, Galatians, and Qumran and reaches a similar conclusion.

50. Klyne Snodgrass, "Spheres of Influence: A Possible Solution to the Problem of Paul and the Law," *JSNT* 32 (1988): 102, rightly contends that even if "works of law" did refer only to identity markers, they would still be a subset of "works" in general.

51. Frank Thielman, "Paul as Jewish Christian Theologian," 385.

binic Judaism, Israel was not an ethnic category.[52] If so, then the new perspective's proposal does not avoid caricaturing ancient Judaism. It merely replaces one alleged caricature with another. These three critics, it seems to me, have the better of the argument.

The third reading of Paul, again represented by Timo Eskola, contends that works of law in the genuine epistles refers not to legalism but to synergism. Works, of whatever kind, are what is necessary to activate God's grace. The ancient Judaism surveyed by Sanders cannot be described merely as covenantal nomism. Rather, once a covenantal nomistic Judaism is set within an eschatological context, obedience to the law is no longer just how to "stay in" God's people but much more how to "get in" the age-to-come. Once this is so, then Judaism becomes a legalistic covenantal nomism whose soteriology is that of synergism.[53] It is this legalistic covenantal nomism which Paul opposes. If so, then an explanation for what is wrong with works that is very similar to that of the Reformers and their heirs comes again into play. Pauline theology is once again seen as a struggle between divine grace and human self-sufficiency rather than being reduced to the tensions between social inclusivism and exclusivism.

In light of the answer suggested to question one, no one of these three readings of Paul is exactly on target. The one that is farthest from the evidence is the new perspective on Paul. In spite of its claims finally to offer a correct picture of Judaism, its view of Middle Judaism is seriously skewed. This throws its entire reading of Paul off center. The heirs of the Reformers correctly see that some ancient Jews were legalists. The post–new perspective interpreters rightly recognize the soteriological synergism of much ancient Palestinian Judaism. Taken together, they give a more accurate picture of the Judaism of Paul's time than do Sanders and his followers. Both the heirs of the Reformers and the post–new perspective interpreters correctly see that the heart of Paul's theological struggle is divine grace versus human self-sufficiency whatever the particular circumstances might be that evoke his letters.[54]

52. Jacob Neusner, "Was Rabbinic Judaism Really 'Ethnic'?" *CBQ* 57 (1995): 281-305.

53. Timo Eskola, "Paul, Predestination and Covenantal Nomism — Re-assessing Paul and Palestinian Judaism," 390-412, and the other bibliography mentioned in n. 11.

54. Krister Stendahl, *Paul among Jews and Gentiles and Other Essays* (Philadelphia: Fortress, 1976), 2, 26, 29, 36-37, argues that the issue in Romans is Jew-Gentile equality in Christ (9–11). Romans 1–8 is a preface to chapters 9–11. The Jews are not a symbol of a timeless legalism. The logical consequence of Stendahl's argument is found in Francis Watson's *Paul, Judaism, and the Gentiles,* where the theology of 1–8 is merely a rhetorical technique to

It is now time to turn to the third of the questions around which this paper is organized. If legalism and synergism were Jewish options in Paul's context, and if Paul opposed all attempts to effect salvation by human initiative, how did the apostle understand God's grace to operate soteriologically after one "gets in" the messianic people of God? How did he avoid the pitfalls of legalism and synergism in the Christian life?

How Did Paul Avoid the Pitfalls of That Which He Critiqued?

Paul worked in a milieu where legalism and synergism were present as religious options in both non-Christian Judaism and in Christian messianic Judaism. His gospel included a critique of both. How did his soteriology avoid both of these alternatives? Again it is helpful in answering the question if we begin with different readings of Paul. This time we focus on only two: the new perspective on Paul and the post–new perspective reading.

E. P. Sanders again serves as the representative of the new perspective. According to Sanders, Paul presents an essentially different type of religiousness from that found in Palestinian Jewish literature. This difference, however, is not at the level of grace and works. Both agree that we are saved by grace and judged by works. The difference is Christ. Christians participate in Christ. This participation results not only in forgiveness of transgressions but also in deliverance from the bondage of sin. Everyone, Jew and Gentile alike, must transfer to the group being saved. From this perspective, what is wrong with Judaism is that it is not Christianity. This synthesis of Paul's thought as participationist eschatology, Sanders believes, is in harmony with his correct view of ancient Judaism.

Timo Laato may serve as a representative of the post–new perspective reading of Paul.[55] From his standpoint as well, Paul's religion is of a different

---

accomplish the end (9–11), a means that has no significance beyond such a function. Both follow F. C. Baur's claim that Romans' significance lies not so much in its doctrinal discussion about sin and grace as in its practical bearing on the relation between Jew and Gentile. The effect: Paul is seen as advocating Jew and Gentile unity in Christ *instead of* justification by grace through faith. One can only say that if the theological justification for Gentile-Jewish equality has no substance, then the end sought by this rhetoric is untenable. A proper reading would hold instead: Paul advocates Jew and Gentile unity in Christ *because of* justification through faith. Cf. Frank J. Matera, "Galatians in Perspective: Cutting a New Path through Old Territory," *Int* 54 (2000): 233-45.

55. Laato, *Paul and Judaism: An Anthropological Approach.*

type from that of ancient non-messianic Judaism. The difference goes back to their respective anthropologies. Palestinian Judaism was optimistic; Paul was pessimistic.[56] If non-Christian Judaism was optimistic, then soteriological synergism was possible. If Paul was pessimistic, then everything depends on God. Like Sanders, Laato believes Paul's soteriology was primarily participationist. One's participation in Christ results not only in forgiveness and deliverance but also in enablement. What is it that enables Christians' works after their entry into Christ? It is their empowerment by God. Everyone, Jew and Gentile alike, then, must transfer to Christ to receive these benefits. What is wrong with non-Christian Judaism is its synergistic soteriology. To maintain this, he contends, does not return one to Ferdinand Weber's view of ancient Judaism. "Paul criticizes the boasting and self-righteousness arising even from covenantal nomism."[57]

The crucial difference here between these two readings is in their presentations of the scope of Pauline soteriology. Sanders rightly pushes beyond justification as forgiveness for transgressions. "People are not just guilty, they are enslaved, and they need to escape."[58] Hence, he interprets justification in Rom 6:6-7 as being set free. Paul, he says, forced the passive verb to mean "changed, transferred, incorporated into another person."[59] Sanders also can speak of Paul's belief that "Christ lives in and through the believer."[60] In Paul's thought, "deeds do flow from the Spirit, not from commandments."[61] He, however, never pursues this aspect of Paul's soteriology. Most likely, it is because he rejects a pessimistic anthropology for Paul.[62] It is left to Laato to focus on this dimension of Pauline thought. He insists that in Paul grace and obedience should not be viewed as successive stages in the Christian life. This would produce a new legalism. He says: "If the ethical norms provoke no good works among the church members, Paul does not urge the lukewarm hearers on to do their part as God has already done his

56. Laato acknowledges his indebtedness in this regard to Hugo Odeberg, *Pharisaism and Christianity* (St. Louis: Concordia, 1964). This point of view is shared by Christiaan Beker, *The Triumph of God: The Essence of Paul's Thought* (Minneapolis: Fortress, 1990), 106, 108, 134.

57. Laato, *Paul and Judaism*, 210.

58. Sanders, *Paul*, 79.

59. Sanders, *Paul*, 48.

60. Sanders, *Paul*, 76.

61. Sanders, *Paul, the Law, and the Jewish People*, 208.

62. Sanders, *Paul, the Law, and the Jewish People*, 80, says that in Romans 7 Paul "overstates human inability to fulfill the law." It was not what he really thought. On pp. 35-36, Sanders dismisses "all are under the power of sin" to the periphery of Paul's thought.

part by reconciling the world in Jesus Christ. The new life depends rather on the Gospel reviving the dead faith. Living faith works then incessantly by love (Gal 5:6)."[63] For Paul, Christians cannot — after a certain stage in their spiritual development — fulfill the law by their own willpower. Citing texts like Phil 1:6; 2:12-13; and Gal 2:20, Laato contends that, in Paul, Christians act because it is God who acts in them. Although Sanders lays weight on Paul's participationist categories, Laato contends, he does not draw the right conclusion from them.[64] Laato concludes: "In view of participatory categories it appears incontestable that the way of staying in according to the Pauline pattern of religion does not correspond to that of the Jewish pattern: Christ does the good works of Christians."[65] Obedience to the law in covenantal nomism is not an equivalent to manifesting the fruit of the Spirit as a way of "staying in." The good works of Christians have their origin in the action of God/Christ/Spirit (monergism), while those of non-Christian Jews and Judaistic Christians arise from human strength (synergism).[66] The non-messianic Jew or Judaistic Christian stays in the covenant through obedience to the law which is possible by human free will. For Paul, obedience to the law depends on the Spirit.[67] The pessimistic and optimistic anthropologies hover in the background as presuppositions for the alternative soteriological stances.[68] In distinguishing between the foreground and the background on Pauline theology, Laato joins the ranks of others like Christiaan Beker[69] and N. T. Wright, who are attempting the same thing.

N. T. Wright, for example, distinguishes between Paul's explicit theology on the one hand which is out in the open, but if studied piecemeal remains unintegrated, and Paul's wider worldview and belief system on the

---

63. Laato, *Paul and Judaism*, 159-60.

64. The statement by Sanders that draws Laato's ire is found in Sanders's article, "Jesus, Paul and Judaism," *ANRW* 25.1:449. Sanders says about Paul and Judaism: "In both cases . . . salvation is by the grace of God, while works (in Judaism, observance of the Mosaic law; in Paul, producing the fruit of the Spirit) are the condition of remaining 'in.'"

65. Laato, *Paul and Judaism*, 161-62.

66. Laato, *Paul and Judaism*, 162.

67. Laato, *Paul and Judaism*, 175-76.

68. Laato, *Paul and Judaism*, 167.

69. Beker, *The Triumph of God: The Essence of Paul's Thought*, employs the categories "coherence and contingency." He claims that the coherent center of Paul's thought is located on a subtextual level, not in one of the contingent symbols of the text. It is an apocalyptic matrix that is the coherent center (134-35). Beker agrees with Laato that "all are under the power of sin" forms the indispensable presupposition of the coherent center of Paul's thought (134).

other, presupposed by his explicit theology.[70] He sees this assumption system located in the belief of many first-century Jews that the Babylonian exile of Israel continued into their own day. So Israel's promised forgiveness of sins and restoration from exile were yet to come. Paul, in this view, claimed the hour of fulfillment had arrived in Jesus' death and resurrection. The particular form of Paul's worldview espoused by Wright is suspect because it is not clear that there was a widespread sense in Middle Judaism that Israel remained in exile. Baruch 4:36 and 5:5-9 say that the return from the exile is in progress; Judith 4:1-5 and 5:17-19 and Josephus, *Antiquities* 4.314, 10.112-13, and 11.1-4 say the exile is over. *M. 'Avot* 1.11 has Abtalion speak in a way that assumes the exile is over but another is a future possibility.[71] At the same time, Wright's general point that an assumption system underlay Paul's explicit theology is persuasive and widely accepted. The question is: What is it? I offer my suggestion.

In an earlier essay[72] I argued that Paul read his scriptures, the scriptures of Israel, in a way that valued certain covenants and not others.[73] Paul makes no mention of the covenants with Noah (Gen 9:8-17), Phinehas (Num 25:10-13), Joshua (Josh 24), Josiah (2 Kgs 23), and Ezra (Ezra 9–10; Neh 9–10). The covenant with David is not central to Paul's thought, although it is echoed in the oral tradition taken up in Rom 1:3-4 ("descended from David according to the flesh") and in the quotation from Isa 11:10 in Rom 15:12 ("The root of Jesse will come, he who rises to rule the Gentiles; in him shall the Gentiles hope"). If so, Paul would see the promise to David fulfilled in the reign of Jesus after the resurrection (1 Cor 15:20-28). Three covenants of the scriptures of Israel receive significant attention in Paul's letters: (1) the covenant with Abraham, (2) the Mosaic covenant, and (3) the new covenant of Jer 31. Of the three covenants that play a significant role in Paul's letters, two are highly valued, while the third's importance is minimized by the apostle.

---

70. N. T. Wright, "Romans and the Theology of Paul," in *Pauline Theology*, vol. 3: *Romans* (ed. David M. Hay and E. Elizabeth Johnson; Minneapolis: Fortress, 1995), 30-67, especially 31-34; *The New Testament and the People of God* (Minneapolis: Fortress, 1992), 268-79.

71. Seifrid, "The 'New Perspective on Paul' and Its Problems," 7-9 (appealing to F. G. Downing).

72. Charles H. Talbert, "Paul on the Covenant," *RevExp* 84 (1987): 299-313.

73. Sanders, *Paul, the Law, and the Jewish People*, 162, argues that Paul's distinctive interpretation of scripture reflects the great convictions that determined his career and theology. Peter Stuhlmacher, "Theologische Probleme des Römerbriefpräscripts," *EvT* 27 (1967): 378, also locates Paul's distinctives in his reading of the scriptures.

The construct that makes the best sense out of the various things Paul says about the covenants throughout his letters may be summarized as follows. (1) The covenant with Abraham furnishes Paul a scriptural way to argue that justification through faith has been God's plan all along for Jew and Gentile alike. Both the focus on God's promise and that on universalism are rooted here. (2) The law (Mosaic covenant) was a temporary phase in God's dealings with his people. In spite of its just requirements, it was impotent because of human sin. With the coming of Christ, the law (Mosaic covenant) has come to an end as a part of ongoing salvation history. (3) The Mosaic covenant has been replaced in salvation history by the prophesied New Covenant of Jer 31 in which God himself enables his people's faithfulness to the relationship. It is this way of reading Israel's scriptures that underlies Paul's explicit theological statements in his letters.

Paul's thought in this regard is seen most clearly when set against the backdrop of Middle Judaism. Different circles valued the covenants differently. For example, the *Psalms of Solomon* refer to the covenant with Abraham (9:9-10; 18:3) and to the Mosaic covenant (10:4), but the covenant central in their thought is the Davidic one (chs. 17, 18). The new covenant of Jer 31:31-34, moreover, is absent from Second Temple Judaism, except for Qumran and Christian messianic Judaism. At Qumran, *new covenant* is used (CD-A VI, 18-19; VIII, 20-21; CD-B XIX, 33-34; XX, 11-13; 1QpHab II, 3) interchangeably with other expressions like *covenant of God, this covenant, covenant of the everlasting community, covenant of loyalty and fidelity*, and others.[74] Qumran saw the new covenant as a return to the original intentions of the Mosaic Torah.[75] This is similar to the earliest exegetical use of Jer 31 in Rabbinic Judaism. *Sifra* on Leviticus has Jer 31 juxtaposed with Lev 26:9 in order to clarify the latter verse. The result: the promise to maintain the covenant in Lev 26 is identified with the making of the new covenant in Jer 31.[76]

Among the early Christian messianic Jewish references to the new covenant are: Gal 4:21-31 (?); 1 Cor 11:25; 2 Cor 3:6, 14; Heb 8:6-13; and Luke 22:20. Some less reliable manuscripts of Mark 14:24 add "new" before covenant, and a similar situation applies in Matt 26:28. In both cases, the "new" was likely

74. Susanne Lehne, *The New Covenant in Hebrews* (Sheffield: JSOT, 1990), 43.

75. Lehne, *New Covenant in Hebrews,* 58; Ellen Juhl Christiansen, *The Covenant in Judaism and Paul* (AGJU 27; Leiden: Brill, 1995), 129-30.

76. Richard S. Sarason, "The Interpretation of Jeremiah 31:31-34 in Judaism," in *When Jews and Christians Meet* (ed. Jakob J. Petuchowski; Albany: SUNY Press, 1988), 99-123. Five later texts understand Jer 31:33-34 to refer to study of the Torah rather than observance of Torah.

added to make explicit what is implicit in the best texts. John 13:34's reference to a "new commandment" assumes a new covenant, just as Revelation 5:9's "new song" also assumes a new deliverance/covenant. Christian messianic Judaism saw the old Sinai covenant as, at best, soteriologically inefficacious.[77] Paul, then, fits into Christian messianic Judaism's way of thinking about a new covenant that replaces an old, inefficacious one. In addition, he focuses on the Abrahamic covenant as a basis for Gentile inclusion in God's people. This view of the covenants, I propose, is at the heart of Paul's assumption system that controls his explicit theological statements. If so, how does it bear on the question at hand? What does Paul's view of the covenants have to do with his positions on divine enablement of the Christian life?

Given his pessimistic anthropology, Paul did not believe that humans could, in and of themselves, be faithful in their relationship with God. Soteriological synergism, therefore, was for him no more an option for "staying in" than for "getting in" the eschatological participation in Christ. The new covenant of Jer 31 provided scriptural warrant for Paul's conviction that God supplied and supplies what a pessimistic anthropology requires if humans are to relate to God faithfully (= be righteous). If this is the coherent assumption system out of which Paul thinks, what are the specific, contingent images/categories that give expression to God's enabling power in the Christian life?

Laato rightly uses the language of indwelling (Gal 2:20; Phil 2:12-13). There are numerous other ways, however, that Paul speaks about human transformation by means of divine enablement/empowerment. Without any attempt to be exhaustive we may mention: touching (2 Cor 3:2-3; 2 Tim 1:6), drinking (1 Cor 12:13), hearing (1 Thess 2:13; Rom 10:17), seeing/contemplating (2 Cor 3:18), being given a gift (Rom 5:17; Phil 3:9), and being clothed (Gal 3:27). Because of the limitations of space, we will limit ourselves to only one: being clothed.

In Paul's context, the image of being clothed or clothing oneself was employed as a way of talking about empowerment/transformation. Several examples suffice. (1) Putting on the actual apparel of another person was believed to convey that person's role to the one being clothed. LXX Numbers 20:25-28 speaks about Aaron's apparel being taken off him and put on Eleazar as part of the succession of the priesthood. The transfer of apparel conveyed a transfer of role. LXX 3 Kings 19:19 tells how Elijah casts his mantle on Elisha as part of his anointing the younger man to succeed him. (2) Putting on the ac-

---

77. Lehne, *New Covenant in Hebrews*, 58.

tual apparel of another conveys the Spirit or transforms a person ontologically. LXX 4 Kings 2:13, 9, 14-15 narrates how when Elijah was being taken up into heaven his mantle fell on Elisha. This is connected in the story with the transfer of the Spirit that had been on Elijah to Elisha. *2 Enoch* 22:8-10 has God tell Michael to clothe Enoch in the garments of glory. When the angel does so, Enoch is transformed and becomes like the angels. The same theme is also found in the early Christian *Martyrdom and Ascension of Isaiah* 8:14-15, where Isaiah learns that on donning the garments of glory he will be transformed. (3) Being clothed with some aspect of another's selfhood empowers one who is so clothed. LXX Judges 6:34 says that the Spirit of the Lord clothed Gideon, empowering him to act as Israel's savior. Pseudo-Philo 20:2-5 has God tell Joshua to clothe himself in Moses' garments of wisdom and belt of knowledge. When he does so, "his mind was afire and his spirit was moved" and he was enabled to lead the people. LXX Baruch 5:2, 9 exhorts Jerusalem to wrap around herself a double garment of the righteousness from God with the promise that God will deliver her with the righteousness that comes from Him. The *Testament of Levi* 18:14 says that in the End Time "all the saints shall be clothed in righteousness." The context shows this means they will be enabled to please God. This mindset is found in the early Christian Hermas, *Vision* 4.1.8-9 and 4.2.4. Hermas, clothed in the faith of the Lord, takes courage, faces the beast, and conquers through angelic help.

Paul's authorial audience[78] would have heard a statement like Gal 3:27 ("as many of you as were baptized into Christ have put on Christ") as a statement of empowering just as much as they would Gal 2:20 about the indwelling Christ's living through believers. To be clothed in Christ means to be transformed by Christ and to be enabled by Christ with Christ's own power. Likewise Rom 13:14's "put on the Lord Jesus Christ" is an exhortation to appropriate the enabling power within one's participation in Christ to "make no provision for the flesh."

Whatever the concrete, contingent image used by the apostle, the import is that the Christian life is enabled by God/Christ/the Spirit. Christian behavior is fruit of the Spirit (Gal 5:22-23); it is a living out of the salvation of the God who is active within, enabling us to will and to work for his good pleasure (Phil 2:12-13); it is a manifestation of the faithfulness of the Son of

---

78. Peter J. Rabinowitz, "Truth in Fiction: A Reexamination of Audiences," *Critical Inquiry* 4 (1977): 121-41; *Before Reading: Narrative Conventions and the Poetics of Interpretation* (Ithaca, NY: Cornell University Press, 1987); cf. also Hans Robert Jauss, "Literary History as a Challenge to Literary Theory," in *Toward an Aesthetic of Reception* (Minneapolis: University of Minnesota Press, 1982), 3-45.

God who lives in and through believers (Gal 2:20).[79] In Paul's mind, Christian obedience is due to divine enablement. Because of his pessimistic anthropology, nothing else would suffice.[80] If there is any human faithfulness in the relation to God, Paul believes it is due to divine empowerment. It is all of grace![81] The scriptural root for this basic assumption is the new covenant of Jer 31. Whatever the contingent image, this is Paul's coherent core. In this way, he, if not his heirs, escaped the pitfalls of the legalism and synergism against which he devoted his ministry.

Viewed in this light, once again the post–new perspective reading of Paul seems more adequate than the new perspective of Sanders. For Paul, grace and obedience are not successive stages in religious life but are bound together in each moment as root and fruit. For the apostle, obedience is not so much motivated by gratitude for past grace as empowered by an enabling God from moment to moment. Laato offers a careful exposition of a dimension of Pauline thought that is underdeveloped in the new perspective on Paul.

At the end of our survey the Reformers and their heirs look a lot less like ignorant villains; the revisionists with their new perspective on Paul appear much less knowledgeable and far less convincing; and the post–new perspective reading of Pauline thought calls for yet another paradigm shift, one that will pay due respect not only to a chastened view of Middle Judaism but also to the theological exegesis of the much-maligned heirs of the Reformers, some of whom are Catholic.

79. Brendan Byrne, *Reckoning with Romans* (Wilmington, DE: Michael Glazier, 1986), 125, contends that the Christian life for Paul is "a continued living out of the 'obedience' of Christ, or, more accurately perhaps, it means Christians allowing Christ to live out in them his continuing obedience and fidelity to the Father (cf. Gal 2:19-20 . . .)."

80. Paul's position is reasonable but not necessary. Qumran (1QS XI, 9-10) and *4 Ezra* (3:19-26) held to pessimistic anthropologies but continued to believe that at least a few individuals could and would themselves obey the law. Paul's creativity is seen in his linking a pessimistic anthropology (like that at Qumran and in *4 Ezra*) with a soteriology of divine enablement (like that of LXX Jer 38:31-34; Isa 2:1-4; and Tob 14:6-7; and the *Apocalypse of Abraham*).

81. Jan Lambrecht and Richard W. Thompson, *Justification by Faith: The Implications of Romans 3:27-31* (Wilmington, DE: Michael Glazier, 1989), 84, conclude their study: "For Paul, Jewish boasting was excluded for one fundamental reason: in the final analysis, everything is grace." If Lambrecht, Thompson, and Byrne are any indication, *sola gratia* is a Catholic as well as a Protestant reading of Paul. The *Joint Declaration on the Doctrine of Justification* by the Lutheran World Federation and the Roman Catholic Church (Grand Rapids: Eerdmans, 2000) confirms it.

Enabling Χάρις: Transformation of the Convention of Reciprocity by Philo and in Ephesians

Jason A. Whitlark

In the ancient Mediterranean world the language of χάρις was commonly associated with the convention of benefaction or patronage and the dynamic of reciprocity. Such a dynamic encouraged the feeling of grateful indebtedness as a means to securing fidelity and emphasized the worthiness of the recipient of χάρις. Conversely, Philo and Ephesians, Hellenistic Jewish and Christian representatives respectively, both employ a notion of χάρις that undermines the rationale of reciprocity. When we examine Ephesians in particular, we will find, contrary to the rationale of reciprocity, that divine χάρις is given to the unworthy according to divine election and that divine χάρις *actually enables human fidelity.* On the other hand, we will see, in accordance with one aspect of the reciprocity rationale, that such beneficence is meant to result in praise to God.

•   •

The rationale of reciprocity is commonly used in the present to motivate and sustain the Christian life. For example, Enriquez Velunta outlines a Christian's response to grace according to the Filipino custom of reciprocity, *utang na loob,* about which he concludes, "It is through people who live their lives as debts of gratitude that God's liberating acts are revealed."[1] Moreover,

---

1. "*Ek Pisteōs eis Pistin* and the Filipino's Sense of Indebtedness," *SBL Seminar Papers, 1998* (2 vols.; SBLSP 37; Atlanta: Scholars, 1998), 1:37.

"reciprocity was at the heart of all forms of benevolence in the ancient Graeco-Roman world. The bestowal of gifts initiated the establishment of long-term relationships that involved mutual obligation and clear status differentials between the transactors."[2] Reciprocity can be defined as "exchange conceptualized as the performance of and requital of *gratuitous* [going beyond what is required] actions."[3] Or in other words, "reciprocity is the principle and practice of voluntary requital, of benefit for benefit (positive reciprocity) or harm for harm (negative reciprocity)."[4] More importantly, positive reciprocity in the ancient Mediterranean world was the means by which enduring faithfulness was secured, whether between the divine and human or among humans.

James R. Harrison has demonstrated that χάρις was a leitmotif for Hellenistic reciprocity systems in general and ancient Mediterranean benefaction in particular.[5] In fact the dual meaning of χάρις highlights the centrality of reciprocity in ancient benefaction, since χάρις could mean either the benefit given or the gratitude shown for such a benefit.[6] The language of χάρις features prominently in the Pauline corpus (100 out of 154 occurrences in the New Testament). Nowhere in the Pauline corpus is the language of χάρις more central and elevated than in the Letter to the Ephesians, where Christians are climactically declared to be saved by χάρις. The question with which this chapter will be primarily concerned is how the Christian auditors of the Letter to the Ephesians would have heard such a declaration. Frederick Danker has already compared Ephesians to an ancient honorific decree bestowed on benefactors as a demonstration of the

2. Stephan Joubert, *Paul as Benefactor: Reciprocity, Strategy and Theological Reflection in Paul's Collection* (WUNT 2.124; Tübingen: Mohr-Siebeck, 2000), 6.

3. Hans van Wees, "The Law of Gratitude: Reciprocity in Anthropological Theory," in *Reciprocity in Ancient Greece* (ed. Christopher Gill, Norman Postlethwaite, and Richard Seaford; New York: Oxford University Press, 1998), 20.

4. Richard Seaford, "Introduction," in Gill, Postlethwaite, and Seaford, eds., *Reciprocity in Ancient Greece*, 1.

5. James R. Harrison, *Paul's Language of Grace in Its Graeco-Roman Context* (WUNT 2.172; Tübingen: Mohr-Siebeck, 2003), 63.

6. Such reciprocity was given expression in the phrases χάρις χάριν γάρ (Sophocles, *Aj.* 522) or χάρις γὰρ ἀντὶ χάριτος (Euripides, *Hel.* 1234). Similarly, there was the notion of repaying χάρις, e.g., Diodorus Siculus 1.86.3 (χάριν ἀποδιδόντας); 1.86.5 (χάρις . . . ἀποδοῦναι); Dio, *Or.* 31.53 (ἀποδοῦναι χάριν); Aristotle, *Eth. Nic.* 1124 B10-12; 1164 B26 (εὐεργέτῃ ἀνταποδοτέον χάριν). *Pietas* served a similar function in the Roman Latin context. *Pietas* involved giving someone their due, especially for benefits bestowed or honor received (cf. Virgil, *An.* 2.536 and Cicero, *Nat. d.* 1.4.116)

beneficiaries' gratitude.[7] Such decrees were laced with the language of χάρις and embodied the rationale of reciprocity in the manifesto clauses typical of such decrees.[8] Would, then, Ephesians and its χάρις language have been heard in terms of reciprocity or something different? Another way to ask this question is, what is the basis or rationale for ongoing faithfulness in the divine-human relationship according to Ephesians? In an effort to answer this question, we will look briefly at the χάρις-convention, i.e., the reciprocity rationale, in ancient Mediterranean benefaction. We will next examine the soteriological implications of that reciprocity rationale. Then we will look at how both Philo and the Letter to the Ephesians use the language of χάρις. What we will see is that Philo and Ephesians understand divine χάρις in such a way that they overturn the rationale of reciprocity with a notion of divine enablement.

Characterization of Benefaction

In this section, we will examine the relational dynamic of Greco-Roman benefaction, namely reciprocity. After briefly describing reciprocity in the ancient Mediterranean world, we will look more in depth at the issues of indebtedness and the selection of the beneficiary. These topics were important to the goal of ancient reciprocity, which was to secure fidelity. Such an examination will prepare us to hear the adaptation that Philo and Ephesians make of the χάρις-convention.

Reciprocity: The Relational Dynamic of Benefaction

The reciprocity of benefaction in the ancient Mediterranean world is best illustrated by Seneca in answer to the question, "why the Graces are three in number and why they are sisters, why they have their hands interlocked, and why they are smiling and youthful and virginal, and are clad in loose and transparent garb." He writes:

> Some would have it appear that there is one for bestowing a benefit, another for receiving it, and a third for returning it. . . . Why do the sisters

7. Frederick W. Danker, *Benefactor: Epigraphic Study of a Greco-Roman and New Testament Semantic Field* (St. Louis: Clayton, 1982), 451-52.
8. Cf. Harrison, *Paul's Language of Grace*, 40-43.

hand in hand dance in a ring which returns upon itself? For the reason that a benefit passing in its course from hand to hand returns nevertheless to the giver; the beauty of the whole is destroyed if the course is anywhere broken, and the most beauty if it is continuous and maintains uninterrupted succession. (*Ben.* 1.3.2-4 [Basore, LCL])

Throughout his discussion on benefaction, Seneca repeatedly returns to this description of reciprocity as a never-ending circle of indebtedness that arises from favorable exchange: "I ought properly, to receive a benefit, then be indebted, then repay" (*Ben.* 5.9.4 [Basore, LCL]).[9] In the honorific inscriptions dedicated to benefactors, we see the same circle of reciprocity in the manifesto clauses. The manifesto clause of an honorary inscription from 200 B.C.E. is typical and reads:

Therefore, in order that the people might continue to be known for expressing appropriate appreciation for those who choose to be their benefactors and in order that physicians to come might show themselves all the more zealous in meeting the needs of the people.[10]

If we were to examine the ancient sources, we would find five fundamental characteristics that identified reciprocity. (1) Reciprocity is a relational bond. (2) Ideally, the bond is long-term and maintained by each party's fidelity to the relationship by means of a sense of indebted gratitude. (3) The bond is a cooperative agreement where both parties undertake specific obligations to maintain the relationship. (4) Cooperation entails mutual dependence, with each party having to rely upon the other for the fulfillment of his or her specific obligations. Finally, we would see that the success of reciprocity was predicated upon an optimistic anthropological assumption.[11]

Since securing fidelity was at the heart of the reciprocity systems of the ancient Mediterranean world, the feeling of indebtedness and the character of the beneficiary were two vital issues that influenced the giving of a benefaction. To these two related issues we now turn.

---

9. Cf. *Ben.* 1.4.3 and 2.18.5.

10. Danker, *Benefactor*, §2.

11. For a detailed examination of these characteristics see Jason Whitlark, *Enabling Fidelity to God: Perseverance in Hebrews in Light of the Reciprocity Systems of the Ancient Mediterranean World* (PBMS; Milton Keynes: Paternoster, 2008), 15-69.

Indebtedness and Benefaction

Even though a loan and a benefaction could be contrasted based upon the durability of the relationship established by each, the language of indebtedness was at home in Greco-Roman benefaction because of the reciprocal dynamic that undergirded the relationship. Aristotle notes the common conception of the benefit as a debt or a loan in *Eth. Nic.* 9.7.1. Both Seneca and Cicero easily apply the language of debt to the benefactor-beneficiary relationship. Seneca relates the giving of benefactions to making a loan (*Ben.* 1.1.2). Seneca regularly emphasizes that the receiver of a benefit should regard the benefit as a debt (*Ben.* 1.4.5). Moreover, the beneficiary who does not repay a benefit is regarded as a worse offender than the one who fails to give a benefit (*Ben.* 1.1.13). Cicero states:

> No duty is more imperative than that of proving one's gratitude.... For generosity is of two kinds: doing a kindness and requiting one. Whether we do a kindness or not is optional; but to fail to requite one is not allowable to a good man. (*Off.* 1.47 [Miller, LCL])

Cicero also reflects in this statement that the feeling of indebtedness for a benefit and the feeling of gratitude are synonymous. This feeling of indebted gratitude was precisely the glue that held together the bond of benefactor and beneficiary.

Not only was the feeling of indebtedness or gratitude important for the longevity of the relationship between human benefactors and their beneficiaries but also between divine benefactors and their human beneficiaries. Robert Parker has argued that in Greek religion, and I would add also Roman, the primary source of anxiety for a worshiper was that the gods might prove ungrateful.[12] For the honor and gratitude the worshipers offered, there was the hope that the gods would be grateful by continuing to bestow their benefits upon their worthy worshipers.[13]

I should point out that although Seneca applies the language of indebtedness to the beneficiary-side of the relationship, he frequently insists

12. Robert Parker, "Pleasing Thighs: Reciprocity in Greek Religion," in Gill, Postlethwaite, and Seaford, eds., *Reciprocity in Ancient Greece,* 105. See also Dieter Zeller, *Charis bei Philon und Paulus* (Stuttgarter Bibelstudien 142; Stuttgart: Verlag Katholisches Bibelwerk, 1990), 14-18. Cf. Virgil, *An.* 2.536 for a similar Roman notion.

13. Cf. Homer, *Il.* 8.236-44, where Agamemnon's complaint is based on such a dynamic between the gods and their human worshipers.

that the benefactor should not view his benefactions as a loan but as a gift (cf. *Ben.* 1.1.9). Seneca regularly recommends to human benefactors the gods, the greatest benefactors, as the models for the giving of benefits. The gods persistently give gifts to the ungrateful (*Ben.* 1.1.9-10; 2.29.5–2.30.1; 4.26.1; 7.31.2; 7.32.1-5).[14] These mutually contradictory rules of the benefactor-beneficiary relationship were devised in order to sustain and guarantee the dynamic of reciprocity. Each participant had a distinct code of virtue (generosity or gratitude) that was necessary to sustain this mutually beneficial relationship.[15] What is important to point out from all these observations is that debt, requital, and gratitude are the language of the reciprocity in Greco-Roman benefaction.

Selection of Benefactor and Beneficiary

Since Greco-Roman benefaction was based on such reciprocal exchange, choosing a benefactor or beneficiary was a matter of serious consideration for both members of this relationship. In *Ben.* 1.1.2, Seneca states that the reason there is so much ingratitude in beneficence is that benefactors "do not pick out those who are worthy of receiving gifts" (Basore, LCL). Thus Cicero, in *Off.* 1.45, records:

> In acts of kindness we should weigh with discrimination the worthiness of the object of our benevolence; we should take into consideration his moral character, his attitude toward us, the intimacy of his relations to us, and our common social ties, as well as those services he has hitherto rendered in our interest. (Miller, LCL)

Cicero goes on to state that the person who is invested with more virtue should be more favored as the object of beneficence (1.46). Seneca encourages benefactors to choose their beneficiaries as wisely as they would choose their debtors if they expect to be requited with gratitude (*Ben.* 1.1.2). Conversely, in a warning to beneficiaries, Seneca states:

---

14. Seneca reflects the belief that the persistent giving of benefits can eventually cultivate gratitude in the beneficiary (cf. *Ben.* 1.2.5; 1.3.1; 2.11.5; 5.1.4). Also see Plutarch, *Dion* 47.4.

15. David deSilva, *Honor, Patronage, Kinship, and Purity: Unlocking New Testament Culture* (Downers Grove, IL: InterVarsity, 2000), 118.

And so it is necessary for me to choose the person from whom I wish to receive a benefit; and, in truth, I must be far more careful in selecting my creditor for a benefit than a creditor for a loan. For to the latter I shall have to return the same amount that I have received, and, when I have returned it, I will have paid all my debt and am free; but to the other I must make an additional payment, and, even after I have paid my debt of gratitude, the bond between us still holds; for, just when I have finished paying it, I am obliged to begin again, and friendship endures. (*Ben.* 2.18.5 [Basore, LCL])

Again, the reason for such cautions is that the one who enters into a benefactor-beneficiary relationship enters a long-term relationship. The threefold nature of reciprocity suggests a continual ongoing relationship of giving and receiving. We see explicitly in Seneca's instructions the major conceptual difference between a benefaction and loan in the Greco-Roman world. A benefaction initiates an indefinite relationship while the relationship established with a creditor is terminated once the debt is repaid.[16] Seneca states that if he were to be ransomed from slavery by some unworthy person then he would receive the ransom "not as a benefit, but as a loan; then I shall repay the money to him. . . . I shall regard him . . . as a banker [as opposed to a friend]" (*Ben.* 2.21.1 [Basore, LCL]). Again, in *Ben.* 3.9.3–3.10.1, Seneca writes:

> Since benefits may be given in one form and repaid in another, it is difficult to establish their equality. Besides, for the repayment of a benefit no date is set, as there is for a loan of money. (Basore LCL)

Moreover, Seneca rebukes as ungrateful a person who does not endure under the obligation to requite benefits received but tries as quickly as possible to requite the benefit in order to be relieved of the obligation, for a benefit binds two people together (*Ben.* 6.40.1-2). This long-term relationship is inherent in the Greco-Roman notion of reciprocity and thus necessitated the careful evaluation of the character of the benefactor or beneficiary.

---

16. Cf. Stephen C. Mott, "The Power of Giving and Receiving: Reciprocity in Hellenistic Benevolence," in *Current Issues in Biblical and Patristic Interpretation* (ed. Gerald F. Hawthorne; Grand Rapids: Eerdmans, 1975), 63.

Soteriological Implications of Reciprocity

From this survey of the ancient literature as it concerns the use of χάρις, we have noted that χάρις is regularly used in a context of reciprocity. If one wants to talk about χάρις, more specifically divine salvation by χάρις, within the context of Greco-Roman benefaction and the dynamic of reciprocity that maintained it, there are some important implications for soteriology. First, with regard to entrance into a relationship with the divine benefactor, either the character of the recipient of divine favor determines whether benefits are given or withheld, or the divine benefits are given initially to the unworthy in hope that the recipient will prove gratefully indebted. Second, regardless of whether the initial benefit was given to the worthy or unworthy, the ongoing nature of the relationship depends upon the beneficiary's willingness to feel gratefully indebted, out of which comes the enduring obedience of the beneficiary.[17] The failure to feel indebted breaks the dance of reciprocity and effectively dissolves the beneficial relationship. In most cases, the failure to appropriately reciprocate divine benefits precipitates divine wrath.[18]

Philo and Ephesians, however, present a use of the benefactor-beneficiary model between God and humans and a use of χάρις that run counter to the expectations established from the above survey. They offer a scheme of salvation and fidelity contrary to reciprocity.[19] The following

17. Stephan Joubert, "ΧΑΡΙΣ in Paul: An Investigation into the Apostle's 'Performative' Application of the Language of *Grace* within the Framework of His Theological Reflection on the Event/Process of Salvation," in *Salvation in the New Testament* (ed. Jan G. van der Watt; NovTSup 121; Atlanta: SBL, 2005), 187-212, seems to suggest that this is in fact the implication of Paul's use of χάρις in his genuine letters. Without directly responding to Joubert's analysis of the genuine Pauline letters, the results of this paper offer a way of conceptualizing Paul's χάρις-language in his genuine letters and of assessing Joubert's exploration of that χάρις-language.

18. Cf. Aristotle, *Rhet.* 2.2.8; Aulus Gellius, *Noct. Att.* 7.14.2-4; Harrison, *Paul's Language of Grace*, 53, 56.

19. Josephus is the clearest Jewish example of how the covenant relationship with God could be reconceptualized according to the benefactor-beneficiary (patron-client) model and the reciprocity that typically maintained it. Paul Spilsbury points out that *Ant.* 4.212 "is a classic statement of the workings of a patron-client relationship. Displays of gratitude for benefactions received are meant, in part, to secure further benefactions" ("God and Israel in Josephus: A Patron-Client Relationship," in *Understanding Josephus: Seven Perspectives,* ed. Steve Mason [Sheffield: Sheffield Academic Press, 1998], 183). Spilsbury goes on to observe concerning 4.190, "The conditional, two-sided nature of the relationship between God and the Hebrews is clearly exemplified in this speech. . . . The basis of the relationship between God and Israel is ultimately God's generosity in providing the law. In order for there to be a

analysis of Philo and Ephesians will demonstrate that God gives not only initial χάρις that establishes a covenant relationship with him, but also continuing χάρις that empowers the beneficiary's fidelity. Thus the logic of reciprocity is undermined and replaced with a rationale of divine enablement in order to secure fidelity to the relationship.

Benefaction of Χάρις in Philo

Philo is a prolific representative of the Hellenistic Jewish world, a subculture in the Greco-Roman world and the subculture in which the Pauline mission thrived. We will examine Philo's use of χάρις in the context of his discussion of God as benefactor. What we will see is that Philo subverts the reciprocity rationale associated with benefaction as it relates to the attainment of the immortal life.

In the Philonic corpus εὐεργέτης (benefactor) occurs fifty-two times. In several of those instances the term is an appellation for God.[20] After objecting to the manner and motives by which Greco-Roman benefaction operates, Philo says of God:

> But God is no salesman, hawking His goods in the market, but a free giver of all things, pouring forth eternal fountains of free bounties (χαρίτων), and seeking no return. For He has no needs Himself and no created being is able to repay His gift. (*Cher.* 123)[21]

Philo, here, appears to represent a philosophic critique of the reciprocity that undergirded Greco-Roman religion.[22] The resources or χάρις that God has are inexhaustible and place him beyond all need of anything from his creation. Furthermore, Philo asserts that all creation belongs to God (*Mut.* 28). Creation is always in the place of the beggar (*Her.* 103). Moreover, all humans stand in need of God's benefaction (*Spec.* 1.152). Consequently, creation has no χάρις to give back to God that would enrich him in any way, for it can only render back what has already freely come from God.

---

relationship, however, God's generosity must be reciprocated by the piety of the Israelites expressed in obedience to God's laws. Piety evokes God's blessings which in turn evoke gratitude from the people. Gratitude ensures God's continued favor on a people who continue to live by the law" (189, 191).

20. Cf. *Leg.* 2.56; *Congr.* 97; *Deus.* 110; *Plant.* 87; *Dec.* 41; *Spec.* 1.209.

21. All quotes from the Philonic corpus are from the LCL.

22. Cf. Plato, *Euthyphro* 14E-15A.

Philo, however, distinguishes between two types of χάρις that come from God. The two types can be classified as general χάρις and particular χάρις. In *Ebr.* 117-19, Philo talks about the universe as a gift from God to all, but virtues are particular gifts given by God to some. Concerning this general χάρις, Philo writes:

> The righteous man exploring the nature of existences makes a surprising *find*, in this one discovery, that all things are a grace (χάριν) of God, and the creation has no gift of grace (χάρισμα) to bestow, for neither has it any possession, since all things are God's possession, and for this reason grace (χάριν) too belongs to Him alone as a thing that is His very own. Thus to those who ask what the origin of creation is the right answer would be, that it is the goodness and grace of God, which He bestowed on the race that stands next after Him. For all things in the world and the world itself is a free gift (χάρισμα) and act of kindness and grace on God's part. (*Leg.* 3.78)

For Philo, creation is a gift or χάρις from God to all who dwell in it. Anything that contributes to the maintenance of creation and enjoyment of it is due to the χάρις of God. In *Congr.* 96 Philo writes concerning the human body, "For its [the body] life and survival, growth and health, come to it by the grace (χαρίτι) of God." All things good in the creation have come from God the benefactor of the whole world (*Sob.* 55). Creation and the enjoyment thereof is God's general χάρις, for all creatures indiscriminately.

The particular χάρις that God gives is that of virtue. This χάρις is not given to everyone.

> For many souls have the desire to repent and not been permitted by God to do so. (*Leg.* 3.213)

> For the life of virtue, which is life in its truest form, is shared by few, and these few are not found among the vulgar herd, none of whom has a part in the true life, but only among those to whom it is granted to escape the aims which engross humanity and to live to God alone. (*Mut.* 213)

This particular χάρις is more important than the general χάρις, for without virtue the soul will never achieve immortality.[23] More significantly, the

---

23. Cf. *QG* 1.6, 10, 56; *Her.* 274; *Conf.* 161.

virtuous life is entirely due to the χάρις of God. In *Leg.* 3.136-37, Philo writes:

> It is necessary that the soul should not ascribe to itself its toil for virtue, but that it should take it away from itself and refer it to God, confessing that not its own strength or power acquired nobility, but He who freely bestowed (χαρισάμενος) also the love of it. . . . For only then does the soul begin to be saved, . . . a readiness to yield the honor to God, the Bestower (εὐεργέτης) of the boon.

The soul's attainment of virtue and thereby immortality is solely the initiative of God.[24] God not only gives the χάρις for entrance into the virtuous life and thereby immortality but also the χάρις for the maintenance of that life as well. Speaking about Isaac's one wife Rebecca whose name means Constancy, Philo says:

> For he [Isaac] has ready beside him in their fullness the gifts of God, conveyed by the breath of God's higher graces (χάρισι), but he wishes and prays that these may remain with him constantly. And therefore I think his Benefactor, willing that His graces once received should stay forever with him, gives him Constancy for his spouse. (*Congr.* 38)

Elsewhere Philo writes:

> The other [perpetual liberation] stands firm through the grace (χάριτι) of the Benefactor, who is that worshipper's portion and possession. (*Sac.* 127)

> He shall do away with fear we feel before Him as Master, and implant in the soul the loyalty and affection that goes out to Him as Benefactor. (*Plant.* 89)

> For this mass of clay and blood . . . holds together and is quickened by the providence of God. . . . The spirit called Pharaoh, whose tyranny rife with lawlessness and cruelty it is impossible to escape, unless Eliezer be born in the soul and looks with hope to the help which God the only Saviour can give. (*Her.* 58, 60)

---

24. Philo emphasizes this point throughout *De Cherubim.* For a concise discussion of this point in *De Cherubim* see Fred W. Burnett, "Philo on Immortality: A Thematic Study of Philo's Concept of παλιγγενεσία," *CBQ* 46 (1984): 450-53.

For Philo the life of virtue is a χάρις from God and maintained by God. There is no room for reciprocity. In other words, God does not give initial χάρις and then rely on humans to make a grateful response to that χάρις in order to maintain the relationship in a perpetual circle of reciprocity. Though God is called Benefactor by Philo, Philo modifies the dynamics of that institution in God's relation to humans especially as it regards granting the life of virtue that leads to immortality. God is the beginning and the end of the life of virtue. God gives χάρις as a benefactor both to begin the life of virtue and to persevere in the life of virtue.

If the above analysis is correct, then how does gratitude function for Philo? Jean Laporte argues that "[t]o take pleasure in one's good deeds, or to consider oneself as their only author without further distinction, is to deny the necessity of God and to introduce impiety at the summit of spiritual life, at the moment when perfection seems close at hand. . . . As a remedy to this perversion, Philo offers thanksgiving, since it is the antidote to self-love."[25] Gratitude, as in reciprocity relationships, retains the function of honoring God for his benefits. Unlike reciprocity relationships, gratitude does not secure loyalty; instead, gratitude is an expression of humility and the acknowledgment of spiritual poverty in an individual who depends wholly on God's power to live unto God.

Ephesians and Salvation by Χάρις

In this next section we will examine the use of χάρις in Ephesians. First, we will explore the meaning of χάρις in all relevant passages in Ephesians. Second, we will look at *when* God gives χάρις for salvation, *to whom* it is given, *to what extent* it is given, and finally *for what purpose* it is given.

Χάρις in Ephesians

Ephesians uses χάρις eleven times with varying nuances of the basic meaning of a benefit.[26] In 4:29, χάρις simply means benefit. Christians are to

---

25. Jean Laporte, *Eucharistia in Philo* (Studies in the Bible and Early Christianity 3; Lewiston, NY: Edwin Mellen Press, 1983), 5. See also his more extensive discussion on pp. 172-78. Cf. Emile Bréhier, *Les idées philosophiques et religieuses de Philon d'Alexandrie* (Etudes de philosophie médiévale 8; Paris: Librairie philosophique J. Vrin, 1925), 298; David Winston, "Philo's Ethical Theory," *ANRW* 21.1:376-77.

26. There were three basic meanings of χάρις in the Greco-Roman world: (1) a charm-

speak only what is good and for edification "in order that it [their words] might give a *benefit* (χάριν) to those who hear" (emphasis mine).

In a more nuanced sense, Eph 4:7 uses χάρις to mean a spiritual gift for the benefit of the body. "But to each one of us the spiritual gift (χάρις) is given according to the measure of the gift of Christ." Lincoln believes that here χάρις is "equivalent to the use of χάρισμα in 1 Cor 12:4 and Rom 12:6" because with the "reference to grace here the writer has in view its outworking in a variety of ways in the individual believers."[27] In 4:11, this grace or these gifts to the church take the form of apostles, prophets, evangelists, pastors, and teachers to the church whose ministries are to establish the saints and build up Christ's body.

The author elaborates on the spiritual gift of apostleship in Eph 3:2, 8, where χάρις is used as a designation for Paul's apostleship. In 3:2, Paul's stewardship of the χάρις (i.e., apostleship) given to him by God is for the benefit of the Gentiles. In 3:8, the author makes explicit that this χάρις was given "in order to preach the gospel to the Gentiles."

Another nuance of χάρις occurs in Eph 1:6, 7; 2:7; and likely 1:2 and 6:24 where χάρις is used to refer to all the benefits collectively given through Christ to the elect. Ephesians 1:3 states the theme of the whole *berakah* in 1:3-14. God has blessed the saints with every spiritual blessing. The rest of the eulogy is a declaration of those blessings. Also, the eulogy makes clear that the locus of these blessings is ἐν Χριστῷ. The saints have been blessed by Christ (1:3, ἐν Χριστῷ), adopted through Jesus Christ (1:5, διὰ Ἰησοῦ Χριστοῦ), have redemption through his blood (1:7, διὰ τοῦ αἵματος αὐτοῦ), are sealed by Christ (1:13, ἐν ᾧ), and all of creation is summed up by Christ (1:10, ἐν τῷ Χριστῷ). After declaring the blessings of election and adoption, the author declares in verse 6 that this is "for the praise of [God's] glorious τῆς χάριτος which he bestowed on us through the beloved."[28]

---

ing or pleasing attraction, (2) favor, and (3) gratitude or thanks. Cf. Zeller, *Charis*, 13-14. Ephesians does not use χάρις in the sense of (1) or (3) — though in 1:16 and 5:20, εὐχαριστῶν and εὐχαριστοῦντες are the terms utilized for thanksgiving and gratitude in Ephesians. Ephesians utilizes nuanced meanings of (2) for χάρις. Concerning the notion of favor, χάρις was understood in two ways. First, there is favor in the sense of a concrete benefit or gift given. Second, there is favor in the sense of a disposition to bless or give a benefit. This is the sense in which Aristotle utilizes the term where he says that χάρις is "the feeling in accordance with which one who has it is said to render a service to one who needs it" (*Rhet.* 2.7.2 [Freese, LCL]). In fact, John Freese translates χάρις in *Rhet.* 2.7.4 as the "feeling of benevolence."

27. A. T. Lincoln, *Ephesians* (WBC 42; Waco: Word Books, 1990), 240.

28. I am treating τῆς χάριτος as an attributed genitive. See Daniel B. Wallace, *Greek*

Here, χάρις appears to designate collectively the blessings of election and adoption bestowed through Christ. In 1:7, the forgiveness of transgressions is "according to the [God's] abundant τῆς χάριτος." Again, χάρις seems to designate here the collective benefits or blessings of God to which the forgiveness of transgressions belongs. Ephesians 2:7 uses the same expression. God is going to show in the coming ages "his surpassing abundant τῆς χάριτος" to the saints.

When we come to Eph 2:5, 8, the meaning of χάρις in 1:6, 7, and 2:7 would suggest that χάρις in 2:5, 8 should be understood in the same way. The saints have been saved by χάρις. The saints are saved by the past and ongoing collective benefits of God, which have just been delineated in 1:3-14. Moreover, 1:3-14 has demonstrated that these collective benefits have come to the saints through Christ. This would suggest that "through faith" in 2:8 should be understood as "through the faithfulness of Christ" (Ephesians' way of saying Christians are justified by the faithfulness of Christ, as in Romans and Galatians).[29]

It is interesting to note that the declaration of God's super-abounding χάρις might have been heard in the light of the abounding benefits Augustus

---

Grammar Beyond the Basics: An Exegetical Syntax of the New Testament (Grand Rapids: Zondervan, 1996), 89, for a discussion of this category. I am using this category for the genitive in 1:7 as well.

29. In these verses, χάρις does not refer to the Christ-event of death and resurrection, which brings salvation to the elect (cf. Markus Barth, *Ephesians: Introduction, Translation, and Commentary on Chapters 1–3* [AB 34; Garden City, NY: Doubleday, 1974], 73-74). As we have seen, χάρις comes to the elect through or by means of Christ. To say that the saints are saved by the Christ-event through or by means of Christ (granting that "through faith" is a reference to Christ) is tautologous. Also to say that χάρις means simply the disposition to bless here in Ephesians does not make much sense. God's disposition to bless is made clear in the opening, 1:3. But there is difficulty in conceptualizing what it means to bestow the disposition to bless on the saints through Christ in 1:6 or to show the saints that disposition in the ages to come in 2:7, unless it is understood as the manifestation of that disposition in the various benefits bestowed. Taking χάρις to refer to collective benefits is the simplest alternative and makes the most sense of these passages. For those who take the disposition position see Peter T. O'Brien, *The Letter to the Ephesians* (PNTC; Grand Rapids: Eerdmans, 1999), 168; J. A. Robinson, *St. Paul's Epistle to the Ephesians: A Revised Text and Translation with Exposition and Notes* (London: Macmillan, 1903), 224; Heinrich Schlier, *Der Brief an die Epheser: Ein Kommentar* (Düsseldorf: Patmos-Verlag, 1963), 34, 115. C. K. Barrett, *Paul: An Introduction to His Thought* (Louisville: Westminster/John Knox, 1994), 89; and Thomas N. Schulz, *The Meaning of Charis in the New Testament* (Genoa: Editrice lanterna, 1971), 57, believe χάρις refers to both action/event and attitude.

bestowed upon the world.[30] According to Augustus's own accounts of his benefactions in the *Res Gestae Divi Augustae,* the benefits that Augustus bestowed upon the Roman Empire were extraordinary and vast. Harrison relates that the imperial propaganda focused on Augustus as the preeminent "world-benefactor." The language of excess (ὑπερβάλλειν, ὑπερβολή) typically accompanied the description of Augustus's benefactions.[31] As a result, Augustus was held forth as a divinely chosen world ruler. Providence had sent him, and he brought worldwide peace, prosperity, hope, and restoration.[32] In a similar way, Ephesians describes God's χάρις as glorious (1:6), abundant (1:7), and surpassingly (ὑπερβάλλον) abundant (2:7). Moreover, the divinely elected Christ reconciles and restores creation (1:10) and unites the peoples of the world (2:11-22). He is the true κοσμοκράτωρ.[33]

While Augustus's benefits were given to increase his own glory and secure the goodwill and fidelity of the imperial inhabitants, is this the way God's super-abounding benefits function in Ephesians? To this question we now turn.

When Is Χάρις Given?

If Christians are saved by "the collective benefits" of God through Jesus Christ, then when are these benefits given to them? In Eph 1:4, the first benefit listed is the grace of election. God elects the saints for adoption as his children *before the foundation of the world.* Furthermore, in 1:11, God's election is "according to the purpose of the One [God] who inwardly works (ἐνεργοῦντος) all things according to the counsel of his will." Other benefits occur in time, such as when the elect are sealed with the Spirit upon hearing the gospel and believing (1:13-14). The χάρις of election, however, is the

---

30. Ethelbert Stauffer, *Christ and the Caesars: Historical Sketches* (trans. K. and R. Gregor Smith; Philadelphia: Westminster, 1955), 90-111, sets up interesting parallels between Augustus and Jesus, suggesting a way the gospel of Jesus might have been heard in the Roman Empire over which the "gospel" of Augustus had cast its shadow.

31. James R. Harrison, "Paul, Eschatology, and the Augustan Age of Grace," *TynBul* 50 (1999): 86-87.

32. Harrison, "Age of Grace," 89. See also the letter from the Asian League in Danker, *Benefactor,* 33, and Dieter Georgi, "Who Is the True Prophet?" *HTR* 79 (1986): 100-126.

33. Cf. Francis Dvornik, *Early Christian and Byzantine Political Philosophy: Origins and Background* (Dumbarton Oaks Studies 9; Washington, DC: Dumbarton Oaks Center for Byzantine Studies, 1966), 1:217-22. Dvornik notes that Alexander was given a similar title and recognized as divine because he united the world.

foundational benefit for the saving benefits that the saints experience in time. Χάρις thus provides entry into the realm of salvation. We can, however, say more.

To Whom Is Χάρις Given?

God gives χάρις to the unworthy. As we saw above, benefits were typically bestowed on the worthy. The giving of benefits to the unworthy was always in the hope that such giving would produce a grateful heart in the benefi-ciary.[34] Ephesians 2:1-3, however, delineates the desperate condition of hu-manity. In 2:1, people are "dead" in their transgressions and sins. To talk about the "living dead" was a familiar topic in the popular philosophy of the Greco-Roman world.[35] Among Hellenistic Jews, Philo speaks about the soul of the wicked as dead to the life of virtue, and if the soul is dead to virtue, then it does not possess immortality. Commenting on Gen 2:17 in *Leg.* 1.105-8, Philo contrasts the natural-death with the penalty-death:

> That death is of two kinds, one that of man in general, the other that of the soul in particular. The death of the man is the separation of the soul from the body, but the death of the soul is the decay of virtue and the bringing of wickedness. . . . That special death properly so called, which is that of the soul becoming entombed in passions and wickedness of all kinds. And this death is particularly the antithesis of the death which awaits us all. The latter is the separation of the combatants that had been pitted against one another, body and soul. The former, on the other hand, is the meeting of the two in conflict. And in this conflict the worse, the body, overcomes, and the better, the soul, is overcome. . . . The penalty-death occurs when the soul dies to the life of virtue, and is alive to only that of wickedness.

The "dead" soul is given over to wickedness with no hope of obtaining virtue and the immortal life. According to Philo, God implants the life of virtue that leads to immortality (cf. *Congr.* 56); consequently, abandonment by God is the worst condition anyone can find him- or herself in since he or she

---

34. Cf. Whitlark, *Enabling Fidelity*, 62-65.

35. Deter Zeller, "The Life and Death of the Soul in Philo of Alexandria: The Use and Origin of a Metaphor," *SPhilo* 7 (1995): 51-54.

will be enslaved to wickedness and will fail to attain immortality (cf. *QG.* 1.73, *Conf.* 166-67, *Det.* 141-42). Likewise, here in Ephesians, the author declares that Christians, both Gentile and Jew, were formerly dead, given over to a life of wickedness living as rebellious, disobedient children (cf. Eph 2:1, 3). More than that, they were the objects of God's wrath because they were born as humans in the present "age of this world" (cf. Eph 2:2).[36] Christians have been delivered out of this hopeless state only because God "made them alive with Christ" (Eph 2:5). They have been saved by χάρις. "God goes beyond the high-water mark set by Seneca, which was for the virtuous to even consider giving to the ungrateful (if they had resources to spare after benefiting the virtuous)."[37]

We still, however, have not demonstrated that the dynamic of the salvation by God's χάρις through Jesus Christ in Ephesians is anything other than reciprocity. At best God chooses the undeserving and delivers them from the expectation of not having to suffer his wrath. But in the light of such super-abounding benefits or χάρις, does the relationship with God proceed along the lines of indebted gratitude, i.e., reciprocity? Does a Christian once he or she has entered into salvation by God's free and unmerited election now stay in by his or her own perseverance in gratitude? We must now examine what is the extent of the salvation by χάρις in Ephesians. What I will demonstrate is that God gives χάρις not just to enter into salvation but also χάρις to remain faithful.

The Extent of Χάρις

The first notion of divine enablement occurs in Eph 1:11. After declaring that the saints have been chosen for adoption and forgiven of their sins through Christ, the author, in Eph 1:11, declares that they have been called because God predestined them. God, who "inwardly works (ἐνεργοῦντος) all things according to the counsel of his will," predestined them. As previously discussed, God's disposition to bless is according to his own determinations. This is not fundamentally different from human benefactors, even Augustus, except that God is able to guarantee and carry out his determinations be-

---

36. O'Brien, *Ephesians*, 162, understands 2:1-3 in the light of Rom 5:12, namely humanity's corporate identity in Adam. See also Lincoln, *Ephesians*, 99, who understands "by nature" in 2:3 to mean "by birth" as in Gal 2:15. Contra Barth, *Ephesians*, 231-32.

37. DeSilva, *Honor, Patronage*, 129.

cause he inwardly works all things in accordance with his will. Later, in Eph 1:19, the author prays that the saints might know "what is the surpassing greatness of his power for us who believe according to the inward working (ἐνέργειαν) of the strength of his might." This is the same power that God worked in Christ when he raised him from the dead and seated him above all rulers and authorities (1:20-21). God does not have to give χάρις in order to secure the indebted gratitude and loyalty of his elect. His irresistible power works in the saints to preserve them "holy, blameless, and in love." Later, in Eph 3:16-20, the agent of this inward empowering is identified. The author declares that God strengthens his saints through the Spirit so that Christ might dwell in their hearts. This statement appears to embody what Paul sets forth in Gal 2:20 — that the indwelling Christ empowers his life so that he lives it out with faithfulness to God.

Another motif of divine enablement and security occurs in Eph 1:13. The author states that the saints are sealed (ἐσφραγίσθητε) by the Holy Spirit, who is a down payment of the future inheritance. Even as the Spirit is the inward empowering agent, the Spirit also functions as the sealing agent. The notion of sealing had multiple connotations in the ancient Mediterranean world. Some of these notions were protection, empowerment, and enablement. We find such notions in the Jewish and Christian contexts. Ezekiel 9:4-6 demonstrates that sealing provides protection against harm. In *T. Job* 5:1-3 the angel seals Job, and Job declares, "Till death I will endure." Here Job is empowered to persevere. In Rev 7:3-4, the angel seals the servants of God so that they will be protected from the devastation that is to come upon the world. In 2 Cor 1:22, God sets his seal upon the saints and gives them the guarantee of the Spirit in their hearts. Ephesians 4:30 declares that the saints have been sealed by the Holy Spirit for the day of redemption. Consequently, Christian auditors would have heard the sealing by the Spirit in Ephesians as God's securing of the bond he has established with his elect until the day they are fully redeemed.

Still another motif for divine enablement is found in Eph 2:6. There, Christians are said to be seated with Christ in the heavenlies. In Eph 1:20-22, Christ has been raised and seated at God's right hand far above all rulers, authorities, powers, lordships, and every name that can be named. They have all been subjected to Christ and placed under his feet. Therefore, if Christians are seated with Christ, they are seated above the powers that formerly worked in them a spirit of disobedience and rebellion (2:2). Christians are not subjected to these powers but seated with Christ to whom are subjected all things. Consequently, the Christian, in his or her struggle against sin and the powers that would subject him or her to disobedience and rebellion, has the resources, power, and possibility to be victorious over these struggles. Again, the saints persevere because God preserves them to the end. What need does God have of reciprocity (indebted gratitude) when he is the one who provides the resources and power to maintain the bond between him and his saints? The saints have nothing to offer back to God that did not originate with God.

In Eph 2:8-10, the author crystallizes the extent of God's saving χάρις. First, in verses 8-9, the author argues that because the saints have been saved by χάρις there is no room to boast. For the saints' salvation from first to last is not from themselves but is a gift from God.[38] Second, in verse 10, God re-creates the Christian for good works, works that God has already prepared for them to do. God gives the Christian a nature to do good works and then provides those works for the Christian to do. From first to last, "getting in" and "staying in" are the result of God's own doing.

In the Homeric world, divine aid does not preclude boasting in human achievement. In fact the gods support the human endeavor to seek immortal fame. For example, Book 5 of the *Iliad* opens with Athena giving "force and courage" to Diomedes so that he might win "glorious renown (κλέος)" (1-3, [Murray, LCL]). Aeneas in his prayer later on recognizes that if Diomedes wins glory, then it comes from Zeus (225). Moreover, Achilles' honor, the central plot line of the *Iliad,* is protected and bestowed by Zeus.[39] Upon killing Hector, Achilles acknowledges that the gods have granted this victory but also that he with the Achaeans has won great glory (*Il.* 22.378-93). We find the ground and foundation for this way of thinking more clearly articulated in Virgil's *Aeneid.* Anchises prays to Zeus, "If by our piety *(pietate)* we earn it, give us your aid" (2.690-91 [Fairclough, LCL]). In both the Greek and Roman worlds victory and thus glory were divine gifts given to the virtuous, pious, and excellent among humans.[40] The author of Ephesians undermines such synergistic reciprocity. There is no human boast before God or in being

---

38. John Calvin, *Commentaries on the Epistles of Paul to the Galatians and Ephesians* (trans. William Pringle; Grand Rapids: Eerdmans, 1957), 227, writes that God not only bestows the first grace but all subsequent grace because "salvation is not a reward or recompense"; if so, then "the praise of grace would not . . . remain unblemished."

39. Cf. *Il.* 1.509-10; 9.607-8. In fact, this is one of the reasons why Achilles turns down all the gifts the Achaean assembly attempts to bestow in order to honor him and thus persuade him to rejoin the fight.

40. J. Rufus Fears, "Theology of Victory at Rome: Approaches and Problems," *ANRW* 17.2:748.

God-chosen. The Ephesian Christians' salvation is for the glory of God alone.

If reciprocity was the scheme by which Ephesians understands salvation by God's χάρις, then we would certainly expect to find such notions in Eph 4–6. This section is universally acknowledged to build on what has gone before in Eph 1–3. If Ephesians is an honorific decree, then typically this second half would be a delimitation of the grateful response of the recipients to the benefactor for his or her benefits. In Eph 4–6, the language of gratitude or indebtedness is never provided as the motivation for walking in a manner worthy of the calling the saints have received. Instead of gratitude, the saints are exhorted to "be clothed in the new person that is created according to God" (4:24). Even this, as Charles Talbert has demonstrated, is a motif of divine enablement. "In Paul's context, the image of being clothed or of clothing oneself was used in talking about empowerment or transformation."[41]

In Eph 6:10-11, the saints are exhorted to "be inwardly strengthened (ἐνδυναμοῦσθε) by the Lord and by the might of his strength" and to "be clothed in the full armor of God." As Lincoln notes, the genitive not only indicates that this armor is what God supplies but also that it is his own armor that he gives.[42] Consequently, the saints fight with God's strength and God's weapons. No doubt the saints are to be thankful as they are exhorted to be in 5:4, 20, yet even giving thanks to God is empowered by the Spirit (5:18).

The Purpose of Χάρις

Ephesians does contain a motif that is common to Greco-Roman benefaction. God in giving χάρις has acted for the praise of the glory of his χάρις (Eph 1:6, 12, 14; 2:7). God will show to his saints for all time the surpassing abundance of his χάρις. Undoubtedly this will elicit eternal praise and thanks from the saints, as Eph 1:3-14 evidences. But to transform grace into debt is to diminish the ends for which God has acted, i.e., for the praise of his glorious grace so that no one may boast before him. As was demonstrated from Greek religious practices above, the worshipers, for all practical reasons, believed that their offerings of honor and gratitude to the gods secured their future favor. In Ephesians, God's favor toward his elect is secured by his own will before the foundation of the world through Jesus Christ, whom he

---

41. Charles Talbert, "Paul, Judaism, and the Revisionists," *CBQ* 63 (2001): 20-21.
42. Lincoln, *Ephesians*, 442.

himself offered for them, and he preserves his elect to the very end for the day of redemption. Certainly gratitude will arise to God for such χάρις to his saints. Gratitude magnifies God's χάρις; it does not secure it.

Conclusion

What then might we conclude about Ephesians' use of χάρις and the reciprocity such language often assumed? Often in cultures where reciprocity is foundational to the structure of the society, benefits bestowed by prominent figures place those who receive benefits under obligations until they are able to repay. Typically, generosity is not meant to be repaid in kind but reciprocated with long-term subordination to the benefactor.[43] Consequently, a "gift economy" becomes a "debt economy." Reciprocity or the χάρις-convention is based on establishing the feeling of indebtedness in order to sustain a long-term relationship.

This type of debt thinking highlights the "dark side" of reciprocity. A modern sociology study by Martin Greenberg and Solomon Shapiro has shown that the psychological state of indebtedness is aversive, and so people are reluctant to accept favors where there is little or no possibility of paying them back.[44] The aversive nature or "dark side" of reciprocity emerges from some of the ancient sources. For example, as cited above, Aristotle writes:

> Benefactors seem to love those whom they benefit more than those who have received benefits love those who have conferred them; and it is asked why this is so, as it seems to be unreasonable. The view most generally taken is that it is because the one party is in the position of a debtor and the other of a creditor; just as therefore in the case of a loan, whereas the borrower would be glad to have his creditor out of the way, the lender actually watches over his debtor's safety, so it is thought that the conferrer of a benefit wishes the recipient to live in order that he may receive a return, but the recipient is not particularly anxious to make a return. (*Eth. Nic.* 9.7.1 [Rackham, LCL])

The speech of Pericles in the *History of the Peloponnesian War* 2.40.4-5 by Thucydides relates a similar notion: "Now he who confers the favour is a

43. Van Wees, "The Law of Gratitude," 41.
44. Martin S. Greenberg and Solomon P. Shapiro, "Indebtedness: An Adverse Aspect of Asking For and Receiving Help," *Sociometry* 34 (1971): 290-301.

firmer friend, in that he is disposed, by continued goodwill toward the recipient, to keep the feeling of obligation alive in him; but he who owes it is more listless in his friendship, knowing that when he repays the kindness it will count, not as a favour bestowed, but as a debt repaid" (Smith, LCL). Part of Seneca's aim in writing *De Beneficiis* was to encourage beneficiaries "not to be fearful of benefits, not to faint under them as if we were weighed down by an intolerable burden" (2.35.3 [Basore, LCL]). Victor Matthews observes after studying specific stories in the Hebrew Bible through the lens of reciprocity that when "an unequal exchange is proposed or imposed . . . a social tension is created that may lead to open hostility or the loss of personal status."[45]

In Ephesians, the bond between God and his elect is an expression of his χάρις. Moreover, his χάρις reaches not only to the admittance into a relationship but also the maintenance of that relationship. The saints' perseverance in holiness, blamelessness, and love is a result of God's inward working. God's bestowal of χάρις upon his rebellious creatures transforms them into obedient children re-created to do the good works that God has prepared for them. God has no need of reciprocity or the χάρις-convention to maintain the bond between himself and his elect. God does not secure loyalty or faithfulness from his saints by maintaining the feeling of indebtedness to him in them. To transform God's χάρις into debt through conceiving of the relationship between him and his saints on the grounds of reciprocity is for the saints to be justified (in an eschatological sense) by their repayments of gratitude and not according to God's χάρις. Finally, the author encourages the saints to pray knowing that God does surpassingly more than what they ask or think (Eph 3:20). Piety in Ephesians seems to be reliance upon God for continual supplies of χάρις and not repayment for χάρις already received.

I will conclude with an apt observation by Richard Hays:

> There is, interestingly, no emphasis in Paul on gratitude as a motive for obedience. (He never says, in effect, "God has done something nice for us, so we should return the favor by doing something nice for God.") Instead, Paul seems to see moral action as a logical entailment of God's redemptive action. For Paul, God's transforming act in Christ conditions

---

45. Victor H. Matthews, "The Unwanted Gift: Implications of Obligatory Gift Giving in Ancient Israel," *Semeia* 87 (1999): 91. Matthews also cites Racine, who states that the donor of a gift too large to be reciprocated can represent enmity on the part of the donor (95). Evelyn Meranda-Feliciano (*Filipino Values and Our Christian Faith* [Manila: OMF Literature, 1990], 70-72) points out the aversive and oppressive ethos of *utang na loob* in Filipino culture.

all of reality. . . . Consequently, much of Paul's moral exhortation takes the form of reminding his readers to view their obligations and actions in the cosmic context of what God has done in Christ.[46]

Though this observation is made from Paul's genuine letters, we can see that such a statement is in character with the deutero-Pauline document under consideration here.[47]

---

46. Richard Hays, *The Moral Vision of the New Testament: A Contemporary Introduction to New Testament Ethics* (San Francisco: HarperSanFrancisco, 1996), 39.

47. Most scholars recognize that Ephesians and Colossians share some type of literary relationship. They also share common elements of divine enablement of the Christian's perseverance. Colossians emphasizes the necessity of perseverance (1:22-23). Such perseverance is divinely enabled because God makes one strong from the strength of his glorious power (1:11) and enables saints to share in the future inheritance (1:12). Christ dwells in the saints, strengthening their future hope (1:27). Paul also labors with the strength Christ provides (1:29). The Colossian Christians are to be clothed with the new man who is being renewed (3:10). All of these motifs are present in Ephesians: divine power that works within, Christ who indwells, and being clothed with the new man.

Between Two Epiphanies: Clarifying One Aspect of Soteriology in the Pastoral Epistles

Charles H. Talbert

In the Pastorals the Christian's "staying in" is accomplished through transformation by the vision of key *exempla* (a philosophic technique) and by the Lord's presence, power, guarding, gift, and by the Lord's deliverance of one from the evil one (Jewish language).

•　　•

The soteriology of the Pastoral Epistles has been discussed with reference to a variety of concerns: e.g., whether salvation is effective for all by virtue of Christ's first epiphany or only becomes effective through faith;[1] whether the PE hold to a view of limited atonement;[2] whether the PE seek to counter an overemphasis on the death of Jesus;[3] whether the PE subsume Christology to soteriology, thereby confining Jesus Christ to his two epiphanies so as to reduce overenthusiasm about the living Christ;[4] whether the PE's soteriology is part of Christian acculturation,[5] reflecting links with Hellenistic moral

---

1. A. Klöpper, "Zur Soteriologie der Pastoralbriefe," *ZWT* 47 (1904): 57-88.

2. I. H. Marshall, "Universal Grace and Atonement in the Pastoral Epistles," in *The Grace of God, the Will of Man* (ed. Clark Pinnock; Grand Rapids: Zondervan, 1989), 51-69.

3. D. Gerber, "1 Tm 1:15b: L'indice d'une sotériologie pensée prioritairement en lien avec la venue de Jésus?" *RHPR* 80, no. 4 (2000): 463-77.

4. L. R. Donelson, *Pseudepigraphy and Ethical Argument in the Pastoral Epistles* (HUT 22; Tübingen: Mohr-Siebeck, 1986), 133-54.

5. J. D. Quinn, "Jesus as Savior and Only Mediator," in *Fede e cultura alla luce della*

philosophy and Philo;[6] whether Paul is not only the authorized bearer of the saving message but also an integral part of that message;[7] whether the PE's soteriology reflects continuity with the genuine Paulines;[8] whether the view of salvation in the three PE differs from letter to letter when they are not studied as a unit.[9] On certain matters, however, there seems to be general, if not universal agreement. First, the PE form a homogeneous group in the NT, standing together in language, style, and theology. It is possible, therefore, to see the contents of any one of the three as casting light on the other two. Each letter must be interpreted in the context of the three-letter collection.[10] Second, the majority opinion among scholars is still that they are pseudepigraphical.[11] Third, in the PE God is Savior (1 Tim 1:1; 2:3; 4:10; 2 Tim 1:8-9; Titus 1:2-4; 2:10; 3:4). Jesus is the human agent who carries out God's plan and, as such, can also be called Savior (2 Tim 1:10; Titus 1:4; 2:13; 3:6). Jesus' saving work is described mainly in terms of two epiphanies: past incarnation (2 Tim 1:10; Titus 1:4; 3:6) and future coming (Titus 2:13). These two poles block any attempt to claim that the resurrection is past already (2 Tim 2:17-18). The first appearing is an expression of God's grace (2 Tim 1:8-9; Titus 3:4-5). The time between the two epiphanies is provided for training (παιδεύουσα — Titus 2:11-12) that will produce progress (ἡ προκοπή — 1 Tim 4:15)[12] in virtuous living (1 Tim 4:7, 15; 2 Tim 3:16; Titus

---

Bibbia: Atti della sessione plenaria 1979 della Pontificia Commissione Biblica (Torino: Editrice Elle Di Ci, 1981), 249-60.

6. Stephen C. Mott, "Greek Ethics and Christian Conversion: The Philonic Background of Titus 2:10-14 and 3:3-7," *NovT* 20 (1978): 22-48.

7. M. Wolter, *Die Pastoralbriefe als Paulustradition* (FRLANT 146; Göttingen: Vandenhoeck & Ruprecht, 1988), 269-70; K. Läger, *Die Christologie der Pastoralbriefe* (HTS 12; Münster: LIT, 1996), 177.

8. I. H. Marshall, "Salvation, Grace and Works in the Later Writings in the Pauline Corpus," *NTS* 42 (1996): 339-58.

9. George M. Wieland, *The Significance of Salvation: A Study of Salvation Language in the Pastoral Epistles* (Milton Keynes: Paternoster, 2006).

10. Marshall, "Universal Grace and Atonement in the Pastoral Epistles," 53-54.

11. L. T. Johnson, "First Timothy 1:1-20," in *1 Timothy Reconsidered* (Colloquium Oecumenicum Paulinum 18; Leuven: Peeters, 2008), 19-39, is a notable exception. He argues that the Pauline School is present and active in the apostle's correspondence during his lifetime, so that an apt analogy is the production of a presidential state of the union address. M. M. Mitchell, "Corrective Composition, Corrective Exegesis," in *1 Timothy Reconsidered*, 41-62, affirms the pseudepigraphy of the PE with a new wrinkle: the author attempts to enlarge and interpret the existing Pauline corpus.

12. In the Greek world this term was used in philosophical circles to depict an individual's process of moral and spiritual development between beginning and perfection.

2:12)[13] and lead to inheritance of the blessed hope (Titus 2:13).[14] Fourth, the PE are letters of moral exhortation.[15] This includes 2 Timothy as well, because a testament/farewell speech functioned to give moral exhortation, just as did paranetic and protreptic letters like 1 Timothy and Titus.[16] Fifth, the ethics of the PE are grounded in their understanding of salvation.[17] Doctrine can provide the basis for instruction that follows. It can also back up instruction that has just been given.[18]

This essay builds upon the prior list of generally accepted conclusions about the PE. It addresses a specific aspect of the soteriology of the PE. How do the PE understand soteriology in the period between election/regeneration (which is clearly by God's grace — 1 Tim 1:14; 2 Tim 1:9; Titus 2:11; 3:7) and departure from this life?

Epictetus, for example, speaks of "one who is making progress" (ὁ προκόπτων) because he has learned from the philosopher (*Diatr.* 1.4.1; cf. also 1.4.4; 1.4.18-21). Philo uses the terminology in the same way. He speaks of three grades of people: ὁ ἀρχόμενος, the one who is just beginning; ὁ προκόπτων, the one who is making progress; and ὁ τέλειος, the perfect or mature person (*Leg.* 3.159). The same use of the terminology is found in later Christian writings (e.g., *Vita Pachomii* 28). In Luke 2:52 the terminology is used of the boy Jesus.

13. Philip H. Towner, *The Goal of Our Instruction: The Structure of Theology and Ethics in the Pastoral Epistles* (JSNTSS 34; Sheffield: JSOT Press, 1989), 110, points out that in Greek thought, *paideia* (training/education) produced virtue. Numbered among the cardinal virtues were σωφροσύνη, δικαιοσύνη, and εὐσέβεια, which occur in adverbial form in Titus 2:11-14 where salvation is viewed from the perspective of the life it produces.

14. This summary reflects the sketch by Margaret Davies, *The Pastoral Epistles* (Sheffield: Sheffield Academic Press, 1996), ch. 3.

15. Mark Harding, *Tradition and Rhetoric in the Pastoral Epistles* (New York: Peter Lang, 1998). Perhaps the closest parallel to the PE are the letters of Seneca. Seneca's letters "to Lucilius represent the only extant extended correspondence of the tutelage of a protégé" (118). Cf., however, Pliny's letter to Maximus, Pliny's junior who is about to become imperial legate in Achaea (*Ep.* 8.24).

16. Craig A. Smith, *Timothy's Task, Paul's Prospect: A New Reading of 2 Timothy* (NTM 12; Sheffield: Sheffield Phoenix Press, 2006), denies that 2 Tim is a farewell speech or a last will and testament. Sean Charles Martin, *Pauli Testamentum: 2 Timothy and the Last Words of Moses* (Tesi Gregoriana, Serie Teologia 18; Rome: Pontificia Universita Gregoriana, 1997), reflects the general consensus.

17. P. Trummer, *Paulustradition der Pastoralbriefe* (BBET 8; Frankfurt: Peter Lang, 1978), 198; Davies, *The Pastoral Epistles,* 62; Frances Young, *The Theology of the Pastoral Letters* (Cambridge: Cambridge University Press, 1994), 48.

18. I. H. Marshall, "Salvation in the Pastoral Epistles," in *Geschichte — Tradition — Reflexion: Festschrift für Martin Hengel,* vol. 3, *Frühes Christentum* (ed. Hubert Cancik et al.; Tübingen: Mohr-Siebeck, 1996), 455.

I

Bultmann helps clarify the issue.[19] In the period after Paul (and a pre-canonical version of the Fourth Gospel), he says, there was a falling away from the truth of the gospel. In the area of soteriology he uses the Shepherd of Hermas to pose the question. In Hermas, baptism (the beginning of the Christian life) brings about salvation only insofar as it frees one from previously committed sins (*Mand.* 4.3.1-3; 4.4). This makes possible a new beginning for life. Henceforth, however, one must lead one's life on *one's own responsibility* in obedience to the commandments of God. In the end, therefore, not baptism but one's own good conduct saves the believer. By contrast Colossians and Ephesians do not view forgiveness as if one's life were now placed under an imperative, the fulfillment of which would be the condition for obtaining salvation. Rather, they believe that with forgiveness the might of sin is broken so that a believer's *obedience is divinely enabled* in the present. The PE also, Bultmann contends, know that the present is under grace as a present reality (2 Tim 1:9-10; Titus 1:3). The Spirit, given by God, aids the Christian in fulfilling one's duty (1 Tim 1:14). Grace is understood as a power that transforms one's present living (Titus 2:11-12). It trains a person for godly living. So the PE represent a somewhat faded Paulinism. Almost everywhere else Christian faith has sunk back into legalism.

Bultmann is not alone in his judgment about salvation in the PE. L. R. Donelson offers a similar assessment. He says that Jesus in his first epiphany revealed the existence of God's salvific plan and taught the required ethical standards. He then made available the means of attaining them by the Spirit given in baptism. At his second epiphany Jesus will reward those who have lived virtuously within the official cultus.[20] M. Davies also contends that the new life is seen in the PE as engendered and sustained by God's Holy Spirit (Titus 3:4-5; 2 Tim 1:7, 14).[21] What follows will reexamine this estimate of the PE's soteriology.

---

19. Rudolf Bultmann, *Theology of the New Testament* (New York: Scribner's, 1955), 2:161-62, 175-80, 183-86, 198.

20. Donelson, *Pseudepigraphy and Ethical Argument in the Pastoral Epistles.*

21. Davies, *The Pastoral Epistles,* 50.

II

What is the story assumed by the three letters? It centers around Paul's departures. He leaves Crete (Titus 1:5); he leaves Ephesus (1 Tim 1:3); he is about to leave this life (2 Tim 4:6).[22] The apostle's aim in his ministry at this point in his life is set forth in Titus 1:1-3 in the context of the three phases of salvation: past (vv. 2b-3 — the good news of Christ promised ages ago), future (v. 2a — hope of eternal life), and present (v. 1 — to further the faith of God's elect and their knowledge of the truth that accords with godliness = Christian growth; cf. also 2 Tim 2:10 where Paul describes his mission as to work so that the elect may obtain future salvation). Titus for sure and 1 and 2 Timothy most likely must be taken as giving instruction that will further this stated goal of developing those qualities that lead to eternal life.[23] Given his departures, Paul's strategy for accomplishing this aim is the employment of two emissaries: Titus (Titus 1:5) and Timothy (1 Tim 1:3; 2 Tim 1:6, 14; 2:2). This strategy involves their formation, to be accomplished largely by means of doctrines, precepts, and exempla. In order to clarify how this strategy works itself out in the PE, we turn to Seneca's letters to Lucilius where the philosopher undertakes a similar effort with his protégé.

At the very beginning it is necessary to state the difference between philosophic inculcation of virtue and the early Christian exhortation in the PE.[24] The central concern of paranetic letters like those of Seneca was to promote an individual's growth in character through moral transformation for the purpose of attaining happiness. The primary aim of early Christian letters of moral transformation like the PE was to promote moral growth of individuals who belong to groups claiming allegiance to a common cause for social even more than individual ends (e.g., *social ends:* Titus 2:5 — so that the word of God may not be discredited; 2:10; 2:8 — so any opponent will be put to shame; 2:10 — so they may be an ornament to the doctrine of God; 1 Tim 3:15 — so you will know how one ought to behave in the household of God; 5:14 — so as to give the adversary no occasion to revile us; 6:1 — so that the name of God and the teaching may not be defamed; *individual ends:* 1 Tim 6:19 — behavior that is storing up for themselves a foundation for the

---

22. Robert Wild, "The Image of Paul in the Pastoral Letters," *TBT* 23, no. 4 (1985): 239-45.

23. Marshall, *Festschrift für Hengel*, 452.

24. John H. Elliott's review of J. de Wahl Dryden, *Theology and Ethics in 1 Peter* (2006) may be found in *RBL*, December 2009, online: http://www.bookreviews.org/bookdetail .asp?TitleId=7248&CodePage=7248. Elliott makes the distinctions given above.

future; 2 Tim 4:7-8 — there is laid up for me the crown of righteousness to be awarded on that Day). Even with such a difference, remarkable similarities abound. We now turn to Seneca.

How did the ancients try to do character formation? Let us focus on one philosopher and pose the question to him.[25] This seems appropriate since it is widely agreed that one role Seneca plays in his letters is that of "a guide to and inspiration for the moral development of his addressee."[26] In several of his moral epistles we get a summary of his answer about how to effect change for the better in the philosophic life.

Life is a gift of the gods; the good life is the gift of philosophy (*Ep.* 90). Indeed, the paramount aim of philosophy is to shape virtuous character (*Ep.* 88.4).[27] Exactly how is the good person formed by philosophy? There are three main ingredients to be considered: precepts (= advice about how to live), *exempla* (= patterns, virtues seen in the lives of others), and doctrines (= presuppositions on which precepts are based and in terms of which they make sense). Doctrines form the foundation. Precepts depend on doctrines; doctrines are the source of precepts (95.12). Doctrines first of all remove the conditions that stand in the way of precepts (95.38), e.g., a wrong idea of God (95.48). They then provide a standard of truth (95.57), e.g., a right view of God (95.48). Precepts, like branches, must be grafted onto a school of philosophy that functions like the roots of a tree (95.60). Moral advice (= precepts) only makes sense within a given philosophical system (and its doctrines). By themselves, however, doctrines are ineffective (95.34-35). Once the doctrines are in place, precepts (= moral advice) must be added (95.34-35). Seneca, however, goes on to say that "the way is long if one follows precepts but short and helpful if one follows patterns *(exempla)*" (6.5-6). He argues:

> Cleanthes could not have been the express image of Zeno if he had merely heard his lectures; he shared in his life, saw into his hidden purposes, and watched him to *see* whether he lived according to his own rules. Plato, Aristotle, and the whole throng of sages who were destined

25. For what follows, cf. Charles H. Talbert, "Matthew and Character Formation," *ExpTim* 121 (2009): 53-59.

26. Brad Inwood, *Seneca: Selected Philosophical Letters* (Oxford: Oxford University Press, 2007), xv.

27. Marcus Wilson, "Seneca's Epistles to Lucilius: A Reevaluation," in *Seneca* (Oxford Readings in Classical Studies; ed. John G. Fitch; Oxford: Oxford University Press, 2008), 59-83, esp. 69.

to go each his different way, derived more benefit from the character than from the words of Socrates. (6.6 [Gummere, LCL]; italics mine)

Exempla provide the embodiment of virtue. People will follow them (95.66). So men like Cato should be set forth for others to emulate (95.72).

Seneca's appeal to *exempla* reflects broad agreement among ancient authors. For example, Xenophon, *Mem.* 4.1.1, says of Socrates: "Socrates was so useful in all circumstances and in all ways that any observer gifted with ordinary perception can see that nothing was more useful than the companionship of Socrates, and time spent with him in any place and in any circumstances" (Marchant, LCL). In 1.2.24-28, Xenophon says, "So long as they were with Socrates, they found him an ally who gave them strength to conquer their evil passions" (Marchant, LCL). Quintilian, *Inst.* 12.29-30, urges readers not to restrict their study to precepts alone but to include noble sayings and deeds (= patterns, *exempla*). He says:

Who will teach courage, justice, loyalty, self-control, simplicity, and contempt of grief and pain better than men like Fabricius, Curius, Regulus, Decius, Mucius and countless others? For if the Greeks bear away the palm for moral precepts, Rome can produce more examples *(exempliis)* of moral performance, which is a far greater thing. (Butler, LCL)

Once the doctrines provide a framework within which moral advice (= precepts) makes sense, then patterns of human embodiment are introduced. They function as more than rhetorical ornaments; they shape the life of the individual.[28] How so? They affect the will and enable moral development. Two dimensions of their effectiveness need to be noted. First, *exempla* show that the virtuous life is possible (72.22). You can do it! Second, they possess a certain efficacy, enabling transformation. There is help to do it!

What was the source of the efficacy of these patterns? It is linked to the ancient view of transformation by vision. Seneca expresses the ancient Mediterranean belief that being in the presence of a deity causes a transformation of the self. Pythagoras, he says, declared that "our souls experience a change when we enter a temple and behold the images of the gods face to face" (*Ep.* 94.42 [Gummere, LCL]). This conviction was widespread in antiquity. *Corpus Hermeticum* says the vision of the gods changes one's whole be-

---

28. Roland G. Mayer, "Roman Historical *Exempla* in Seneca," in Fitch, ed., *Seneca*, 299-315, esp. 314.

ing (10.6); the vision of deity transforms; it is being born again (13.3).[29] Philo, *Embassy* 1.5, says seeing God yields virtue and nobility of conduct; *Prelim. Studies* 56 says that in the mind that has the vision of God, God enables the acquisition of virtue. In 2 Cor 3:18, Paul says that Christians who behold the face of the Lord are being changed from one degree of glory to another.

The same effect, it was believed, was bestowed by one's contact with a true philosopher (as we have seen above). The contact with a true philosopher was, moreover, not limited to one's being with and beholding the teacher in person. When separated from Socrates, his disciples still benefited from his pattern. Xenophon, *Mem.* 4.1.1, speaks about the recollection of Socrates by his disciples, when they were separated from him, as an aid to virtue. "The constant recollection of him in absence brought no small good to his constant companions and followers" (Marchant, LCL). Further, books and the use of imagination played a part. Seneca, *Ep.* 52.7 and 11.8-10, advocates looking to the ancients for models with whom to associate. In *Ep.* 25.6, he says that if one cannot be in a philosopher's presence, one should come to know him through books, acting as if he were constantly at one's side. Vision of the philosopher, in person or mediated through books, was viewed as transforming just as was the vision of the gods.

The same effect, it was also believed, resulted from the vision of a good king. Plutarch, in his *Lives,* "Numa" 20.3, speaks of the effect that the second king of Rome had on subjects and neighbors alike:

> For not only was the Roman people softened and charmed by the righteousness and mildness of their king, but also the cities round about, as if by some cooling breeze or salubrious wind wafted upon them from Rome, began to experience a change of temper, and all of them were filled with a longing desire to have good government, to be at peace, to till the earth, to rear their children in quiet, and to worship the gods. (Perrin, LCL)

This being with a righteous king was sometimes spoken of in terms of vision. In the Pythagorean Diotegenes' *On Kingship,* fragment 2, one hears that as the king has righteousness in himself, he is able to infuse it into the entire

---

29. Brian Copenhaver, *Hermetica: The Greek Corpus Hermeticum and the Latin Asclepius in a New English Translation, with Notes and Introduction* (Cambridge: Cambridge University Press, 1992), 31, 49-50.

state when they *see* him live. Of the king he says: "so will he succeed in putting into order those who *look* upon him. . . . For to *look* upon the good king ought to affect the souls of those who *see* him no less than a flute or harmony" (italics mine).[30] The vision of the good king, like that of a deity or true philosopher, was believed to effect change in the personhood of the one who gazed upon him. This is transformation by vision.

So, if the ancients believed that doctrines established the foundation for character formation and that precepts gave concrete guidance, they were of one mind that without *exempla* or patterns of virtue embodied there could be no significant change in the self. *Exempla* functioned as performative language, language that provided more than information and that served as a catalyst for an auditor's action.[31] It was only a vision of the good that effected transformation over the long haul.[32]

III

How would the PE have fit into the ancient context sketched above? First of all, ancient auditors would have recognized the three ingredients used by moral philosophers to effect moral transformation in individuals: doctrines, precepts, and *exempla*. Most of the material in the PE falls under one of the three headings: doctrines, precepts, *exempla*. Under *doctrine* one would classify Titus 1:1-3; 2:11-14; 3:4-8a; 1 Tim 1:8-11; 1:15; 2:5; 3:16; 4:4; 4:10; 5:18; 6:13, 14-16; 2 Tim 1:9-10; 2:8; 2:11-13; 3:16-17. Under *precepts* one would classify Titus 1:5-9; 2:1-6, 9-10; 3:1-3; 3:9-11; 1 Tim 2:1-4; 2:8-15; 3:1-13; 4:7-9; 5:1-7; 5:9-17; 5:19-23; 6:1-2; 6:6-10; 6:17-19; 2 Tim 1:6-7; 1:8, 13-14; 2:1-7; 2:14-17a; 2:22-26; 3:14-15; 4:1-2, 5. Under *exempla* one would classify Titus 2:7-8 (Titus is the model); 1 Tim 1:12-14, 16 (Paul is the model); 4:12-16 (Timothy is the example); 6:11-14

---

30. E. R. Goodenough, "The Political Philosophy of Hellenistic Kingship," *YCS* 1 (1928): 55-102, esp. 72.

31. Cf. J. L. Austin, *How to Do Things with Words* (Cambridge, MA: Harvard University Press, 1962).

32. Discomfort with the language of imitation is widespread. E.g., Morna Hooker, *Pauline Pieces* (London: Epworth Press, 1979), 79-80, calls imitation soteriologically inadequate; John H. Elliott, "Backward and Forward 'In His Steps,'" in *Discipleship in the New Testament* (ed. Fernando Segovia; Philadelphia: Fortress, 1985), 184-209, says imitation reflects a moralizing trend. The common basis for such judgments is the conviction that Jesus must be not only an example of virtue but also the *means* to attainment of virtue. Ancients, however, believed that *exempla* not only displayed virtue but also enabled it. Transformation by vision was the foundation upon which such a view rested.

(Timothy is the model); 2 Tim 1:11-12 (Paul is the example); 2:9-10 (Paul is the model); 3:10-12 (Paul is the example); 4:6-8, 16-18 (Paul is the example). Polemical material present in the PE does, of course, fall outside the three main types of formation material (Titus 1:10-16; 1 Tim 1:3-7; 1:19b; 4:1-3; 5:8; 6:3-5; 2 Tim 1:15; 2:17b-19; 3:1-9, 13; 4:3-4). It is a rhetorical technique, however, also used by ancient moralists to assist in the formation of a person. Polemic is used to arouse a feeling of antipathy towards the false teachers.[33]

What is the relation between doctrines and precepts in the PE? Precepts arise out of doctrines in the PE just as they do in Seneca's model. Titus 2:1 states it plainly. Titus is to teach what is consistent with sound doctrine. Other passages in the PE sound the same note (Titus 1:16 — some claim to know God but deny him by their actions; Titus 2:11-12 — the grace of God appeared, training us to live properly; Titus 3:8b — those who believe right doctrine devote themselves to good works; 1 Tim 1:3, 5 — the aim of good instruction is love from a pure heart; 1:9-10 — some have behavior that is contrary to sound doctrine; 2:10 — good works are proper for those who profess reverence for God).

What is the relation between precepts and exempla? *Exempla* function as a catalyst for good performance in the PE just as they do in pagan authors.[34] The teacher becomes an example of theory put into practice (Isocrates, *Soph.* 16-18). His example presents a character sketch to be imitated (Isocrates, *Ad Nic.* 79, 75, 77; *Demon.* 36). Self-testimony can serve as an example (Seneca, *Ep.* 71.7; 6.3-5; 94.73-74). Imitation, however, is *not* a reproduction (Seneca, *Ep.* 84.8-11). Above all, an *exemplum* stirs the audience's spirits (Cicero, *De or.* 3.27.104-05; Quintilian, *Inst.* 5.11). No clearer statements can be had for the ancients' understanding of the transformative effect of *exempla* than that of Plutarch. In *Virt. prof.* 84D, he says that one's being in the presence of a good person has the effect: "Great is his craving all but to merge his own identity in that of the good man" (Babbitt, LCL). In *Per.* 1-2, Plutarch elaborates:

> Since, then, our souls are by nature possessed of a great fondness for learning and fondness for seeing, it is surely reasonable to chide those

33. Harding, *Tradition and Rhetoric in the Pastoral Epistles,* 211; cf. Luke T. Johnson, "2 Timothy and the Polemic against False Teachers: A Re-examination," *Ohio Journal of Religious Studies* 6, no. 7 (1978/79): 1-26.

34. For comprehensive coverage of personal examples in antiquity, see Benjamin Fiore, *The Function of Personal Example in the Socratic and Pastoral Epistles* (AnBib 105; Rome: Biblical Institute Press, 1986).

who abuse this fondness on objects all unworthy either of their eyes or ears, to the neglect of those which are good and serviceable. . . . our intellectual vision must be applied to such objects as, by their very charm, invite it onward to its own proper good. Such objects are to be found in virtuous deeds; *these implant in those who search them out a great and zealous eagerness which leads to imitation.* . . . But virtuous action straightway so disposes a man that he no sooner admires the works of virtue than he strives to emulate those who wrought them. . . . The Good *creates a stir of activity towards itself, and implants at once in the spectator an active impulse; it does not form his character by ideal representation alone; but through the investigation of its work furnishes him with a dominant purpose.* For such reasons I have decided to persevere in my writing of Lives. (Perrin, LCL; italics mine)

If one asks what in the PE enables the training of believers between their regeneration by God's grace (Titus 2:11-14; 3:4-7) and the epiphany of judgment (2 Tim 1:18; 4:8), at one level it is the performative language of *exempla* above all, but of course also polemic. In this, the PE share with Hellenistic moral philosophers two major techniques that are catalysts for progress in virtue. Believers are not left to their own resources to form themselves. *Exempla* and polemic, as performative language, enable progress in virtue. This the PE share with the moral philosophers.

IV

At another level there is the distinctively Christian dimension to enablement of the believers' progress between regeneration and judgment. Bultmann (1 Tim 1:14 — Spirit; Titus 2:11-12 — grace as power; 2 Tim 1:9-10 and Titus 1:3 — the present is under grace as a present reality), Donelson (the Spirit given at baptism), and Davies (Titus 3:4-5; 2 Tim 1:7, 14 — Holy Spirit) all locate this distinctive largely in the Holy Spirit's activity. Such a claim bears investigation. Let us now look carefully at the texts appealed to by these authors.

We begin with Titus 2:11-12, which says "the grace of God has appeared for the salvation of all people, training us . . . to live sober, upright, and godly lives in the world, awaiting our blessed hope." The text says the incarnation occurred for everyone's salvation; it also says believers await the blessed hope. The period in between the former and the latter epiphanies is a time of training/teaching about how to live. The enabling of this journey is not at all clear from this text. Where in this text is grace as power in the present? Where is the activity of the Holy Spirit in the between time?

Titus 3:4-5 says that God's goodness appeared in the incarnation, saving us by renewal in the Holy Spirit so that we might become heirs in the hope of eternal life. Here the Holy Spirit is explicitly active in the beginning of the Christian life. The Spirit's activity in the period between regeneration and eternal life, however, is not spelled out.

2 Timothy 1:6-7 refers to the Spirit given to Timothy as part of his being set apart for special ministry (cf. 1 Cor 12:4-11). It is probably to be understood in terms of texts like Deut 34:9 (Joshua is full of the spirit of wisdom because Moses had laid hands on him), Num 11:16-17, 24-25 (the seventy elders receive a share of Moses' spirit by a similar ritual gesture), Acts 13:1-3 (prophets and teachers in Antioch lay hands on Barnabas and Saul as a part of sending them off on mission), and perhaps *b. Sanh.* 13b-14a (Johannan ben Zakkai ordains his disciples with a ritual imposition of hands). What is imparted to Timothy is a Spirit of power. Here, as in Acts, the Spirit functions to empower a witness for mission/ministry. The Spirit is here not given at baptism but at a time of appointment to a special ministry.[35]

2 Timothy 1:9-10 and Titus 1:3 speak only about the beginning of the Christian life due to the first epiphany of Christ and about Paul's ministry of preaching. Having looked at the texts appealed to by Bultmann, Donelson, and Davies, one can only conclude that the claim that the Holy Spirit given at baptism enables the Christian's moral and spiritual progress between conversion and judgment is unproven.

Are there other texts that might lend their support? Let us look at several additional texts in 2 Tim. In 1:8 Timothy is told, "Do not be ashamed then of testifying to our Lord, nor of me his prisoner, but take your share of suffering for this gospel in the power of God." Here the power of God enables Timothy's endurance of suffering because of his bearing testimony to the Lord (cf. Acts 5:41). In 1:11-12 the Lord is deemed able to guard until the day of judgment the gospel entrusted to Paul.[36] Here again enabling power is

---

35. Ernst Käsemann, "Das Formular einer neutestamentlichen Ordinationsparänese," in *Exegetische Versuche und Besinnungen* (Göttingen: Vandenhoeck & Ruprecht, 1960), 1:101-8, regards 1 Tim 6:11-16 as the first extant formula of instruction given at ordination. It is probably anachronistic to refer to Timothy's "ordination," but some type of ceremony is in view.

36. I am reading τὴν παραθήκην μου in 1:12 as an objective genitive (God deposits the tradition with Paul) rather than as a subjective genitive (Paul deposits his soul with God). This has the advantage of giving to the word "deposit" the same meaning in all three pas-

related to an apostolic mission. In 1:14 we hear that the Holy Spirit who dwells within Paul and Timothy is the power of God that faithfully preserves the gospel message from one generation to the next.[37] In 2:7 God will give Timothy the gift of understanding "so that he can carry out his catechetical task"[38] (cf. Matt 13:11-12, 23). Enablement is again related to mission. In 3:11 the Lord rescued Paul from all his persecutions. Again, divine power enables mission. In 4:17-18 we come to the last enablement passage in 2 Timothy. Because of its importance, it may be quoted in full, distinguishing the two verses. Verse 17 reads: "The Lord was present with (παρέστη) me and empowered (ἐνεδυνάμωσεν) me to proclaim the word fully, that all Gentiles might hear it, and I was rescued out of the mouth of a lion." Verse 18 reads: "The Lord will rescue me from every evil work and will save me for his heavenly kingdom." Let us look first at verse 17. In verse 17 we meet the formula, "the Lord was with him." The definitive work on the formula has been done by van Unnik.[39] He says it is most commonly used with individuals. It involves the empowering or enablement of someone involved in a divine task. Interestingly, he says, the formula "being with" is used in a virtually synonymous way with "being filled with the Spirit." So, it refers to the dynamic activity of God's Spirit enabling people to do God's work by protecting, assisting, and blessing them. It is no surprise then to hear Paul say that God's being with him empowered him. For what was he empowered? In verse 17 it is for the task of preaching. Indeed, throughout the PE so far the focus in the interim between two epiphanies is on the Lord's enablement of his witnesses who are on mission. So far there has been an absence of emphasis on the divine enablement of one's training/education. In 2 Tim 4:18, however, we find what has eluded us to this point. There is here likely an echo of the Lord's Prayer (Matt 6:13 — deliver us from evil or the evil one).[40] Here Paul says the Lord will deliver him from every evil. For what purpose? For his involvement in mission? No. It is to "save me for his heavenly kingdom." At this point there is a reference to the Lord's saving activity of an individual in the be-

---

sages where it occurs (cf. 1 Tim 6:20; 2 Tim 1:14) (so C. K. Barrett, *The Pastoral Epistles* [Oxford: Clarendon, 1963], 96-97).

37. Raymond F. Collins, *1 & 2 Timothy and Titus: A Commentary* (NTL; Louisville: Westminster/John Knox, 2002), 214.

38. Collins, *1 & 2 Timothy and Titus*, 222.

39. W. C. van Unnik, "Dominus Vobiscum: The Background of a Liturgical Formula," in *New Testament Essays: Festschrift for T. W. Manson* (ed. A. J. B. Higgins; Manchester: Manchester University Press, 1959), 270-305.

40. Collins, *1 & 2 Timothy and Titus*, 286-87.

tween time in order to enable him to reach the heavenly kingdom. In verse 18, grace is experienced not only at the beginning of the Christian life and not only in the empowerment of Christian witnesses in the present time, but at least in this one spot it is clearly operative for an individual's deliverance from evil or the evil one so that he may make it into the future salvation.

From this brief survey, what can we conclude? The PE see God's grace undergirding the believer's existence in its beginning (regeneration) (e.g., Titus 3:4-7), in its fulfillment (e.g., 2 Tim 4:8), and in its progress from beginning to fulfillment (e.g., for the individual's defense and deliverance, enabling inheritance of the heavenly kingdom [e.g., 2 Tim 4:18] and for the Lord's servant on mission, enabling a successful service [e.g., 2 Tim 4:17]). The disparity of examples of divine empowerment of individual believers in the period of training (Titus 2:12), of which there are very few, and examples of God's enabling those on mission is surely due to the purpose of the three-part correspondence. Paul's departures demand his employment of two emissaries who must be formed in order to ensure the continued well-being of the Pauline churches. The emphasis, therefore, is on divine enablement of Paul, Titus, and Timothy in the period between the first and second epiphanies of the Lord. This enablement operates on two levels: that of the moral philosophers like Seneca with their use of *exempla*[41] based on the concept of transformation by vision[42] and that of the distinctively Christian experience of the Lord's being with/the Holy Spirit's presence and power/the Lord's gift of understanding/the Lord's rescue. There is, then, continuity with the understanding of soteriology in the undisputed Pauline letters.

---

41. For Paul's use of *exempla*, cf. 1 Cor 4:16; 11:1; Phil 3:12-16; 1 Thess 1:6-7; 2:14; 2 Thess 3:7. Cf. Acts 20:35.

42. One should not think that the notion of imitation is non-Jewish. Josephus (*Ag Ap.* 2.204) says that the Law orders that children "shall be taught to read, and shall learn both the laws and the deeds of their forefathers, in order that they may imitate the latter."

Fidelity and New Covenant Enablement in Hebrews

Jason A. Whitlark

This essay examines the soteriology of "getting in" and "staying in" in Hebrews. What will be demonstrated is that "getting in" is grounded in God's gracious election while "staying in" is grounded in God's enablement of fidelity foretold in Jeremiah's prophecy of a new covenant. Hebrews, however, interprets the accomplishment of the inward empowerment promised in the new covenant through Jesus' purification of the conscience that brings the believer into God's presence where he or she finds ongoing grace and mercy. The association of divine enablement for faithfulness with inward purification is not new in Hebrews but is grounded in the Jewish scriptures that are central to the thought world of Hebrews.

•   •

The soteriology in Hebrews has presented interpreters of this document with several unique challenges. Among them is the document's singular focus on perseverance and its rigorist position that does not allow a second repentance for apostates. In the first three centuries of the Common Era, some Christians used Hebrews to argue that the lapsed should not be readmitted into the Christian fellowship, thus effectively barring them from the hope of salvation.[1] In more modern times, in those streams of Protestant Christian-

---

1. Cf. Philaster, *Haer.* 41, who cites Heb 6:4-6 as problematic in Hebrews' reception in the West.

ity that have originated primarily out of the Reformed tradition, the debate over Hebrews centers upon whether genuine Christians can lose their salvation.[2] Both of these viewpoints about Hebrews' soteriology have often caused it to be treated as a subcanonical text in the NT.

In light of this problematic, even disturbing, soteriology, few interpreters of Hebrews have grasped the significance or role of the new covenant prophecy from Jeremiah, which is quoted in its entirety in Heb 8:8-12. In Jeremiah, the prophecy of a new covenant was given as the solution to Israel's and Judah's continual apostasy from God, for in its fulfillment would come the necessary forgiveness of sins *and* divine transformation and power for fidelity to God, that is, God would write his laws on their hearts and they would know God. Moreover, this new covenant relationship would be enduring, as indicated by the prophecy which follows that of the new covenant, namely, Israel and Judah will be "a nation before [God] forever" and the rebuilt city of Jerusalem will "never again be uprooted or overthrown."[3]

This emphasis in the new covenant on the divine enablement of the people's faithfulness is often minimized in interpretations of Hebrews. For example, when David deSilva speaks about the internality of the new covenant in Hebrews, he seems to believe that knowledge of what pleases God is the extent of what is given to the believer.[4] Moreover, his almost exclusive emphasis upon honor and shame strategies in the rhetoric of Hebrews suggests that behavior is controlled heteronomously (from without), whereas Hebrews' emphasis on the conscience and internality of the new covenant would suggest a behavior that is controlled from within.[5] Petrus Gräbe lim-

---

2. E.g., Clark Pinnock, "From Augustine to Arminius: A Pilgrimage in Theology," in *The Grace of God, the Will of Man: A Case for Arminianism* (ed. Clark H. Pinnock; Grand Rapids: Zondervan, 1989), 17. In fact, Pinnock attests that the examination of Hebrews facilitated his shift away from "Augustine" to "Arminius." Cf. Grant R. Osborne, "Soteriology in the Epistle to the Hebrews," in *Grace Unlimited* (ed. Clark H. Pinnock; Minneapolis: Bethany House, 1975), 159.

3. The author of Hebrews possibly picks up on this connection between the new covenant and an enduring Jerusalem in Jeremiah since, after his exposition of the new covenant in 8:1–10:18, he introduces the inviolable heavenly Jerusalem as his Christian audience's promised hope in the latter part of his discourse.

4. David A. deSilva, *Perseverance in Gratitude: A Socio-Rhetorical Commentary on the Epistle "to the Hebrews"* (Grand Rapids: Eerdmans, 2000), 326-27.

5. Zeba Crook (*Reconceptualizing Conversion: Patronage Loyalty, and Conversion in the Religions of the Ancient Mediterranean* [BZNW 130; New York: De Gruyter, 2004], 184-86) explicitly confirms my observation. He accepts that the ancient Mediterranean world was an honor-shame culture. Therefore, he concludes that it was less important what one believed

its the benefits of the new covenant in Hebrews to the forgiveness of sins at the conclusion of the prophecy, while the middle part of the prophecy in Jeremiah (the assurances of the Torah in the heart, knowledge of God, and the covenant formula) remains unstressed in Hebrews.[6] Susan Lehne has specifically identified the soteriological pattern in Hebrews with E. P. Sanders's covenantal nomism. She writes:

> In Sanders' terms, the paranetic appeals are never about "getting in," but always about "staying in" the NC, while the warnings are about the danger of "dropping out," that is, losing the elect status of κεκλημένοι/ μέτοχοι that Christ won for NC people.[7]

She goes on to identify the new covenant dynamic with the reciprocity that is characteristic of the old covenant and of Sanders's covenantal nomism. In this paradigm, the "indicative" comes to be identified with God's initial act of grace through Jesus Christ that marks out the beginning of the Christian life or creates the possibility for it, while the Christian's own responsive gratitude for that initial grace is the power for the continuance in that life, i.e., fulfillment of the "imperative."[8]

When, however, we turn to the majestic benediction of Hebrews (13:20-21), we find that it is predicated upon the fulfillment, through Jesus' high priestly ministry and mediation, of the new covenant promises that constitute the central part of the Jeremiah prophecy. Thus, the author prays

---

or internally preferred than that one showed the appropriate behavior, i.e., loyalty to one's benefactor. At least one Jesus tradition was explicitly critical of this perspective. The Matthean Jesus (Matt 15:8-9a) castigates the religious leaders for this superficial "loyalty," quoting the prophet Isaiah, "These people honor me with their lips but their hearts are far from me. They worship me in vain."

6. Petrus Gräbe, *Der neue Bund in der frühchristlichen Literatur: unter Berücksichtigung der alttestamentlich-jüdischen Voraussetzungen* (FB 96; Würzburg: Echter Verlag, 2001), 118, 127-28. See also Sebastian Fuhrmann, "Failures Forgotten: The Soteriology in Hebrews Revisited in the Light of Its Quotation of Jeremiah 38:31-34 [LXX]," *Neot* 41 (2007): 295-316.

7. Susanne Lehne, *The New Covenant in Hebrews* (JSNTSup 44; Sheffield: Sheffield Academic Press, 1990), 107.

8. This is also deSilva's position about the relational or covenantal dynamic in Hebrews (*Despising Shame: Honor Discourse and Community Maintenance in the Epistle to the Hebrews* [SBLDS 152; Atlanta: Scholars, 1995], 209-75); deSilva, *Perseverance in Gratitude,* 59-64. See my discussion of the relational dynamic of reciprocity in the ancient world along with its critique by some Jewish streams (e.g., Jeremiah) in *Enabling Fidelity to God: Perseverance in Hebrews in Light of the Reciprocity Systems of the Ancient Mediterranean World* (PBMS; Carlisle: Paternoster, 2008), 1-126.

for his audience in the benediction that God would *"equip you* with all good things *so that you may do his will* and *work in us* that which is pleasing before him through Jesus Christ." Thus, I will argue in this essay that the divine transformation, divine enablement, and the enduring covenant relationship predicted in Jeremiah's prophecy of a new covenant have central significance for the soteriology of Hebrews. The soteriology is something more than covenantal nomism, but a new covenant piety that is continuously enabled by God from the beginning to the end of the Christian sojourn in this present age.

Interpreting Fidelity in Hebrews

If we desire to understand the divine-human relational dynamic in Hebrews, then, as stated above, we must look first to its interpretation of the new covenant for our clue. The new covenant is the primary metaphor for the divine-human relationship in Hebrews. There are some key supports for this assertion. First, the Jeremiah prophecy is the most extensive Old Testament quote in Hebrews (and in the NT). Second, the quotation of the Jeremiah prophecy (8:8-12) occurs in the central expository unit on the priesthood of Jesus, beginning at 5:1 and concluding at 10:18.[9] In chapter 8 the author explains the change in covenant that has come along with the change in priesthood previously demonstrated in chapter 7. Jesus, the Melchizedekian high priest, mediates the new covenant. Third, the covenant motif is the organizing principle of the discourse in Hebrews.[10] The main rhetorical feature of the sermon, syncrisis, supports this observation. Underlying the various syncrises in Hebrews is the demonstration of the superiority of the new covenant over the old. In fact, this syncritical project in Hebrews possibly arose out of the prophecy of the new covenant in Jeremiah, who himself contrasts the new covenant with the old. Furthermore, the progymnasmatic instruction about syncrisis states that a syncrisis of two subjects (in Hebrews the old and new

9. Here I follow those commentators who see the exhortations in 4:14-16 and 10:19-23 framing the exposition of Jesus' high priesthood. Hebrews 4:14-16 is transitional from an exhortation to an exposition, while 10:19-23 is transitional from an exposition to an extensive exhortation. On 4:14-16 and 10:19-23 as parallel texts that function as an *inclusio* in Hebrews' structure, see the original proposal by Wolfgang Nauck, "Zum Aufbau des Hebräerbriefes," in *Judentum, Urchristentum, Kirche: Festschrift für Joachim Jeremias* (ed. Walther Eltester; Berlin: Alfred Töpelmann, 1960), 200-203.

10. Cf. Lehne, *The New Covenant in Hebrews,* 103.

covenants) is not between the "whole" subjects but between their analogous parts.[11] Hebrews' syncrises are arranged by moving from one representative subject of the old and new covenants to another — from their mediators (1:1-14; 2:5-18), to their inaugurators (3:1-6), to their priests and their cultic ministries and sacrifices (5:1-10; 7:1–10:18), and finally to their representative mountains (12:18-24). This new covenant relationship at the heart of Hebrews' exposition implies election of the covenant community (getting in) and proclaims its enablement for ongoing faithfulness to God (staying in). Let us now turn to the demonstration of these points in Hebrews.

Divine Election: Getting In

We can at one level say that "getting in" according to Hebrews involves both hearing the message of salvation that was first delivered by the Lord (2:1-4; 10:32) and believing it (4:2; 10:39). We can, however, say more than this. Hebrews is rich with divine election themes. These themes are especially prevalent in chapter 2. In 2:11, the author refers to the "many sons" who are led to glory as "those who are sanctified" (οἱ ἁγιαζόμενοι; 10:14). In the same verse, God is referred to as the one who sanctifies (ὁ ἁγιάζων).[12] In the Old Testament, ὁ ἁγιάζων was a reference to God. The specific sense of this terminology is that God has set apart Israel from the other nations to worship him. This setting apart for service is a way to talk about God's choosing or election. We find such a meaning in Lev 22:31-33 (LXX):

> Keep my commands and follow them. I am the LORD. Do not profane my holy name. I must be acknowledged as holy by the Israelites. I am the LORD who sanctifies you (ὁ ἁγιάζων ὑμᾶς) and who brought you out of Egypt to be your God. I am the LORD.

Here God's sanctifying of Israel is associated with his deliverance of Israel out of Egypt to be his people and to worship him.[13] In Ezek 20:12 (LXX),

11. Cf. the progymnasmatic instruction regarding syncrisis by Apthonius (*Prog.* 43 [Kennedy, 114]) and Nicolaus (*Prog.* 59 [Kennedy, 162]).

12. Others have seen a reference to Jesus. Cf. William L. Lane, *Hebrews 1–8* (WBC 47a; Dallas: Thomas Nelson, 1991), 58; Harold W. Attridge, *The Epistle to the Hebrews* (Philadelphia: Fortress, 1989), 88n.107; Paul Ellingworth, *The Epistle to the Hebrews: A Commentary on the Greek Text* (Grand Rapids: Eerdmans, 1993), 163.

13. Cf. Exod 31:13 (LXX).

God declares that he sanctified Israel (ὁ ἁγιάζων αὐτούς). Elsewhere, in Ezek 37:28 (LXX), God declares, "Then the nations will know that I the Lord sanctify Israel (ὁ ἁγιάζων αὐτούς), when my sanctuary is among them forever." In all these instances, for Israel to be sanctified by God means for God to choose Israel from among all the nations to be his people and to serve him. Moreover, in Ezekiel, this sanctifying is a restoration by God of the relationship his people violated. Thus, in all the examples, "sanctifying" (ἁγιάζων) is a reference to that choice being enacted in time by God so that God's choice of Israel is now apparent to all the nations. Likewise, Hebrews now applies this terminology to the Christians as those who have been consecrated by God or chosen by him in order to serve God (cf. 9:14).[14]

We encounter yet another election motif in Heb 2:13. The verse is a citation of Isa 8:18 put on the lips of the exalted Jesus. Jesus upon his entrance into his glory declares, "Here am I, and the children God has given to me." In Isa 8:18, the children that God gives to the prophet are the remnant of Israel that awaits God's deliverance. Likewise, in Hebrews, the children are those awaiting God's deliverance from this present age to the glory and honor of the world to come (cf. 2:5-9). Again, in both contexts, both Hebrews and Isaiah, the notion of election is implicit — God gives the children to the prophet and to Jesus because they belong to him; he has chosen them.

Other election terminology is found in Heb 2:16 where the "many sons" that Jesus leads to glory are referred to as "Abraham's seed." The immediate allusion of this phrase is to Isa 41:8-10. Paul Ellingworth has shown through key lexical overlap between the text of Hebrews and the passage in Isaiah that the cumulative allusion in Hebrews is to this whole passage from Isaiah.[15] In verse 8 of Isaiah, Yahweh describes Abraham's seed as those "whom I have chosen" for deliverance from captivity. If the allusion is the entire passage in Hebrews, then "Abraham's seed" is another way of talking about those who have been chosen by God in order to be rescued by Jesus from the Devil and death.[16]

---

14. Cf. David Peterson, *Hebrews and Perfection: An Examination of the Concept of Perfection in the "Epistle to the Hebrews"* (Cambridge: Cambridge University Press, 1982), 150. Peterson notes that sanctification is something that is already effected by Christ (10:10, 29; 13:12). It is a designation for Christians, not for an ongoing process.

15. Ellingworth, *Hebrews,* 176.

16. Interestingly, if we are dealing with an allusion to all of Isa 41:8-10, the focus of this passage is not only on God's election that brings about deliverance but also on his preservation of "Abraham's seed."

In Heb 2:17, we come across a reference to "the people" (τοῦ λαοῦ).[17] Likewise, we read in Heb 13:12 that Jesus sanctifies "the people" (τὸν λαόν) through his own blood. In Hebrews, "the people" designates the new covenant community (cf. 4:9; 8:10; 10:30).[18] Ὁ λαός (τοῦ θεοῦ) was a technical term in the LXX for Israel as a nation chosen by God. Strathmann describes the theological significance of this term in the LXX when it serves as a designation for Israel:

> Because Yahweh has separated Israel to himself as a peculiar possession, they are a holy people. They do not have to become a holy people by cultic or moral sanctification: they are this in virtue of the divine distinction. . . . This relation of possession is by the free act of Yahweh. He chose Israel, Dt. 4:37; 7:6; 14:2; Ψ 134:4.[19]

In various NT references the term is, likewise, laden with a notion of a gracious divine election (cf. Acts 15:14; Acts 18:10; Rom 9:24-25; 1 Pet 2:9-10).[20] As with the "seed of Abraham," this term became a religious designation used by the early Christians affirming that God himself called out and brought into existence the Christian community for his worship and praise.

Possibly the clearest notion of the divine election of those who experience the benefits of Christ's mediation occurs in Heb 9:15. There we are told that Jesus' death redeems from the sins committed under the first covenant so that those who are called (οἱ κεκλημένοι) might receive the eternal inheritance. Οἱ κεκλημένοι is a perfect passive pointing to the divine initiative of God who calls.[21] Being called is often synonymous with being chosen. For instance, in Isa 41:9 (LXX), to which the author of Hebrews has previously alluded in 2:16-18, to be called is equated with being chosen.[22] This equating of calling with divine election is made explicit in Heb 5:4. The high priest does not take the honor of this office by his own initiative but must be called (καλούμενος) by God, which is another way of saying that he must be chosen by God.

We encounter a final election motif in Heb 12:23. Here we are given a pic-

---

17. This statement is reminiscent of Heb 9:28, where Jesus "bore the sins of the many."
18. Attridge, *Hebrews*, 398.
19. Strathmann, "λαός," *TDNT* 4:35.
20. See the discussion of Strathmann, *TDNT* 4:54-56.
21. Cf. Attridge, *Hebrews*, 255n.19.
22. Commenting on Rom 8:29, Charles Talbert (*Romans* [Macon, GA: Smyth & Helwys, 2002], 225) writes, "'[C]alling' focuses on the divine choice."

ture of the Christian's eschatological hope. The Christian pilgrim has come "to the assembly of the firstborn inscribed permanently (ἀπογεγραμμένων) in heaven."[23] This description is a proleptic encounter with the *"ultimate complete company of the people of God,"* since we seem to be dealing here with a post-judgment picture of God's people rejoicing with the angelic host before him.[24] The inscription of names in heaven is what is of interest here. A heavenly registry in which the names of the redeemed were recorded was common in apocalyptic literature. Daniel 12:1 states that all whose names are written in the book will be delivered from times of distress. Revelation 13:8 refers to the redeemed as those having names that have been inscribed in the book of life from the creation of the world.[25] In these passages, the inscription of names in a heavenly registry is a reference to both election and divine protection. Craig Koester notes that the passive voice (ἀπογεγραμμένων) in Heb 12:23 is used here to suggest that the people on the registry are registered by God's initiative.[26] The perfect tense points to the abiding nature of that choice, in other words, the preservation of those inscribed or chosen.[27]

All of these election motifs in Hebrews affirm that the foundation of the benefits the Christian pilgrims receive through Jesus Christ resides in the elective will of God. Moreover, God's election is gracious in that God does not choose the worthy for his benefits.[28] The new covenant in Jeremiah,

23. My translation follows William L. Lane (*Hebrews 9–13* [WBC 47b; Dallas: Thomas Nelson, 1991], 467-68) in order to bring out the meaning of the perfect participle. James Moffatt (*A Critical and Exegetical Commentary on the Epistle to the Hebrews* [Edinburgh: T. & T. Clark, 1924], 217) states that the whole phrase emphasizes God's election.

24. Peterson, *Hebrews and Perfection*, 162. The phrase ἐκκλησίᾳ πρωτοτόκων may be and has been taken by some (Käsemann, Spicq, Montefiore) with the previous verse as a reference to the myriad of angels. The description, "permanently ascribed in heaven," however, is never used of angels. Further, ἐκκλησία and πρωτότοκος are "rooted in the description of Israel in the Pentateuch." Also, πρωτότοκος in the plural was "an apocalyptic title applied to the redeemed community." See Lane (*Hebrews 9–13*, 468-69) for this discussion and the evidence presented in favor of the latter assertions. I understand that Heb 12:23 refers to the ultimate complete company of God's people across the ages and not merely to the faithful dead (i.e., "the spirits of the perfected righteous") because the author includes the living faithful to be among that joyful assembly ("for you have come," 12:22).

25. See also Exod 32:32-33; Ps 69:28; 1 *En.* 104:1; *Apoc. Zeph.* 3:7; Luke 10:20; Phil 4:3.

26. Craig R. Koester, *Hebrews* (New York: Doubleday, 2001), 545.

27. Hans Friedrich Weiss (*Der Brief an die Hebräer* [Göttingen: Vandenhoeck & Ruprecht, 1991], 680) recognizes the paradox evident here. He observes that those who are presently on their way to the heavenly Jerusalem already have their names enrolled there.

28. *Contra* deSilva's (*Perseverance in Gratitude*, 116-17) interpretation of Heb 2:13a, which would seem to suggest that Jesus chooses the worthy.

which is at the heart of Hebrews' expositions, was God's solution to the people's rebellion against God (not a response to their worthiness) demonstrated by their failure to keep the old one. The operative assumption in Hebrews is similar to that assumed by Jeremiah, namely, that the audience of Hebrews was defiled by their "dead works" (9:14) and stood in need of divine forgiveness because of an "evil conscience" (10:22).[29] Thus, God's election in Hebrews is free and gracious and stands at the beginning of the Christian pilgrimage to the heavenly Jerusalem. It is the foundation of the Christian's experience of the benefits of Jesus' high priestly ministry and the reason for his saving ministry. Moreover, God's elective purpose is for his children to realize the "glory and honor" he intended for them in the world to come and that they now see in the exalted Son, Jesus (cf. 2:5-9).[30] The realization of that purpose requires perseverance in their Christian confession (cf. 3:6; 4:14; 10:23). Thus, we need to discuss Hebrews' representation of human transformation and ongoing divine enablement that is a primary blessing of the new covenant relationship for the realization of God's promise.

29. This is especially true if we understand "dead works" in Hebrews to be a reference to pagan idolatry (cf. deSilva, *Perseverance in Gratitude*, 216-17). A parallel expression is found Acts 14:15, where the people of Lystra are exhorted to turn "from these worthless things (idols) to the living God." Further, in Hebrews, the "evil conscience" seems to be related to the "evil heart" in 3:12. In the exhortation of chapter 3, an evil heart abandons or turns away from God. Thus, 10:22 could be understood in the sense that Jesus' cleansing preserves the believer from apostasy, which is in line with Ezekiel's and Jeremiah's understanding of cleansing (see below), or a reference is being made to the former idolatrous state of the believers when they rejected God, especially if we understand "dead works" to refer to idolatry in 9:14. Of course, the evil conscience might just be the consciousness and conviction of sin that defiles a person (cf. Attridge, *Hebrews*, 288).

30. Hebrews opens with the declaration of the Son's enthronement in the world to come and thus the guarantee of God's promise (cf. 1:6). The interpretation of οἰκουμένην in 1:6 hinges on whether one equates it with its use in 2:5 and finds Christ's exaltation after his incarnation (when he was made a little lower than the angels) in 2:5-9 determinative for what the author describes in 1:6. I have chosen to side with those commentators who have advocated this position. Also when the author of Hebrews refers to the present "shakable" order, he uses the term κόσμος (4:3; 9:26; 10:5; 11:7; 11:38; cf. 9:1 [κοσμικόν]). Cf. Kenneth L. Schenck, "A Celebration of the Enthroned Son: The Catena of Hebrews 1," *JBL* 120 (2001): 469-85, esp. 477-79; deSilva, *Perseverance in Gratitude*, 96-98, 278; Lane, *Hebrews 1–8*, 27; Albert Vanhoye, "L'οἰκουμένη dans l'Épître aux Hébreux," *Bib* 45 (1964): 248-53. *Contra* Ceslas Spicq (*L'Épître aux Hébreux* [vol. 2; Paris: Librairie Lecoffre, 1977], 17), Moffatt (*Hebrews*, 10-11), and Attridge (*Hebrews*, 55-56) among others who believe the Son's entrance into the world in 1:6 is a reference to the incarnation. To see 1:6 as a reference to the incarnation was also a popular interpretation among the early Christians (cf. Erik M. Heen and Philip D. W. Krey, eds., *Hebrews* [ACCS NT 10; Downers Grove, IL: InterVarsity, 2005], 22-23).

Divine Enablement: Staying In

"Staying in" for Hebrews is of vital importance. It is the singular concern of the exhortations. Without perseverance and longsuffering, the Christian will not receive the promised inheritance or life in the world to come for which he or she was chosen (6:12; 10:36). Thus, concerning the maintenance of this new covenant relationship, Hebrews emphasizes two aspects of the Jeremiah prophecy at the conclusion of its discussion of Jesus' Melchizedekian priesthood: (1) God will write his law upon the heart, and (2) God will remember the sins of the people no longer (10:16-17). Our primary concern will be examining how Hebrews represents the fulfillment of these two promises. For in these promises the elective purposes of God come to fruition. From the perspective of Hebrews, what we will see is that the transformation and divine enablement for faithfulness promised in the new covenant are tied to the removal of transgressions before God also promised in the new covenant. Failure to see this connection has caused some[31] to downplay in Hebrews that aspect of the prophecy in Jeremiah which is focused on the divine enablement of fidelity, namely, the writing of the law on the hearts and minds of the people.

The Cultic Reinterpretation of the New Covenant Promises

A New Covenant and a New Cult

In order to unpack this connection of human transformation and ongoing divine enablement with the forgiveness of sins in Hebrews, we must first understand the cultic reinterpretation of the new covenant in Hebrews. Though the prophecy in Jeremiah or its surrounding context does not mention the cult or sacrifice, Hebrews filters its interpretation of the new covenant through the cult of the old covenant. Moreover, in Hebrews, a new covenant implies a new cult: "For when there is a change in priesthood, of necessity there is also a change in Law" (7:12) and "[Jesus] has obtained a superior ministry by as much as he is the mediator of a better covenant, which is given on the basis of better promises" (8:6).

Thus, we can expect the author of Hebrews to use cultic language in order to express notions of human transformation and enablement that fulfill the new covenant blessings — blessings that empower the people's fidel-

31. See introduction above.

ity to God. Precisely in the cultic language of purification of the conscience, approaching God, and perfection, in Hebrews we find those notions of transformation and divine enablement of fidelity promised in the new covenant. To these concepts we now turn our attention.

The Cultic Language of New Covenant Blessings

Perfection of the worshiper or believer in Heb 7:1–10:18 is tied to the realization of the new covenant benefits by the believer.[32] For the author, after he declares in 10:14 that Christ "by one offering has *perfected* forever those who are sanctified," goes on to delineate the new covenant blessings in 10:15-18 prophesied by Jeremiah (i.e., the law written on the hearts and minds of the people and God's non-remembrance of sins).

Hebrews 10:14 also grounds perfection and, thereby, the realization of the new covenant promises in Jesus' Melchizedekian priesthood and heavenly cult. Perfection is the goal of Jesus' cultic ministry. While perfection was unachievable under the old covenant and its Levitical priesthood (cf. 7:11), Jesus' Melchizedekian priestly ministry perfects forever those who are sanctified. Again, the new covenant promises are given a cultic foundation and reinterpretation as already indicated in Heb 8:6. Now let us consider both the transformation and divine enablement of God's restored people in the cultic interpretation of the new covenant promises in Hebrews.

Transformation of the Worshiper

In Heb 7:1–10:18, perfection of the worshiper is accomplished when his or her conscience has been cleansed. The antithesis of this statement is found in

32. The classic definition of perfection is found in Aristotle, *Metaph.* 5.16. Most discussions of perfection in Hebrews agree that the fundamental meaning of its perfection language has to do with *attaining an end* (Aristotle's fourth meaning). For deSilva, "the completion of a process that involves a rite of passage from one state to another" informs all the uses of perfection in Hebrews (*Perseverance in Gratitude,* 196. For his complete discussion of the multifarious aspects of perfection in Hebrews, see 194-204). Kenneth Schenck (*Cosmology and Eschatology in Hebrews: The Settings of the Sacrifice* [SNTSMS 143; Cambridge: Cambridge University Press, 2007], 71) understands the essential meaning of perfection in Hebrews to be "the purpose which God has intended for that particular item in the plan of salvation history." These perspectives are not mutually exclusive but related. In the case of the perfection of the believer in 7:1–10:18, the transference from the state of defilement to purity with respect to the conscience that enables one to approach God is the fulfillment of God's salvific purposes foretold in the Jeremiah new covenant prophecy.

9:9 concerning the Levitical priesthood and the sacrifices offered through it: "The gifts and sacrifices offered were not able to perfect (τελειῶσαι) the worshiper with reference to the conscience (κατὰ συνείδησιν)." A similar statement is found in 10:1-2. There the argument states that the sacrifices continually offered by the Levitical priests were not able to perfect (τελειῶσαι) those who were approaching (τοὺς προσερχομένους) God. If they could have perfected the worshiper, then they would have ceased to be offered, because the conscience of the worshiper would have been cleansed (κεκαθαρισμένους). Here, again, we find that the cleansing of the conscience leads to perfection that empowers the worshiper's approach to God, but such a cleansing and perfection was not available under the old covenant Levitical system.

On the other hand, Christ's high priestly ministry, which includes his once-and-for-all sacrifice, "has perfected forever the sanctified" (10:14). This perfection includes the present effect of Christ's ministry that "cleanses our conscience (καθαριεῖ τὴν συνείδησιν) from dead works so that we can serve (λατρεύειν) the living God" (9:14b). This inward cleansing transforms the defiled state of the believer (cf. 9:14a) and empowers the believer to approach God. This logical connection is made explicit in 9:14. The believer is cleansed *so that* he or she may worship/serve God.[33] The author elsewhere makes this logical connection when he exhorts his audience to approach (προσερχώμεθα) God *because* they have been given a "sincere heart (ἀληθινῆς καρδίας)" and a "heart sprinkled from an evil conscience (ῥεραντισμένοι τὰς καρδίας ἀπὸ συνειδήσεως πονηρᾶς)" (10:22). Whereas the old covenant cult only provided an *outward* purification of the "flesh" (9:13), Jesus' high priestly ministry and the new covenant based upon it bring about *inward* transformation through the cleansing of the conscience (9:14). Thus, Peterson can conclude that cleansing of the conscience is the most significant element of the perfection of the believer.[34]

Furthermore, Christ's priestly mediation that cleanses the conscience is the ongoing experience of the believer throughout his or her pilgrimage to the heavenly Jerusalem. We can think of an initial decisive cleansing experienced at the beginning of the sojourn that transforms the human condition.[35] But Hebrews also represents this transformation as abiding and the

---

33. "To serve" is the Greek term λατρεύειν. This term carries cultic and worship connotations in the LXX (Num 16:9; Deut 10:12; 11:13, 28; 28:14; 29:17; Josh 22:5; 1 Macc 2:19, 22). In Heb 9:9, the substantive participle, τὸν λατρεύοντα, practically means "worshiper" (cf. 9:1).

34. Peterson, *Hebrews and Perfection*, 136, 155.

35. The reference in 10:22, having "our bodies washed with pure water," is possibly a

experience of an empowered approach to God as ongoing.[36] First, Heb 9:14 states that Jesus "cleanses (καθαριεῖ) our conscience." By putting καθαριεῖ in the future tense (but with present force for the audience of Hebrews), the cleansing of Jesus is not relegated to a past action but is represented as a present experience.[37] Second, in Heb 10:2, we read that if the sacrifices offered under the old cultus were effective, then they would have ceased because they would have cleansed once and for all (ἅπαξ κεκαθαρισμένους) the conscience of the worshiper. Of course, the argument follows that Jesus' sacrifice accomplishes what the old cultus could not (cf. 10:5-18, esp. v. 10). The use of the perfect tense, κεκαθαρισμένους, with ἅπαξ conveys that the cleansing that the old cultus could not effect but that Jesus did effect was a past completed act with continuing effect. Third, in Heb 10:14, Christ perfects forever the sanctified. The use of the perfect tense, τετελείωκεν, with the adverbial phrase εἰς τὸ διηνεκὲς indicates the abiding quality of what Jesus has done for the believer.[38] Thus, the high priestly ministry of Christ also has permanent results for the Christian pilgrim.[39] Since cleansing was an element of perfection of the believer in Hebrews, we may deduce that cleansing has decisive and ongoing validity for the believer. Fourth, in Heb 10:22, we read that Christ "has sprinkled (ῥεραντισμένοι) the heart from an evil conscience." Again, the perfect tense participle, ῥεραντισμένοι, not only indicates a past, completed, decisive cleansing of the believer's conscience, but the cleansing also has an ongoing abiding effect in the believer's present experience.

This subjective experience of a cleansed conscience is realized through the objective declaration of God's non-remembrance of sins as prophesied in the new covenant, which is inaugurated through Jesus' Melchizedekian priesthood (cf. 10:17-18).[40] God's "non-remembrance of sins" prophesied in

---

reference to the initiatory right of baptism that accompanied the experience of having "our hearts sprinkled from an evil conscience."

36. Cf. Barnabas Lindars, "The Rhetorical Structure of Hebrews," *NTS* 35 (1989): 385.

37. Ellingworth (*Hebrews*, 456) describes καθαριεῖ as a gnomic future and parallels the present tense verb ἁγιάζει in verse 13. Καθαριεῖ appears as a future tense due to the representation of the sanctifying effects of the old covenant sacrifices in the present tense.

38. Hebrews 7:28 has already used a similar statement and syntax with reference to Christ. Christ "has been perfected forever (εἰς τὸν αἰῶνα τετελειωμένον)." This phrase refers to Jesus' exaltation to the unshakable, abiding realm where he performs his permanent priestly ministry.

39. Peterson, *Hebrews and Perfection*, 148-49.

40. Fuhrmann ("Failures Forgotten") is certainly correct to argue that God's forgiveness is not to be grounded on the imagery of expiation in the cultic sacrifice but on God's non-remembrance of transgressions promised in the new covenant. Fuhrmann has also

the new covenant is thereby tied to the purification of the believer's own conscience — the transformative experience that enables the worshiper's approach to God — achieved by Jesus' sacrifice and priestly ministry.

While purification of the conscience is a transformative experience of the worshiper, the perfection achieved through this purification enables the equally important approach into God's presence. The one whose conscience has been cleansed is perfected and thereby able to approach God confidently. Moreover, this transformative experience of Jesus' Melchizedekian priestly ministry and the subsequent approach to God bring about the worshiper's ongoing fidelity to the new covenant relationship with God.

Empowerment in God's Presence

As previously stated, the benefit of perfection within the context of cult is the ability to approach God: "For the Law perfected nothing, but a better hope is introduced by which we draw near to God" (7:19).[41] This approach to God (προσέρχεσθαι) is a key theme in Hebrews (cf. 4:16; 7:25; 10:1, 22; 11:6, 12:18, 22).[42] Only the one who has been perfected is able to approach God in the present and in the future.[43] There are two aspects about the present approach that are important for our consideration. First, the confident ap-

---

made a strong case for seeing the subject of the infinitive phrase, τὸ ἱλάσκεσθαι τὰς ἁμαρτίας τοῦ λαοῦ, in Heb 2:17 as a reference to God and not Jesus (308-12). Fuhrmann thus rejects the notion that Jesus' sacrifice is ever expiatory in Hebrews. It is only covenant-making. Fuhrmann might, however, have overstated his case. In Hebrews 9, Jesus' sacrifice is both a covenant sacrifice (thus he inaugurates a new covenant) and a cultic sacrifice (thus he cleanses the conscience and expiates sin). While Jeremiah does not tie God's non-remembrance of sins to any cultic activity, Hebrews understands the new covenant to be grounded upon a new cult, which leads to this blending of imagery of covenant and cultic sacrifice in Jesus' death and priestly ministry in Heb 9. Additionally, the statement, "without the shedding of blood there is no forgiveness of sins" (9:22), is tied to the purifying function of the cultic sacrifice, which suggests that Jesus' sacrifice is both covenant-making and expiatory. The author then states that Jesus' sacrifice cleanses heavenly things (9:23-24), which again suggests that his sacrifice is expiatory with reference to God. There might be a notion of propitiation with God in 9:15-22, if we follow Scott W. Hahn's ("A Broken Covenant and the Curse of Death: A Study of Hebrews 9:15-22," *CBQ* 66 [2004]: 416-36) arguments that Jesus' death absorbs the curse of death for the sins committed under the first covenant.

41. Peterson, *Hebrews and Perfection*, 128.

42. Cf. LXX Exod 19:6; 34:32; Lev 9:5; 22:3; Deut 4:11; 5:23 where προσέρχεσθαι is used to refer to the people's coming into God's presence.

43. Peterson, *Hebrews and Perfection*, 126. Cf. Paul Johannes Du Plessis, *TELEIOS: The Idea of Perfection in the New Testament* (Kampen: J. H. Kok, 1959).

proach to God is necessary for fidelity in the midst of trial and temptation: "Let us, therefore, approach (προσερχώμεθα) the throne of grace with confidence so that we may receive grace and mercy and we might find timely help" (4:16; cf. 10:19-22).[44] The "grace and mercy" sought in 4:16 should be understood as divine power and intervention for perseverance, since perseverance is the singular concern of the exhortations and need of the audience in Hebrews. Thus in this approach to the throne, God is present to the worshiper to uphold and sustain him or her.[45] Second, the confident approach into God's presence in the present time is a partial realization of the believers' future hope. In their approach to God, they are given a foretaste of their future glory and hope, for in this present approach and experience of God's presence they proleptically join the joyful assembly of the angels and perfected spirits of the righteous in their enjoyment and praise of God. In this way also, God himself continually renews the worshiper's hope in this present age of trial and testing.

Through this language of a cleansed conscience or a true heart that empowers one to approach God so that he or she may receive necessary grace and mercy, we can see the fulfillment of the new covenant promises. Hebrews reinterprets the promises of inscribing the law on the hearts of the people, of knowing God, and the experience of the forgiveness of sin in the new covenant through these cultic metaphors.[46] Our author has precedents from the Jewish scriptures for understanding the cultic language of purification or cleansing as the fulfillment of the divine enablement and transformation promised in the new covenant.

Purification in the Old Testament: The Conceptual World of Hebrews

Purification in the Old Testament is not merely a transaction with God, but a transformation of the human condition that enables service and fidelity to

44. Hebrews 13:9 might represent a similar notion, where the author exhorts the audience that it is good for their hearts to be established or strengthened by grace.

45. The "throne of grace" here seems to be a reference to the symbolic images of the ark of the covenant, which represented God's throne, and the Day of Atonement. When the high priest on the Day of Atonement applied the blood to the mercy seat of the ark, God's kingly presence was then able to dwell with the Israelites for their benefit.

46. Cf. Erich Grässer, *An die Hebräer: Hb 7,1–10,18* (vol. 2; EKKNT 17; Zurich: Benziger, 1993), 101-2, for a similar line of reasoning; Koester, *Hebrews,* 444.

God. When we examine cultic practices in the OT, the cleansing of the tools sanctifies them for use in the cult and worship of God. Leviticus 8:15 (LXX) relates that Moses cleansed the altar with blood and, thus, was sanctified so that atonement could be made upon it: "He cleansed (ἐκαθάρισεν) the altar.... He sanctified (ἡγίασεν) it so that atonement can be made upon it." On the Day of Atonement, the high priest "sprinkles upon the altar the blood [of the sacrifice] with his finger seven times and cleanses (καθαριεῖ) it and consecrates (ἁγιάσει) it from the uncleanness (τῶν ἀκαθαρσιῶν) of the children of Israel" (Lev 16:19 [LXX]). God's presence is now able to dwell among the people beneficially, and the tabernacle is able to be used in the ongoing worship of God. Similarly, in 2 Macc 2:18, Judas Maccabeus rededicates the temple that has been defiled. In order for the temple to once again be employed in the worship of God, it had to be cleansed (ἐκαθάρισεν; cf. v. 19).

The ceremonial cleansing of both the objects employed in worship and the worshiper as well was necessitated by the dangerous holiness of God. In Lev 22:3 (LXX), we read that the one who approaches God unclean (ἀκαθαρσία) will be destroyed (ἐξολεθρευθήσεται). Further, the failure to regard God as holy precipitated God's wrath. Fire from God's presence consumed Aaron's sons, Nadab and Abihu, because they offered this enigmatic unauthorized fire. God, however, makes clear that their death was a result of the failure to honor him and regard him as holy (cf. Lev 10:3). God was ready to destroy all the Israelites for their idolatry when they worshiped the golden calf at Sinai (cf. Exod 32:9-10). God's wrath broke out against the Israelites who engaged in sexual immorality with the Moabite women (cf. Num 25). The holiness of God which consumes and destroys unclean, sinful humans makes the approach to God dangerous. The author of Hebrews appears to pick up on this line of thinking when he admonishes his audience that those who deliberately continue to sin are left with the fearful expectation of judgment and raging fire that will consume God's adversaries (cf. 10:26-27). Also, to fall into the hands of the living God is a fearful prospect (10:31). Thus, we understand the importance of cleansing and the need of assurance that one will be accepted with God. Only when one is enabled to come into the divine presence can he or she experience God's empowering presence that sustains fidelity to him.

The ceremonial cleansing of the cult also became a metaphor for the inward spiritual cleansing the worshiper required in order to approach God and serve him. In Ps 23:3-4 (LXX) the psalmist asks, "Who shall ascend to the hill of the LORD? And who shall stand in his holy place?" The psalmist replies that the one who has "clean hands and a clean heart (καθαρὸς τῇ καρδίᾳ)" may ascend to the holy place. Conversely, in Ps 50 (LXX), the psalmist confronts the guilt of his sin before God. He pleads with God to cleanse (καθάρισόν) him from his sin (v. 4; cf. v. 9). Only God can do this. He seeks for God to "create in [him] a clean heart (καρδίαν καθαρὰν κτίσον) and to renew a right spirit (πνεῦμα εὐθὲς ἐγκαίνισον) in [his] inward parts" (v. 12). Marvin Tate writes, "The divine activity results in a new order of existence, a new arrangement, or a new emergence shaped by the divine power and will."[47] If the Lord does not grant these things, then the psalmist will be forever cast from God's presence and will not have the experience of God's sustaining holy spirit (cf. v. 13). In other words, the psalmist will not be a cleansed and sanctified vessel in which God's empowering presence may dwell. Only out of this experience of the divine presence comes a willing spirit to sustain him (πνεύματι ἡγεμονικῷ στήρισόν με; v. 14). Only when God has granted the psalmist's request for a clean heart will he then be able "to teach transgressors [God's] ways" (v. 15). Here we see that the individual who is defiled by sin can neither experience God's gracious presence nor serve him. God must cleanse the person from his or her sin and create in him or her a clean heart, which is equated with being renewed with a right spirit. Moreover, the purified individual is sustained by God's presence in order to remain faithful to him. Only then can he or she serve God. We see in Ps 50 (LXX) that the language of inward cleansing and purification is the language of divine enablement and transformation.

We find a similar movement in Isa 6:1-8 (LXX). Isaiah is confronted with the vision of Yahweh seated upon his throne in the heavenly temple. Yahweh is surrounded by seraphim who declare Yahweh's holiness before Isaiah (cf. vv. 1-4). Isaiah, then, curses himself because he is a man of unclean (ἀκάθαρτα) lips in the presence of a holy God (v. 5).[48] In his defiled state, he cannot serve Yahweh or enjoy his presence. The seraph, however, takes a burning ember from the altar which cleanses (περικαθαριεῖ) Isaiah from his sins (v. 7). Only then is Isaiah able to serve Yahweh and deliver Yahweh's message to Israel (cf. v. 8). Again, we have the movement from defilement from sin, to an inward cleansing, to the ability to remain in God's presence and serve him. This spiritual inward purification transforms the defiled human condition so that those called by God may enjoy him and faithfully serve him.

---

47. Marvin E. Tate, *Psalms 51–100* (WBC 20; Dallas: Word Books, 1990), 23.

48. In Matt 15:11, the Matthean Jesus associates uncleanness with what comes out of a person's mouth. In verse 18, the mouth and the heart are related. The mouth gives vent to what is in the heart.

We discover analogous notions among the prophetic books of Jeremiah and Ezekiel. Jeremiah 40:8 (LXX) relates God's promise to restore Israel: "I will cleanse (καθαριῶ) them from all the guilt of their sin against me, and I will not remember their sins concerning which they sinned against me and rebelled from me." Here, we have God's non-remembrance of sins (as in the new covenant prophecy) related to the cleansing from sin. Again, Hebrews seems to share this understanding of the relationship between these two ideas. The result of God's cleansing is that Jerusalem "shall be to me a name of joy, a praise and glory before all the nations of the earth who hear of all the good that I do for them" (v. 9). Implicit in this prophecy is that once God cleanses the people they will faithfully and joyfully serve and honor him, thus becoming "a name of joy" and "a praise and glory before all nations." This cleansing delivers God's people from their apostasy and transforms them into faithful worshipers. Jeremiah 32:29 (LXX), however, relates what happens when God "will not cleanse with cleansing (καθάρσει οὐ μὴ καθαρισθῆτε)." Israel will not go unpunished but will bear the stroke of the sword that God summons against all the inhabitants of the earth who fail to honor him.

What is implicit in the prophecy of Jer 40:8 is explicit in Ezek 36:24-33. Ezekiel 36:24-33 (LXX) is another prophecy of God's restoration of Israel. Here, God will cleanse the people from all their uncleanness and idolatry (καθαρισθήσεσθε ἀπὸ πασῶν τῶν ἀκαθαρσιῶν ὑμῶν καὶ ἀπὸ πάντων τῶν εἰδώλων ὑμῶν; v. 25). The nature of this cleansing is then elaborated in the next verse. God will give a "new heart" and a "new spirit" to his people and will remove their rebellious unfaithful "heart of stone." The result of this transformation is that God "will cause [Israel] to follow [his] statutes and be careful to observe [his] judgments" (v. 27). Again, this restoration of Israel to a faithful, enduring relationship with God is summarily declared to take place on the day God cleanses the people (ἐν ἡμέρᾳ ᾗ καθαριῶ ὑμᾶς; v. 33). Elsewhere, Ezek 37:23 (LXX) states that God will save Israel from their apostasy when he cleanses them (καθαριῶ αὐτούς).[49] At that time Israel will belong to God in an enduring personal relationship because God has cleansed

---

49. The ideas in Ezek 37 and possibly 36 are perhaps more relevant to Hebrews than merely background, because Ezek 37:26 talks about an "everlasting" covenant God will make with his people upon their restoration. In Heb 13:20, the author calls the new covenant the "eternal covenant," which seems to link together Jeremiah's prophecy of a new covenant with Ezekiel's prophecy of an eternal covenant. Ezekiel 36–37 also shares with Jeremiah's prophecy of a new covenant the need for God's transformation of the human condition that enables his people's faithfulness to the renewed covenant relationship.

them from their idolatry, thus enabling their faithfulness to him. The cleansing is so complete that the land will never become defiled again. Thus the cleansing has an abiding transformative benefit. In both Jeremiah and Ezekiel, Israel's restoration from their defiled, rebellious condition is dependent upon God's cleansing them. This cleansing, moreover, is transformative and enables faithfulness to the renewed relationship with God.

In both the cultic setting and the spiritual inward application of the cultic imagery of cleansing, the scriptures of the author of Hebrews state that cleansing is the necessary transformative act that consecrates a person or object for service to God. In Ps 50 (LXX) and the prophetic books of Isaiah, Jeremiah, and Ezekiel, God's cleansing of the people takes on broader notions than the mere forgiveness of sin. While cleansing includes this, it also denotes the transformation of the human heart or spirit, which leads both to the ability to worship and serve God as well as to ongoing faithfulness to the relationship. Again, the author of Hebrews draws upon this stream of thought when he declares that the blood of Christ cleanses the worshiper's conscience so that he or she can worship/serve the living God (9:14), or that the believer has been given a sincere heart (10:22), or that his or her heart has been sprinkled from an evil conscience (10:22). Thus, through this transformative purification and ensuing present approach to God enabled by Jesus' high priestly ministry, the worshiper encounters the divine presence. In God's presence, the believer receives God's divine enabling to remain faithful even in the midst of trial and temptation (cf. 4:16). In God's presence, the believer also experiences the joyful anticipation of his or her future hope as a member of that joyful assembly that exults in God in the coming new heavenly Jerusalem (cf. 12:22-23).

Conclusion

In conclusion, precisely through the cultic understanding of divine enablement of the worshiper's life in the language of perfection, purification, and approach in Hebrews, which has its roots in the OT, we see the fulfillment of the new covenant promises often ignored by interpreters of Hebrews — that is, that God will write the law on his people's hearts and minds and that they will know him from the least to the greatest. While Hebrews is extremely earnest about the need for Christians to persevere in their Christian confession and in their solidarity with the persecuted Christian community, Hebrews represents a profound understanding of God's ongoing faithfulness and enablement of the new covenant relationship into which he has called those he has chosen. Jesus' once-and-for-all-time Melchizedekian priestly ministry transforms those God has called by cleansing their conscience so that they might come into his presence, where in the present time they receive power from God for faithfulness in the midst of trial and a foretaste of their future hope. The durability of the relationship is grounded on more than the believer's sense of gratitude for what God has previously done in order to provide the hope of salvation. The relationship is grounded on the ongoing encounter of God's gracious presence and help, an encounter enabled by Jesus' Melchizedekian high priestly ministry.

PART II

Gospels

Indicative and Imperative in Matthean Soteriology

Charles H. Talbert

Matthean soteriology is neither legalistic nor covenantal nomistic. It is grounded in grace from first to last, including one's "staying in." Jesus' being with a disciple, granting revelation to a disciple, protecting a disciple by the name, and a disciple's being with Jesus are all ways the Evangelist speaks about divine enablement between the beginning and the consummation of the Christian's career.

• •

In virtually all New Testament scholarship it is believed that, at least to some degree, the relation of the indicative (gift) and imperative (demand) in Matthew constitutes a theological problem for Christians. A spectrum of representative opinion will indicate some of the shades of judgment about this issue.

The Perceived Problem

(1) Some scholars contend that Matthew is legalistic.[1] Willi Marxsen is typical. He contrasts two types of ethics. On the one hand, if God is conceived as

---

1. B. W. Bacon, "Jesus and the Law: A Study of the First 'Book' of Matthew (Mt 3-7)," *JBL* 47 (1928): 203-31, speaks of the "neo-legalism" of Matthew. Hans Windisch, *Der Sinn der Bergpredigt* (WUNT 16; Leipzig: Hinrich, 1937), would fall also into this camp. He sees the

one who sets requirements and makes his relationship with people dependent on their fulfilling these requirements, then the practice of ethics promises realization of the relationship. It is assumed that humans are capable of meeting the admission requirements. On the other hand, if God is conceived as one who has already come to humans with love — without any precondition — then the relationship already exists and humans can act (ethics) — out of gratitude. It is assumed that humans can act rightly only if they are enabled by God's prior act. The former type, Marxsen thinks, is a Pharisaic ethic; the latter, a Christian ethic. Marxsen, moreover, believes that Matthew represents a type one ethic. Matthew's imperative, then, consists of admission requirements for entering the kingdom of heaven. He says, further, that to avoid this conclusion, one must demonstrate that Matthew undergirds the imperatives with an indicative that enables the doer to follow the imperatives. He does not believe this can be done.[2] That is, Matthew's demand/imperative constitutes God's requirement of humans if they are to attain a relationship with him. There is no prior indicative/gift/grace that bestows a relation, unconditionally, quite apart from human performance and to which human performance can respond.

Marxsen's position is problematic on two counts. On the one hand, Matthew clearly sees getting into Jesus' community as due to divine initiative. The disciples are called (4:18-22) before Jesus gives the Sermon on the Mount. Matthew 28:19-20 specifies that the nations are to be made disciples and baptized before they are taught to observe all that Jesus commanded. That the kingdom has been inaugurated in Jesus' ministry (12:28) means that repentance (4:17) is a response to a prior act of God. Matthew is clearly not legalism. A divine indicative enables one's entry into the community of Jesus' disciples. On the other hand, Marxsen represents a perspective on Pharisaic Judaism that is pre–E. P. Sanders,[3] or for that matter pre–G. F. Moore.[4] Most modern scholars would regard a Pharisaic ethic not as legalism (in which one gets into the covenant relation by works of law) but as covenantal

---

Sermon on the Mount as admissions requirements for entering the kingdom of heaven. Hans Kvalbein, "The Kingdom of God in the Ethics of Jesus," *ST* 51 (1997): 60-84, esp. 79, reflects the same stance.

2. Willi Marxsen, *New Testament Foundations for Christian Ethics* (Philadelphia: Fortress, 1993), 238.

3. E. P. Sanders, *Paul and Palestinian Judaism* (Philadelphia: Fortress, 1977); *Paul, the Law, and the Jewish People* (Philadelphia: Fortress, 1983).

4. George F. Moore, *Judaism in the First Three Centuries* (3 vols.; Cambridge, MA: Harvard University Press, 1927-1930).

nomism (in which one gets into the covenant by grace and obeys the law thereafter out of gratitude). To such scholars, Marxsen's description of a type two ethic (= his Christian one) sounds very much like the covenantal nomism modern scholars associate with Pharisaic Judaism. The issue of Matthew's ethic is better focused by certain other scholars (e.g., Eskola;[5] Laato[6]) as whether or not Matthew represents legalistic covenantal nomism (in which one gets into the covenant relation by grace and then stays in it and gets into the age-to-come by works of law). This legalistic covenantal nomism is seen in contrast to a new covenant piety in which God or Christ or the Holy Spirit enables one to be obedient in an ongoing way after one's having gotten into the relation. That is, in new covenant piety one gets into the relation by grace and stays in the covenant relation by grace and gets into the age-to-come by grace. In this view, the life of a disciple is by grace from start to finish. This grace is not a substitute for obedience to God's will but is the enablement of it. The question to be pursued must be refined beyond Marxsen's statement of it. Properly put, the issue is: Does Matthew see the imperative as admission requirements, either initially into Jesus' community or ultimately into the age-to-come, that humans must meet in order to gain either or both of these benefits? Most scholars today believe that entry into Jesus' community is by grace for the reasons cited above. The current debate is over what follows in the disciple's life. Is there an indicative that underlies and enables fulfillment of the imperative in disciples' lives after their entry into the community of Jesus?

(2) Other scholars believe Matthew reflects covenantal nomism. That is, Matthew is believed to employ an indicative/grace for the disciple to get into the relationship but is believed to have no developed notion of grace for staying in or for getting into the age-to-come. Petri Luomanen[7] and Kari Syreeni[8] are representatives of this stance. They each speak of Matthew as reflecting a defective covenantal nomism. Since Luomanen's work is more comprehensive, we focus on it. He contends that Matthew wanted to under-

---

5. Timo Eskola, "Paul, Predestination and Covenantal Nomism — Reassessing Paul and Palestinian Judaism," *JSJ* 28 (1997): 390-412; *Theodicy and Predestination in Pauline Soteriology* (WUNT 2/100; Tübingen: Mohr-Siebeck, 1998).

6. Timo Laato, *Paul and Judaism: An Anthropological Approach* (SFSHJ 115; Atlanta: Scholars, 1995).

7. Petri Luomanen, *Entering the Kingdom of Heaven: A Study on the Structure of Matthew's View of Salvation* (WUNT 2.101; Tübingen: Mohr Siebeck, 1998).

8. Kari Syreeni, *The Making of the Sermon on the Mount* (AASFDHL 44; Helsinki: Suomalainen Tiedeakatemia, 1987).

stand Jesus' proclamation within the framework of traditional covenantal nomism and so pass it on to his Jewish contemporaries. There are differences, of course, between Matthew's content and that of non-Christian Judaism, but from a structural point of view Matthew has much in common with covenantal nomism. God's election forms the starting point. This grace enables one's getting into the people of God. It remains a presupposition, however, that is not spelled out. Jesus' atonement, which is restricted to staying in rather than to inclusion, functions very much as sacrifice did in non-Christian Jewish covenantal nomism. This is an aid to one's staying in. It is part of the synergism of staying in and getting into the age-to-come. This position is subject to the criticisms of people like Eskola and Laato who regard synergism in the post-entry period as legalistic covenantal nomism. If Matthew represents covenantal nomism, then the indicative sees to one's getting in but is not solely responsible for one's staying in or for getting into the age-to-come.

(3) Another group of scholars believe Matthew has both an indicative and an imperative but that the former does not control the latter. At least three shades of opinion must be noted. (a) Some see the imperative as explicit in Matthew but regard the indicative as only implicit. Mohrlang[9] and Meyer[10] are two representatives of this shade of opinion. Since Mohrlang's work is the more comprehensive we will focus on his views. He is concerned with the question of how the concept of grace enters into Matthew's understanding of ethics. He summarizes:

> Matthew does not exploit this assumed structure of grace, and does not build his ethics explicitly upon it (rarely is ethical behavior motivated by considerations of grace); for the most part, it remains in the background, simply taken for granted — the largely unspoken context in which the Gospel is set.[11]

Second and third summary statements add clarification. The second: "The concept of Jesus' continuing presence with the community is as little explicitly integrated with the evangelist's ethics as his view of the Spirit."[12] The

9. Roger Mohrlang, *Matthew and Paul: A Comparison of Ethical Perspectives* (SNTSMS 48; Cambridge: Cambridge University Press, 1984).

10. Ben F. Meyer, *Five Speeches That Changed the World* (Collegeville, MN: Liturgical Press, 1994), 47.

11. Mohrlang, *Matthew and Paul*, 80.

12. Mohrlang, *Matthew and Paul*, 112.

third: Matthew's Gospel with its emphasis on demand and obedience results in a Gospel "almost totally devoid of explicit reference to God's aid in the moral-ethical realm."[13] For these scholars, only the imperative is explicit; the indicative is merely implicit.

(b) Others believe both indicative and imperative are present in Matthew but that the link between them is not clearly spelled out. Ulrich Luz is an example.[14] The indicative and imperative are there. The miracle stories, for example, have a central function of announcing salvation (= the indicative) in the earthly career of Jesus. It is not the kerygma of the death and resurrection of Jesus that conveys the indicative in Matthew, however; it is rather the abiding presence of Jesus in the community. Jesus' ethics constitute the imperative.[15] Both components, indicative and imperative, stand together. Their relationship does not seem clearly defined, however. It is not clear how demand and gift belong together. This is a weakness in Matthew's theology.[16]

(c) David Seeley argues that Matthew contains multiple perspectives that cannot be blended into a smooth unity.[17] On the one hand, there is the claim that Jesus' atoning death provides salvation. Jesus is the one who brings salvation. On the other hand, there is a focus on Jesus as the spokesman who describes a way of life to be followed. Salvation in this perspective does not involve Jesus. It takes place between a person and God the Father. Whether it occurs or not depends on the person's own initiative. There is no need for Jesus' atoning death. Jesus is, however, the end-time judge who decides on the basis of a person's deeds in this life. There is nothing that would lead one to see the first perspective as the underlying structure embracing all else. So in Matthew, the emphasis on the law is very much at odds with the parts of Matthew that focus on Jesus as redeemer. Matthew never consolidates these two portraits of Jesus presented by the building blocks he used. "We can see Matthew wrestling with his traditions, and we can see them wrestling back. In this case, they seem to have won the match."[18] Matthew never quite brings the two, the indicative and the im-

---

13. Mohrlang, *Matthew and Paul,* 114.

14. Ulrich Luz, "The Disciples in the Gospel according to Matthew," in *The Interpretation of Matthew* (2d ed.; ed. Graham Stanton; Edinburgh: T. & T. Clark, 1995), 115-48.

15. Luz, "The Disciples in the Gospel according to Matthew," 129-30.

16. Luz, "The Disciples in the Gospel according to Matthew," 132-33.

17. David Seeley, "Deconstructing Matthew," in *Deconstructing the New Testament* (BibIntSer 5; Leiden: Brill, 1994), 21-52.

18. Seeley, "Deconstructing Matthew," 52.

perative, together. "They are . . . there, like an unharmonious choir demanding to be heard."[19]

(4) Yet another group of scholars see indicative and imperative as present in Matthew and attempt to explain how the indicative has priority. Hubert Frankemölle[20] and David Kupp[21] are representative of this stance. Both affirm that the concept of Jesus' presence with the disciples, rooted in the Old Testament view of God's compassionate and caring presence among his people, is Matthew's leading idea. Out of the God-with-us theme Matthew's entire plot is constituted. The expressions "with us/you" and "in your midst" are synonyms in both OT and in Matthew.[22] Over one hundred occurrences of this formula are found in the OT, mostly in the historical books and mostly with individuals, though sometimes with the whole people. The formula mostly drops out of use in post-biblical Judaism. The formula signals empowerment of God's people. This formula applied to Jesus (1:23; 18:20; 28:19-20) is a part of Matthew's Christology that makes possible his soteriology.[23] This is a significant advance toward understanding the relation of indicative and imperative in Matthew. It enables one to see how God is present in Jesus; how Jesus is present with the disciples or in their midst; how this presence enables both church discipline (18:20) and mission (28:20). On at least these two fronts the indicative is clearly prior to the imperative and God's grace explicitly enables his people's obedient response in the period subsequent to their entry into Jesus' community. In the form in which it is presented, however, the proposed quilt is too small to cover the whole Matthean bed. Where, for example, is the indicative that covers ethical activity of the disciple? More work needs to be done in the direction these scholars are pointing.

It is usually thought, then, that Matthew emphasizes the imperative at the expense of the indicative, demand over gift. If one wanted to try to falsify this perception, what would be necessary? Two things at least! First, one would need to identify Matthew's indicative, if there is one. Second, one would need to show how this indicative, if there is one, controls Matthew's

19. Seeley, "Deconstructing Matthew," 52.

20. Hubert Frankemölle, *Yahwebund und Kirche Christi* (NTAbh 10; Münster: Verlag Aschendorff, 1974), n.p.; *Matthäus Kommentar* (vol. 2; Düsseldorf: Patmos Verlag, 1997), 552-60. His influence is seen in Santi Grasso, *Il Vangelo di Matteo* (Roma: Edizioni Dehoniane, 1995), 683.

21. David D. Kupp, *Matthew's Emmanuel: Divine Presence and God's People in the First Gospel* (SNTSMS 90; Cambridge: Cambridge University Press, 1996).

22. Frankemölle, *Yahwebund und Kirche Christi*, 32.

23. Kupp, *Matthew's Emmanuel*, 220.

imperative. In the pages that follow these two points will be pursued. We begin with the first.

Identifying Matthew's Indicative

How would one recognize Matthew's indicative, if there is one? It seems obvious that Matthew does not operate in the Pauline conceptual world (e.g., divine indwelling). Could it be that there are other conceptual worlds besides those used by Paul for speaking about divine enablement of human activity? If so, then the failure to recognize Matthew's indicative may be due to the reader's failure to recognize the First Evangelist's conceptual repertoire. It is my contention that Matthew has a strong indicative if one knows where to look. In attempting to clarify Matthew's conceptual world we will need to indicate both (1) the type of narrative approach he uses and (2) at least some of the techniques employed in such a type of approach. We begin with the former: the type of narrative approach used.

Matthew begins and ends his Gospel with narratives that attest repeated divine inbreaks into human affairs. Here God very much has the initiative and humans respond. For example, the birth narratives begin with a miraculous conception of Jesus (1:18) about which Joseph is reassured by an angel of the Lord (1:20-21). The wise men from the East are directed to Jesus by a miraculous star (2:2) and are sent on their way by a warning in a dream (2:12). Joseph is warned by an angel of the Lord to flee to Egypt (2:13). After Herod's death an angel tells Joseph it is safe to return to Israel (2:19-20). At the end of the Gospel, when Jesus dies the earth shakes, rocks are split, and many bodies of saints are raised and appear to many in Jerusalem (27:51-53). In connection with the stories of Jesus' resurrection, there is a great earthquake and an angel descends from heaven, rolls back the stone from before the tomb (28:2), frightens the soldiers nearly to death (28:4), and tells the women that Jesus has been raised (28:6). The beginning and ending of the First Gospel are full of explicit divine interventions into human affairs. The main body of the Gospel, containing the five big teaching sections (chs. 5–25), is narrated in a very different way. Especially when the text concerns disciples' obedience to the teachings of Jesus, divine intervention appears to be either absent or well hidden in the background. Hence the problem about the indicative and the imperative in the First Gospel. There are different ways to explain such shifts in the narrative.

Gerhard von Rad attempts to understand the different types of approach to God's action in history in OT narrative by setting up a dichotomy between an early view and a later one. The older idea of God's action in history involved Yahweh's immediate visible and audible intervention (e.g., Gen 28:17; similar to the beginning and ending of Matthew's Gospel). A later idea dispenses with any outwardly perceptible influence of Yahweh on history. God's guidance comes in hidden ways (e.g., the narrative of the wooing of Rebecca, the Joseph stories, Ruth, the history of the succession to David; more like Matt 5–25). A new way of picturing Yahweh's action in history led to a new technique in narrative.

> For an era which no longer experienced Yahweh's working mainly in the sacral form of miracles . . . could therefore no longer satisfactorily express its faith in a sacral narrative-form. . . . Nature and History . . . became secularized, and was as it were, overnight released from the sacral orders sheltering it. In consequence, the figures in stories now move in a completely demythologized and secular world. . . . In order to show Yahweh at work, these story-tellers have no need of wonders or the appearance of charismatic leaders — events develop apparently in complete accord with their own inherent character.[24]

Psychological processes (e.g., Saul's love-hate relation with David) dominate in a world that has gotten into the habit of looking on human affairs in such a secular way.[25]

Meir Sternberg is surely right, however, when he notes that in the Hebrew Bible the books mix overt and implicit guidance by God.[26] The difference in style is due not to a historical development in the way God's activity in the world was seen but to a "compositional alternative of treatment, in the interests of plotting and variety."[27] Take Genesis for example. In Genesis, one starts out with: God said, and it was so. This has a long-range effect on one's perceptual set.

> It develops a first impression of a world controlled by a prime mover and coherent to the exclusion of accident. Reinforced at strategic junc-

24. Gerhard von Rad, *Old Testament Theology* (vol. 1; Edinburgh: Oliver & Boyd, 1962), 52-53.

25. Von Rad, *Old Testament Theology*, 1:56.

26. Meir Sternberg, *The Poetics of Biblical Narrative* (Bloomington: Indiana University Press, 1985), 106.

27. Sternberg, *The Poetics of Biblical Narrative*, 106.

tures by later paradigms and variants, it also enables the narrative to dispense with the continual enactment of divine intervention that would hamper suspense and overschematize the whole plot.[28]

This way of dealing with the divine activity (indicative) he calls "omnipotence behind the scenes." It is seen at work, for example, in the stories about Joseph and about David's accession to the throne. In the NT, other scholars have seen the same technique at work in the activities of Paul in Acts 23–28, for example.[29] I would suggest, then, that what is to be looked for are techniques that are appropriate to a narrative style that often deals in "omnipotence behind the scenes." It is this type of narrative that one encounters in Matt 5–25, insofar as disciples are concerned. It is, therefore, for techniques that allow the evangelist to speak in terms of "omnipotence behind the scenes" that one is to search.

There are at least four techniques, about which I know, that fit such a method of narration and that are found in Matthew. They may be summarized as: (1) I am with you/in your midst; (2) invoking the divine name; (3) it has been revealed to you/you have been given to know; and (4) being with Jesus. Each of these devices will need to be examined in order.

I

Let us begin with the formula "with you" or "in your midst," a technique of speaking about divine enablement that has already been the subject of some discussion in NT circles. The definitive work on the formula itself was done by W. C. van Unnik in 1959.[30] He examined the more than one hundred passages

28. Sternberg, *The Poetics of Biblical Narrative*, 105.

29. On Acts, see Robert Tannehill, *The Narrative Unity of Luke-Acts*, vol. 2: *The Acts of the Apostles* (Minneapolis: Fortress, 1990), 294, and Charles H. Talbert and J. H. Hayes, "A Theology of Sea Storms in Luke-Acts," in *SBL Seminar Papers, 1995* (Atlanta: Scholars, 1995), 333. Behind 1 Sam 17–2 Sam 5 there is the same "omnipotence behind the scenes" (cf. 1 Sam 18:12, 14 — the Lord was "with David"; 2 Sam 5:10 — David became great because the Lord was "with him").

30. W. C. van Unnik, "*Dominus Vobiscum:* The Background of a Liturgical Formula," in *New Testament Essays: Studies in Memory of T. W. Manson* (ed. A. J. B. Higgins; Manchester: Manchester University Press, 1959), 270-305. Cf. also Manfred Görg, "Ich bin mit Dir: Gewicht und Anspruch einer Redeform im Alten Testament," *TGl* 70 (1980): 214-40, who wants to classify the phrase's use in three categories: (1) God's promises to someone; (2) a statement about someone; (3) a blessing on someone.

using this formula in the LXX and grouped them in about six categories.[31] He noted that the formula is found rarely in Psalms and prophets but frequently in the historical books (in narrative!). It is used mostly with individuals but sometimes with the nation. It involves the empowering or enablement of someone or some group involved in a divine task. Certain early Christian writers also used the formula (e.g., Luke 1:28; Acts 7:9-10; 10:38; 18:9-10; John 3:2; 8:29; 14:16-17; 16:32; Rom 15:33; 2 Cor 13:11; Phil 4:9; 2 Thess 3:16; 1 Cor 14:25; 2 Tim 4:22; Matt 1:23; 28:20; 18:20). Josephus and Philo, however, do not retain the formula. Later Jewish exegetical material, moreover, does not use the phrase as the OT did. One of the most interesting observations made in this essay by van Unnik is about the connection between this formula and the Spirit. The relation between God's "being with" someone and the Spirit's involvement is too frequent to be accidental.[32] Consider these examples: Joseph (Gen 39:23 — God was with Joseph; 41:38 — God's Spirit was in Joseph); Moses (Exod 3:12 — God will be with Moses; Num 11:17 — the Spirit is upon Moses); Joshua (Josh 3:7 — God will be with Joshua; Deut 34:9 — Joshua was full of the Spirit); Gideon (Judg 6:12 — God is with Gideon; Judg 6:34 — the Spirit of the Lord took possession of Gideon); Saul (1 Sam 10:7 — God is with you; 1 Sam 10:6 — the Spirit came upon you); David (1 Sam 18:12, 14 — the Lord was with David; 1 Sam 16:13 — the Spirit came upon David); Israel (Hag 2:4 — I am with you; Hag 2:5 — my Spirit abides among you); Jesus (Acts 10:38 — God was with him; God anointed him with the Spirit); Mary (Luke 1:28 — the Lord is with you; 1:35 — the Holy Spirit will come upon you); Jesus' disciples (John 14:16 — to be with you; 14:17 — Spirit dwell with you and in you); church at Corinth (1 Cor 14:24-25 — one convicted declares God is among them because of prophecy, which is a manifestation of the Spirit). Van Unnik concludes that the expression "with you" refers to the dynamic activity of God's Spirit enabling people to do God's work by protecting, assisting, and blessing them.[33] Given this background, one would have to conclude that when Matthew uses the formula "with you" or "in your midst" he is speaking of God's prior enabling activity (= the indicative), activity that empowers those to whom it applies to do the tasks set before them. It also may explain why Matthew's discussion of the Spirit is so underdeveloped. This formula (with you/in your midst) was an alternative, but less explicit, way of speaking of God's activity among his people.

---

31. For a full list of references, see Van Unnik, *"Dominus Vobiscum,"* 300-301n.37.

32. Van Unnik, *"Dominus Vobiscum,"* 286.

33. Van Unnik, *"Dominus Vobiscum,"* 293.

In Matthew, scholars have frequently noted the use of the phrase "with you" or "in your midst" in three texts: 1:23; 18:20; and 28:20. The first (1:23) says that the one to be born will be called Emmanuel (which means, God with us). This is Matthew's controlling image when speaking of the divine presence in Jesus. The ripple effect of this statement is seen throughout the Gospel: for example, 3:17 (the voice from heaven at the baptism); 8:23-27 (what sort of man is this?); 12:6 (something greater than the temple is here); 12:18 (I will put my Spirit upon him); 14:32-33 (those in the boat worshiped him); 9:8 and 15:29-31 (after Jesus' acts, God is glorified); 17:5 (the voice from heaven at the transfiguration); 21:9 and 23:39 (the one who comes in the name of the Lord); 28:9, 17 (worshiped him). The auditor is never allowed to forget that when Jesus is active God is present. What Jesus does and says, God is doing and saying through him. In Matthew, Jesus mediates the divine presence; he is God with us.

There are more "with us" phrases in Matthew than the remaining two (18:20 and 28:20). They may be grouped in terms of where they fit on a timeline in salvation history. Regarding Jesus' earthly life, consider the following: 9:15 (can the wedding guests fast while the bridegroom is with them?); 17:17 (how long am I to be with you?[34]); 26:11 (you do not always have me [with you]); 26:18 (keep the Passover with my disciples); 26:20 (he sat at table with the twelve disciples); 26:36 (Jesus went with them to Gethsemane).[35] For the period between Jesus' resurrection and parousia there are the oft-noticed duo: 18:20 (where two or three are gathered in my name, there am I in the midst of them); 28:20 (I am with you always, to the close of the age). For the period of the age-to-come there is 26:29 (I shall not drink again until that day when I drink it new with you in my Father's kingdom). In Matthew's schema, when Jesus is with the disciples, God is present with them.[36] Moreover, in most cases the presence is obviously an enabling one.[37]

---

34. Whereas Mark 9:19 has πρός, Matt 17:17 has μετά to correspond with the motif elsewhere.

35. M. E. Boring, "Matthew" (NIB 8; Nashville: Abingdon, 1995), 356, notes: Matthew understands his narrative to "work at two levels, both portraying the pre-Easter story and being transparent to the post-Easter situation. Thus the disciples are already addressed as though they live in the time after Easter."

36. G. Braumann, "Mit euch, Matth 26:29," *TZ* 21 (1965): 161-69.

37. D. Vetter, *Yahwes Mit-Sein — ein Ausdruck des Segens* (AT 1/45; Stuttgart: Calwer Verlag, 1971), starts with J. Pedersen's contention that the "expression that Yahweh . . . is with one is only another term for the blessing" (*Israel* 1-2 [London: Cumberlege, 1946-1947], 194) and attempts to validate the claim, successfully, I think. If so, then for Yahweh to bless one is

This is one way that the First Evangelist speaks about divine enablement of the disciples. It is subtle and can be missed very easily if one has not first been sensitized by the evidence from the OT background.

II

A second technique that is employed by the First Evangelist to speak about divine enablement of disciples (= the indicative) is associated with "the name." (1) In the scriptures of Israel the name was considered part of the personality.[38] So the name is used interchangeably with the person (Ps 7:17; 9:10; 18:49; 68[67]:4; 74[73]:18; 86[85]:12; 92[91]:1; Isa 25:1; 26:8; 30:27-28; 56:6; Mal 3:16; also in the NT — Acts 1:15; 5:41; 18:15; Rev 3:4; 11:13; 3 John 7; Matt 6:9).[39] (2) The OT used the name as a way of speaking about the presence of God involved with humans. For example, when one swears (1 Sam 20:42; Lev 19:12), curses (2 Kgs 2:24), or blesses (2 Sam 6:18), invoking the name of Yahweh, the name thus pronounced evokes Yahweh's presence, attention, and active intervention.[40] Or again, the name of Yahweh is said to assist humans (Ps 54[53]:1 — in response to prayer, where name is used in synonymous parallelism with might/power [cf. Jer 10:6]; Ps 89[88]:24 — where God's steadfast love's being with him is used in synonymous parallelism with "in my name shall his horn be exalted"; Ps 20[19]:1 — in response to prayer, where name is used together with God's protection [cf. Prov 18:10]). The same motif of divine assistance is found in the NT related to the name of Jesus (1 Cor 6:11 — where the name of the Lord Jesus is used in parallelism with the Spirit of God, and the two are credited with the converts' being washed, sanctified, and justified; Acts 4:12 — where we are saved only through the name of Jesus; Acts 10:43 — where forgiveness comes in his name; 1 John 5:13 — where eternal life comes through his name; Mark 9:39 — where mighty works are in his name; Acts 3:6 — where the lame man is told to walk, in the name of Jesus [cf. Acts 9:34 — where the language is "Jesus Christ heals you, walk," indicating the interchangeability of name and person]; Acts 4:7 — "by what name or power do you do this?"; Rom 10:13 — where "those who call on the name of the Lord [Christ] will be saved").

---

equivalent to God's being with that one. Both refer to the divine power within a person or people that issues in success.

38. Hans Bietenhard, *"onoma," TDNT* 5:243.
39. Bietenhard, *"onoma," TDNT* 5:257.
40. Bietenhard, *"onoma," TDNT* 5:255.

(3) In the NT one meets the phrase "to be baptized in the name of." Three different prepositions are used in such phrases for "in": for example, Acts 2:38 (ἐπί); Acts 10:48 (ἐν); and Acts 8:16; 19:5; 1 Cor 1:13, 15; Matt 28:19 (εἰς). Although W. Heitmüller thought there was a difference between ἐν and ἐπί on the one hand and εἰς on the other,[41] the three prepositions do not seem to offer significantly different meanings (cf., e.g., Justin, *1 Apol.* 61, who uses ἐπὶ ὀνόματος with his trinitarian formula whereas Matthew uses εἰς).[42] Generally speaking, "in the name of" conveys the meaning "under the authority of," or "with the invocation of." Given its background/roots, however, it can also carry the connotations of "in the presence of" ("name" and "presence" are concepts that are interchangeable — cf. Ps 89:24; 1 Cor 6:11) and/or "in the power of" ("name" and "power" are parallel concepts — cf. Ps 54:1; Acts 4:7).[43] Since name and person are interchangeable (cf. Acts 3:6 with 9:34), moreover, there does not seem to be any significant difference between being baptized in/into the name of Christ and being baptized into Christ.

Matthew 28:19-20 indicates that evangelization involves new disciples' being baptized into the name of the Father, the Son, and the Holy Spirit. At least three inferences may be drawn. In the first place, certainly implied is that such a one is in a relation of belonging to/being under the authority of the Father, Son, and Holy Spirit. This bonding is reflected in Matt 10:40 (whoever receives you receives me, and whoever receives me receives him who sent me); in Matt 18:5 (whoever receives one such child in my name receives me); and in Matt 25:31-46 (as you did it to the least of these [followers of Christ],[44] you did it to me). This cannot be all that is implied, however. In the second place, Matt 18:20 shows that the invocation of Jesus' name evokes his presence among the disciples. By extension, whenever the disciples pray the "Our Father" (6:9-13), the invocation of the name of the Father would evoke his presence in and provision for the disciples' lives (including leading not into temptation and delivering from the Evil One). To invoke the name of God unleashes the power that makes intelligible the words, "with God

41. W. Heitmüller, *Im Namen Jesu* (FRLANT 2; Göttingen: Vandenhoeck & Ruprecht, 1903). Heitmüller thought the εἰς derived from banking and so meant "become the property of."

42. Lars Hartman, *"Into the Name of the Lord Jesus": Baptism in the Early Church* (Edinburgh: T. & T. Clark, 1997), 38-45; Rudolf Schnackenburg, *Baptism in the Thought of St. Paul* (Oxford: Basil Blackwell, 1964), 19-23.

43. Bietenhard, *"onoma," TDNT* 5:271.

44. Sherman W. Gray, *The Least of These My Brothers, Matthew 25:31-46: A History of Interpretation* (SBLDS 114; Atlanta: Scholars, 1989).

nothing is impossible" (19:26). In the third place, there is at least the possibility and perhaps the probability that the First Evangelist understood Christian baptism in terms of Matt 3:11 (he will baptize you with the Holy Spirit).[45] If so, then the Spirit's presence is presumed by Matthew to be a part of the disciples' lives to enable them.[46] To be baptized into the Triune Name, therefore, is to enter into a bonded relationship that will provide one with the divine resources to enable one's following the guidance of what comes next (= all that I have commanded you). This is a second technique used by the First Evangelist to indicate the indicative in disciples' lives after their entry into the community of Jesus.

III

A third technique employed by the First Evangelist to indicate the divine indicative/gift/grace in the lives of Jesus' disciples is associated with the concept of revelation by the Father and/or Jesus to them. In Matt 11:25-27, in a context of chapters 11–13 where the focus is on revelation and concealment,[47] the Matthean Jesus offers thanks to his Father that he has revealed "these things" to babes rather than to the wise. In light of the previous paragraph (11:20-24), "these things" must refer to the kingdom's breaking in through the ministry of Jesus (so eschatological secrets having to do with the divine plan of salvation for the world). The larger context would indicate, moreover, that the "babes" are Jesus' disciples. Jesus then states that "no one knows the Son except the Father, and no one knows the Father except the Son and anyone to whom the Son chooses to reveal him." The second part of this statement portrays Jesus as the one with a knowledge of heavenly mysteries and as the one who can reveal them to others. Two backgrounds have been proposed as an aid to understanding this text. The first is wisdom. Just as God knows wisdom (Job 28:12-27; Sir 1:6-9; Bar 3:32), so also the Father

45. Hartman, *"Into the Name of the Lord Jesus,"* 153, thinks this is how Matthew likely understood Christian baptism. So also J. Andrew Overman, *Church and Community in Crisis: The Gospel according to Matthew* (Valley Forge, PA: Trinity Press International, 1996), 409, says that in baptism in the name of the Spirit, John's prophecy of 3:11 is fulfilled.

46. Blaine Charette, *Restoring Presence: The Spirit in Matthew's Gospel* (JPTSS 18; Sheffield: Sheffield Academic, 2000), 137.

47. Celia Deutsch, *Hidden Wisdom and the Easy Yoke: Wisdom, Torah and Discipleship in Matthew 11:25-30* (JSNTSS 18; Sheffield: JSOT, 1987), 42; Frances Taylor Gench, *Wisdom in the Christology of Matthew* (Lanham, MD: University Press of America, 1997), 95.

knows the Son. Just as wisdom knows God (Wis 8:4; 9:1-18), so the Son knows the Father. Just as wisdom makes known the divine mysteries (Wis 9:1-18; 10:10), so also Jesus reveals God's hidden truth. Just as wisdom calls people to take up her yoke and find rest (Sir 51:23-30), so Jesus extends a similar invitation.[48] The second is the Teacher of Righteousness. The similarity with the Teacher of Righteousness at Qumran has been noted at least since the 1950s.[49] God has disclosed the mysteries to the Teacher of Righteousness (1QpHab VII, 4-5; 1QH IV, 27-28) and he has disclosed them to many others (1QH IV, 27-28 [= Col XII]; 1QH II, 13-18 [= Col X]). In both cases the revelation has to do with the proper understanding of the eschatological moment. This, the Matthean Jesus' disciples have been given by the Son. Both sets of comparative materials enable one to read the Matthean text in light of ancient Jewish thought. The two sides of the revelatory focus are treated in Matthew in other texts.

This theme of revelation comes up again in chapter 13. Here the focus is on the revelatory function of the Son. In 13:10-17 Jesus tells his disciples: "To you it has been given to know the secrets of the kingdom of heaven (cf. 13:16-17). . . . For to him who has will more be given, and he will have abundance." The latter part of the statement surely points to a post-Easter setting when the revelation will continue. In 13:16-17 Jesus says to them: "Blessed are your eyes, for they see, and your ears, for they hear. Truly, I tell you, many prophets and righteous men longed to see what you see, and did not see it, and to hear what you hear, and did not hear it."[50] The disciples are recipients of revelation. In 13:23 the good soil is interpreted to mean the one "who hears the word and understands it . . . [and] bears fruit." (Note: Mark 4:20 has "hear the word and accept it"; Luke 8:15 has "holds it fast in an honest and good heart"; only Matt 13:23 has "understands it.") So the understanding is given by Jesus to the disciples and it produces fruit. That is, the revelation is empowering, enabling in their daily lives. The emphasis on "understanding" continues to the end of the section on parables. In 13:51, only in Matthew does Jesus ask the disciples: "Have you understood all this?" They answer: "Yes." The Son has made his revelation to them and it has been effective/enabling/empowering. They will bear fruit as good soil.

48. Boring, "Matthew," 274.

49. E.g., W. D. Davies, "Knowledge in the DSS and Matthew 11:25-30," *HTR* 46 (1953): 113-39.

50. If "blessing" is the equivalent to "being with" in biblical thought, as Pedersen and Vedder contend (see n. 37), then the language of blessing associated with the revelation to the disciples in 13:11-12, 16-17 speaks of their divine empowering. Cf. also 16:17.

That the Father knows the Son was the first part of the sentence in 11:27. The Son's revelation to the disciples has been confirmed in chapter 13. Now several passages indicate the Father's role in the revelatory process as well. (a) In 15:13 Jesus says: "Every plant that my heavenly Father has not planted will be uprooted. Let them alone; they are blind guides." The reference is to scribes and Pharisees. The language contrasts these "wise ones" with the disciples/babes. There are echoes of the parable of the weeds among the wheat (13:24-30). The blind ones are planted not by the Father but the enemy. They are to be left alone until the judgment. They have not been given the revelation. (b) In 16:16-17 Peter makes his confession: "You are the Christ, the Son of the living God." Jesus responds: "Blessed are you [remember 13:16]. . . . Flesh and blood has not revealed this to you, but my Father who is in heaven." The Father knows the Son and has revealed his identity to Peter. (c) In 17:5-6, on the mount of transfiguration, a voice comes from heaven to the three disciples: "This is my beloved Son, with whom I am well pleased; listen to him." This echoes an earlier declaration (to John the Baptist at least) at the baptism in 3:17: "This is my beloved Son, with whom I am well pleased." One more passage attests the Father's role in revelation. (d) In 7:1-12 we find a thought unit that makes two main points. First, verses 1-5 contend that one should not judge others until having first judged oneself. Second, verses 6-12 affirm that it is necessary to discern between good and bad (v. 6), that this may be done with wisdom gained from God through prayer (vv. 7-11), and that any judgments made as a result should be in line with the golden rule (v. 12).[51] In this text, moral discernment is the result of prayer to the disciples' Father in heaven. One should remember that such insight is considered empowering by Matthew, as is the invocation of the Father's name! In sum: a third technique used by the First Evangelist to indicate his involvement of omnipotence behind the scenes in the enablement of Jesus' disciples is associated with the concept of revelation — by Jesus and by the Father. There is yet another!

IV

The fourth technique employed by Matthew to point to the divine indicative in the lives of Jesus' followers is linked to the notion of their being "with Jesus." Writings of this period speak of four types of teachers with adult fol-

---

51. W. D. Davies and D. C. Allison, *The Gospel According to Saint Matthew* (vol. 1; ICC; Edinburgh: T. & T. Clark, 1988), 626-27, 667-91.

lowers: (1) philosophers (e.g., Socrates); (2) sages (e.g., Sirach); (3) interpreters of Jewish law (e.g., scribes, Pharisees, Essenes); (4) prophets or seers (e.g., John the Baptist; the Egyptian Jew mentioned by Josephus, *J.W.* 2.261-73; *Ant* 20.169-72; Acts 21:38).[52] When auditors of Matthew's Gospel heard the story of Jesus and his followers, into which of these categories would they have unconsciously slotted Jesus and the disciples?

The overall picture of Jesus and his disciples in Matthew can be sketched with about four strokes of a brush. (a) In the First Gospel Jesus gathers followers, either through a summons (4:18-22; 9:9) or attraction (4:23-25). (b) They follow him (4:20, 22; 4:25; 9:9). (c) They are with him (the Twelve — 17:1, Jesus took with him Peter and James and John; 26:51, one of those with Jesus; 26:69, you were with Jesus; 26:71, this man was with Jesus; the crowds — 15:32, they have been with Jesus three days). (d) They derive benefit from his company (crowds — 4:25, healings; 8:1-4, healing; 9:10, tax collectors and sinners accepted; 14:13-20, feeding; 19:2, healing; the Twelve — 8:23, safety in a storm; 19:27-29, eschatological benefits promised; 17:1-8, vision of Jesus and message from heaven).

For a Mediterranean auditor of this Gospel, the closest analogy to Jesus and his disciples would have been a philosopher and his disciples. The four strokes with which the Gospel paints Jesus and his followers would have seemed familiar from depictions of philosophers in antiquity.[53] (a) Philosophers gathered disciples either by summons (e.g., Aristophanes, *The Clouds,* has Socrates tell Strepsiades to "follow me"; Diogenes Laertius, *Lives of Eminent Philosophers* 2.48, tells of Socrates meeting Xenophon and saying "follow me" and learn) or by attraction (Philostratus, *Life of Apollonius* 1.19, says Damis was drawn to Apollonius). (b) A philosopher's disciples followed him (e.g., Philostratus, *Vit. Apoll.* 1.19, has Damis say to Apollonius: "Let us depart . . . you following God, and I you"; 4.25 has Demetrius of Corinth follow Apollonius as a disciple; Josephus, influenced by the philosophical schools, depicts the Elijah-Elisha relation as that of philosopher-teacher and disciple. In *Ant.* 8.354, Elisha follows Elijah as his disciple). (c) The disciples are with him (e.g., Philostratus, *Vit. Apoll.* 1.19, has Damis stay with the philosopher and commit to memory whatever he learned; Josephus, *Ant.* 8.354, says that Elisha was Elijah's disciple and attendant as long as Elijah was alive). (d) The

---

52. Pheme Perkins, *Jesus as Teacher,* Understanding Jesus Today (Cambridge: Cambridge University Press, 1990), 1-22.

53. Vernon K. Robbins, *Jesus the Teacher: A Socio-Rhetorical Interpretation of Mark* (Philadelphia: Fortress, 1984), 89-105, offers further data.

disciples receive benefit from being in the company of the philosopher. Several examples suffice. Xenophon, *Mem.* 4.1.1, says of Socrates:

> Socrates was so useful in all circumstances and in all ways, that any observer gifted with ordinary perception can see that nothing was more useful than the companionship (συνεῖναι) of Socrates, and time spent with him (μετ' ἐκείνου) in any place and in any circumstances. (Marchant, LCL)

In *Mem.* 1.2.24-28, Xenophon says: "So long as they were with (συνήστην) Socrates, they found him an ally who gave them strength (ἐδυνάσθην) to conquer their evil passions" (Marchant, LCL). Seneca, *Ep.* 6.5-6, says in the same vein:

> Cleanthes could not have been the express image of Zeno, if he had merely heard his lectures; he also shared his life, saw into his hidden purposes, and watched him to see whether he lived according to his own rules. Plato, Aristotle, and the whole throng of sages who were destined to go each his different way, derived more benefit from the character than from the words of Socrates. It was not the classroom of Epicurus, but living together under the same roof, that made great men of Metrodorus, Hermarchus, and Polyaenus. (Gummere, LCL)

In his *Ep.* 94.40-42, Seneca says association with good men is an aid to virtue. "We are indeed uplifted by meeting wise men; and one can be helped by a great man even when he is silent" (Gummere, LCL). In the Cynic epistles, Crates says: "It is not the country that makes good men, nor the city bad ones, but rather time spent with good men and bad. Consequently, if you want your sons to become good men and not bad, send them . . . to a philosopher's school" (Crates, *Epistle 12*, 1-5 [Worley]). It was the association with the teacher that gave the disciples their benefits and made them better people.

These statements about the benefits disciples received from "being with" a philosopher do not refer to the disciples' imitation of their teacher but rather to their being enabled by their association with him. This is a philosophic variation on the general Mediterranean belief that one's being in the presence of a deity causes transformation of the self.[54] Pythagoras, for example, declared

---

54. See J. A. Fitzmyer, *Paul and His Theology* (2d ed.; Englewood Cliffs, NJ: Prentice Hall, 1989), 69-70, and the bibliography listed there.

that "our souls experience a change when we enter a temple and behold the images of the gods face to face" (Seneca, *Ep.* 94.42 [Gummere, LCL]). This conviction was widespread in antiquity (e.g., *Corp. herm.* 10:6; 13:3; Philo, *Vita* 1.158-59; 2.69; *Legat.* 1.5; *Contempl.* 2.11, 13, 18; 4.34; *Congr.* 56; *Praem.* 114; 2 Cor 3:18; 1 John 3:6; *Diogn.* 2:5). In all such cases it is a matter of human transformation by vision. In the case of the philosopher, the vision is not of a god but of a god-like man. The effects are the same: human transformation.

The benefits, it was believed, were not limited to being with the philosopher in person. (a) Recollection had its impact. Xenophon, *Mem.* 4.1.1, speaks about the recollection of Socrates by his disciples when they were separated as an aid to virtue. "The constant recollection of him in absence brought no small good to his constant companions and followers" (Marchant, LCL). (b) Books and the use of the imagination also played a part. Seneca, *Ep.* 52.7 and 11.8-10, advocates looking to the ancients for models with whom to associate. In *Ep.* 25.6, he says that if one cannot be in a philosopher's presence, one should come to know him through books, acting as if he were constantly at one's side. *Epistles* 25.5, 11.10, and 11.8 advocate using the imagination to picture one's teacher as ever before him and himself as ever in the teacher's presence. The presence of the disciples with their master through books and imagination was regarded, however, as second best. Seneca, *Ep.* 6.5, writes: "The living voice and the intimacy of a common life will help you more than the written word" (Gummere, LCL). The point of all this is that disciples' being with their teacher was an aid to personal transformation. Being with him conveyed benefits in their moral progress. Being with him enabled them to do better and to be better people. Plutarch captured part of why that is so. In "Progress," 84d, he says that one's being in the presence of a good and perfect man has the effect: "great is his craving all but to merge his own identity in that of the good man" (Babbitt, LCL).

Matthew used the idea of disciples being with their teacher to convey part of his indicative. During Jesus' earthly career his disciples were with him. They heard him teach and saw him act. They saw the correspondence between his life and teaching. They could ask him questions and hear his answers. This common life would have been assumed by ancient auditors to have provided enablement for the disciples' progress in their formation by Jesus. For example, in the Sermon on the Mount Jesus says to his disciples that they are salt and light (5:13-14) and are sound trees that bear good fruit (7:17-18). That is, Jesus assumes some transformation of the disciples' characters has taken place. From the Gospel's plot the only thing that has occurred so far that could explain their transformation is the fact that, having been called, they followed Jesus (4:20, 22). That is, they were with him and this association had a transforming quality to it.

If being in a philosopher's presence was regarded as transforming by the ancients in a way that was more than disciples' imitation of their master, so likewise the disciples' being with Jesus in Matthew speaks of more than their imitation of him. Transformation by vision is heightened in the First Gospel by the fact that Jesus is depicted as divine. In Matthew, God is present in Jesus (1:23). The Evangelist, as a consequence, speaks of the worship of Jesus before his resurrection (e.g., 2:11; 8:2; 9:18; 14:33; 15:25; 20:20 — all unique to Matthew) as well as after (28:9, 17 — also unique to Matthew).[55] Since in 4:10 Jesus says that worship belongs to God alone and since Jesus does not reject the worship, he must be viewed as Emmanuel, the one in whom and through whom God is present (1:23). By presenting Jesus as an appropriate object of worship, the Evangelist "does, for all practical purposes, portray Jesus as divine."[56] Hence the disciples' being "with him" has not only the philosophic frame of reference but also the overtones of being changed by beholding deity. In Matthew, then, for the disciples to be "with Jesus" is for them to be transformed by their vision of God-with-us.

After Jesus' departure, they could have been with him early on, in part, through their memory and recollection of him. Later it would have been through their reading of the First Gospel. They were with Jesus as they moved through the narrative plot with him. The being with him made possible by the story powered their transformation. The power of the story to enable change is captured in an old Hasidic tale related by Gershom Scholem. It bears repeating.

> When the Baal Shem had a difficult task before him, he would go to a certain place in the woods, light a fire and meditate in prayer — and what he set out to perform was done. When a generation later the "Maggid" of Meseritz was faced with the same task he would go to the same place in the woods and say: We can no longer light the fire, but we can still speak the prayers — and what he wanted done became reality. Again a generation later Rabbi Moshe Leib of Sassov had to perform this task. And he too went into the woods and said: We can no longer light the fire, nor do we know the secret meditations belonging to the prayer, but we do know

55. Mark A. Powell, "Worship," in *God with Us: A Pastoral Theology of Matthew's Gospel* (Minneapolis: Fortress, 1995), 28-61, focuses on worship in the First Gospel.
56. Powell, "Worship," 58.

114

the place in the woods to which it all belongs — and that would be sufficient; and sufficient it was. But when another generation had passed and Rabbi Israel of Rishin was called upon to perform the task, he sat down on his golden chair in his castle and said: We cannot light the fire, we cannot speak the prayers, we do not know the place, but we can tell the story of how it was done. And the story-teller adds, the story which he had told had the same effect as the actions of the other three.[57]

Being with him and experiencing the vision of God-with-us — in person, by means of recollection, or by means of the book (the First Gospel) — was a powerful assistance in their life of obedience.[58]

How Matthew's Indicative Controls His Imperative

The four techniques discussed above function in the Gospel of Matthew to provide an indicative of divine enablement that underlies the imperative in an ongoing way. The purpose of this section of the paper will be to show how this is so.

We may begin with Matt 28:19-20. On the basis of all power being given (by God) to him (cf. Matt 11:27; Dan 7:13-14), the Matthean Jesus issues a command to his followers. As you go, make disciples, baptizing them and teaching them (28:19-20a). A promise follows: "I am with you always, to the close of the age" (v. 20b). Jesus' promise is that he will empower them so they can fulfill the mission he has just commanded them to undertake. How else could the work of Jesus be accomplished if he did not enable it? (Indeed, 13:37 says that it is the Son of Man who sows the seed!) There is a widespread consensus that 28:18-20 is the key to understanding the whole Gospel.[59] For this reason some have sought to use 28:20 as the indicative underlying the imperative throughout the First Gospel.[60] This seems impossible, however. Matthew 28:19-20 limits the presence of Jesus with the disciples to their mis-

---

57. Gershom G. Scholem, *Major Trends in Jewish Mysticism* (New York: Schocken Books, 1946), 349-50. I am grateful to Professor Joseph Sievers for pointing me to this text.

58. Another story that illustrates how being with an idealized figure over time transforms selfhood is Nathaniel Hawthorne's "The Great Stone Face" (1850), in *Hawthorne's Short Stories* (ed. Newton Arvin; New York: Alfred A. Knopf, 1975), 357-75.

59. Most recent literature references O. Michel, "Der Abschluss des Matthäus-Evangeliums," *EvT* 10 (1950-1951): 21.

60. Boring, "Matthew," 159, 504.

sion.[61] Jesus is with those evangelizing. What about those being evangelized (baptized and then taught to observe all Jesus commanded)? Matthew 28:19-20 is silent about this dimension. Matthew 19:26 — "all things are possible with God" — surely is the general answer to this question. The issue is: How does Matthew see this divine enablement worked out?

The four techniques that speak of divine activity in a behind-the-scenes way are relevant here. (1) Revelation enables both the confession of Jesus (16:17) and the bearing of abundant fruit (13:23 — which surely includes ethical living). (2) Baptism in the name of the Father, Son, and Holy Spirit opens the door to divine assistance. (a) For example, when two or three are gathered in Jesus' name, then he is present in their midst (18:20). This logion, which seems to be a Christian variant of a non-Christian Jewish saying about the Shekhinah's presence in the midst of two or three who discuss Torah (*m. 'Avot* 3:2b [3]; *'Abot R. Nat.* [B] 34),[62] is set in the context of church discipline.[63] It indicates that when Christians are involved in the task of settling church disputes among its members, the presence of Jesus is with them to empower their decisions.[64] (b) Or when disciples are brought before hostile authorities, "what you are to say will be given you in that hour; for it is not you who speak, but the Spirit of your Father speaking through you" (10:19-20). Here a combination of revelation given to disciples is combined with the activity of the Spirit in whose name one has been baptized (remember 3:11). (c) Or again, when disciples invoke the name of their heavenly Father (6:9-13; 7:7-11), this evokes his answering response (e.g., leading us not into temptation; delivering us from the Evil One; giving us discernment about the difference between good and evil). (3) Jesus' being with his disciples, moreover, affects the way they behave (9:15 — "Can the wedding guests mourn as long as the bridegroom is with them?") and comes to their aid when their faith is weak (17:17, 19-20). (4) When the disciples are with Jesus their character is shaped for the better. The Gospel assumes one's actions arise out of one's character (12:35 — "The good man out of his good treasure brings forth good, and the evil man out of his evil treasure brings forth evil";

61. Pierre Bonnard, *L'Evangile selon Saint Matthieu* (2d ed.; Commentaire du Nouveau Testament; Neuchâtel: Delachaux & Niestlé, 1970), 419, 457.

62. Joseph Sievers, "Where Two or Three . . . : The Rabbinic Concept of Shekhinah and Matthew 18:20," in *Standing Before God* (ed. Asher Finkel and L. Frizzell; New York: Ktav, 1981), 171-82.

63. J. Duncan M. Derrett, "'Where Two or Three Are Convened in My Name' . . . : A Sad Misunderstanding," *ExpTim* 91 (1979): 83-86.

64. Bonnard, *L'Evangile selon Saint Matthieu,* 275.

15:18-19 — "What comes out of the mouth proceeds from the heart, and this defiles a man. For out of the heart come evil thoughts, murder, adultery, fornication, theft, false witness, slander."). The Sermon on the Mount assumes Jesus' disciples have been transformed (5:13, 16 — "You are the salt of the earth"; "You are the light of the world"; 6:22; 7:17-18).[65] How is this possible (in the plot of the First Gospel)? All that has gone before is their call and their following Jesus, that is, being with him (4:18-22). Being with him, it is implied, has changed their character. As one moves along through the Gospel, it is not difficult to see how this took place. When Jesus teaches with a "focal instance" (e.g., 5:38-42) it requires the reorientation of the hearer's values;[66] when he teaches in certain parables that shatter one's old world (e.g., 20:1-15) and help form a new one, it necessitates a reorientation of life.[67] When Jesus' proverbs jolt their hearers out of the project of making a continuity of their lives (e.g., Matt 5:44; 16:25; 19:24), it demands a reorientation.[68] When Jesus behaves in certain provocative ways before them (e.g., 8:2-3; 9:10-13; 12:1-14) it forces a disciple to a reorientation of life. When the disciples encounter Jesus' healing as visual teaching (e.g., 15:29-30), they join the crowds in their glorifying the God of Israel (15:31).[69] Being with Jesus is a constant aid to transcending one's old ways, to being transformed by the renewing of their minds (Rom 12:2). From these observations it seems clear that no area of life is left untouched by one or more of Matthew's four techniques for alluding to divine assistance in a disciple's experience.

Another angle of vision about the relevance of the four techniques is to look at how they relate to the five major teaching sections of the First Gospel (i.e., Matthew's imperative = all that I have commanded you). (1) The link with Matt 18 is explicit. Both the name of Jesus and Jesus' presence in the disciples' midst are employed. (2) A connection with chapter 13 is seen in the revelation by Jesus to the disciples of the eschatological plan of God. (3) Matthew 10 is covered under 28:20's "with you" in your mission and by the invocation of the name of the Spirit of the Father who speaks through the disci-

65. Meyer, *Five Speeches That Changed the World*, 47.

66. Robert Tannehill, *The Sword of His Mouth* (SemeiaSt 1; Philadelphia: Fortress, 1975), 67-77.

67. William A. Beardslee, "Parable Interpretation and the World Disclosed by the Parable," *PRSt* 3 (1976): 123-39.

68. William A. Beardslee, "Uses of the Proverb in the Synoptic Gospels," *Int* 24 (1970): 61-73.

69. Samuel Byrskog, *Jesus the Only Teacher* (ConBNT 24; Stockholm: Almqvist & Wiksell, 1994), 274-75.

ples. (4) The Sermon on the Mount utilizes the invocation of the name in prayer to the Father and speaks of discernment being given to those who ask. The disciples' being with Jesus explains how their character could be salt and light. (5) In the eschatological chapters of the fifth teaching section, 26:29 comes into play. Jesus will be with his disciples even beyond the resurrection/ judgment when they share the messianic banquet together. There is no big teaching section that does not have a link to one or more of Matthew's techniques for speaking about the enabling presence of God in the disciples' lives.

Two reminders are helpful at this point. First, one should remember that these techniques are functionally virtually interchangeable in a biblical context. (a) The presence of God "with you" is virtually synonymous with "assistance by God's name" (Ps 89[88]:24 — "My faithfulness and my steadfast love shall be with him, and in my name shall his horn be exalted"; remember Matt 18:20). (b) The presence of God "with you" is an alternative way of saying "God's Spirit is in your midst" (Hag 2:4-5 — "Take courage, all you people of the land, says the Lord; work, for I am with you, says the Lord of hosts, according to the promise that I made with you when you came out of Egypt. My Spirit abides among you; fear not"; cf. Luke 1:28, 35). (c) The presence of God "with you" is closely associated with revelation given to one (1 Kgs 1:37 — the Lord be with Solomon; 4:29 — God gave Solomon wisdom and understanding; cf. John 14:16-17, 26). (d) "In the name of" and Spirit are closely linked (1 Cor 6:11 — in the name of the Lord Jesus Christ and in the Spirit you were washed, sanctified, justified). Anyone familiar with this biblical way of speaking would have been sensitive to Matthew's use of his conceptual repertoire. Second, one should remember that in the First Evangelist's scheme of things, when the narrative speaks of Jesus' presence, it is God who is with us in Emmanuel (1:23).

At every point in a disciple's life and at every stage of salvation history, therefore, Matthew speaks of the divine indicative, divine enablement for the whole of a disciple's existence from its beginning unto the messianic banquet! Granted, all of this is unobtrusive, almost invisible to the eye that is focused on the surface of the plot of the Gospel. That is as it should be, however, given that in chapters 5–25, as far as disciples are concerned, the Evangelist is telling his story in terms of omnipotence-behind-the-scenes. This is not the way Paul or the Fourth Evangelist would tell the story, but it is Matthew's way. Matthew's way, moreover, involves him in neither soteriological legalism nor legalistic covenantal nomism. Like Paul, his soteriology is by grace from start to finish. He just uses a different conceptual repertoire. Surely he cannot be faulted for that!

Salvation, Grace, and Isaiah's New Exodus in Mark

Michael W. Martin

In recent scholarship, the case has been made that Mark portrays Jesus as the divine warrior of the Isaianic New Exodus who leads Israel out of captivity and into God's eternal βασιλεία. The present study takes this perspective as a starting point for addressing the question of whether Mark is legalistic, synergistic, or characterized by the principle of *sola gratia*. The study argues that three Markan portraits of the divine warrior Jesus as, respectively, liberator, shepherd, and covenant-maker collectively point to a soteriology wherein both "getting in" the people who undertake the New Exodus and "staying in" through to that journey's end in the good-age-to-come are a matter of divine enablement.

• •

This side of E. P. Sanders's *Paul and Palestinian Judaism*,[1] inquiry into the soteriology of any early Christian writing may be pursued with a view to the book's position concerning the basis for "getting in" and "staying in" covenant relationship with God, to use Sanders's shorthand. That is, one can ask whether a book's soteriology is legalistic (one "gets in" by obedience and "stays in" by obedience), synergistic (one "gets in" by grace but "stays in" by obedience and, therefore, "gets in" the good-age-to-come by obedi-

---

1. *Paul and Palestinian Judaism: A Comparison of Patterns of Religion* (Philadelphia: Fortress, 1977).

ence),[2] or characterized by new covenant piety (one "gets in" by grace and "stays in" by grace).[3]

This essay puts this question to the Gospel of Mark, arguing that a recent development in Markan scholarship — namely, the proposal that Mark tells the story of the Isaianic New Exodus (hereafter INE), portraying Jesus as the divine warrior who leads Israel out of captivity and into the eschatological age — provides new resources for answering this new problem.[4] According to this perspective, the introductory citation (1:1-3) and the prologue of Mark (1:1-15) together introduce the Gospel story as the anticipated INE, while the threefold structure of the body of Mark ("Galilee-and-beyond," along the "Way," and "to Jerusalem") conforms to the threefold conceptual framework of Isaiah ("the nations," along "the Way," to Jerusalem).[5] Part one of each narrates Israel's deliverance, part two her exodus journey, and part three her arrival in Jerusalem. Unlike the first exodus, however, the deliverance and exodus journey of the INE leads to Israel's eschatological salvation. That is, what Israel enters into at the end of its second exodus is God's end-time βασιλεία. Jerusalem, as the destination of the journey, is in Isaiah's depiction the center of this reign and what it effects, the new heaven and the new earth. Thus we may ask, in the present study, what does Mark's portrayal of the INE say or assume about (a) "getting in" the people who undertake the INE journey, and (b) "staying in" through the duration of this journey?[6]

2. That is, legalistic covenantal nomism; cf. Timo Laato, *Paul and Judaism: An Anthropological Approach* (SFSHJ 115; Atlanta: Scholars, 1995); Timo Eskola, "Paul, Predestination, and Covenantal Nomism — Reassessing Paul and Palestinian Judaism," *JSJ* 28 (1997): 390-412; *Theodicy and Predestination in Pauline Soteriology* (WUNT 2/100; Tübingen: Mohr-Siebeck, 1998).

3. In this third religious pattern, human obedience may be required, but it is divinely enabled; thus the either/or polarity of Sanders's covenantal nomism formula ("gets in" by grace, "stays in" by obedience) is inappropriate for this model.

4. This development is represented chiefly by Joel Marcus, *The Way of the Lord: Christological Exegesis of the Old Testament* (Louisville: Westminster/John Knox, 1992); Rikki E. Watts, *Isaiah's New Exodus in Mark* (Biblical Studies Library; Grand Rapids: Baker, 1997); and Sharyn Dowd, *Reading Mark: A Literary and Theological Commentary on the Second Gospel* (Macon, GA: Smyth & Helwys, 2000).

5. So Watts, *Isaiah's New Exodus*, 123-36.

6. This question may be answered not just with regard for disciples of Jesus who followed in the INE "way" during his earthly ministry, but also for those who do so post-Easter. As Marcus observes, "the whole genius of Mark's Gospel is to overlay the story of Jesus' earthly ministry with the postresurrectional story of Mark's church, and this overlay implies that Jesus' 'way' continues in the time of the church" (*Way of the Lord*, 44; see also *The Mystery of the Kingdom* [SBLDS 90; Atlanta: Scholars, 1986], 69-71).

The study will argue, in answer to this question, that both are a matter of God's grace. That is, the study will show that in Isaiah, the divine warrior Yahweh is portrayed as a deliverer who graciously sets Israel free from captivity to her enemies, a shepherd who graciously sustains and transports Israel along the journey's way, and a covenant-maker who graciously enables everlasting covenant relationship with Israel by divinely enabling her covenant fidelity. Hence in Isaiah, the success of each of the three stages of the New Exodus is attributable to God's grace. The study will show, more importantly, that the Markan Jesus is depicted as this same divine warrior who undertakes these same three roles in the INE journey, graciously securing Israel's entrance into the good-age-to-come.

The argument of the study will proceed under three headings: "The Divine Warrior as Deliverer," "The Divine Warrior as Shepherd," and "The Divine Warrior as Covenant-Maker." In each of these sections, attention will be given first to Isaiah's depiction of the divine warrior in the role in question and, in particular, to the implications of that depiction for divine enablement and human agency in the New Exodus. Attention will then be given to the Markan depiction of the same and its correspondence to the Isaianic template.

The Divine Warrior as Liberator

The Divine Warrior as Liberator in Isaiah

The announcement of Israel's impending liberation from Babylon is centered in the exilic portions of Isaiah, chapters 40–55. The opening oracle (40:1-11) of this section declares the "gospel" that Israel's captivity has come to a conclusion. A voice cries out, "Prepare the way of the Lord. Make straight in the desert a highway for our God," thereby framing the return from Babylon to the promised land as a new exodus. In view of the present problem of captivity, the "herald of good news" exhorts exiled Jerusalem, "Do not fear," and the other exiled cities of Judah, "Here is your God!" The voice announces God as a powerful warrior coming to do battle on behalf of Israel: "See, the LORD God comes with might (LXX: μετὰ ἰσχύος), and his arm rules for him; his reward is with him, and his recompense before him." The oracle closes with the portrait of Yahweh carrying off his people to Jerusalem as booty.[7]

7. In conformity with the practice reflected in Isaiah and the Hebrew Bible generally,

For the remainder of Isaiah, the portrait of Yahweh as a warrior who (once again) liberates his people from captivity is recurring (40:25-26; 41:10; 42:10-17; 43:14-21; 45:13; 47:4; 49:24-26; 51:9-11, 12-16; 52:10; 54:5; 56:1-2; 58:8-9; 59:15b-21; 63:1-6; 63:8-14).[8] Several themes and motifs that emerge in connection with this portrait are of particular note for Mark: the depiction of Israel as "prey" to be taken back from "the mighty one," "captives" from "the tyrant" (49:24); similarly, the portrait of Israel as "plunder" (42:22), and her captors as "plunderers" (42:24); the recurring command, "Do not fear/be afraid" (40:9, 10; 41:10, 13, 14; 43:1, 5; 44:2, 8; 51:7, 13; 54:4; cf. 51:12), particularly in connection with Yahweh's command of the seas (43:1-2; 51:12-16); the portrait of Yahweh coming "with strength" (μετὰ ἰσχύος: LXX 40:10; 42:13; 63:1) and via descent through rent heavens (64:1); and the "bowing/stooping" of captors before the victorious divine warrior (46:1-2; cf. 65:12).

Because Israel's liberation from Babylon and other nations is characterized as a second exodus analogous to the first, exodus imagery plays a prominent role in the portrait of Yahweh as her liberator (43:2; 51:9-11; 52:10; 57:14; 58:8-9; 62:10; cf. 11:15-16; 63:8-14). Not surprisingly, the battle that secured Israel's release from Egypt, the miraculous victory at the Reed Sea, is treated as paradigmatic for the coming liberation of Israel. "When you pass through the waters," Yahweh declares, "I will be with you" (Isa 43:2; cf. 11:15; 43:16-17; 51:9-11). Just as the first battle, through the division/drying/subduing of the sea (Exod 14:16; 15:4-5), reflected Yahweh's much-celebrated redemptive mastery of primordial chaos (Gen 1:2, 6-9; Job 26:8-13; 38:8-11; Ps 65:6-7; 74:12-15; 89:9-10; 93:1-5; 104:2-9; Jer 5:22; Nah 1:3-4; 2 Esd 6:41-43), so shall its INE reenactment:

> Awake, awake, put on strength, O arm of the LORD!
> Awake, as in days of old, the generations of long ago!
> Was it not you who cut Rahab in pieces, who pierced the dragon?
> Was it not you who dried up the sea, the waters of the great deep;
> who made the depths of the sea a way for the redeemed to cross over?
> So the ransomed of the LORD shall return. . . .
>
> (Isa 51:9-11a; cf. 11:15-16; 44:27;
> 45:18-19; 50:2; 51:14-15)

---

this study employs the masculine pronoun for Yahweh/God with the understanding "he" transcends sexuality and gender and is imaged by male and female alike (Gen 1:27).

8. On this depiction as background for Mark, see Watts, *Isaiah's New Exodus*, 140-43.

In this connection, we may observe with Rikki Watts that Yahweh's war-faring in Isaiah is fundamentally directed not so much against Babylon and the nations as against their gods and idols.[9] It is the redemptive ordering of the "hosts" at creation (40:25-26) that anticipates the eschatological reenactment of the same (24:21-22, where Yahweh imprisons the hosts at the end of history; 34:1-5, where Yahweh's defeat of the hosts precedes his defeat of the nations), securing the INE in its fullest sense — as an exodus from the destructive reign of false gods into the redemptive reign and newly created order of Yahweh.

Accordingly, in the final chapters of Isaiah (56–66), which presume a post-exilic context, Israel remains in captivity and awaiting Yahweh's return to Zion as her redeemer, *despite* having already been freed from Babylon. The ultimate problem she faces is not so much her continuing subjugation to the nations as it is her subjugation to their false gods — now described for the first time in LXX Isaiah as "demons" (65:3, 11).[10] Only when Yahweh puts on his armor and returns to Zion as her redeemer (59:15b-20; cf. 56:1-2; 58:8-9) to rid her of her idolatry (65:1-7; cf. 57:1-13) and its attendant unrighteousness and injustice (59:15b-20; cf. 59:1-15a), will the work of liberation be complete. Then and only then will the full hope of the INE — the renewal of creation that follows in the wake of Yahweh's enthronement in Jerusalem (65:8-25; cf. 55:12-13; 66:22-23) — be realized.

Soteriological Implications

In its portrayal of the divine warrior as Israel's liberator, Isaiah frames the human problem as one of captivity: Israel, like all the nations, is in bondage to the false gods — the demons — of this world and must be set free if she is to undertake the INE to restored Jerusalem/Creation. This perspective has important implications for an understanding of the pattern of religion assumed in Isaiah.

First, it shows that post-election grace is required for Israel — both corporately and individually — to experience eschatological salvation. To

9. Watts, *Isaiah's New Exodus*, 141-42; Watts notes in support that both "the anti-idol promises . . . (40:18-20; 41:9-20; 44:9-20; 46:5-7 [8])" and "the trial speeches . . . are primarily directed against the gods who epitomize the wealth and power of oppressors (41:1-5, 21-29; 43:8-13; 44:6ff and 45:18-25)" (141).

10. Watts calls attention to this, noting the growing tendency in the intertestamental period to identify idols with demons (*Isaiah's New Exodus*, 157).

express the matter in Sanders's terms, Isaiah proclaims a coming liberation from captivity to idols/demons that is crucial not to "getting in" the people of God who undertake the INE, but rather, to "staying in."

Second, in framing Israel's problem as one of captivity to the false gods of the nations, Isaiah assumes a negative anthropology that precludes the possibility, apart from Yahweh's promised redemption, of post-election obedience and, therefore, the viability of patterns of religion — namely, legalism and covenantal nomism — that require it. Israel is and will remain, until her anticipated liberation, utterly devoid of righteousness and justice (cf. 59:1-20) — and the same is true, of course, for all the nations.

The Divine Warrior as Liberator in Mark

While much new remains to be said concerning the depiction of Jesus in Mark as the divine shepherd and covenant-maker of the INE, sufficient evidence has already been gathered demonstrating the Gospel's close identification of Jesus with the INE liberator. Among the key points:

- The programmatic citation (1:2a) and quotation (1:3) of Isa 40:3, with Exod 23:20//Mal 3:1 sandwiched in between, in the opening sentence of Mark closely identifies Jesus' "way" with the divine warrior's INE "way."[11]
- χαθὼς γέγραπται (1:2) identifies "the good news of Jesus Christ" (1:1) with the "good news" (Isa 40:9) of Yahweh's INE coming.[12]
- The exaggerated appearance in the wilderness at the beginning of the story of "all" Jerusalem and people from the "whole" Judean countryside (1:5) reflects the contemporary Jewish expectation, based on Isa 40:3 ("In the wilderness prepare the way of the LORD"), that the wilderness setting would be the INE staging ground for the people when Yahweh's apocalyptic war of liberation begins.[13]

11. See Marcus, *The Way of the Lord*, 12-47; Watts, *Isaiah's New Exodus*, 53-90; Dowd, *Reading Mark*, 3-10. For Exod 23:20//Mal 3:1 as a Markan interpolation, see Watts, *Isaiah's New Exodus*, 53-90.

12. See Robert A. Guelich, "'The Beginning of the Gospel': Mark 1:1-15," *BR* 27 (1982): 5-15; but cf. Marcus, *The Way of the Lord*, 20n.31; Watts, *Isaiah's New Exodus*, 56n.23.

13. Marcus, *The Way of the Lord*, 24, taking cues from Ulrich W. Mauser, *Christ in the Wilderness: The Wilderness Theme in the Second Gospel and Its Basis in the Biblical Tradition* (SBT 39; Naperville, IL: Allenson, 1963), 5-52, 58-61, 107, 137.

- The rent heavens at the beginning of Mark's story (1:10) recall Yahweh's coming via the same (Isa 64:1) at the outset of the INE.[14]
- The theme of "strength" associated with Jesus' coming (1:7), as well as the importance of this motif in his confrontation with Satan (3:27) and the demonic "Legion" (5:4), recalls the Isaianic motif of Yahweh's coming "with strength" (Isa 40:10; 42:13; 63:1),[15] and particularly the "strength" he displays in his mastery of idols/hosts (40:26).
- The "binding" of Satan (3:27) evokes the heavenly hosts' eschatological imprisonment as the precursor to Israel's salvation (Isa 24:21-22; cf. 34:1-6).[16]
- The "plundering" of the "property" from the "strong man" (3:27) reflects the depiction of Israel as prey/captives taken from the mighty one/tyrant (Isa 49:24),[17] and as "plunder" reclaimed from her captors (Isa 42:22).
- The theme of "destroying/perishing" (ἀπόλλυμι in its active and middle forms) ties together as a single pattern of confrontation Jesus' conflicts with demons (1:24; 9:22), religious political leaders (3:6; 11:18; cf. 12:9), and the sea/chaos (4:38). Collectively, these confrontations reflect Yahweh's anticipated "destroying" of enemies in connection with the INE (LXX 41:11; 60:12; cf. 1:25; 11:13; 13:9, 11; 14:22, 25; 15:1, 2; 23:1, 14; 29:14, 20; 30:25; 32:3).
- Jesus' healings of the blind, deaf/dumb, and lame are best understood against the background of Isaiah as the expected signs of the INE's inauguration (cf. Isa 35:4-6).[18]
- The depiction of healing and storm-stilling as conflict comparable to demon-expulsion — and of sickness and storm as adversaries comparable to demons — serves literarily to associate Jesus' healing and storm-stilling with his warfaring/liberating mission. That is, both the healing of 1:40-45 and the storm-stilling of 4:35-41 entail a rebuke (1:43; 4:39) and a command for silence (1:44 [cf. 7:36]; 4:39), as in Jesus' battles with demons (rebuking: 1:25; 3:12; silencing: 1:25, 34;

---

14. Watts, *Isaiah's New Exodus*, 102-8.

15. Watts, *Isaiah's New Exodus*, 159.

16. Ernest Best, *The Temptation and the Passion: The Markan Soteriology* (2d ed.; Cambridge: Cambridge University Press, 1990), 12-13, notes the wide attestation to "binding" as an image for rendering powerless (Tob 8:3; *1 En.* 10:4-7; 18:12-16; 21:1-6; 54:4-5; *T. Levi* 18:12; *Jub.* 48:15; Rev 20:2).

17. Watts, *Isaiah's New Exodus*, 146-56.

18. Watts, *Isaiah's New Exodus*, 169-77.

3:12).[19] Moreover, the sickness of 1:40-45 is depicted in semblance of a demon, as an "unclean" thing that "departs" the person at Jesus' command (1:42; cf. 1:26; 5:13; 7:29; 9:26).[20] Likewise, the storm of 4:35-41 is depicted in semblance of a demon, seeking the disciples' "destruction" (4:38; cf. 1:24; 9:22), becoming silent at Jesus' command (4:39; cf. 1:34), and evoking by its submission to Jesus amazement among witnesses (4:41; cf. 1:27).[21]

- The bowing down of those afflicted by demons (3:11; 5:6; 7:25) and sickness (1:40) reflects the INE expectation that Israel's demonic captors (46:1-2; cf. 65:12) will bow down to the divine warrior in defeat.

- Jesus' stilling of the storm (4:35-41) and drowning of the demonic "Legion" (5:1-13) together constitute the reenactment, per INE expectation (Isa 43:2, 16-17; 51:9-11; cf. 11:15), of the iconic moment of Israel's liberation in the first exodus, Yahweh's miraculous victory at the Reed Sea (Exod 14–15).[22]

This latter point, perhaps the most telling, deserves further attention. The reenactment occurs in two stages, the storm-stilling constituting the expected reenactment of the miraculous crossing, and the expulsion of the "Legion" constituting the reenactment of the drowning of Pharaoh's army in the sea. In both events, Jesus plays the role of the INE divine warrior, providing safe passage for his followers across the chaotic sea and defeating the demonic army of the oppressor (the δαιμόνια; cf. LXX Isa 65:3, 11), per Isaianic expectation. Several narrative details drawn from Exodus and Isaiah are enlisted in service of the portrait:[23]

The Storm-Stilling as Yahweh's Victory over the Sea/Chaos

- The setting of evening/the sea (4:35) evokes the setting of the Reed Sea crossing (Exod 14:20-23), which is itself patterned on the setting of

19. Cf. Dowd, *Reading Mark,* 54.

20. Cf. Howard Clark Kee, *Community of the New Age: Studies in Mark's Gospel* (Philadelphia: Westminster, 1977), 35; followed by Dowd, *Reading Mark,* 19.

21. Cf. Dowd, *Reading Mark,* 54.

22. Cf. J. Duncan M. Derrett, "Contributions to the Study of the Gerasene Demoniac," *JSNT* 3 (1974): 2-17; Dowd, *Reading Mark,* 51-55; Watts, *Isaiah's New Exodus,* 157-63.

23. For many of the details below, see Derrett, "Contributions to the Study," 2-17; Dowd, *Reading Mark,* 51-55; Watts, *Isaiah's New Exodus,* 157-63.

Yahweh's mastery of the chaotic, primordial sea at creation (the "darkness" over "the face of the deep"; Gen 1:2).

- The miraculous crossing via divine mastery of the sea recalls the Reed Sea crossing (Exod 14:1–15:21) and its expected INE reenactment (Isa 11:15-16; 43:2, 16-17; 51:9-11).
- Per INE expectation (11:15-16; 51:9-11; cf. 44:27; 45:18-19; 50:2; 51:14-15), Jesus' reenactment of the Reed Sea crossing (like the original event itself) evokes Yahweh's defeat of primordial chaos:
  - The windstorm's beating and swamping of the boat reflect the depiction of the threat of the primordial chaos-like storm in Ps 107:23-25.
  - Jesus' subduing of the wind and sea through his words (4:39) recalls Yahweh's defeat/delimitation of the primordial sea by the same at Creation (Gen 1:1-2, 6-9; Job 26:8-13; 38:8-11; Ps 65:6-7; 93:1-5; 104:6-9; 2 Esd 6:41-43).
  - The rebuke ("He rebuked"; 4:39a), silencing ("Peace!"; 4:39b), and stilling ("Be still!"; 4:39b) of the wind and the sea recall Yahweh's much-celebrated rebuking (Ps 104:6-9; Nah 1:4; cf. Job 26:11), silencing (Ps 65:6-7; cf. Ps 107:29), and stilling (Job 26:12; Ps 89:9-10; cf. Ps 107:29) of the same in the battle with primordial chaos at Creation.
- "Why are you afraid?" (4:40) evokes the needlessness of fear at the INE sea crossing: "Do not fear, for I have redeemed you. . . . When you pass through the waters, I will be with you" (Isa 43:1-2; also 51:12-16).
- The baffled disciples' question, "Who is this that controls wind and wave?" could only evoke, ironically, Yahweh-at-Creation/the Reed Sea in a Jewish context.

The Expulsion of the Legion as Yahweh's Victory over the Demonic Army

- The aforementioned theme of "strength" needed to subdue the demoniac, as well as his "bowing down" upon seeing Jesus, serve as initial clues that the episode belongs to larger patterns of INE conflict running across Mark.
- The presence of demons, tomb-dwelling, and pigs recalls LXX Isaiah 5:1-7[24] and the condition of idolatrous Israel as she awaits Yahweh's expected INE deliverance.

---

24. Heinrich Julius Holtzmann, *Der Synoptiker* (HKNT 1.1; Tübingen: Mohr, 1901), 160-62; John F. Craghan, "The Gerasene Demoniac," *CBQ* (1968): 522-36.

- The use of military terminology frames the unclean spirit as an enemy army and the conflict as a battle.[25]
  - The spirit's name is "Legion" (5:9), a military loan word referring to a unit of 6000 soldiers ("for we are many").
  - ἀποστείλῃ (5:10) in a military context is a technical term used for the ordering of troop movements.
  - The odd use of ἀγέλη (5:11) in connection with swine is best explained by the military theme — it can refer to a group of military trainees.
  - ἐπέτρεψεν (5:13) in a military context connotes a military command.
- The outcome of the conflict, the drowning of the "Legion" in the sea (5:13), reflects the drowning of Pharaoh's army in the Reed Sea.
- ὥρμησεν (5:13) is similarly employed by Josephus (*Ant.* 2.340) and Philo (*Mos.* 2.254) for the "rush" of the Egyptian army into the sea.[26]

Soteriological Implications

In view of the sketch above, it is clear that Jesus is portrayed in Mark as the divine liberator of the INE. This portrait, moreover, offers some initial clues that the Gospel subscribes neither to a legalistic nor covenantal nomistic soteriology, but rather, to a "new covenant piety" soteriology wherein "staying in" is a matter of grace. First, similar to the Isaianic view that Israel, like all the nations, is captive ultimately to idols/demons, Mark maintains that Israel, like all the nations, is captive to Satan and his allied demonic forces (unclean spirits, sickness, political/religious oppression, chaos). Thus, a clear act of post-election grace is needed in Markan perspective, as in Isaianic perspective, for Israel/humanity to undertake the INE journey and thereby experience eschatological salvation.

Second, in describing the fundamental problem facing Israel/humanity as one of captivity to Satan, Mark assumes, like Isaiah, a negative anthropology that precludes the possibility of freely offered obedience on the part of humans. Under such a condition, patterns of religion that require such obedience — i.e., legalism and covenantal nomism — are not viable options. It is in view of this negative assessment of the human predicament, moreover, that we can begin to make sense of Jesus' assertion to the rich man that "No one is good but God alone" (Mark 10:18).

---

25. For the terms below, see Derrett, "Contributions to the Study," 2-17.
26. Derrett, "Contributions to the Study," 2-17.

The Divine Warrior as Shepherd

The Divine Warrior as Shepherd in Isaiah

In the annunciation of the New Exodus in Isa 40:1-11, the final image of Yahweh as he prepares to embark on the highway of return is a pastoral one: having liberated the people of Israel, he feeds and gathers them as a shepherd does a flock, and then sets off on the journey, leading and carrying them on the way:

> See, the Lord God comes with might (LXX: μετὰ ἰσχύος)
> and his arm rules for him;
> his reward is with him,
> and his recompense before him.
> He will feed his flock like a shepherd;
> he will gather the lambs in his arms,
> and carry them in his bosom,
> and gently lead the mother sheep.
>
> (Isa 40:10-11)

The dual image of the divine warrior as liberator and shepherd of the INE is derived, appropriately, from the original exodus story as celebrated in the song of Moses:

> In your steadfast love you led
> the people whom you redeemed;
> you guided them by your strength (LXX: τῇ ἰσχύι σου)
> to your holy pasture.
>
> (Exod 15:13)

Moses' song becomes the basis for the subsequent remembrance of God in song as a shepherd generally (e.g., Ps 23) and as the shepherd of the exodus specifically (Ps 77:19-20; 78:51-53).

For the remainder of Isaiah, the image of Yahweh as the shepherd of the New Exodus is a recurring one.[27] Frequently he is depicted engaged in the four shepherding activities mentioned in the annunciation oracle: feeding (40:11; 49:9-10; 51:14-16), gathering (40:11; 43:5; 54:7; 56:6-8; 60:4-7; 66:18;

---

27. So Watts, *Isaiah's New Exodus*, 177-78.

cf. 11:12), carrying (40:11; 46:3-7; cf. 49:22; 60:4; 63:9), and leading (40:11; 49:10; cf. 42:7; 43:8; 48:21; 49:10; 63:13-14). These activities continue to be associated with the shepherd metaphor (49:9-13), and their depiction is often with allusion to the original exodus (Isa 43:16-20; 49:9-12; 51:9-11, 14-16; 63:9-14).[28] Accordingly, the activities occur across sea (43:16-20; 51:14-16 [cf. vv. 9-11]), through wilderness (43:16-20; 48:21; 49:10), and over mountains (49:9-11) as reenactments of the first exodus — and in explicit connection, appropriately, with the "way" (40:3-11; 42:15-16) of the INE.

The "feeding," specifically, occurs along "the way" amidst scorching wind and sun and in prevention of hunger and thirst (49:9-10). Reenacting the manna miracle, Yahweh provides "bread" (51:14-16; cf. Exod 16:1-22), and reenacting the miracles at Marah and at Meribah in Rephidim, Yahweh supplies water (Isa 48:21; 43:16-20; Exod 15:22-25; 17:1-7; Num 20:1-13). The "feeding" occurs out of Yahweh's "compassion" for Israel's hunger and thirst (49:9-11) — a theme picked up in Mark. The proof that Israel will indeed "not lack bread" is seen in Yahweh's control of the sea both in creation and the exodus (51:14-16). Thus Israel can be assured that she will not suffer hunger and death at the hands of her enemies, whether cosmic or political. The "feeding" of Israel is resumed, too, upon arrival in Jerusalem, when Yahweh hosts the people at a great end-time banquet celebrating his enthronement and everlasting covenant in Israel (25:6-10; 55:1-13).

The "gathering" of Israel like sheep begins at the outset of the INE. Yahweh gathers captive Jerusalem and then carries/leads her off along the INE (40:11). Yahweh's gathering continues, however, to the very end of the INE, when Yahweh brings captive sons and daughters of Israel from the farthest reaches of the world (43:5). The gathering even encompasses "foreigners who join themselves to the Lord," so that Yahweh's house becomes a "house of prayer for all peoples" (56:6-8). Thus the earlier promise that "these [prisoners] shall come from far away" (49:12) awaits a surprising fulfillment. Yahweh's "compassion," which motivates the gathering of the "suffering ones" (49:12-13), is extended even to Gentiles.

The "leading" (49:9-11) of Israel — also the "guiding" (49:9-11; 42:16) and "bringing" (42:16) — is along the "way" of the second exodus. Yahweh shepherds Israel across the sea (43:16-20), desert (49:9-11; LXX 48:21) and mountains (49:9-11), as in the first exodus. The theme of darkness/blindness

---

28. Cf. Bernhard W. Anderson, "Exodus Typology in Second Isaiah," in *Israel's Prophetic Heritage* (ed. Bernhard W. Anderson and Walter Harrelson; New York: Harper, 1962), 177-95.

is of particular importance in the portrayal of Yahweh's guidance. In 49:9-11, Shepherd Yahweh leads and guides the flock after summoning her from a captivity of "darkness." In 42:7, he is pictured opening the "eyes of the blind" and bringing out "those who dwell in darkness." In 43:8, he brings out those "who are blind, yet have eyes, who are deaf, yet have ears." In 42:16, he declares, "I will lead the blind by a road (LXX: ὁδός) they do not know, by paths they have not known I will guide them. I will turn darkness before them into light, the rough places into level ground."

Finally, Yahweh's "carrying" of Israel takes her back to Jerusalem (40:1-11), just as she was carried by Babylon into captivity (cf. 39:6). It is a reenactment of the first exodus, when Yahweh lifted/carried the wilderness generation (63:9), leading them through the waters of the Red Sea (63:12-13) and giving them "rest" in the desert (63:14; cf. Exod 16:23). Yahweh's carrying of individual Israelites is said to be from birth/conception to old age/turning gray (46:3-4). It is a metaphor for salvation (46:4, where "carry" is parallel to "save"). The carrying/saving Yahweh is contrasted with idols, which are carried by worshipers and do not save (46:7).

Soteriological Implications

The portrait of Yahweh as shepherd of the INE, with its associated images of Yahweh's feeding, gathering, leading, and carrying the sheep along the "way," vividly illustrates Israel's soteriological need, beyond election and liberation, for God's pastoral care. Apart from Yahweh's feeding, the sheep would not survive the INE journey to the eschaton. Apart from Yahweh's gathering, not only Babylonian captives, but captive Jews from across the globe and even Gentiles, would never see the new Jerusalem/Creation. Apart from Yahweh's leading, the "blind" flock would never find its way to Zion. And apart from Yahweh's carrying — the metaphor that perhaps more than any other argues against synergism — Israel would never reach the age-to-come.

Collectively, these four images of post-election grace span the distance between Israel's liberation and her entrance into the good-age-to-come, illustrating the truth that salvation in Isaiah is a matter of grace from first to last. The images point, moreover, to a transformation of Israel that takes place from the time of her new beginning as a people (her liberation) to the time of her "return" in its fullest, eschatological sense. The metaphor of Yahweh's leading/healing of the blind points to a transformation of the heart and its perceptiveness, for in Isaiah, blindness and deafness are metaphors for the hardheartedness and imperceptiveness Yahweh inflicted upon Israel when in ironic retribution he remade her in the image of her blind, deaf, imperceptive idols (6:9-10; 44:17-18).[29] The metaphor of gathering points to a transformation of the eschatological faith community in terms of its ethnic constitution. The metaphor of feeding gives poetic expression to Israel's nourishment and renewal at the hand of Yahweh, while the metaphor of carrying/bearing — whether applied in connection with the corporate journey (40:11) or the individual lifespan (46:3-4) — points to Yahweh's patient forbearance of a people utterly unable to reach eschatological salvation by their own stamina and ability.

The Divine Warrior as Shepherd in Mark

The opening oracle of Isa 40–55 (40:1-11), as noted above, concludes with the image of the victorious liberator, Yahweh, preparing to embark on the second exodus. Having (a) liberated the people of Israel, he (b) feeds and gathers them as a shepherd does a flock, and then (c) sets off on the highway, carrying and leading them on the way. The expectation, of course, is that he will (d) return to Zion with the people (cf. 40:9).

The Gospel of Mark, which treats Isa 40:1-11 as programmatic for the entire story,[30] takes its cue from this fourfold conceptual progression in its fourfold depiction of Jesus as the INE divine warrior. (a) Mark 1:14–6:13 introduces Jesus as the INE liberator of the people.[31] (b) Mark 6:30–8:21, we will argue, introduces Jesus as the INE shepherd who feeds and gathers the flock in the wilderness. (c) Mark 8:22–10:52 introduces Jesus as the INE shepherd who leads the blind along "the way" up "to Jerusalem," metaphorically "bearing" them in pastoral patience. Finally, (d) Mark 11:1–16:8 depicts

29. Cf. G. K. Beale, "Exodus vi 9-13: A Retributive Taunt Against Idolatry," *VT* 41 (1991): 257-78.

30. See, esp., Marcus, *The Way of the Lord*, 1-29.

31. In announcing the Isaianic "good news" both in word (his powerful teaching) and deed (his ministry of casting out demons and healing) (1:14–3:12), and in preparing (3:13–6:13) and sending (6:7-32) his disciples/apostles to do the same, Jesus enters into conflict with demons, sickness, the political and religious leadership, and chaos (on these literary divisions, see Dowd, *Reading Mark*, 15-28, 29-62, and 63-64 respectively). This work is collectively interpreted as the binding and plundering of Satan (3:23-27), and unpacked in INE terms as a reenactment of the Reed Sea crossing: after miraculously bringing his disciples safely across the sea (4:35-41), the divine warrior drowns Satan's pursuing armies in the same (5:1-13).

Jesus as the enthroned king and covenant-maker of the INE who has re-turned/will return with his followers to Zion. Elements (b) and (c), which belong to Jesus' pastoral activity as the INE shepherd, are the concern of the present section, and will be treated under separate headings below.

Each of the four sections features, moreover, an INE reenactment of an iconic exodus event that is related to the section's central theme. (a) Mark 1:14–6:13 (liberation) features the INE reenactment of the defeat of Pharaoh's army in the sea (4:35–5:13). (b) Mark 6:30–8:21 (feeding/gathering the sheep) features parallel INE reenactments of the manna miracle in the wilderness, one in Jewish territory (6:30-52), and one in Gentile territory (8:1-21). (c) Mark 8:22–10:52 (leading/bearing the blind flock along "the way") fea-tures the INE reenactment on the "way" up to Jerusalem of Moses' encoun-ter with God's glory on the holy mountain (9:2-8). (d) Mark 11:1–16:8 (en-thronement and covenant ratification) depicts the expected INE reenactment on Mt. Zion of Yahweh's first covenant banquet with Israel at Mt. Sinai (14:22-25).

The fourfold progression in both Isaiah and Mark, it should be noted, is cumulative in nature. That is, while God's liberating work is the focus of the first stage of the INE, it is not limited to it, but continues even to the end of the INE, when he liberates Jerusalem from its own unrighteousness/un-righteous leaders. And while God's shepherding activity is the focus of the second and third stages, it is not limited to these, but continues even to the end of the INE, when God gathers Jewish exiles/the nations from the ends of the earth, feeds them at the covenant banquet, and in response to the dark-ness that covers the earth, provides everlasting guidance via the dawn of his rising upon Zion. Finally, while God's covenant-making activity as the en-throned king upon arrival in Jerusalem is the focus of the fourth stage, all other activities are drawn up into this activity.

In presenting this argument, the present study proposes a major modi-fication of Watts's tripartite, INE-derived outline for Mark ("from 'Galilee and beyond' [1:14/16-8:22/27], along the 'Way' [8:22/27-10:45–11:1], to 'Jerusa-lem' [10:45/11:1–16:8]," corresponding to Isaiah's "from 'the nations,' along the 'Way,' to 'Jerusalem'").[32] Essentially, the present study treats the feeding and gathering section (6:30–8:21) as an additional fourth unit. The success of the argument will depend on establishing 6:30–8:21 as a distinct literary unit on par with the others.

---

32. Watts, *Isaiah's New Exodus*, 123.

Michael W. Martin

The Shepherd's Feeding and Gathering in the Wilderness (6:30–8:21)

The portrayal of Jesus as a shepherd who feeds and gathers his sheep in the wilderness occurs primarily in the two miraculous feeding stories (6:30-52; 8:1-21), which form an *inclusio* around 6:30–8:21, demarcating it as a literary unit. Before we examine the stories themselves, it will be helpful to note their common structure and their role within the larger piece.

Both stories feature a detailed parallel structure consisting of the following elements in the following order: (a) a crowd follows Jesus into the desert; (b) the crowd grows hungry; (c) the question is raised concerning whether to send the crowd home; (d) Jesus highlights the need to feed them; (e) the disciples, in response, are incredulous; (f) Jesus asks, "How many loaves do you have?"; (g) the disciples answer; (h) the people are commanded to sit down; (i) Jesus takes the loaves, prays a word of blessing or thanksgiving, breaks the loaves, and gives the loaves to the disciples; (j) the disciples distribute the food; (k) the crowd eats and has its fill; (l) the number of baskets of broken pieces the disciples take up is reported; (m) the crowd's number is reported;[33] (n) the disciples depart in a boat to the other side; (o) Jesus confronts an adversary (the sea, the Pharisees); (p) Jesus and the disciples return in the boat; (q) the disciples fail to "understand" about the loaves while returning in the boat.

In both feeding episodes, moreover, items (n), (o), and (p) above constitute an intercalated story that interrupts the feeding story before its conclusion with (q). Thus both stories may be seen as parallel "Markan sandwiches":

The Jewish Feeding
A   Provision of Bread: The Miracle in the Desert (6:30-44)
  B   Confrontation with Adversary across the Sea (6:45-51a)
A′ Provision of Bread: The Disciples' Misunderstanding (6:51b-52)

---

33. R. T. France notes with ambivalence the long-standing suggestion concerning the potential "significance in the numbers, in that five (books of the law) and twelve (tribes of Israel) are clearly 'Jewish' numbers, while four (corners of the earth) and seven (completeness) point to a worldwide dimension to the Messiah's mission" (*The Gospel of Mark: A Commentary on the Greek Text* [NIGTC; Grand Rapids: Eerdmans, 2002], 306). The fact that Jesus calls pointed attention to the numbers, however, and in an attempt to remedy the disciples' lack of understanding concerning the meaning of the parallel miracles (8:18-21), lends credence to the suggestion. So, too, does the parallel structure we are proposing for 6:31–8:21.

The Gentile Feeding
A   Provision of Bread: The Miracle in the Desert (8:1-9)
  B   Confrontation with Adversary across the Sea (8:10-13)
A' Provision of Bread: The Disciples' Misunderstanding (8:14-21)

The high degree of parallelism between the two episodes — and especially their common portrait of Jesus as the feeding/gathering INE shepherd — serves to underscore a crucial theological point in Mark, namely, that Gentiles are included in the eschatological gathering/feeding of the flock.[34] This is in keeping, of course, with the Isaianic expectation, which envisions Yahweh's "gathering" not only of all Israel (Isa 43:5), but the nations (56:6-8). The point is further underscored by the overall chiastic design of the literary unit the feeding stories bracket, Mark 6:30–8:21:[35]

A — Jewish Feeding (6:30-52)
  B — Jewish Healings (6:53-56)
    C — Clean and Unclean (7:1-23)
  B' — Gentile Healings (7:24-37)
A' — Gentile Feeding (8:1-21)

On the one hand, the central portion of this structure establishes the new basis of purity common to Jewish and Gentile members of the gathered eschatological flock, namely, what comes out of the heart — and not what enters a person in accordance with Mosaic food laws. Not surprisingly, the Isaianic account of Yahweh's complaint (Isa 29:13) that the people honor him with their lips and not their heart (Mark 7:6) is the scriptural basis for the argument of the section. On the other hand, it is the first and last sections of this arrangement that are vital to framing Jews and Gentiles alike as "the flock" in the first place. Moreover, in returning to the motif of the shepherd's feeding and gathering of the flock in 8:1-21 (A'), the writer sets the stage for what follows both in Isaianic expectation (40:11) and in the Markan narra-

34. On the Gentile identification of the crowd, see Dowd, *Reading Mark,* 75-79; but cf. the discussion of Watts, *Isaiah's New Exodus,* 181-82, which at the very least suggests the crowd is symbolically, if not historically, Gentile.

35. Cf. the chiastic proposals of Watts (*Isaiah's New Exodus,* 223n.9) and Dowd (*Reading Mark,* 65), and the longstanding parallelism proposal described and critiqued by Robert H. Gundry (*Mark: A Commentary on His Apology for the Cross* [Grand Rapids: Eerdmans, 1993], 395), none of which takes into account the crucial parallel sandwiching of 6:30-52 and 8:14-21 and their consequent function as an *inclusio* demarcating 6:30–8:21 as a literary unit.

tive itself (8:22–10:52), namely, the leading and carrying of the sheep along "the way."

Turning to the two stories themselves, we observe that both depict Jesus' miraculous provision of bread as the INE reenactment (Isa 40:11; 49:9-11; 51:14-16) of the manna miracle (Exod 16:1-22; Neh 9:15; Ps 78:17-32; 105:40), incorporating allusions to both the original exodus story[36] and the INE in the portrait.[37]

In the story of the Jewish feeding (6:30-52), the depiction begins an introductory scene. The disciples, returning from their mission (6:7-13), are "gathered" (6:30) to Jesus and report what they have done and taught. In response, Jesus calls them away to a "deserted place," so that they may "rest," for as Mark explains, "many were coming and going, and they had no leisure to eat." The mention of gathering, rest, and eating in connection with a "deserted place" (6:31; also vv. 32, 35) recalls the setting of the original exodus, where Shepherd Yahweh first provided "food" (16:1-22) and commanded "rest" (16:23) for the gathered flock (cf. Exod 15:13). The picture of the crowd "coming and going," meanwhile, is an allusion to the portrait in Numbers 27:15-17 of the appointed shepherd who comes in and goes out before the congregation, leading and bringing them, "so that [they] may not be like sheep without a shepherd." What transpires with the disciples in this opening scene — their being gathered to Jesus, and their planned resting and eating in the desert — anticipates in outline form what will transpire for the multitudes, first in Jewish territory, and then in Gentile territory. But in those episodes the disciples are summoned as agents of Jesus' pastoral activity, just as they were summoned previously as agents of Jesus' liberating work of teaching, healing, and casting out demons (3:13–6:32).[38]

Accordingly, in 6:33, the Jewish multitude is pictured being gathered like sheep to Jesus and his disciples: they see them, recognize them, and hurry on foot to join them in the desert — so eager to follow, in fact, that when they see Jesus/the disciples "going" to the desert by boat (again, an allusion to the "coming and going" of Num 27:15-17), they arrive there ahead

36. On the allusion to exodus traditions in what follows, see Mauser, *Christ in the Wilderness.*

37. On allusions to both, see below; cf. Watts, *Isaiah's New Exodus,* 178-79; Dowd, *Reading Mark,* 67-70.

38. Mark 6:30-32 may be viewed as a "hinge" text that completes the narration (6:7-32) of the disciples' mission (narration intercalated, ominously, by the story of John's execution) and, simultaneously, introduces the narration of the gathering/feeding of the flock (6:30–8:21).

of them. That they come "from all the towns" reflects the INE motif of Yahweh's gathering of dispersed Israel (Isa 43:5; 49:12).

In the description of Jesus' emotional reaction upon seeing the waiting crowd on the shore, the pastoral motif becomes explicit: he has "compassion" for them, "because they were like sheep without a shepherd." The image recalls the recurring portrait of the INE shepherd's "compassion" for his sheep (49:9-11, in the context of feeding; 49:12-13, in the context of gathering), while the phrase "sheep without a shepherd" is taken directly from Num 27:15-17.

One recognizes, then, in the disciples' proposal to "send them away" their failure to grasp their own pastoral responsibility for the crowd, and in Jesus' response ("You give them something to eat") the call to join Jesus in taking up that responsibility. It may be that their incredulous reply ("Are we to go and buy two hundred denarii worth of bread, and give it to them to eat?") reflects similar incredulity concerning the ability of Yahweh to feed the people in the first exodus (Num 11:21-22; Ps 78:19-20).

The command for the crowd to lie down on green grass certainly resumes the pastoral motif, echoing the language of Ps 23:2 ("He makes me lie down in green pastures")[39] as it casts Jesus in the role of putting the flock to pasture per Isaianic expectation (49:9-11). In this moment, we witness the crowd's sharing in the "rest" that was planned for the disciples but never occurred, since the crowd in its eagerness to join Jesus and the disciples had "hurried" to the desert and arrived before them (6:33). (It would seem sharing in Jesus' pastoral vocation means sharing in its harried pace.)

The subsequent grouping of the crowd by hundreds and fifties recalls Exod 18:21, while the crowd's eating until "filled" recalls the outcome of the manna miracle in Exod 16:8, 12. In this moment, the crowd again shares in what was planned for the disciples — leisure to eat — but never occurred.

Related to the expected INE provision of bread is the theme of Yahweh's mastery of watery chaos: the latter, evident in both creation and Is-

---

39. Because the psalm employs the image of Yahweh as a shepherd who leads in righteous "paths," it is probably read by the evangelist through the lens of Isaianic expectation and, moreover, employed as a template for what is narrated in Mark 6:30-56: Jesus' compassion for the "sheep without a shepherd" ("The LORD is my shepherd"), his provision of food ("I shall not want"), his command to sit down on green grass ("He makes me lie down in green pastures"), his stilling of the storm ("he leads me beside still waters"), and his healings in Gennesaret/beyond ("he restores my soul"); cf. A. Heising, "Exegese und Theologie der alt- und neutestamentlichen Speisewunder," *ZTK* 86 (1964): 80-96; Rudolph Pesch, *Das Markusevangelium* (2 vols.; HTKNT 2; Freiburg: Herder, 1976, 1977), 1:350n.11.

rael's deliverance at the Reed Sea, is cited as proof in Isaiah that Yahweh will care for Israel in her new wilderness journey — as proof that she will "not lack bread" (Isa 51:14-16). The same linking of these themes is evident in the Markan intercalation of the "walking on water" episode (6:45-51a) within the story of Jesus' miraculous provision of bread. The effect is to tie the second iconic exodus event to the first, just as Isaiah does, so that Jesus' INE provision of manna is seen to be of a piece with his Reed Sea–like mastery of wind and wave.

Multiple allusions to the battle with watery chaos both at the exodus and at creation accomplish the portrayal. First and most obviously, Jesus is depicted walking across the sea. In Israel's collective memory, this is what "Shepherd" Yahweh did both in creation and at the exodus.

> I am the LORD, your Holy One, the Creator of Israel, your King. Thus says the LORD, who makes a way in the sea, a path in the mighty waters, who brings out chariot and horse, army and warrior; they lie down, they cannot rise, they are extinguished, quenched like a wick. (Isa 43:15-17)

> . . . who alone stretched out the heavens and trampled the waves of the Sea. (Job 9:8)

> Your way was through the sea, your path, through the mighty waters; yet your footprints were unseen. You led your people like a flock by the hand of Moses and Aaron. (Ps 77:19-20)

The mention of the disciples facing a "hostile wind" that "torments" them (6:48) at "evening" (6:47) recalls both the adversarial nature of Yahweh's "path-making" across the waters at both creation and the Reed Sea crossing, and the setting of those stories at evening/amidst darkness (Gen 1:2; Exod 14:20-21). Jesus' intention to "pass them by" (6:48) reminds of God's saving action in the Exodus (cf. Exod 33:19-23; 34:6; 1 Kgs 19:11), while Jesus' order for the disciples not to be afraid (6:50) echoes the same command issued by Yahweh at the anticipated INE reenactment of the Reed Sea crossing (Isa 43:1-2; 51:12-16). Occurring as it does in the midst of this cluster of allusions, Jesus' identification of himself to his disciples with the self-designation Yahweh employed in the exodus, "I am" (ἐγώ εἰμι, Mark 6:50; cf. MT and LXX Exod 3:14), cannot be a coincidence, but rather, is the obvious answer to the question that the disciples have been asking since the previous sea confrontation: "Who is this that even the wind and the sea obey him?" (4:41).

The outcome of Jesus' triumphant striding — the wind's ceasing — also points the disciples to the answer. The disciples, however, can only be "utterly astounded" by the event because "they did not understand about the loaves" (6:52). Evidently, what they had witnessed in the desert should have assisted them in comprehending what they had witnessed on the waters.

The second feeding story, that which occurs in Gentile (8:1-21) territory, again depicts Jesus' miraculous provision of bread as the INE reenactment by Yahweh of the first manna miracle. Once again, there is the general resemblance: Jesus miraculously supplies the hungry crowd with bread in the "desert place." Again, there is the progression of gathering (8:1), resting (8:6), and eating until filled (8:8), recalling several interrelated exodus and INE motifs. Jesus' "compassion" (8:2) for the crowd — this time, explicitly, because they are without food — again brings to mind the INE shepherd and his "compassion" for the flock as he feeds and gathers them.

Other exodus and INE motifs not seen in the first story also appear. The "three days" the crowd spends with Jesus in the desert (8:2) recall Exodus 5:1-3 and, specifically, Moses' request that the people be allowed to feast in the wilderness for that amount of time. Jesus' concern that, if he sends them away hungry to their homes, "they will faint on the way" (8:3), echoes the recurring motif of the "way" in Isaiah, and in particular, Isaianic portraits of the Shepherd feeding the sheep on the "way" lest they die from hunger (51:14). Perhaps most importantly, Jesus' observation that "some of them have come from a great distance" (8:3) on this same "way" recalls the INE shepherd's gathering of prisoners who "come from far away" (Isa 49:12) — including "foreigners who join themselves to the LORD" (56:6-8). The allusion is poignant given the Gentile context of the feeding.

Finally, just as the Jewish feeding story was intercalated with a sea-crossing/confrontation episode that furthered the allusions to exodus/INE in support of the ongoing portrait of Jesus as the INE Shepherd, so too is the Gentile feeding story, only in this case, the sea-crossing is not miraculous and the adversary is not cosmic. Rather, the adversary confronted by Jesus across the sea is the Pharisees, who have come to argue with him. In so doing, they ask for a "sign from heaven" — a likely allusion to the giving of manna "from heaven" (Exod 16:4; Ps 78:23-24; John 6:31). They make the request, moreover, "to test him" — a further allusion to Exod 16:4-5, where the manna is given by God to the skeptical people in order "to test them." In response to the cynical request, Jesus sighs, insisting no sign will be given to "this generation" — words intended to recall the rebuke of the people in the Song of Moses (Deut 32:5, 20; cf. Ps 95:10). The timing of the exchange (not to mention its intercalated literary position within the Gentile feeding story) points to an irony that is lost on the Pharisees, that what Jesus denies to them — the sign of manna from heaven — he has just granted to a Gentile multitude.

With the close of the larger section (6:30–8:21), extended reflection on the shepherdly themes of gathering and feeding comes to an end, and the themes do not reappear in Mark until the end of the Gospel. We recall that in Isaianic expectation, Yahweh's pastoral "gathering" of the people at the outset of the INE (40:11) is resumed upon his arrival in Zion, when he "gathers" all his captive people from the "ends of the earth" (Isa 41:9; cf. 43:5; 49:12; 56:6-8). In a similar fashion, Mark depicts Jesus resuming his pastoral "gathering" of the people "from the ends of the earth to the ends of heaven" (13:27) upon his arrival in Zion at his second coming. Also in Isaianic expectation, Yahweh hosts his people at a grand enthronement/covenant banquet upon arrival in Zion, serving them rich food and well-aged wine. This expectation, too, finds its fulfillment in Mark, as we note below in the section devoted to Yahweh's covenant-making activity.

Leading and Carrying "On the Way" to Jerusalem (8:22–10:52)

The oracle announcing the INE (Isa 40:1-11), as we have said, concludes with the image of the INE shepherd feeding and gathering his sheep, and then carrying and leading them on the New Exodus "way." Correspondingly in Mark, the depiction of Jesus as a shepherd who feeds and gathers his sheep in 6:31–8:22 is immediately followed by the depiction of Jesus leading and, in the one scene of the unit that reenacts an iconic Sinai event (Moses' ascent of Sinai), metaphorically "carrying" his disciples "on the way" in 8:22–10:52. The integrity and coherence of the unit as a distinct section of Mark is widely recognized in Markan scholarship.[40] So, too, is its employment throughout of the (Isaianic) motif, "on the way," as a unifying theme.[41] In this connection, we note that in Isaianic expectation, the "way" is a path "up to Jerusalem." Correspondingly, in Mark 8:22–10:52, the three "passion predictions" of the unit anticipate Jesus' suffering in Jerusalem, while in 10:32-34 "the way" is explicitly framed as a path that leads "up to Jerusalem." Moreover, we have observed that in Isaiah, the theme of darkness/blindness is intertwined with the theme

40. For the evidence surveyed briefly below and additional arguments, see Marcus, *The Way of the Lord*, 31-37; Watts, *Isaiah's New Exodus*, 124-32, 221-94; and Dowd, *Reading Mark*, 83-116.

41. As Marcus notes, "on the way" (8:27; 9:33-34; 10:32, 52) would be an appropriate title for the section.

of the shepherd's guidance along "the way." The sheep are called from darkness, and must be led by the shepherd along the way because they are blind. Correspondingly in Mark, the theme of blindness is widely recognized as playing a critical role in 8:22–10:52. This is evident in the well-known intercalated structure of the section, wherein the journey narrative, a tripartite unit constructed around the three passion predictions, is bracketed by the only two stories in Mark wherein blind men are healed:

A — Healing of a blind man in two stages (8:22-26)
  B — Passion Prediction Unit #1 (8:27–9:29)
  B′ — Passion Prediction Unit #2 (9:30–10:31)
  B″ — Passion Prediction Unit #3 (10:32-45)
A′ — Healing of a blind man immediately (10:46-52)

The intercalation is not accidental. In the final verses immediately preceding the unit, Jesus excoriates the disciples in Isaianic terms as "blind" for failing to "understand" the loaves (8:17-21). Moreover, the partial, "walking-as-trees" vision of the blind man in 8:22-26 is widely seen as reflecting Peter's partial, "walking-as-trees" understanding of Jesus' identity in 8:27-33 — an understanding that has no place for Jesus' suffering and death. Thus in the three passion predictions and ensuing discussions that follow, Jesus may be seen as articulating a clearer "vision" of his identity. The "way" to Jerusalem is a "way" that leads to the cross, and it is one in which the "blind" disciples are, per Isaianic expectation, called to follow.

Further underscoring the motif of the INE "way" in the section is the transfiguration scene, a reenactment, as we have said, of Moses' ascent of Sinai (Exod 24:15-18//34:29-35). In leading the disciples up the mountain, Jesus may be seen fulfilling the INE expectation concerning the divine shepherd whose path across the "mountain" becomes the exodus "way" (LXX 40:3-4; 49:11; cf. 41:18; 45:2), and who pastures the sheep on the "bare heights" (49:9; cf. 41:18).[42] Jeremias, following Strauss, counts six allusions to Sinai.[43] Marcus charts them as follows:[44]

---

42. Jesus is also portrayed in this scene, as Marcus notes, as the prophet like Moses (Deut. 18:15). Even in this portrayal, however, there is close identification with Yahweh, for Jesus, like Moses in Jewish tradition, is transfigured, enthroned, and deified so that he shares in Yahweh's kingship, divinity, and glory (Marcus, *The Way of the Lord*, 80-93).

43. J. Jeremias, "Μωυσῆς," *TDNT* 4:869n.228; cf. Joachim Gnilka, *Das Evangelium nach Markus* (2 vols.; EKKNT 2; Zurich: Benziger Verlag, 1978, 1979), 2:32.

44. Marcus, *The Way of the Lord*, 82; cf. J. A. Ziesler, "The Transfiguration Story and

Michael W. Martin

Mark		Exodus
9:2a	six days	24:16
9:2a	three disciples	24:1, 9
9:2b	ascent of mountain	24:9, 12-13, 15, 18
9:2b-3	transfiguration	34:29
9:7b	God reveals self in veiled form through cloud	24:15-16, 18
9:7b	voice out of cloud	24:16

Marcus adds to Jeremias's list the astonishment of the crowd after Jesus' return from the mountain (9:15), which recalls the astonishment of the Israelites concerning Moses' transfigured face (Exod 34:29-35).[45] Farrer and Hobbs note, too, the similarity between Moses' confrontation of faithless Israel upon his return from the mountain (Exod 32:7-35) and Jesus' confrontation with the "faithless generation" (Mark 9:19; cf. Deut 32:16-20) upon his return from the mountain (Mark 9:14-28).[46] The words "faithless generation" (Mark 9:19), however, recall the displeasure of Yahweh, not Moses, with the wilderness generation after the golden calf incident (Exod 32:7-35; cf. Deut 32:5, 16-20). In this same vein, Jesus' exasperated question in the same verse, "How long must I bear/carry [ἀνέξομαι] you?" recalls Shepherd-Yahweh's bearing/carrying [ἀνέχομαι; LXX Isa 46:3-4] the sheep along the INE "way" (Isa 40:3, 11).

Soteriological Implications

The Markan portrait of Jesus as the divine shepherd of the New Exodus, like the Isaianic portrait on which it is modeled, further illustrates Israel's/humanity's need for post-election grace if the INE "return" in its fullest sense is to be experienced. Apart from the shepherd's feeding, the flock would "faint

---

the Markan Soteriology," *ExpT* 81 (1970): 263-68; Mauser, *Christ in the Wilderness,* 111-18; B. D. Chilton, "The Transfiguration," *NTS* 27 (1980): 114-25; Morna D. Hooker, "What Doest Thou Here Elijah?" in *The Glory of Christ in the New Testament: Studies in Christology in Memory of George Bradford Caird* (ed. L. D. Hurst and N. T. Wright; Oxford: Clarendon, 1987), 59-70; Watts, *Isaiah's New Exodus,* 126-27; Dowd, *Reading Mark,* 90.

45. Marcus, *The Way of the Lord,* 82-83; cf. J. M. Nützel, *Die Verklärungserzählung im Markusevangelium* (FB 6; Würzburg: Echter Verlag, 1973), 160-61.

46. Austin M. Farrer, *A Study in St. Mark* (Westminster: Dacre, 1951), 110; E. C. Hobbs, "The Gospel of Mark and the Exodus" (Ph.D. diss., University of Chicago, 1958), 45-46.

along the way" (8:3). Apart from the shepherd's gathering, the flock would be divided and dispersed and would never see Jerusalem. Apart from the shepherd's leading, the blind flock would remain in darkness and lose its way. And apart from the shepherd's carrying — as in Isaiah, the metaphor that perhaps more than any other underscores Israel's/humanity's complete soteriological dependence on the shepherd — the flock would never reach its home.

As in Isaiah, so in Mark, these four images of post-election grace collectively span the distance between liberation from captivity and entrance into the good-age-to-come, illustrating that in Markan soteriology salvation is a matter of grace from first to last. The images, moreover, point to a divine transformation of the community as it journeys to its destination. As in Isaiah, blindness and deafness in Mark are treated as metaphors for hardheartedness and imperceptiveness (4:12; 8:17-21). Thus Jesus' leading of the "blind" disciples on the way even as he heals those who literally cannot see may be viewed as foreshadowing the post-Easter fulfillment of Isaiah's prophecy concerning God's eschatological transformation of the heart/vision of the sojourning flock. Similarly, the image of Jesus gathering Jews and Gentiles alike as his flock signals the prophesied reconstitution of the eschatological community as multi-ethnic. The metaphor of Jesus feeding the flock in the wilderness is suggestive of the community's prophesied need for divine renewal and revitalization while undergoing the INE, while Jesus' metaphorical "bearing" of "this faithless generation" underscores the community's utter need, given its wilderness-generation-like faithlessness, for divine patience and forbearance in the eschatological exodus.

The Divine Warrior as Covenant-Maker

The Divine Warrior as Covenant-Maker in Isaiah

Upon arrival in Jerusalem at the conclusion of the INE, Yahweh enters into his reign as king, renewing Israel and all creation. A problem remains, however, as Yahweh begins his reign. Israel was sent into exile because she had broken covenant with Yahweh. Even as Yahweh returns to Jerusalem, he still finds injustice and unrighteousness prevailing and must once again go to war, liberating Jerusalem from herself. Given this situation, the question remains: What will be the basis of lasting relationship between righteous Yahweh and unrighteous Israel in the good-age-to-come? Three oracles address this question, depicting Yahweh as the creator of an "everlasting covenant" with Israel that assures her enduring righteousness: 55:1-13 (cf. 25:6-10), 59:15b-21, and 61:1-11.

The first of these, 55:1-13, opens with Yahweh's call to join him in a lavish feast (55:1-2) celebrating, per the ancient custom, his ascension to the throne. Summoning Israel to listen, Yahweh announces at the feast,

> I will make with you an everlasting covenant,
> my steadfast, sure love for David.
> See, I made him a witness to the peoples,
> a leader and commander for the peoples.
> See, you shall call nations that you do not know,
> and nations that do not know you shall run to you,
> because of the LORD your God,
> the Holy One of Israel,
> for he has glorified you.

(55:3-5)

By "everlasting," a contrast is intended with the first covenant made with Israel, a covenant that was conditional and, as the exile demonstrates, did not last. Also, an analogy is intended: the new covenant with Israel will be like the Davidic covenant, and in two regards. First, it will be rooted in Yahweh's "steadfast, sure love" for Israel, just as Yahweh's covenant with David was rooted in the same. Second, it will be rooted, like the Davidic covenant, in God's commitment to the nations. Just as David was appointed under the Davidic covenant to call the nations to Jerusalem as their leader and commander, so Israel will be appointed to do the same under their new covenant.

Having described the unconditional terms of the covenant, Yahweh then summons Israel ("the wicked" and "the unrighteous") to abandon their "ways" and "thoughts," to return to Yahweh, and to receive "pardon." The reason they must do this is then declared by Yahweh:

> For my thoughts are not your thoughts,
> nor are your ways my ways,
> says the LORD.
> For as the heavens are higher than the earth,
> so are my ways higher than your ways
> and my thoughts than your thoughts.

The summons, thus framed, introduces a tension. Israel is to abandon her own unrighteous ways/thoughts, and yet, Yahweh's ways/thoughts remain entirely beyond her grasp. Indeed, they are as distant as the heavens are from the earth. How, then, can Israel possibly heed the call to repentance and adopt righteous ways/thoughts in place of unrighteous? Certainly, more than mere "pardon" (55:7) is needed, and that is precisely what Yahweh is depicted providing at the climax of the oracle (55:10-13).

In view of the great distance between the ways/thoughts of Yahweh and Israel, Yahweh presents the transformative power of his "word" as the solution, likening it to rain and snow that "come down from heaven" and "do not return" until they have brought life on earth, "giving seed to the sower and bread to the eater." Yahweh's word, he confidently declares, "shall not return to me empty, but it shall accomplish that which I purpose, and succeed in the thing for which I sent it." And what is the "thing for which [he] sent it"? It is, namely, the much-needed transformation not only of Israel, but all creation — a transformation that will itself be an "everlasting sign" Israel that will "not be cut off":

> For you shall go out in joy,
> and be led forth in peace;
> the mountains and the hills before you shall break forth into singing,
> and all the trees of the field shall clap their hands.
> Instead of the thorn shall come up the cypress;
> instead of the briar shall come up the myrtle;
> and it shall be to the LORD for a memorial,
> for an everlasting sign that shall not be cut off.
>
> (55:12-13)

Pictured here is the restoration of creation to an Edenic state, a world no longer plagued by thorn and briar, but rather, bursting in praise of its Creator. Pictured, too, is Israel walking, finally, in the "way" of Yahweh — a "way" unpacked climactically as one of going out in joy, being led forth in peace, surrounded on every side by a worshipful creation.

The portrait in 55:1-13 of Yahweh's covenant-making banquet may be seen as an expansion of the earlier portrait of this same banquet in 25:6-10. In the latter, Yahweh appears at the end of history on Mt. Zion hosting a feast of "rich food" and "well-aged wine" for "all peoples." At this same time, moreover, he "destroy[s] . . . the shroud that is cast over all the peoples, the sheet that is spread over all nations" — that is, he "swallows up death forever." The metaphor of the "shroud" and "sheet" may refer to the garments of mourners or the temple/tabernacle curtain (Exod 26:36; 27:16; Num 3:31). More likely it is intended as poetic invocation of both simultaneously, since both can be seen as metaphors for death's alienation of humanity from God.

The portrait in 55:1-13//25:6-10 of Yahweh's covenant-making banquet also sets the stage for subsequent depictions of covenant ratification in 59:15b-21 and 61:1-11, both of which oracles continue to locate Yahweh's covenant-making activity in Zion/Jerusalem.

In Isaiah 59, Israel is again accused of unrighteous ways and thoughts. In a passage famously quoted by Paul (Rom 3:15-17) to show that Israel is, like all humanity, "under sin," the prophet declares:

> Their feet run to evil,
> and they rush to shed innocent blood;
> their thoughts are thoughts of iniquity,
> desolation and destruction are in their highways.
> The way of peace they do not know,
> and there is no justice in their paths.
> Their roads they have made crooked;
> No one who walks in them knows peace.
> Therefore justice is far from us,
> and righteousness does not reach us.
> We wait for light, and lo! There is darkness;
> and for brightness, but we walk in gloom.
>
> (59:7-9)

Other oracles from the post-exilic portions of Isaiah, it should be noted, lay the blame for this situation especially at the feet of Israel's rulers (see, e.g., 56:9-12).

Once again, Yahweh's covenant-making activity is presented as the ultimate solution to Israel's unrighteousness. Displeased with injustice in Israel, and seeing there is no leadership in Israel that will intervene (59:15b-16), Yahweh dresses himself in armor — righteousness, salvation, vengeance, fury — and "delivers" Israel from itself (59:17-20). Arriving in Zion as its "Redeemer," Yahweh turns Jacob from transgression (59:20), announcing his covenant as the means of the transformation:

> And as for me, this is my covenant with them, says the LORD: my spirit that is upon you, and my words that I have put in your mouth, shall not

depart out of your mouth, or out of the mouths of your children, or out of the mouths of your children's children, says the LORD, from now on and forever. (59:21)

In this text, some important themes seen earlier in 55:1-13 reemerge. First, Israel's covenant fidelity is once again guaranteed by Yahweh's internal empowering. According to 55:1-13, that internal empowering was accomplished by Yahweh's "word," which was likened to precipitation that descends from and returns to heaven, having renewed and transformed Israel and all creation. In this passage, the internal transformation of Israel is accomplished via Yahweh's Spirit, which is placed "upon" her, and via Yahweh's words, which are "put in" her mouth. Evidently, Yahweh's Spirit has the same transformative and renewing power as his word. Second, as in 55:1-13, so in this account the covenant is depicted as something that will, in contrast to the former and now abrogated covenant, last forever. That is, with this covenant, Yahweh's words will remain in the mouths of Israel, generation after generation, "from now on and forever."

The annunciation of the covenant in 59:21 gives way, appropriately, to the song of triumph for Zion in Isa 60. Whereas earlier Zion was depicted in a state of unrighteousness/darkness (59:9), on this side of Yahweh's covenant-making she is exhorted:

> Arise, shine; for your light has come,
> and the glory of the LORD has risen upon you.
> For darkness shall cover the earth,
> and thick darkness the peoples;
> but the LORD will arise upon you,
> and his glory will appear over you.

The image of darkness covering the earth, followed by the dawn of Yahweh's rising in Zion, thus serves as a final, climactic metaphor for the transformation Yahweh effects in Israel via the new covenant.

The third depiction of Yahweh's covenant-making activity in Isaiah, 61:1-11, takes up many of the same themes evident in the first two oracles. Once again, Yahweh is seen arriving in Zion as its deliverer (61:1-7), bringing "righteousness" to Israel (61:3), and establishing an "everlasting covenant" with her out of a love of justice (61:8). Once again, too, the covenant that he establishes is everlasting because he enables Israel's fidelity. That is, Yahweh clothes Zion/Israel in "garments of salvation" and a "robe of righteousness"

(61:10), and Yahweh causes righteousness/praise to "spring up" in Israel, just as the earth and the garden cause seeds to bring forth shoots (61:11). The latter metaphor, too, renews the theme of internal enabling, likening righteousness to something planted within by a sower.

Soteriological Implications

Isaiah's portrait of Yahweh as covenant-maker provides still further confirmation that, in Isaianic soteriology, "staying in" no less than "getting in" is a matter of grace. All three oracles pertaining to the coming covenant locate its establishment not only post-election, but at the dawn of the good-age-to-come. All three oracles, moreover, treat this covenant as the means by which God will internally enable righteousness, or covenant fidelity, for the duration of the everlasting good-age-to-come. In granting, according to the terms of this covenant, his Word, words, and Spirit as transformative gifts, Yahweh assures that Israel will not violate this covenant as they did the last.

Evident, too, in the giving of these gifts is a negative anthropology that acknowledges the soteriological insufficiency of the first covenant and the covenantal nomistic pattern of religion it entailed — an insufficiency rooted not in the covenant itself but in God's human, covenant partners. Left to her own devices, even liberated, post-exilic Israel has once again become like the nations, "wicked" and "unrighteous," following evil "ways" and "thoughts." Wholly incapable of knowing Yahweh's "ways" and "thoughts," something of Yahweh must be given to her if she is to display lasting covenant fidelity. The covenant Isaiah envisions provides this in the gifts of Yahweh's Word, words, and Spirit. These not only result in the radical transformation of Israel, but of the nations and all creation. This transformation is wholly dependent on God. Israel no more bears responsibility for the righteousness that "springs up" in place of her unrighteousness than does creation for the cypresses and myrtles that "spring up" in place of her briars and thorns.

The Divine Warrior as Covenant-Maker in Mark

The portrayal of Jesus as the INE covenant-maker is seen primarily in the final section of Mark devoted to Jesus' time in Jerusalem (11:1–16:8) and, especially, in the interrelated scenes of the covenant feast (14:22-25) and crucifixion (15:16-39). Once again, allusions to both the original exodus story and the story of the INE are incorporated in the portrait.

Key to the portrayal are the words concerning the cup at the institution of the Lord's Supper:

> Then he took a cup, and after giving thanks he gave it to them and all of them drank from it. He said to them, "This is my blood of the covenant, which is poured out for many."

Scholarship is in agreement that the phrase "blood of the covenant" alludes to Exod 24:8 and the sacrificial blood that ratified the first covenant in the story of the exodus: "See the blood of the covenant that the LORD has made with you in accordance with these words." In view of this allusion, Jesus' words may be seen as providing a crucial interpretation of his death — indeed, the only explicit interpretation provided in Jerusalem — as the blood sacrifice that ratifies the covenant. But what covenant? Given that Mark has narrated the entire story of Jesus as the story of the expected INE, the answer that most naturally commends itself is the everlasting covenant Yahweh establishes with Israel at the climax of the INE.[47] Several details in the Markan account confirm such a reading.

In Isaianic prophecy, the covenant is announced on the holy mountain of Zion at a covenant feast. As such, it is a reenactment of the ratification of the first covenant, which was instituted at the holy mountain of Sinai and in connection with a covenant feast. Correspondingly in Mark, the covenant is announced in Zion at a ratification banquet — and at the feast, no less, that not only celebrated the first exodus but, in Jesus' day, had come to be invested with expectation of Israel's future deliverance. And, per Isaianic expectation, this covenant ratification is a reenactment of the first covenant's ratification, as the allusion to the "blood of the covenant" — and, perhaps, the presence of "the twelve" (14:17; cf. Exod 24:1-8) — makes clear.[48]

---

47. Because they read Mark against the background primarily of Isaiah, both Watts and Dowd make this identification. Watts, however, focuses on Jesus' role as the suffering servant of the covenant meal/crucifixion (*Isaiah's New Exodus*, 351-65), while Dowd only briefly explores the manner in which Jesus plays the complementary role of the divine warrior/host of the meal (*Reading Mark*, 144-45). What follows is an expansion on Dowd's line of reading. In exploring Jesus' role as divine warrior of the covenant banquet, however, I do not intend to discount Watts's convincing analysis. As Watts himself observes, Jesus often plays multiple roles in single scenes (see, e.g., Watts on Jesus' baptism, *Isaiah's New Exodus*, 91-121).

48. Cf. Watts, *Isaiah's New Exodus*, 352-55.

In Isaianic expectation, too, the covenant banquet occurs as the climax of a series of events: Yahweh liberates his people, shepherds them along the "way" up to Jerusalem, and arrives in Jerusalem as its conquering king. In Mark, the covenant banquet occurs after the same series of events: Jesus, the divine warrior, has liberated his people (1:14–6:32), shepherded them along the "way" up to Jerusalem (6:30–10:52), and arrived in Jerusalem as its conquering king (11:1-11). In Isaianic expectation, moreover, Yahweh finds injustice reigning in Jerusalem upon his arrival and goes to battle against the leaders who perpetrate it. Similarly in Mark, Jesus finds injustice reigning in Jerusalem (see, e.g., 11:15-19; 12:1-12; 12:38-40) and enters into confrontation with the leadership that upholds it (11:1-11; 11:27–12:44; 13:1-37).[49]

In Isaiah's account, the covenant banquet is simultaneously a celebration, as we have said, of Yahweh's enthronement, for the inauguration of the covenant commences in concert with the inauguration of Yahweh's expected reign. So, too, in Mark, the covenant banquet celebrates Jesus' enthronement, for Jesus reinterprets the Passover meal as pointing not to events from the first exodus but, rather, to his death — which in Mark *is* his enthronement. As T. E. Schmidt convincingly argues, the crucifixion scene (15:16-32) is narrated as an ironic imperial triumphal procession, depicting Jesus, among other things, as the deified king who is enthroned in connection with ritual sacrifice.[50]

It is clear, too, that in Isaianic prophecy, the covenant banquet inaugurates nothing less than the consummation of history: Yahweh has returned to dwell among his people in Jerusalem, has inaugurated everlasting covenant relationship with them, and has entered into his reign in the age-to-come, re-creating the heavens and the earth. In Mark, the covenant banquet is likewise nothing less than the inauguration of the consummation of history, only the evangelist introduces into the banquet scene a "now-and-not-yet" tension not present in Isaiah. While the divine warrior of Mark has returned to Jerusalem prior to the banquet per Isaianic expectation, he expects to be crucified and resurrected and so announces a second coming (13:26). Only at this second, triumphal arrival will the expected dissolution/re-creation of the cosmos prophesied by Isaiah begin (13:24-25; cf. Isa 13:10; 34:4; 50:2-3; 55:12-13; 65:17-25; 66:22-23). And though the divine warrior hosts the covenant banquet in Jerusalem, sharing his cup with the people per

---

49. Cf. Watts, *Isaiah's New Exodus*, 295-368; Dowd, *Reading Mark*, 117-37.

50. T. E. Schmidt, "Mark 15.16-32: The Crucifixion Narrative and the Roman Triumphal Procession," *NTS* 41 (1995): 1-18.

Isaianic expectation, the banquet is apparently to be interrupted — presumably by the Passion — since Jesus announces that its resumption will not occur until "I drink [the cup] anew with you" in the future. Moreover, while the banquet is apparently a celebration of the enthronement that will occur on the cross, the banquet's resumption will nevertheless not occur until the day that Jesus drinks the cup "new in the kingdom of God." Thus Jesus' reign, like the banquet that celebrates it, is both "now" and "not yet."

Also in Isaiah, the enthroned king destroys the shroud/sheet (25:7) in connection with his covenant-making feast (55:1-13//25:6-10). Whether the burial shroud, temple shroud, or both are in view, the image suggests, as we have said, the divine destruction of the alienation of death (Isa 25:8). In Mark, this event is depicted when Jesus' covenant-ratifying death destroys the temple shroud (15:38). Here again, though, a "now-and-not-yet" tension not seen in Isaiah is present. While death may be "swallowed up forever" at Jesus' crucifixion, to quote the Isaianic unpacking of the shroud's destruction (Isa 25:8), and while Jesus' resurrection (16:1-8) may serve as confirmation that this Isaianic expectation is met, death nonetheless remains a shared experience of Mark's readers beyond Jesus' crucifixion (13:8-20) — one that must be endured until "the end" (13:13).

The resurrection itself, too, fulfills another Isaianic hope concerning Yahweh's covenant-making activity. In Isaiah, the annunciation of the covenant (59:21), as we have said, is immediately followed by Zion's triumph song (60:1-22), which celebrates a marvelous development: the darkness covering the earth (60:2a) gives way to the dawn of the enthroned covenant-maker's rising (60:2b) upon Zion. Undoubtedly Mark has this song of triumph in view in its depiction of darkness covering the earth at the moment of Jesus' death (15:33) and, subsequently, the dawn of Jesus' rising in Zion (16:2, 6).

Finally, beyond the resurrection, Mark occasionally provides brief, allusive glimpses into the post-Easter life of the covenant people, and these too suggest fulfillment of INE hopes concerning Yahweh's covenant-making activity.

First, the portrait of the covenant banquet in Isa 55:1-13//25:6-10 depicts the divine warrior hosting, remarkably, "all peoples" (25:6) at his table even as he destroys the shroud and swallows up death forever (25:7-8). In Mark, the fulfillment of this expectation is symbolized by the serving of the bread of Jesus' body at the covenant banquet. The thanksgiving prayer Jesus offers at this moment echoes, as commentators often note,[51] the two prior

---

51. See, e.g., France, *The Gospel of Mark*, 262.

prayers of thanksgiving Jesus spoke when serving bread to followers in the wilderness wanderings — first in Jewish, then in Gentile, regions:

> *Jewish Feeding:* Taking the five loaves and the two fish, he looked up to heaven, and blessed and broke the loaves, and gave them to his disciples to set before the people. (6:41)
>
> *Gentile Feeding:* And he took the seven loaves, and after giving thanks he broke them and gave them to his disciples to distribute. (8:6)
>
> *Covenant Meal:* . . . he took a loaf of bread, and after blessing it he broke it, gave it to them, and said, Take; this is my body. (14:22)

The allusion serves to depict Jesus as the host of "all peoples" (Isa 25:6a), Jew and Gentile alike, at the covenant banquet, and his body as the "rich food" (Isa 25:6b) served at the feast.[52] Thus in Markan Christology, the death of Jesus is experienced in the church's celebration of the Eucharist not only as the event that "swallows up death forever" in fulfillment of Isaiah 25, but also, correspondingly, as the event that nourishes life in the period of the church's "wilderness wandering" — that is, in the time between the banquet's inception in the upper room and its end-time resumption with Jesus "in the kingdom."

Second, Isaiah depicts the everlasting covenant as the solution to the people's recalcitrant unrighteousness: the terms of the covenant are that God will place his Spirit upon the people, and his words forever within their mouths, as a divine source of righteousness, renewal, and transformation. In Mark, there are only a few, brief allusions to the Spirit, and these are made without much introduction concerning who/what the Spirit is. Presumably, the writer expects readers to have some prior understanding of the Spirit's identity in these instances. Given the importance of the INE as background for reading Mark, it would seem that Isaiah's portrait of the Spirit more than any other was expected to inform this prior understanding, and, indeed, Mark provides some confirmation of this expectation virtually every time the Spirit is mentioned. In 1:8-10, the Spirit's descent upon Jesus at his baptism after the heavens are rent (1:10) recalls, as we have said, the Isaianic expectation of the divine warrior's coming via rent heavens at the outset of the

---

52. Sharyn Dowd observes that the presence of "all" (14:23) of Jesus' disciples at the covenant meal "required that both the Jews and the gentiles in the Markan community cross significant boundaries in order to be joined to Jesus and to each other." She notes, too, the comparable presence of "all peoples" (Isa 25:6) at the great end-time banquet (*Reading Mark*, 145).

INE (Isa 64:1), as well as the sending of the Spirit upon the "Servant" (Isa 42:1; 61:1), with whom Jesus is also identified in Mark. Jesus' subsequent (post-Easter) baptizing, correspondingly, of "you" (gathered Israel; cf. 1:5) with the Holy Spirit (1:8) fulfills the Isaianic expectation of the covenant-maker's pouring out of the Spirit upon the people. The Spirit's sending of Jesus into the wilderness for forty days of testing (1:12-13) recalls the Spirit's guidance of Israel in the wilderness during the forty years of testing (Num 11:16-17, 25-29),[53] which is remembered in Isaiah as an anticipation of the provision of the Spirit in the second exodus (Isa 59:21; 63:11). The scribes' blaspheming of the Spirit (3:29-30) constitutes the INE reenactment of the wilderness generation's grieving of the Spirit, with the result that they become the enemy of the divine warrior (Isa 63:10).[54]

Thus when one arrives at the final mention of the Spirit in 13:11 — the only passage in Mark that looks ahead explicitly to the post-Easter life of the church beyond the appearance in Galilee (16:7) — it is not surprising that the Spirit's role in the life of believers is described in terms that bear remarkable resemblance to Isa 59:21. Just as the latter anticipates Yahweh's placing of his Spirit upon the people and his words within their mouths as a source of divine enablement, so too in Mark 13:11, Jesus teaches his disciples that in their coming trials before governors and kings (13:9), they will not have to rely on themselves for words, "for it is not you who speak, but the Holy Spirit." Assumed in this statement is Yahweh's expected provision, per the terms of the everlasting covenant, of his Spirit and words.

Soteriological Implications

In view of the Markan portrait of Jesus as the divine covenant-maker of the INE, we have further cause to conclude with regard to Markan soteriology that "staying in" the community that undertakes the INE journey is no less a matter of grace than "getting in." If Jesus' liberating activity secures the freedom of the elect to embark on the INE, and if Jesus' shepherding activity se-

---

53. Watts observes that in the prologue Jesus is depicted fulfilling multiple INE roles simultaneously: "Davidic-messianic-'Servant', who is at once 'Servant' Israel and Israel's deliverer, and Son of God" (*Isaiah's New Exodus*, 91-121, at 91). In his baptism/forty-day wilderness testing, Jesus plays the INE role of Servant Israel, reenacting the Reed Sea crossing/forty-year wilderness testing under the Spirit's direction.

54. C. K. Barrett, *The Holy Spirit and the Gospel Tradition* (London: SPCK, 1970), 104-5; Watts, *Isaiah's New Exodus*, 151.

cures their safe passage, then Jesus' covenant-making activity secures the full range of hopes associated with the arrival. That is, when Jesus the divine warrior ratifies his covenant, the shroud is destroyed, death is swallowed up, darkness covering the earth is met by the dawn of his rising upon Zion, his Spirit is placed upon the people, his words are placed within their mouths, and his reign is inaugurated. In short, it is only by these final, divine acts of grace, in addition to all that preceded them, that the elect can enter into the salvation belonging to the good-age-to-come.

Conclusion

The "New Perspective" on Paul has ushered in an era in NT scholarship wherein soteriological inquiry into ancient Jewish writings, including those of the Christian messianist variety,[55] may be conducted with a view to their perspective concerning the place of grace in salvation, both with regard to "getting in" and "staying in" the people of God. This study has argued that Mark, in conformity to Isaiah, maintains that salvation is a matter of grace from start to finish. That is, the study has shown that in Mark, "staying in" the community that undertakes the INE journey is no less a matter of grace than "getting in," for it is entirely dependent upon the Isaianic divine warrior's delivering, shepherding, and covenanting with the elect. Thus Mark, together with Isaiah, may be counted among those Jewish writings that hold to the principle of *sola gratia*.[56]

---

55. On the understanding of Judaism assumed in this statement, see Gabriele Boccaccini, *Middle Judaism: Jewish Thought, 300 B.C.E. to 200 C.E.* (Minneapolis: Fortress, 1991).

56. E.g., Jeremiah, *Apocalypse of Abraham*, and Tobit — so Charles H. Talbert, "Paul, Judaism, and the Revisionists," *CBQ* 63 (2001): 1-22, esp. 2n.5.

"I Have Prayed for You":
Divine Enablement in the Gospel of Luke

Andrew E. Arterbury

This essay compares the outcomes of Judas and Peter within Luke's Gospel in the hope of better understanding Lukan soteriology. Both Judas and Peter are heavily influenced by Satan in Luke's passion narrative as they betray and deny Jesus. Yet, whereas Judas apparently apostatizes, Peter perseveres as one of Jesus' disciples. The only explanation that Luke provides, however, for the perseverance of Peter's faith or faithfulness (πίστις) is found in Luke 22:32. There, Jesus' prayer and God's implied, though unseen, work behind the scenes are credited with enabling Peter to survive Satan's sifting. Consequently, important soteriological and Christological implications are found in Luke 22:31-34.

•   •

Discipleship and Apostasy

In his treatment of divine enablement in the Fourth Gospel, Charles Talbert provides some helpful soteriological categories that can be applied profitably to Luke's writings as well. First, Talbert refers to the point at which discipleship begins. Here he references John 1:12 — "as many as received him, he gave them authority to become children of God."[1] Likewise, in Luke's

---

1. Charles H. Talbert, "The Fourth Gospel's Soteriology between New Birth and Resurrection," *PRSt* 37 (2010): 133.

writings, one can easily cite passages that appear to narrate or refer to the point at which discipleship begins (e.g., Luke 5:1-11; 5:27-28; 8:26-39; 18:31-43; 19:1-10; Acts 2:41-42; 8:26-39; 10:23-48; 16:25-34).[2] Second, Talbert refers to the end of the discipleship process as the "soteriological consummation." Talbert cites John 6:40 as an example — "everyone who sees the Son and believes in him . . . I will raise him up on the last day."[3] Again, Luke includes numerous texts that evoke imagery related to the soteriological consummation (e.g., Luke 13:22-30; 14:15-24; 16:19-31; 17:22-37; Acts 3:20-21; 13:48; 14:22; 17:31).[4] Talbert, however, primarily discusses the period between the beginning and the end of the discipleship process in John's Gospel. He simply refers to this middle period as "the period between new birth and departure from this life."[5] In this essay, I will similarly focus on Luke's depiction of the middle period of the discipleship process.

For example, at numerous points in Luke's Gospel, Luke appears to address problems related to the middle phase of the discipleship process. In particular, Luke highlights apostasy as a very real threat for Jesus' followers, who are between the point at which discipleship begins and the soteriological consummation.[6] Succumbing to the temptation of apostasy then seemingly jeopardizes a disciple's status as a member of God's covenant people in the age-to-come. In short, in Luke's writings, that a person begins the process of discipleship does not necessarily mean that the person will remain on that pathway to its completion.

For instance, consider the Parable of the Sower (Luke 8:4-8) along with

---

2. I am assuming that the author who wrote the Gospel of Luke also wrote the Acts of the Apostles to serve as a sequel to the Gospel. See, e.g., Mikeal C. Parsons and Richard I. Pervo, *Rethinking the Unity of Luke and Acts* (Minneapolis: Fortress, 1993).

3. Talbert, "The Fourth Gospel's Soteriology," 133.

4. See, e.g., I. Howard Marshall, "Salvation," in *Dictionary of Jesus and the Gospels* (ed. Joel B. Green and Scot McKnight; Downers Grove, IL: InterVarsity, 1992), 722. Marshall describes "final salvation" as "a future state of being saved as opposed to being lost, and in the imagery of the Gospels signifies entry to the heavenly banquet instead of exclusion."

5. Talbert, "The Fourth Gospel's Soteriology," 133. In regard to discipleship as a process, see also Charles H. Talbert, "Discipleship in Luke-Acts," in *Discipleship in the New Testament* (ed. Fernando F. Segovia; Philadelphia: Fortress, 1985), 62-75, esp. 66-67.

6. I. Howard Marshall, *The Gospel of Luke: A Commentary on the Greek Text* (NIGTC; Grand Rapids: Eerdmans, 1978), 820-21. Marshall refers to apostasy as a disciple's "falling" as a believer. See also Schuyler Brown, S.J., *Apostasy and Perseverance in the Theology of Luke* (AnBib 36; Rome: Pontifical Biblical Institute, 1969), 146-48. Brown links apostasy with "the trial of faith" for individuals in Luke, whereas apostasy in Acts encompasses both a failure of faith and a failure to remain united with the community of faith.

Jesus' interpretation of that parable (Luke 8:9-15). Jesus describes the rocky soil as those who "have no root; they believe only for a while and in a time of testing fall away" (Luke 8:13, NRSV). Using our discipleship categories, Jesus seems to suggest that the rocky soil illustrates the problem of those who begin as disciples but do not survive the middle phase of the discipleship process. They "fall away." They do not persevere as disciples until their soteriological end. "Apostasy is the outcome."[7] Of course, those labeled as the thorny soil fall into a similar trap. Those described as thorny soil "are choked by the cares and riches and pleasures of life, and their fruit does not mature" (Luke 8:14). Here, too, Jesus seems to describe those who are initially counted among Jesus' disciples, but who do not continue on that path until the age-to-come. They fail to persevere as disciples.

Jesus expresses a similar perspective in Luke 12:1-12. He warns his "disciples" (Luke 12:1b) and says, "I tell you, everyone who acknowledges me before others, the Son of Man also will acknowledge before the angels of God; but whoever denies me before others will be denied before the angels of God" (12:8-9). Thus, Jesus again implies that not all of those who begin the discipleship journey will remain on that path to its end. Instead, if Jesus' *disciples* fail to acknowledge him publicly, their status as disciples and soteriological insiders will be revoked. Even then, Jesus provides words of gracious assurance to accompany his words of warning. For instance, in Luke 12:11-12, Jesus goes on to tell his disciples, "When they bring you before the synagogues, the rulers, and the authorities, do not worry about how you are to defend yourselves or what you are to say; for the Holy Spirit will teach you at that very hour what you ought to say." Notice, however, that Jesus' assuring words pertain to the provisions that God will supply to his disciples. The ability to withstand the crisis does not appear to reside within the disciples; rather, help comes from the outside.

In addition, consider Luke's narration of the failures of Ananias and Sapphira in Acts 5:1-11. Their actions in Acts resemble those of Judas in Luke.[8] Ananias and Sapphira are initially grouped among the community of disciples, but in the end they function as the negative counterparts to Barnabas, a faithful believer (Acts 4:32-37). They function as enemies of God.[9] Satan fills their hearts, they lie to the Holy Spirit, and they keep back proceeds, which they had promised to give to the community of believers (Acts 5:3). In

---

7. John Nolland, *Luke* (3 vols.; WBC 35a-c; Dallas: Word, 1989-1993), 1:388.
8. Brown, *Apostasy and Perseverance*, 98.
9. Mikeal C. Parsons, *Acts* (Paideia; Grand Rapids: Baker Academic, 2008), 75.

the end, they appear to be people who begin the discipleship process but who fail to persevere until the soteriological consummation. Schuyler Brown notes that the Ananias and Sapphira pericope illustrates "the lesson that discipleship is no guarantee of perseverance."[10]

Yet, the threat of apostasy in Luke's writings is most prevalent in the passion narrative and especially in the context of the Last Supper. For example, I. Howard Marshall argues that "thoughts of apostasy, self-seeking and betrayal" are "thematic throughout the Supper scene."[11] Perhaps the prominence of apostasy in Luke's passion narrative is not surprising given that only Luke, among the Synoptic Gospels, includes references to Satan and his activity in the passion narrative.[12] Furthermore, Luke magnifies the threat of apostasy at the Last Supper when he locates Jesus' prediction of Peter's denial in the upper room as opposed to the Mount of Olives as we see in Mark and Matthew.[13] Consequently, Marshall describes Satan's aim in Luke's passion narrative as "procuring the apostasy of all the disciples."[14] Joseph Fitzmyer adds "that no disciple . . . will be safe from a test to his/her loyalty and fidelity."[15]

In fact, perhaps the best way to demonstrate the threat that apostasy poses to Jesus' disciples in the middle period of discipleship in Luke's Gospel is to look closely at the experiences of Judas and Peter. Both disciples are impacted by a cosmic struggle that is larger than their own experiences.[16] In particular, both are heavily influenced by Satan in Luke's passion narrative. Peter, however, perseveres and eventually serves as a trustworthy and authoritative spokesperson for God in the book of Acts, whereas Judas meets his demise seemingly on both a physical and a spiritual level. We therefore need to investigate more closely the differences between the outcomes of Judas and Peter in Luke's writings.

In short, in Luke's writings, apostasy functions as the most dangerous threat facing Jesus' disciples in the period between the beginning of disciple-

---

10. Brown, *Apostasy and Perseverance,* 98.

11. Marshall, *The Gospel of Luke,* 818.

12. Joseph A. Fitzmyer, S.J., *The Gospel According to Luke (X–XXIV)* (AB 28a; New York: Doubleday, 1985), 2:1424.

13. Fitzmyer, *The Gospel According to Luke,* 2:1421.

14. Marshall, *The Gospel of Luke,* 818. Nolland (*Luke,* 3:1031) likewise claims that "the passion period" in Luke is "a time of special Satanic onslaught."

15. Fitzmyer, *The Gospel According to Luke,* 2:1423.

16. In regard to the cosmic battle imagery, see, e.g., G. B. Caird, *Saint Luke* (Westminster Pelican Commentaries; Philadelphia: Westminster, 1963), 235.

ship and the soteriological consummation. Yet, I will show that hope emerges from Jesus' prayers and God's behind-the-scenes work to sustain Jesus' disciples during this middle phase. In other words, in Luke's writings, God acts behind the scenes to provide Jesus' disciples with the strength they need to remain faithful disciples.[17] Without this divine assistance, Jesus' disciples appear helpless in the face of trials, temptations, and satanic sifting.

Judas and Peter as Disciples

Near the beginning of Luke's Gospel, both Peter and Judas are called by Jesus to follow him and to serve as apostles (Luke 5:1-11; 6:12-16). Moreover, both Peter and Judas clearly embark on the discipleship journey and can therefore be described as insiders who are in the middle phase of the discipleship process throughout much of Luke's Gospel.[18] Thus, for most of Luke's Gospel, both are between the soteriological beginning point and the final consummation. For instance, unlike Mark and Matthew who highlight betrayal as part of Judas's core identity from the beginning (Mark 3:19 — Ἰούδαν Ἰσκαριώθ, ὃς καὶ παρέδωκεν αὐτόν — "Judas Iscariot, who betrayed him"; Matt 10:4 — Ἰούδας ὁ Ἰσκαριώτης ὁ καὶ παραδοὺς αὐτόν — "Judas Iscariot, the one who betrayed him"), Luke more clearly separates Judas's treachery from his discipleship (Ἰούδαν Ἰσκαριώθ, ὃς ἐγένετο προδότης — "Judas Iscariot, who became a traitor") in Luke 6:16. In essence, while Luke foreshadows Judas's later misdeeds from the beginning, Luke does not set Judas apart from the other disciples at the beginning. Rather, Judas's identity will eventually change from that of disciple to traitor, but Luke does not simultaneously treat Judas as a disciple and a traitor.

Even in the context of the Last Supper, Luke initially reinforces the portraits of both Judas and Peter as disciples of Jesus. Luke does this in two

17. For a discussion of Matthew's use of "omnipotence behind the scenes" as a narrative technique for describing God's enabling work among believers, see Charles H. Talbert, "Indicative and Imperative in Matthean Soteriology," *Bib* 82 (2001): 521-22. Talbert builds upon the work of Gerhard von Rad (*Old Testament Theology* [New York: Harper, 1962], 1:52-53) and Meir Sternberg (*The Poetics of Biblical Narrative* [Bloomington: Indiana University Press, 1985], 106). Talbert writes, "Sternberg is surely right, however, when he notes that in the Hebrew Bible the books mix overt and implicit guidance by God." Talbert goes on to cite Acts 23–28 as an example of Luke's use of this same narrative technique.

18. Brown, *Apostasy and Perseverance*, 86-88. See also Caird (*Saint Luke*, 235), who concludes that Judas "must at one time have been an enthusiastic disciple."

significant ways. First, in Luke 22:3b, Luke refers to Judas as "one of the twelve." In addition, contrary to Mark and Matthew, in Luke Judas clearly partakes of the Last Supper with Jesus and the disciples before Jesus predicts Judas's betrayal (Luke 22:14-23).[19] Hence, Judas partakes of the same bread and wine that symbolize "the new covenant" in Luke's Gospel along with the other disciples (Luke 22:17-20).

Furthermore, when the Lukan Jesus predicts Judas's betrayal, Judas's betrayal is narrated as one of many failures by Jesus' disciples chronicled in Luke 22. For instance, in consecutive order, Jesus identifies Judas as a betrayer (Luke 22:21-23), chastises the disciples for debating who among them is the greatest (Luke 22:24-27), informs Peter that he will deny Jesus three times (Luke 22:31-34), and questions the disciples about their sleep-induced laxity at the Mount of Olives (Luke 22:39-46). Immediately thereafter, Judas betrays Jesus (Luke 22:47-54a), and Peter denies Jesus (Luke 22:54b-61).[20] Thus, even when the association is a negative one, Luke locates Judas among the other disciples up to, during, and just after the Last Supper.[21]

Hence, in Luke 22, the author verbally groups Judas with "the twelve" (22:3b), visually groups Judas with the disciples at the Last Supper (22:14-23), and conceptually groups Judas with the disciples in their missteps (22:14-61). From a soteriological perspective, Luke appears to reinforce Judas's insider status just prior to Judas's acts of betrayal. Consequently, Judas appears to be in the middle phase of the discipleship process along with many other disciples in Luke's Gospel. His identity is not qualitatively different. Instead, Judas and Peter are on similar trajectories up through Peter's denial in Luke 22:61. They are both disciples who face the ominous threat of apostasy.

Second, unlike Matthew and Mark, the primary contrast in Luke's passion narrative is not between Judas and Peter, but rather between Satan and Jesus.[22] For example, Luke interprets the misdeeds of both Judas and Peter within the framework of a cosmic struggle that begins in the temptation scene in Luke 4:1-13. In Luke 4:13, the devil bombards Jesus with temptations.

---

19. In both Mark and Matthew, Jesus openly identifies Judas as a betrayer prior to partaking of the Last Supper (Mark 14:17-21; Matt 26:20-25). Furthermore, it is unclear in both Mark and Matthew whether Judas actually partakes of the Last Supper with Jesus and the eleven. Thus, on a conceptual level, Judas is separated from the other disciples at an earlier juncture in those Gospels.

20. Marshall, *The Gospel of Luke*, 810, 818.

21. Fitzmyer, *The Gospel According to Luke*, 2:1424.

22. Fitzmyer, *The Gospel According to Luke*, 2:1425; and Marshall, *The Gospel of Luke*, 821.

In Luke 22, Satan tenaciously opposes Jesus' disciples.[23] In particular, Satan enters into (εἰσέρχομαι) Judas and apparently guides his treacherous actions (Luke 22:3). While most scholars rightly maintain that Judas remains culpable in his betrayal of Jesus (see, e.g., Luke 22:3-6; Acts 1:25),[24] from Luke's vantage point Satan functions as the puppet master behind Judas's duplicity.[25] Thus, Luke interprets Judas's betrayal as a satanic act that is simply carried out through a complicit Judas. Judas's betrayal provides evidence of a broader battle between Satan and Jesus.

Likewise, Jesus informs Peter in Luke 22:31 that "Satan has demanded to sift" him and all of the disciples "like wheat."[26] In fact, Jesus relays this information about Satan's sifting to Peter even before Jesus prophesies about Peter's denial (Luke 22:34). Consequently, by referring to Satan's sifting prior to Peter's denial, Luke has also interpreted Peter's denial as an outgrowth of Satan's influence. According to Luke, "Peter's fall is part of Satan's scheme."[27]

Hence, up through the Lukan Last Supper, Judas and Peter are portrayed as disciples who face similar circumstances and remain on similar trajectories. As a result, in Luke's passion narrative, the primary contrast is not between the moral character of Judas and Peter. Instead, both Judas and Peter experience downfalls that derive from the work of Satan. Luke interprets both Judas's betrayal and Peter's denial as manifestations of a broader battle.[28] As further evidence of this broader battle, Luke alone adds Jesus' in-

---

23. Luke Timothy Johnson, *The Gospel of Luke* (SP 3; Collegeville, MN: Liturgical Press, 1991), 346. Johnson claims that Satan tests the disciples at the end of Jesus' ministry (Luke 22:31) in a manner similar to that of the temptation that Jesus experienced at the beginning of his ministry (Luke 4:1-13).

24. See, e.g., Brown, *Apostasy and Perseverance*, 92-94; David Michael Crump, *Jesus the Intercessor: Prayer and Christology in Luke-Acts* (WUNT 2/49; Tübingen: Mohr, 1992), 164; David L. Tiede, *Luke* (ACNT; Minneapolis: Augsburg, 1988), 383, 388; and David E. Garland, *Luke* (Zondervan Exegetical Commentary; Grand Rapids: Zondervan, forthcoming). Regarding Luke 22:21-38, Garland writes, "Judas . . . was not 'fated' to do what he did but became a consenting 'conspirator.'"

25. Caird (*Saint Luke*, 235) says, "Judas betrayed Jesus because Satan entered him, because he became the cats-paw of the Enemy in the final stages of the campaign which Jesus had been waging against Satan's kingdom ever since the day of his baptism." See also Nolland (*Luke*, 3:1030-31), who points out that Judas's betrayal takes place "at the initiative of Satan." He contends that "Judas falls entirely under Satan's spell."

26. Luke employs the plural form of the second person pronoun (ὑμεῖς, "you"). As a result, Luke implies that Satan has demanded to sift all of the disciples.

27. Marshall, *The Gospel of Luke*, 818.

28. Marshall, *The Gospel of Luke*, 820.

structions to the disciples in Luke 22:35-38, instructing them to purchase a sword and prepare for battle.

Consequently, by reinforcing the portrayal of Judas as both an insider and a fellow disciple late in Luke's Gospel, it enables Luke's readers to see Judas's betrayal more clearly as an act of apostasy. Luke shows his readers that "it is possible to eat with Jesus and still betray him. . . . Presence at the Lord's table is no guarantee against apostasy." Moreover, Judas's downfall provides "a warning for Luke's community about a danger for which to be alert."[29] In particular, as we see from the narrative, Peter and the other disciples are no safer than Judas. They all face the same threat. The same Satan who enters Judas and drives him to apostasy also demands the opportunity to sift all of the disciples (22:31). All of them run the risk of apostasy, of falling away from following Jesus.[30] All of them run the risk of failing to experience a positive soteriological end after having embarked on the discipleship journey.

Peter, in particular, appears to be in a precarious state. For instance, recall that in Luke 12:8-9, Jesus claims that "everyone who acknowledges me before others, the Son of Man also will acknowledge before the angels of God; but whoever denies (ἀρνέομαι) me before others will be denied (ἀπαρνέομαι) before the angels of God." Notably, Luke employs the same verb again in Luke 22:34 when Jesus predicts Peter's denial (ἀπαρνέομαι) and in Luke 22:61 when Peter recalls Jesus' prophecy after having denied (ἀπαρνέομαι) that he was one of Jesus' disciples.

Consequently, at first glance, one might wonder whether Peter's denials of Jesus would likewise be deemed acts of apostasy. One might anticipate that neither Judas nor Peter would survive the middle stage of discipleship in Luke's Gospel. Yet, surprisingly, Luke demonstrates that Peter survives Satan's sifting as well as the middle phase of the discipleship process. Luke never portrays Peter as an apostate despite his denials of Jesus. Instead, whereas Luke portrays Judas as an apostate, he portrays Peter as one who perseveres despite his failures.

---

29. Charles H. Talbert, *Reading Luke: A Literary and Theological Commentary on the Third Gospel* (rev. ed.; Macon, GA: Smyth & Helwys, 2002), 237. See also Brown, *Apostasy and Perseverance*, 83; and Marshall, *The Gospel of Luke*, 807.

30. Marshall, *The Gospel of Luke*, 818.

The Divergent Paths of Judas and Peter

Judas

Regardless of the similarities of Judas's and Peter's discipleship and failures, their paths diverge drastically in the concluding sections of Luke and most certainly in Acts. Ultimately, our conclusions about Judas and Peter should be drawn from their final depictions in Luke's writings. Both at the ending of Luke and the beginning of Acts, Luke portrays Judas as a failed, former disciple who will not experience a positive soteriological end. Judas not only fails Jesus through his acts of betrayal, but Luke is careful to demonstrate in Acts that Judas never shows any contrition whatsoever.[31] Judas is now an apostate.[32] Using Jesus' logic in the Parable of the Sower, Judas's story follows a similar trajectory to that of the rocky or thorny soils (8:13-14).

For example, after the betrayal pericope in Luke 22:47-54a, Judas's name is never mentioned again in Luke's Gospel. Notice that Cleopas and his friend return to Jerusalem from the village of Emmaus and provide a report about the resurrected Jesus to "the eleven" (Luke 24:33). Similarly, the author begins the book of Acts by once again naming the apostles (Acts 1:13; cf. Luke 6:14-16). Here, Luke omits Judas Iscariot's name altogether from the list of apostles and consequently only mentions the other eleven names (cf. Acts 1:26). By the end of the Gospel and the beginning of Acts, Luke is actually highlighting the void that has been left by Judas.

Not only does Luke choose to omit Judas's name, but, in Acts, Luke never shows Judas participating in any of the actions associated with Jesus' disciples. Judas is not among those who converse with the resurrected Jesus, hear the exhortations of the angelic messengers, visit the Mount of Olives, gather in an upper room, or devote themselves to prayer (Acts 1:3-14; cf. Luke 22:39-46, where Judas likewise appears to be absent). Instead, Judas's betrayal is interpreted as a fulfillment of the scriptures (Acts 1:16; cf. Ps 69:25). Here again, rather than focus narrowly on Judas's disobedience, Luke focuses broadly on matters of salvation history. Judas's act of betrayal is not only directed by Satan, but also fulfills scripture.

Next, in Acts 1:16b-17, Luke continues to highlight the void left by Judas's elimination from the new covenant community of disciples. Peter refers to Judas as the one "who became (γίνομαι) a guide for those who ar-

---

31. Caird, *Saint Luke*, 235.
32. Brown, *Apostasy and Perseverance*, 82-84.

rested Jesus — for he was numbered among us and was allotted his share in this ministry." Here again, Luke portrays Judas as a disciple, who later underwent a radical change. Luke then goes on to characterize Judas's fate in the narration of Judas's death in Acts 1:18-20. In particular, Judas's gruesome death depicts him as a recipient of divine judgment.[33] Finally, we are informed that Judas must be replaced (1:25). His absence leaves a void that must be filled by one who witnessed both the ministry and resurrection of Jesus (1:22).

In short, a soteriological insider has become an outsider. Judas, who began as a disciple, has ended by traveling a different path. He has become an apostate.[34] Judas's tragic outcome provides us with an example of a disciple who does not survive the middle phase of discipleship. He began the discipleship journey, but he will not experience a positive soteriological consummation.

Peter

Even though Peter denies Jesus in Luke 22:54-61, he remains a disciple and a soteriological insider throughout the remainder of Luke's writings. For example, already in Luke 22:62, Peter weeps bitterly over his failures. In addition, in Luke 24:8-12, when the women report the news of Jesus' resurrection, they report it to the eleven (24:9). Likewise, Cleopas and his friend report their encounter with Jesus to the eleven (24:33). In both instances, Peter is still numbered as an apostle and a soteriological insider whereas Judas has been left out. Moreover, Peter retains a position of prominence in Luke's Gospel when he is the first to run to the empty tomb to investigate the report of the women (24:12).

Of course, Peter's role as a prominent leader in the community of believers in Acts is without question. In his second volume, Luke repeatedly portrays Peter as a faithful prophet, who resembles Jesus in numerous ways.[35] For example, in Acts 1, Peter is among the disciples in an upper room

---

33. Brown, *Apostasy and Perseverance*, 82; and Charles H. Talbert, *Reading Acts: A Literary and Theological Commentary on the Acts of the Apostles* (New York: Crossroad, 1997), 32.

34. Luke Timothy Johnson, *The Acts of the Apostles* (SP 5; Collegeville, MN: Liturgical Press, 1992), 38.

35. See, e.g., Johnson, *The Acts of the Apostles*, 53-55; and Talbert, "Discipleship in Luke-Acts," 64.

who are devoting themselves to prayer (Acts 1:12-14). In addition, Peter interprets Judas's betrayal for the other disciples (1:15-20a) and calls for the addition of a twelfth apostle to replace Judas (1:20b-26). Peter is the interpreter of the Pentecost event as well as the one who exhorts others to "repent and be baptized" (Acts 2:1-40). Peter and John heal a lame man (Acts 3:1-10); and after being filled with the Holy Spirit, Peter speaks with great boldness as he challenges the religious leaders and elders in Jerusalem (Acts 4:1-22). Many other examples could be cited, but it is safe to say that Peter functions as a trustworthy and authoritative disciple in Acts. He is not an apostate. He survives the period between the beginning of discipleship and the soteriological consummation.

Luke 22:31-34

Yet, we must ask how Peter remains on the path of discipleship when Judas does not. The comments that Luke provides in this regard are brief but noteworthy. Luke never indicates that Peter's perseverance depends upon the contrition that he exhibits in Luke 22:62 or even upon his later faithful actions, though perhaps they play a role. Instead, Jesus' comments in Luke 22:31-34 provide Luke's readers with the only clear explanation for the perseverance of Peter's discipleship.

In Luke 22:31-32, after informing Peter (here, "Simon") that Satan has demanded to sift him like wheat along with the other disciples, Jesus assures Peter that Peter will not suffer the same fate as Judas. Instead, Jesus informs Peter that he has prayed specifically for Peter.[36] In particular, Jesus has prayed that Peter's faith or faithfulness (πίστις) will not fail (22:32a).[37] Moreover, Jesus is confident that God will respond to his petition and intervene on Peter's behalf.[38] Jesus is likewise confident that God's assistance is sufficient to sustain Peter's faith when Peter's faith or faithfulness would have otherwise faltered.[39] Hence, Luke credits Jesus' prayer and God's behind-the-scenes work for Peter's perseverance.

36. Notice Luke's use of the second person singular pronoun — σύ ("you").

37. Many prefer the translation "faithfulness" in this context. See, e.g., Darrell L. Bock, *Luke 9:51–24:53* (Baker Exegetical Commentary of the New Testament; Grand Rapids: Baker Academic, 1996), 1743; and Fitzmyer, *The Gospel According to Luke*, 2:1425.

38. See, e.g., Fitzmyer, *The Gospel According to Luke*, 2:1422; and Marshall, *The Gospel of Luke*, 820.

39. Parsons (*Acts*, 212), while discussing Acts 15:6-12, observes that "a basically pessi-

Seen from the perspective of a cosmic struggle, however, it is important to observe that Jesus' petitions easily outweigh Satan's demands. If the Satan imagery in this passage reflects the view of Satan that is found in the book of Job as is commonly asserted, then both Jesus and Satan are appealing to God.[40] Satan asks for the opportunity to sift the disciples and is apparently granted permission to do so by God.[41] Consequently, Satan hopes that "the unwillingness of each disciple may be brought to light," thereby allowing him the opportunity to "accuse them."[42] In essence, Satan wants to expose the duplicity and shortcomings of Jesus' disciples. He desires their downfall.

Alternatively, Jesus also petitions God, but Jesus seeks to secure divine aid for his disciples so that they will survive the onslaught of the adversary. Jesus knows about the disciples' shortcomings even before the disciples commit them. Yet, Jesus desires the perseverance of his followers nonetheless. Consequently, Jesus petitions God to sustain Peter in the midst of Peter's satanic sifting (Luke 22:32).

Thus, in the end, Jesus, the "Advocate," is shown to be much stronger than Satan, the "Adversary."[43] Jesus pleads for the intervention of God, who ultimately sides with Jesus and enables Peter to survive Satan's sifting.[44] The

---

mistic anthropology" is present in the book of Acts. As a result, both salvation and righteousness must be enabled by the grace of God. I would agree and add that similar assumptions are found in Luke 22:31-34 as well.

40. See, e.g., Charles H. Pickar, "The Prayer of Christ for Saint Peter," *CBQ* 4 (1942): 135. Nolland (*Luke,* 3:1072) adds, "'Asked for you all' makes best sense in connection with the kind of image of Satan that is found in Job 1–2: Satan needs God's permission to bring the kind of difficulties upon people that, he (Satan) hopes, will reveal their lack of integrity in their devotion to God."

41. Crump, *Jesus the Intercessor,* 160. See also Nolland, *Luke,* 3:1072.

42. Werner Foerster, "σατανᾶς," *TDNT* 7:157.

43. Crump, *Jesus the Intercessor,* 155-57, 161. See also E. Earle Ellis, *The Gospel of Luke* (Grand Rapids: Eerdmans, 1983; repr., Eugene, OR: Wipf & Stock, 2003), 256; and Foerster, "σατανᾶς," 7:157. Foerster argues that the reference to Satan's fall from heaven in Luke 10:18 "denotes primarily the end of the possibility of accusing before God." Foerster goes on to explain "that though Satan's activity in general is not ended, with the total cessation of the ability to accuse he has also lost his power to harm wherever the power of Jesus is at work." Consequently, Foerster argues that we do not see so much of a cosmic battle in the Synoptics. Instead, we see Jesus powerfully disarming Satan (7:159-60).

44. Werner Foerster, "Lukas 22,31f.," *ZNW* 46 (1955): 129-33. Foerster argues that Jesus provides "priestly intercession" for Peter with the goal of countering Satan's accusations. Many, however, have argued against the notion of "priestly intercession." See, e.g., Fitzmyer, *The Gospel According to Luke,* 2:1425.

endurance of Peter's faith is completely dependent upon Jesus' prayer and God's unseen, though implied, assistance.[45] Somehow, God's unseen, intervening work maintains Peter's faith, ensures Peter's survival during the middle stage of discipleship, and prepares Peter for the age-to-come. In short, Peter is not ultimately responsible for his own perseverance in the middle phase of discipleship in Luke's Gospel. Instead, God enables Peter's perseverance as a result of Jesus' prayer. Divine aid prevents Peter's apostasy. Whereas Satan directs Judas's actions, Jesus and God ultimately direct Peter's actions.

Of course, the effectiveness of Jesus' prayer and God's work behind the scenes does not end at the point that Peter shows remorse for his denials in Luke 22:62. Instead, Jesus confidently commissions Peter to strengthen his fellow believers (τοὺς ἀδελφούς σου — "your brothers") once Peter has "turned back" (ἐπιστρέφω) (22:32).[46] Jesus never doubts that God's divine enablement behind the scenes will triumph. He knows that his request for divine assistance will overcome Satan's impact on Peter even before Peter has denied knowing Jesus. Consequently, Jesus goes on to outline the ministry that Peter will have whenever he returns from his double-minded actions.

In retrospect, the reference to Jesus' prayer for Peter in Luke 22:31-34 should perhaps cause us to reexamine other Lukan passages that include references to both Jesus' prayers and Peter's discipleship. In other words, while divine enablement of Peter's faith and ministry is alluded to in Luke 22:31-34, in retrospect Jesus' prayers for God's assistance in Peter's life as a disciple appear to be thematic throughout Luke's writings. For example, prior to the calling of the disciples, Luke alone emphasizes that Jesus prays all night (6:12-16).[47] Thus, before Peter even begins to follow Jesus and before Jesus even gives the name of "Peter" to Simon (6:14a), Jesus' all-night vigil appears to invite God's behind-the-scenes work. Consequently, from the beginning, a link exists between Peter's discipleship, Jesus' prayers, and the behind-the-scenes work of God.

---

45. Fitzmyer (*The Gospel According to Luke*, 2:1423) claims that "Peter's faith is something that stems not from himself alone; in Luke, it depends on Jesus' prayer." See also Caird, *Saint Luke*, 240; Talbert, "Discipleship in Luke-Acts," 67-71; and Garland, *Luke*, forthcoming. Garland writes, "Peter is up against something more than the weakness of the flesh (Mark 14:38). It will not be his strength of resolve but Jesus' intercession that prevents the process of sifting from reaching its intended end — the destruction of his faith."

46. On Luke's use of ἐπιστρέφω in an intransitive sense referring to a moral or religious "return" or "turning back," see, e.g., Fitzmyer, *The Gospel According to Luke*, 2:1425; and Marshall, *The Gospel of Luke*, 822.

47. P. T. O'Brien, "Prayer in Luke-Acts," *TynBul* 24 (1973): 114-15.

Similarly, notice the link between Jesus' prayers and the enlightenment of Peter in Luke 9:18-20. Only Luke indicates that Jesus is praying (9:18) just prior to Peter's confession that Jesus is the Christ (or Messiah) (9:20, cf. Matt 16:13-23; Mark 8:27-33). Consequently, Peter's enlightenment also appears to be connected to Jesus' prayers and God's behind-the-scenes work. Luke "wishes us to understand that the petition of Jesus had been effective since the Father has revealed to Peter the secret of His Messianic person and dignity."[48] Moreover, Peter's understanding of the identity of Jesus is likewise connected to the Lukan transfiguration as well (9:28-36). Again, Luke indicates that Jesus is praying (9:29) just prior to the time that Peter awakens (9:32) and a voice from heaven announces Jesus as God's Son and Chosen One (9:35). In fact, Luke is the only one who tells us that Jesus "took Peter, James, and John 'on the mountain to pray,' verse 28 (the infinitive προσεύξασθαι expresses purpose)."[49] Thus, Peter's grasp of Jesus' identity is undeniably connected to Jesus' prayers and God's assistance.

Then, at the Last Supper in Luke 22:31-34 as we have already seen, Jesus' prayer and God's assistance enable both Peter's faithfulness as a disciple (22:32a) and Peter's future ministry to his fellow disciples (22:32b). Consequently, in hindsight, Jesus' prayers and God's behind-the-scenes assistance may well be integral in the beginning stage of Peter's discipleship, the revelation that produced Peter's understanding of Jesus' identity, the perseverance of Peter's faith, and finally the strengthening ministry that Peter will have.[50] Thus, when Jesus alludes to the behind-the-scenes assistance of God in Luke 22:31-34, we should not be surprised. There has been a correlation between Jesus' prayers, God's work, and Peter's maturation as a disciple throughout Luke's Gospel.

Of course, Luke greatly magnifies the divine enablement of Peter in the book of Acts. In Acts, the exalted Jesus and the Holy Spirit enable Peter to move far beyond his mistake-ridden patterns that we see in Luke. Instead, due to divine enablement, Peter goes on to perform the kinds of works and proclaim the kinds of words that Jesus did and said prior to his ascension. For example, Peter and John heal a lame man in Acts 3. Yet, Peter proclaims that the healing takes place in Jesus' name rather than in his own name (Acts

---

48. O'Brien, "Prayer in Luke-Acts," 115.
49. O'Brien, "Prayer in Luke-Acts," 115.
50. Crump, *Jesus the Intercessor*, 157. Crump claims that "Luke has grounded not only this ongoing perseverance, but also the initial perception and confession of Jesus as the Christ, in the power of Jesus' prayers."

3:6; 4:10). Peter is not the source of healing. The healing derives from an external, intervening source.

Similarly, before Peter speaks boldly to the members of the Sanhedrin in Acts 4, Luke informs his readers that Peter is first filled with the Holy Spirit (Acts 4:8). By pointing out the Holy Spirit's involvement, Luke "demonstrates that Jesus' prophetic words in Luke 12:11-12 are coming true. 'When they bring you before the synagogue . . . do not worry . . . for the Holy Spirit will teach you. . . .'"[51] Thus, the implication in Acts 4:1-22 is that the Holy Spirit divinely enables Peter's speech.

Likewise, after Peter and John are released, they rejoin an assembling of believers (Acts 4:23). Corporately, they pray for divine assistance in both their speech and their deeds (4:29-30). They pray, "And now, Lord, look at their threats, and grant to your servants to speak your word with all boldness, while you stretch out your hand to heal, and signs and wonders are performed through the name of your holy servant Jesus." At that point, all those who pray together are filled with the Holy Spirit and begin to speak "the word of God with boldness" (Acts 4:31). Without a doubt, the Holy Spirit serves as a conduit for the divine enablement of Peter in Acts.

Thus, divine enablement provides the best explanation for Peter's maturation and perseverance as a disciple in Luke's Gospel, as well as Peter's bold speeches and miraculous deeds in Acts. Through Jesus' prayers, God's behind-the-scenes work, and the arrival of the Holy Spirit in Acts, Peter is repeatedly empowered to do what he otherwise appears to be powerless to do on his own. From the beginning of his discipleship and throughout the middle phase of the discipleship process, divine assistance enables Peter's faith or faithfulness (πίστις).

Provisions for All of the Disciples

It would be a mistake, however, to assume that Jesus only secures divine assistance for Peter in Luke's writings. Instead, divine enablement seems to be available for all of the disciples who are between the beginning and the end of the discipleship process. Even Jesus' description of his prayer in Luke 22:32 likely alludes to divine aid for all of the disciples, not only Peter.

Jesus informs Simon that Satan has asked for permission to sift all of the disciples, and apparently the request has been granted for Satan to sift all

51. Parsons, *Acts*, 62.

of them (22:31).[52] In addition, David Crump has persuasively argued that Jesus' prayer for divine enablement in Luke 22:32 included the other disciples who would also be sifted.[53] Among other clues, Crump notes that Jesus begins Luke 22:31 by referring singularly to Simon but then moves on to use the plural form of the word "you," meaning "you all," before returning to the singular form of "you" in 22:32. Thus, "while Jesus is speaking to Peter, he is actually discussing an issue of significance to the entire group."[54] Crump ultimately concludes that "neither Satan's testing nor Jesus' prayer were for him [Peter] alone, thereby also accounting for the plural ὑμᾶς. Consequently, the fact that Jesus explicitly refers only to having prayed for Peter does not exclude the strong implication that he had actually been praying for all of the apostles," with the sole exception of Judas.[55] Peter is merely functioning "as the representative spokesman for the apostles."[56] Peter functions as an example of both the failure and the restoration that the disciples will experience. Thus, by "reading between the lines," Crump interprets Jesus' intent as follows: "Satan has demanded all of you that he might sift you as wheat, but I have prayed for you all that your faith will not fail; and furthermore, for you Peter I have prayed with the intention that when you have turned back you will strengthen your brothers."[57] Hence, "Satan tries to secure the apostasy of Jesus' disciples, but Jesus' prayer protects them."[58]

Of course, even apart from the actual names that Jesus utters to God while making intercession in Luke 22:32, the references to Jesus' prayer and to Peter's strengthening ministry in Luke 22:31-32 are important windows onto God's behind-the-scenes assistance that is extended to all of Jesus' disciples in Luke and eventually in Acts. In essence, both Jesus' prayers and Peter's strengthening ministry point Luke's readers to the conduits of God's divine enablement that are available to all of Jesus' disciples. In particular, even apart from important discussions about the role of the Holy Spirit in Acts,

52. Crump, *Jesus the Intercessor*, 157. Crump writes, "The conclusion to be derived from all this is that Satan has demanded of God that he be allowed to try all of the disciples in such a way as to demonstrate the precarious nature of their faith in Jesus and so bring about their final apostasy."

53. Crump, *Jesus the Intercessor*, 157. Crump says, "Thus *the perseverance of the disciples' faith, the survival of the Satanic trials, is shown to be founded upon the intercession of the earthly Jesus.*" See also Pickar, "The Prayer of Christ," 136.

54. Crump, *Jesus the Intercessor*, 161.

55. Crump, *Jesus the Intercessor*, 161, 166.

56. Crump, *Jesus the Intercessor*, 161.

57. Crump, *Jesus the Intercessor*, 161.

58. Talbert, *Reading Luke*, 238.

the practice of prayer and the community of believers serve as vehicles of God's behind-the-scenes enablement in Luke and Acts.

Prayer

Jesus specifically teaches his disciples to request divine assistance for themselves just as Jesus himself prayed for God's intervention on behalf of his disciples.[59] In fact, prayer functions as the primary means whereby all those in the middle phase of discipleship, the points between the beginning of discipleship and the soteriological consummation, are able to request the divine aid that will sustain them. For instance, Jesus himself both provides a model and instructs his disciples to request divine enablement through prayer in Luke 11:1-4 and Luke 22:39-46. In both passages, Jesus himself prays (Luke 11:1; 22:41-44), and in both passages Jesus instructs his disciples to beseech God for divine aid (Luke 11:2-4; 22:40, 46). In essence, prayer is the human activity that acknowledges the need for God's assistance, requests its benefits, and submits to its guidance.[60]

Notice the model prayer that Jesus provides for his disciples in Luke 11:2-4. The humans are the passive participants at every turn. All of the actions are accomplished from the outside. The petitions for the coming of the Father's kingdom, for bread, for forgiveness of sins, and importantly for the deliverance from temptations or trials are all requests for divine action. In all four petitions, God is the agent who provides the resources the disciples need. Especially illuminating in light of our discussion about Peter and Judas, Jesus assumes that the Father can and will provide the means whereby the disciples can overcome the time of temptation or trial that in turn enables them to persevere until the end (11:4).

In addition, notice Jesus' warnings in Luke 21:34-36. In particular, Jesus commands his disciples to assume a defensive posture when discussing the coming of the Son of Man along with the devastating events that will precede his coming. Only the Lukan Jesus says:

59. See, e.g., Wilhelm Ott, *Gebet und Heil: Die Bedeutung der Gebetsparänese in der lukanischen Theologie* (Munich: Kösel, 1965). Ott argues that throughout his writings, Luke is teaching his readers to incorporate prayer into their Christian practice.

60. O'Brien, "Prayer in Luke-Acts," 112. O'Brien argues that "prayer is shown to be the means by which God has guided the course of redemption history, both in the life of Jesus and in the period of the church's expansion." See also Stephen S. Smalley, "Spirit, Kingdom and Prayer in Luke-Acts," *NovT* 15 (1973): 59-71.

Be on guard so that your hearts are not weighed down with dissipation and drunkenness and the worries of this life, and that day does not catch you unexpectedly, like a trap. For it will come upon all who live on the face of the whole earth. Be alert at all times, praying that you may have the strength to escape all these things that will take place, and to stand before the Son of Man. (Luke 21:34-36)

When describing the act of being weighed down in Luke 21:34, Luke employs a subjunctive aorist passive form of βαρέω. While the disciples' posture of watchfulness is important, the most powerful forces appear to be external to the disciples. A defensive posture is unquestionably prescribed, but the disciples are portrayed in passive roles as opposed to active roles. External forces act upon the disciples. Consequently, the proper course of action that allows disciples to avoid "the trap" and have the strength to escape the impending threat is prayer. In essence, the act of being alert and the act of praying function as synonyms. Without a petition for external aid and intervention, external crises will surely overtake the disciples.[61]

Similarly, notice Jesus' deeds and words as he prays at the Mount of Olives. Luke "specifies that the disciples 'followed him' (22:39). There is not the effort in Luke to put distance between Jesus and the disciples that we find in Matthew and Mark. They are with him in his trials."[62] Here, the disciples are clearly portrayed as insiders who are between the beginning and the end of the discipleship process. In addition, given the threat of apostasy and the ominous nature of Satan's sifting in Luke's Gospel, Luke presents prayer as the proper "weapon of a disciple . . . in the face of satanic attack in an hour of darkness."[63] In particular, Jesus provides "an example in his use of prayer as protection against the temptation to lapse."[64]

Moreover, Jesus twice instructs his disciples to pray as a means of divine enablement that will allow them to persevere to the end (22:40, 46). By praying to God, all of Jesus' disciples, like Peter, can survive periods of testing, temptation, or trial.[65] Thus, throughout Luke's Gospel, Jesus teaches his disciples that

---

61. O'Brien, "Prayer in Luke-Acts," 120. O'Brien writes, "The temptations to which the Christians are exposed can be endured and overcome only through prayer."

62. Talbert, *Reading Luke,* 241.

63. Talbert, *Reading Luke,* 241.

64. Talbert, *Reading Luke,* 241.

65. Allison A. Trites, "The Prayer Motif in Luke-Acts," in *Perspectives on Luke-Acts* (ed. Charles H. Talbert; Danville, VA: Association of Baptist Professors of Religion, 1978), 168-86, esp. 185.

God provides the means whereby one survives the middle phase of discipleship. God's divine enablement, which is requested through prayer, is clearly the answer to surviving the times of temptation and the threat of apostasy. This dynamic applies not only to Peter, but to all of Jesus' disciples. Hence, prayer is an important doorway to the unseen, strengthening work of God.[66]

The Community of Believers

Furthermore, divine enablement is routinely extended to Jesus' followers in Luke's writings via other believers. Recall that Jesus instructs Peter to strengthen the other disciples (his "brothers" or fellow "believers") once he has returned (22:32). Consequently, even if Jesus does not explicitly reference all of the disciples in his prayer as Crump argues, at the very least, the logic of Luke 22:31-32 indicates that Jesus has secured divine assistance for Peter, who in turn is commissioned to strengthen his fellow disciples when he has turned back from his acts of denial. Thus, a chain reaction is envisioned. As surely as Jesus' prayers serve as a provision for faltering disciples, so too Peter's strengthening ministry will also function as Jesus' second provision for his faltering disciples.[67] In essence, the strengthening work of God will flow through Peter to all the disciples.

Consequently, at the very least, the same divine assistance that strengthens Peter's faith also strengthens the other disciples. Thus, Peter's strengthening ministry is a manifestation of God's divine enablement made possible because of Jesus' effective prayer and God's behind-the-scenes enablement of Peter. For example, Peter's interpretation of Judas's betrayal (Acts 1:15-20), Peter's instructions to locate a twelfth disciple (1:21-26), and Peter's sermon in Acts 2:14-36 likely all strengthen his fellow believers (see, e.g., Acts 2:37-47). Thus, Peter's ministry to the other disciples functions as an outgrowth of God's work behind the scenes to buttress Peter's faith and ministry along with the faith of the other disciples.

---

66. We see a continued emphasis on prayer in Acts. From the beginning, the disciples are praying in an upper room as they wait for the empowerment that Jesus promised (Acts 1:8, 12-14). The believers then rely upon prayer at pivotal points throughout the book (see, e.g., Acts 1:24; 2:42; 6:4; 8:15; 10:4; 10:9; 12:5; 16:25).

67. Nolland, *Luke*, 3:1073. See also Caird, *Saint Luke*, 240; and Fitzmyer (*The Gospel According to Luke*, 2:1422), who says that Peter "will have the task of strengthening their dedication to Jesus . . . but not by virtue of any trait or character, but simply because he will be assisted by the effective prayer of Jesus."

Of course Peter's initial strengthening ministry soon morphs into the much broader ministry of the community of believers in the book of Acts. For example, we soon learn that Peter is not the only believer in the book of Acts credited with a strengthening ministry. Instead, Paul, Barnabas, Judas (Barsabbas), and Silas are all "depicted in a strengthening role" (Acts 15:41; 16:5; 18:23).[68] Moreover, as the summary statements in Acts show, the exalted Jesus and God are continuously enabling the church to strengthen, grow, and carry out Jesus' ministry. Notice, for example, Acts 2:41-47. The empowered apostles perform signs and wonders (2:43), which in turn strengthens the community of believers (2:41-47). Yet, even then, the Lord is credited with adding to the number of those being saved (2:47b). God is working behind the scenes through the community of believers to strengthen other believers. In short, in Luke's writings, God often works behind the scenes through Jesus' disciples and the community of believers to sustain those who are between the beginning and the end of the discipleship process.

Conclusion

After demonstrating that the ideas of a beginning, middle, and end to the discipleship process are all present in Luke's writings, and after demonstrating that apostasy poses a very real threat during the middle phase of discipleship in Luke's writings, we have asked how a disciple perseveres during the middle period. In particular, we have asked how a disciple in Luke's writings remains within the bounds of the new covenant relationship until arriving in the age-to-come. To look for clues, we examined the fates of Peter and Judas in Luke and Acts.

In our investigation, we observed that neither Judas nor Peter is a match for Satan in Luke 22. Both apostles stumble. Furthermore, the severity of Judas's and Peter's sinful actions appear to be similar, but the final outcomes of Judas's and Peter's discipleship are not similar. Clearly Peter survives the middle period of the discipleship process whereas Judas does not. Peter stays within God's covenant people despite his denials of Jesus. Yet, Judas's betrayal removes him from the life of a disciple. When Luke articulates how Peter's fate ends in an unpredictably positive manner, he points to the petitions of Jesus in Luke 22:32. Jesus' prayers for Peter and God's unseen

---

68. Fitzmyer, *The Gospel According to Luke*, 2:1426.

work behind the scenes sustain Peter's faith (πίστις) and enable him to remain on the discipleship path.

Furthermore, our comparison of Judas's and Peter's experiences has both soteriological and Christological implications. Luke appears to work with a pessimistic anthropology in Luke 22:31-32. Satan's schemes and the temptation to apostatize appear to be far more powerful than the good intentions of Jesus' disciples (e.g., Luke 22:33-34). Yet, the determinative powers reside outside of the human realm. Divine assistance enables one to persevere through the discipleship process, thereby positively positioning the disciple for the age-to-come. Moreover, Jesus' disciples are taught to yield themselves to that divine empowerment through a variety of means like prayers for assistance and the strengthening ministry provided by the community of believers. Hence, from a soteriological perspective, Jesus' disciples ultimately persevere because they are divinely enabled to do so.

Yet, the soteriological implications in Luke's writings are closely linked to Christological implications. Luke clearly portrays Jesus as the one who advocates for his followers and counters the Accuser. Jesus is portrayed as the protector who strengthens the weak. Unlike Satan, who seeks to expose the weaknesses of human faith and/or faithfulness, Jesus is an advocate for his disciples. He desires to buttress human faith and/or faithfulness. Rather than seeking to eliminate weak disciples, Jesus seeks to aid, strengthen, and rescue them. Furthermore, Luke shows that God sides with Jesus' advocacy rather than Satan's accusations. Jesus' petitions and God's behind-the-scenes empowerment reveal their true natures. Through Jesus' ministry, God has decisively intervened in order to divinely enable perseverance for Jesus' disciples who are between the beginning of the discipleship process and the soteriological consummation.

The Fourth Gospel's Soteriology between New Birth and Resurrection

Charles H. Talbert

In the Fourth Gospel one way of speaking of radical grace between the new birth and departure from this life is by means of the formula "Christ in the disciple" and "the disciple in the Lord." The former employs the language of the Jewish scriptures, meaning Jesus' indwelling enables a disciple's life. The latter uses the classical Greek formula, meaning the disciple is "in Jesus' hands," another way of saying that a disciple's existence is empowered by Jesus.

· ·

Introduction

Most interpreters see the Fourth Gospel's soteriology as grounded in grace (divine initiative/enablement).[1] O'Day goes so far as to claim this Gospel is

1. D. A. Carson, *Divine Sovereignty and Human Responsibility: Some Aspects of Johan-*

As a seminary student, my first adult exposure to the Fourth Gospel was in a class taught by Bill Hull on the Gospel of John. It opened my eyes to a whole new world. When his Broadman commentary on John came out, I read it with great appreciation for its close reading of the Gospel text. Hull's continuing interest in my career over the years has, on occasion, resulted in some tangible blessings for me and, on occasion, some real frustrations for him. For his continued affirmation of my calling as a New Testament scholar, I remain forever grateful. It is a great pleasure to be able to express my appreciation for him with this essay.

the most radical example of salvation by grace anywhere in the New Testament.[2] This is true for discipleship's beginning (e.g., John 1:12 — "as many as received him, he gave them authority to become children of God"). It is also true for soteriological consummation (e.g., 6:40 — "everyone who sees the Son and believes in him . . . I will raise him up on the last day"). What of the period between the new birth and departure from this life? Is this aspect of a disciple's life also dependent on radical grace? If so, how does divine enablement operate in this segment of discipleship? It is this question that this essay addresses. It will be addressed by means of a focus on John 15:1-17, where one finds what has come to be called "the reciprocity of immanence," or "mutual indwelling," or "reciprocal union."

The relevant data, of course, extend beyond John 15. There are, in the Fourth Gospel, three certain couplets. First, the Father is in the Son (10:38; 14:10; 17:23) and the Son is in the Father (10:38; 14:10; 17:21). Second, Jesus is in the disciples (6:56; 14:20; 15:4, 5) and the disciples, individually (6:56; 15:5) and collectively (14:20; 15:4), are in Jesus (6:56; 14:20; 15:4, 5).[3] Third, disciples, collectively, are in the Father and the Son (17:21) and the Father and the Son are with the individual disciple (14:23). A fourth couplet is possible. The Spirit of truth is with and in the disciples (14:17 — indicating that "with" and "in" are virtual synonyms) and the disciples are in Spirit and truth (4:23-24 — a hendiadys, so Spirit of truth[4]).[5] In all four couplets the divine person is "in" the human disciple and the disciple is said to be "in" the divine person. A variation on this theme is when disciples abide in Jesus and Jesus' words abide in the disciples (15:7),[6] or when disciples are to abide in Jesus' love (15:9

---

nine Theology against a Jewish Background (New Foundations Theological Library; Atlanta: John Knox, 1981), 198, says of John, "Christian life is based at all points upon grace; as it proceeds, one grace is exchanged only for another."

2. Gail O'Day, *The New Interpreter's Bible* (vol. 9; Nashville: Abingdon, 1995), 664.

3. T. E. Pollard, "The Father-Son and God-Believer Relationship according to St. John: A Brief Study of John's Use of Prepositions," in *L'Evangile de Jean: Sources, redaction, théologie* (ed. M. de Jonge; BETL 44; Gembloux: J. Duculot, 1977), 363-70, wrongly reduces the Fourth Gospel's mutual indwelling (divine and human) to the community of believers.

4. C. H. Dodd, *The Interpretation of the Fourth Gospel* (Cambridge: Cambridge University Press, 1953), 342; Raymond E. Brown, *The Gospel According to John: Introduction, Translation, and Notes* (AB 29-29A; 1st ed.; Garden City, NY: Doubleday, 1966, 1970), 180.

5. David L. Mealand, "The Language of Mystical Union in the Johannine Writings," *DRev* 95 (1977): 21, and Edward Malatesta, *Interiority and Covenant: A Study of* einai en *and* menein en *in the First Letter of Saint John* (AnBib 69; Rome: Biblical Institute Press, 1978), 31, contend that no Johannine text says disciples are "in Spirit."

6. Barclay Newman and Eugene Nida, *A Translator's Handbook on the Gospel of John*

— probably Jesus' love for them). From such data is derived the use of the language of "mutual indwelling" or its equivalent. Although the "mutual indwelling" is found more widely in the Fourth Gospel, this project will concentrate on 15:1-17 because this text is focused on the issue of the soteriological relation of Jesus and the disciples between new birth and resurrection. To understand the "in" terminology here will enable one's grasp of such language elsewhere and when used more broadly than in the relation of Jesus and disciples.[7]

There has been little success in locating the social context and origins of such language. Without such comparative materials there are few controls on the ascribed meaning of the language. Virtually every possibility has been suggested and eliminated.[8] No consensus has emerged, leaving room for this paper's argument. We begin by examining 15:1-17's location in the Gospel as a whole.

Clarifying the Place of 15:1-17 in the Fourth Gospel

In John 13–17 the Johannine Jesus turns his attention from the world to his disciples. After the supper with its washing of feet and the departure of the betrayer (13:1-35), there is a farewell speech in two parts (13:36–14:31 and 15:1–16:33), with the expected predictions and exhortations, that ends with a lengthy prayer in chapter 17.[9] John 15:1-17 begins the second version of the

---

(London: United Bible Societies, 1980), 483, say that there is no difference between Jesus' remaining in his disciples and his words' remaining in them.

7. This essay will not deal with the language of mutual indwelling in the Johannine epistles. One can only note at this point that Judith M. Lieu, *I, II, & III John* (NTL; Louisville: Westminster/John Knox, 2008), 73-74, 160, emphasizes the differences between the Fourth Gospel's and 1 John's usage. The differences are probably overstated, because once one understands the context within which such language is to be understood, the variations are seen to be complementary, not contradictory.

8. Jürgen Heise, *Bleiben: Menein in den Johanneischen Schriften* (HUT 8; Tübingen: Mohr-Siebeck, 1967), provides a *TWNT*-type volume that is long on details and short on interpretation. Klaus Scholtissek, *In Ihm Sein und Bleiben* (HBS 21; Freiburg: Herder, 2000), is the most comprehensive study of the issue. He provides a comprehensive survey of the history of research, allowing this essay to focus elsewhere.

9. Although influences from ancient literature on consolation may be found in John 13–17 (so George L. Parsenios, *Departure and Consolation: The Johannine Farewell Discourses in Light of Greco-Roman Literature* [NovTSup 117; Leiden: Brill, 2005]), the view that this material fits the genre of ancient farewell speeches seems secure.

farewell speech.[10] It is a distinct subunit held together by an inclusion (the language about bearing fruit recurs at v. 16) and set off from what follows in 15:18–16:4 (the world's hatred) by a focus on relations between Jesus and his disciples. The unit is composed of two main parts: verses 1-6 and verses 7-17, each with its own organization.[11]

Verses 1-6 break into two paragraphs that loosely correspond to one another.[12]

15:1-4	*15:5-6*
I am the true vine (1a)	I am the vine (5a)
Every branch of mine (2a)	You are the branches (5b)
The fate of unfruitful branches (2b)	The fate of unfruitful branches (6)
Necessity of abiding for fruit bearing (4)	Necessity for abiding for fruit bearing (5c)

Verses 7-17 are arranged in a chiastic pattern: ABCDEFE′D′C′B′A′.[13]

A — v. 7a: If my words abide in you,

  B — v. 7b: Ask what you will and it will be done for you.

    C — v. 8: Bear fruit and so prove to be my disciples.

      D — v. 9: As the Father loved me, so I have loved you.

        E — v. 10: If you keep my commandments, you will abide in my love.

          F — v. 11: The purpose of these words is joy.

        E′ — vv. 12-14: You are my beloved if you do what I command you.

      D′ — v. 15: What I heard from the Father, I made known to you.

---

10. Mary L. Coloe, *Dwelling in the Household of God: Johannine Ecclesiology and Spirituality* (Collegeville, MN: Liturgical Press, 2007), 155-58, explains the dual versions of the farewell speech as a *relecture*. The reread text looks back on the original text and develops its meaning further, applying it to a different context. The final text is a rereading of the original text. This hypothesis addresses a diachronic problem and does not affect the type of reading performed in this essay.

11. Others make the break at verse 8 (e.g., Herman Ridderbos, *The Gospel of John: A Theological Commentary* [Grand Rapids: Eerdmans, 1997]), or at verse 11 (e.g., Frances J. Moloney, *Glory Not Dishonor: Reading John 13–21* [Minneapolis: Fortress, 1998]).

12. Charles H. Talbert, *Reading John* (rev. ed.; Macon, GA: Smyth & Helwys, 2005), 220.

13. Raymond E. Brown, *The Gospel According to John*, 2:667.

C′ — v. 16a: I chose you to bear fruit.
B′ — v. 16b: Whatever you ask the Father he may give it to you.
A′ — v. 17: This I command you. . . .

John 15:1-17 begins with the last of the "I am" sayings. The other six (6:35; 8:12; 10:7; 10:11; 11:25; 14:6) have focused on "coming to Jesus"; this one focuses on those who have already come. The questions addressed in the final "I am" saying are two: first, *how* can God's people function faithfully, and second, *what* would that look like? Jesus' answer to the first is: by means of a mutual abiding. His answer to the second is: fruit-bearing (understood as loving one another as Jesus has loved them, 15:12, 16-17). Having located 15:1-17 in its context within the Fourth Gospel, it is now necessary to search for its Mediterranean social location. We begin with a survey of the key options.[14]

Clarifying 15:1-17's Place in the Ancient Mediterranean World

The Johannine Jesus here claims to be the true vine (= people of God, cf. Isa 5:1-7; Jer 2:21; Mark 12:1-11) just as earlier he contended that he was the true bread, the true light, the true shepherd, the true life, the true way. He is the true reality to which each metaphor points. His disciples, he says, are the branches connected to him, drawing life from him, and producing fruit from such a connection. If the connection is broken, bearing fruit ceases. The connection between the vine and its branches is described by the language of mutual indwelling. "Abide in me, and I in you" (v. 4); "the one who abides in me and I in him, bears much fruit" (v. 5). New Testament interpreters see the language as conveying a range of meanings that run from mystical union of the communion, not absorption, type,[15] through the most intimate union conceivable between God and humans but not mysticism,[16] to fellowship.[17] Personal intimacy is the common denominator for this range of meanings. The language used (mutual indwelling, reciprocal union) conveys, perhaps unintentionally, an equal involvement of the two parties in such intimacy.

14. For a comprehensive survey, cf. Scholtissek, *In Ihm Sein und Bleiben.*
15. Mealand, "Language of Mystical Union." Jey J. Kanagaraj, *Mysticism in the Gospel of John* (JSNTSup 158; Sheffield: Sheffield Academic, 1998), 264, contends that the union is not absorption into or an ecstatic state but communion.
16. C. H. Dodd, *The Interpretation of the Fourth Gospel,* 197.
17. Barnabas Lindars, *The Gospel of John* (NCB; Greenwood, SC: Attic, 1972), 489.

Does one find such a conceptual world elsewhere in early Christianity either before or after the Fourth Gospel? In the canonical Pauline corpus the language of mutual indwelling used for the relation of Christ and God is rare (2 Cor 5:19 when read one way could be taken as God was "in" Christ; Col 3:3 says Christians' life is hid with Christ "in" God). Nowhere, however, are the two expressions used together in a formula of reciprocity. Paul, of course, knows the language of Christians being "in" Christ (e.g., 2 Cor 5:17; Phil 4:13) as well as that of Christ being "in" Christians (e.g., Gal 2:20; 2 Cor 13:5). Again, however, there is no formula of reciprocity. Paul also can say that Christians are "in" God (Col 3:3) and that God is "in" Christians (Phil 2:13), but not within a formula of reciprocity. The closest Paul comes to reciprocity is in Rom 8:9, where he says "you (pl.) are not 'in' flesh but 'in' Spirit since the Spirit of God dwells 'in' you (pl.)" (cf. Christians "in" the Spirit, Eph 2:18; Spirit in Christians, 1 Cor 3:16; 6:19).

After the Fourth Gospel, Ignatius of Antioch uses similar language. Christ is "in" the Father (*Rom.* 3:3) but nothing is said about the Father being "in" Christ. Christ is "in" the Christian (*Magn.* 12:1; *Rom.* 6:3). The Christian is "in" Christ (*Eph.* 10:3; 11:1; 20:3; *Trall.* 2:2). The Christian is "in" the Son and the Father, and "in" the Spirit (*Magn.* 13:1). God is in Christians (*Eph.* 15:3). The two sides of the indwelling are used but not together in a couplet as in John 6, 14, and 15. These data from Christian writers before and after the Fourth Gospel show John was not the lone user of such language in the early church, but his usage still had its distinctives. The Christian evidence, moreover, does not provide the key to understanding the precise meaning of the language of indwelling. Is such language found outside of Christian sources?

There are Greco-Roman sources that, on the surface, seem analogous. Seneca offers an example. In *Ep.* 41, the first-century Stoic writes: "God is near you, he is in you, he is within you. . . . a holy spirit indwells within us, one who marks our good and bad deeds, and is our guardian. As we trust this spirit, so are we treated by it. Indeed, no person can be good without the help of God" (41.1 [Gummere, LCL]). Here God indwells a person. In 41.5 the person's "abiding in" is mentioned. He says that when a soul rises superior to other souls, it is stirred by a force from heaven. A greater part of it still abides in that place from when it came down to earth. "Just as the rays of the sun do indeed touch the earth, but still abide at the source from which they are sent, even so the great and hallowed soul, which has come down in order that we may have a nearer knowledge of divinity, does indeed associate with us, but still cleaves to its origin; on that source it depends, thither it turns its gaze and strives to go" (Gummere, LCL). Note that in both parts of the mutual indwelling the emphasis is on divine enablement.

Corpus Hermeticum also uses similar language.[18] For example, *Corp. herm.* 11.6 says, "The one who makes exists in all things." *Corp. herm.* 11.18 says, "All things are in God." Or in *Corp. herm.* 9.9 one hears: "all things that exist are in God. . . . He is in all things." The proximity of the two expressions to one another in the same tractate comes close to a formula of mutual indwelling. In this context to be in God is to be dependent on God. For God to be in something is for it to be enabled by God. In both cases it is divine agency to which the language refers.

Iamblichus, *On the Pythagorean Way of Life* 240, offers analogous data.[19] He says of the Pythagoreans: "They encouraged one another not to disperse the god within themselves (μὴ διασπᾶν τὸν ἐν ἑαυτοῖς)." Their zeal aimed at "some kind of mingling (θεοκρασίαν) and union with God (τὴν πρὸς τὸν θεὸν) and at communion with intellect (τὴν τοῦ νοῦ κοινωνίαν) and the divine soul (τῆς θείας ψυχῆς)." For no one could find anything better "than this kind of friendship (φιλίας)." This type of friendship in antiquity was understood to yield a unity of action. Lucian, *Toxaris* 61-62, says the union of three friends is like a person with six hands and three heads. "Indeed, to my mind Geryon was three persons acting together in all things, as is right if they are really friends" (Harmon, LCL).[20] The surface similarities of these Greco-Roman examples to the Fourth Gospel are offset by the fact that they do not belong to a theistic worldview.

Hellenistic Judaism might offer help in locating the intellectual milieu in Mediterranean antiquity for the Fourth Gospel's formula of mutual indwelling. The LXX knows of God's dwelling in humans (e.g., Deut 6:15 — ἐν σοί; Hos 11:9 — ἐν σοί; Lev 26:12 — ἐν ὑμῖν; Jer 14:9 — ἐν ἡμῖν; Ezek 37:27-28 — ἐν αὐτοῖς).[21] There is no example, to my knowledge, of an exact

18. C. H. Dodd appealed especially to the Hermetica for parallels to the Fourth Gospel. The critical text of *Corp. herm.* may be found in A. D. Nock and A. J. Festugière, *Corpus Hermeticum* (2 vols.; Paris: Société édition 'Les belles lettres,' 1954-1960). The most recent English translation is that of Brian P. Copenhaver, *Hermetica* (Cambridge: Cambridge University Press, 1992).

19. John Dillon and Jackson Hershbell, eds., *On the Pythagorean Way of Life by Iamblichus* (Atlanta: Scholars, 1991).

20. Lucian, *Toxaris* (trans. A. M. Harmon; LCL; Cambridge, MA: Harvard University Press, 1936), 205.

21. The LXX prefers "in" to "in the midst of."

parallel to Israelites abiding in God. The examples sometimes offered may or may not fit (e.g., Ps 18:30 — take refuge in God; Ps 3:2 — no salvation for him in God).[22]

Among the deuterocanonicals/OT Apocrypha, the Wisdom of Solomon has a notion of mutual indwelling applied to wisdom. On the one hand, in every generation Wisdom passes into (εἰς) holy souls (7:27), making them friends of God (7:14); Wisdom, however, will not enter into (εἰς) a deceitful soul nor dwell in (κατοικήσει ἐν) a body enslaved to sin (1:4). The language of "being with" seems virtually synonymous with that of "dwelling in." For example, the author says he was determined to take Wisdom to "live with me" (συμβίωσιν), knowing she would give him good counsel (8:9); he says Wisdom's "being present with" him (συμπαροῦσα μοι) enabled him to learn what is pleasing to God (9:10). When Wisdom is "in" a person, that person is enabled by Wisdom. In Wisdom of Solomon 7:27, for example, we hear that when Wisdom passes into holy souls, she makes them friends of God. On the other hand, nothing defiled gains entrance into (εἰς) Wisdom (7:25); God loves no one so much as the one who "lives with" (συνοικοῦντα) Wisdom (7:28). Here again, the mutual indwelling is seen as empowering and enabling. In 7:21-22, to gain entrance into Wisdom is to have her instruct one.

Philo uses the language of God's indwelling Israel (e.g., *Somn.* 1.148 — I will walk in you [ἐν ὑμῖν] and I will be your God; 2.248 — the same as in 1.148). He also speaks of humans being in God (*Det.* 48.4 — he lives life "in God"; *Deus* 12.2 — the soul rests "in God"; *Ebr.* 62.2 — the joy that is "in God"). In the latter instances the meaning relates to God's enabling power in the life of the virtuous. There is no place in Philo, to my knowledge, where he uses a formula of mutual indwelling. Overall, with the possible exception of the Wisdom of Solomon, Hellenistic Judaism does not provide a neatly formulated converse to the idea that God dwells in his people. Although the language of "in God" may be found, it is never in a formula of mutuality. The nearest to a formula of reciprocity we get is in such expressions as "I will be your God and you will be my people" (Lev 26:12), and "I will be his father and he shall be my son" (2 Sam 7:14).[23]

An interesting and helpful recent proposal that has been made regards Jesus in the Fourth Gospel as a broker standing in between the Patron (the

---

22. Mealand, "The Language of Mystical Union," 29, contends that the LXX does not speak of Israel/Israelites dwelling in God as a result of God's dwelling in them.

23. Mealand, "The Language of Mystical Union," 29.

Father) and the clients (the disciples).[24] As such he belongs to the worlds of both God-Patron and that of the disciples-clients. He is "in" both worlds (in the Father and in the disciples). This allows him to perform his primary role, that of intermediary or go-between. He mediates God's benefaction to God's clients; he in turn prays to God for the clients and urges the disciples to pray to the Father in his (Jesus') name. The disciples have a dual duty. They have a duty to acknowledge Jesus as their broker (i.e., his special relation to the Father) and to keep his commandments. They also owe God, their patron, acknowledgment and honor (i.e., believe in God). Broker is a modern social-science category that accurately describes the go-between role in the ancient Patron-client relationships. As such it correctly sees Jesus' role between the Father and the disciples. It offers little help, however, in understanding the language of mutual indwelling. To say the broker belongs to both worlds does not define the soteriological dimension of discipleship between new birth and resurrection.

The seeming futility of a search for parallels to the Johannine formulas of reciprocity has led some scholars to seek an explanation from within the Fourth Gospel itself. As Jesus is in the bosom of the Father (1:18), so the beloved disciple is in the bosom of the Son (13:23).[25] This reflects the Johannine community's experience of a new level of intimacy in the relation to Jesus, the Father, and the Spirit. While true, insofar as it goes, this position provides insufficient controls on possible meanings of the formula of reciprocity. At this point, we move to an alternative proposal.

A Tentative Proposal of the Meaning of John's Reciprocity Formulas

The proposal that follows will separate the argument for an understanding of the Son's being in disciples from that of the disciples' being in Jesus. When the argument is complete, I hope the reader can see why the separation was made. We begin with a focus on Jesus' abiding in disciples.

24. Jerome H. Neyrey, *The Gospel of John* (NCB; New York: Cambridge University Press, 2007), 245-46, 260-61. Neyrey's position is built on a base established by Bruce J. Malina, *The Social World of Jesus and the Gospels* (New York: Routledge, 1996), 143-57, and Bruce J. Malina and Richard L. Rohrbaugh, *Social-Science Commentary on the Gospel of John* (Minneapolis: Fortress, 1998), 115-19, 301.

25. Edwyn Clement Hoskyns, *The Fourth Gospel* (ed. Francis Noel Davey; London: Faber & Faber, 1947), 442-43; O'Day, *New Interpreter's Bible*, 9:729.

Jesus Abides in the Disciples

Although there have been claims that John 15:1-17 and its farewell speech context as a whole should be understood within a new covenant context,[26] not until Chennattu's published dissertation did we have an extensive argument for the hypothesis.[27] What follows immediately is indebted to her. At the very beginning, she argues, the reader must understand that discussions of covenant relationships do not necessarily use the term "covenant" (e.g., Deut 26:16-19). The absence of the term in John 13–17 is no obstacle, then, for reading the farewell speech within a covenant context. The Old Testament covenant relation between Yahweh and Israel, she continues, involved such things as *election* (e.g., Deut 7:6-8 — Yahweh has chosen Israel and loves her), Yahweh's *presence* (e.g., Lev 26:11-12 — Yahweh says, my tabernacle will be in you [ἐν ὑμῖν]; I will be your God and you will be my people), *knowledge* of God (e.g., Deut 7:9 — experience of Yahweh's covenantal love and loyalty is presupposed in accepting Yahweh as God), *peace* (e.g., Num 25:12; 1 Kgs 2:33 — Yahweh's covenant grants peace to participants), *promises* (e.g., of land, Deut 1:8; of God's presence, Lev 26:11-12; of guidance, Isa 41:10), *loving* Yahweh,[28] cleaving to him, keeping the commandments (Deut 11:22; 13:3-4; 10:20; 30:16), *joy* (e.g., Deut 27:7 — rejoicing at a meal celebrating covenant renewal), a *meal* to celebrate establishment of the covenant (e.g., Exod 24:9-11), exhortation *not to fear* (e.g., Deut 1:21; 31:8), and exhortation to *witness* to future generations (e.g., Deut 6:7, 20-25). When all of these components are taken together, their reflection of the covenant between Yahweh and Israel is convincing.

Turning to John 13–17 one notices such things as a *communal meal* (John 13; cf. Gen 26:26-30; 31:43-54; Exod 24:5-11; Deut 27:6-7 [cf. rejoice]), the giving of a *new commandment* (John 13:34-35; 15:17; cf. Deut 5), a promise that the *divine presence* will dwell among the disciples (John 14:16-17, 23, 26; 15:4, 5,

---

26. E.g., Carson, *Divine Sovereignty,* 510-16; J. W. Pryor, "Covenant and Community in John's Gospel," *RTR* 48 (1988): 44-51. Both are working off of E. Malatesta, *Interiority and Covenant,* who argued such a case for 1 John.

27. Rekha M. Chennattu, *Johannine Discipleship as a Covenant Relationship* (Peabody, MA: Hendrickson, 2006).

28. "Love" and "hate" are generally recognized as treaty terms both in the Ancient Near Eastern treaties and in the OT covenant (e.g., Deut 30:16; Josh 24:14-15). The vassal who observes the stipulations of the treaty (keeps the commandments) is said to "love" his suzerain (cf. Deut 5:10; 7:9; 10:12-13, etc.). The one who breaks the treaty "hates" the overlord (cf. Deut 7:10).

26; 16:7-11, 13-15; cf. Exod 25:8; 29:45-46; Lev 26:11-12), *knowledge* of God (John 14:7, 17, 20-21, 26, 27; 17:3; cf. Exod 29:44-45), *love* God and *keep the commandments* (John 14:15, 21, 23-24; 15:10, 12, 14, 17; Deut 11:22; 13:3-4),[29] an *election* motif (John 15:16; cf. Deut 7:6-7), *guidance* by God (John 16:12-15; cf. Exod 15:13, 17; Deut 1:33), *rejoicing* (John 15:11; 16:16-24; cf. Deut 27:7). The cluster of such motifs and language and their similarity to the covenant motifs and language of the Old Testament make it plausible to read John 13–17 within a covenant context. If so, then the language of a divine presence "in" the disciple individually or the disciples corporately would be analogous to the presence of Yahweh in (the midst of) Israel. Leviticus 26:11-12 LXX conveys the significance of such a presence. "I will put my tabernacle (σκήνην) in you (ἐν ὑμῖν) . . . and I will walk in you (ἐν ὑμῖν), and I will be your God and you will be my people." God's presence seals the covenant between Yahweh and Israel, entitling the people to God's protection, guidance, and provision, that is, Yahweh's gracious enabling of their existence. If the Ancient Near Eastern covenant formulas give perspective on the divine presence "in" the disciples, what enables an understanding of the disciples' being "in God/Jesus/Spirit"?

The Disciples Abide in Jesus

To date it has been easier to understand what John 15:4, 5 meant by Jesus' abiding in the disciples than to grasp exactly what it meant for the disciples to abide "in Jesus." Newman and Nida voice the difficulty in their advice to translators of John 3:21 ("The one who is doing the truth comes to the light in order that his works may be manifest that they have been wrought 'in God'"). They advise avoiding translating "in God" because this phrase has at best "zero meaning for the average reader of English."[30] Before the TLG was available, however, C. H. Dodd already noted that there is "an ancient and persis-

---

29. Loving Yahweh and keeping his commandments are accompanied sometimes in Deuteronomy by "cleaving to him" (cf. Deut 11:22 LXX = προσκολλᾶσθαι αὐτῷ; 13:3-4 LXX = αὐτῷ προστεθήσεσθε; 10:20 LXX = καλληθήσῃ). T. F. Glasson, *Moses in the Fourth Gospel* (SBT 40; Naperville, IL: Allenson, 1963), argues that μένειν ἐν in John 15 is a translation of ב דבק in these texts with "cleave to." The reason he gives is that Isaac E. Salkinson and Christian D. Ginsburg in *The New Testament in Hebrew and English* (London: Trinitarian Bible Society, 1940), translate μείνατε ἐν ἐμοί in John 15:4 (abide in me) by ב דבק (cleave to). If so, then "abide" is the equivalent to "cleave." This, of course, leaves open the question of the meaning of the "in."

30. Newman and Nida, *A Translator's Handbook on the Gospel of John*, 94.

tent usage in which the phrase (ἐν θεῷ) is exactly parallel with similar prepositional phrases used with reference to men."[31] He pointed to Sophocles' *Oedipus Coloneus*, where Antigone begs the elders to allow her and her father to stay. She says (line 247), we are "in you as in a god" (ἐν ὑμῖν ὡς θεῷ). This means she and her father are dependent on the elders' power. In Sophocles' *Oedipus Tyrannus*, there is a prayer (line 314) to the seer for salvation from defilement, for "we are in you" (ἐν σοὶ γάρ ἐσμεν). Fagles translates, "We are in your hands."[32] To be "in the seer" is to be dependent on him for deliverance. In Pindar's *Olympian Odes*, we hear that "the issue is ἐν θεῷ," which is translated by LCL as "in God's hands" (13.104 [Sandys]). The next line makes this explicit. "We shall leave this to Zeus to accomplish." Philostratus says the Ephesians belong to Artemis. They could be addressed as being ἐν Ἀρτέμιδι (*Ep.* 65). Again the meaning is something like "in Artemis' hands, dependent on her power, under her protection." This usage is also found in the *Corpus Hermeticum*. For example, in *Corp. herm.* 9.9 we read: "All things that exist are in god." This is followed by, "They have come to be by god's agency, and they depend from on high." The meaning of "in god" is clear. All things are dependent on the deity, for their being and for their continuation. In Philo the idiom is found repeatedly (e.g., *Det.* 48.4, to be "in God" means to be the recipient of God's power; *Deus* 12.2 uses the idiom to mean to be dependent on God for the outcome; *Ebr.* 62.2 uses the idiom to mean that something is derived from or is given by God). The Apostolic Fathers reflect the same usage. In *1 Clement* 30.6, "Let our praise be in God, and not from ourselves," means "in recognition of our reliance on God." In Ignatius of Antioch, *Eph.* 6:2, "good order in God" means "in dependence on God." A TLG search reinforces these illustrative examples with many more. Dodd's summation is to the point. "The preposition indicates complete dependence on a person, whether human or divine."[33] An auditor of the Fourth Gospel would, then, have likely heard John 15:4's words of Jesus, "abide in me," to mean "continually live in dependence on me." Bultmann accurately captures the gist. "*En* denotes the union in which the 'one who abides' allows himself to be determined by him in whom he 'abides.'"[34]

---

31. Dodd, *The Interpretation of the Fourth Gospel*, 187-88.

32. Robert Fagles, trans., *Sophocles: The Three Theban Plays* (New York: Penguin, 1984), 176. Dodd, *The Interpretation of the Fourth Gospel*, 188, translates, "We are dependent on you as on God."

33. Dodd, *The Interpretation of the Fourth Gospel*, 188.

34. Rudolf Bultmann, *The Gospel of John: A Commentary* (Philadelphia: Westminster, 1971), 534n.6.

At this point it is possible to bring the two types of abiding together into their original unity in John 15:4-5. When Jesus speaks of his abiding "in" the disciples, it "refers to the determination of a person's being by the thing which 'is' or 'remains' in him."[35] When Jesus speaks of the disciples' abiding "in" him, it means they are dependent on, determined by, the one in whom they abide. They are in his hands. Such an understanding of the two types of abiding in 15:4-5 fits perfectly with the Johannine context where Jesus is the vine and the disciples are the branches. Thus both halves of the reciprocal union have a similar function. For Jesus to be "in" a disciple means that one is enabled by the deity. For a disciple to be "in" Jesus means that one is in Jesus' hands. This is no relationship of equals.

It is *not* a *mutual* or *reciprocal* indwelling. Again, Bultmann captures the soteriological essence of the metaphor. He says:

> The imagery of the relationship of the tendril to the vine shows us at once that the believer's relationship to the revealer is not one of personal loyalty, in which what is given and what is demanded are always equally shared by both sides, even if the gift from one side had founded the relationship. . . . The loyalty that is demanded is not primarily a continued being *for*, but a being *from;* it is not the holding of a position, but of allowing oneself to be held.[36]

For the party with higher status "to be in" the party with lower status means the former *enables* the latter.[37] For the party with the lower status "to be in" the party with higher status means the former is *dependent on* the latter.[38]

At this point the *new* covenant emphasis becomes clear. The existence of God's people is continually enabled by the one with whom they are in relationship. Not only does Jesus abide in them and so determine their existence, enabling their lives and their fruit-bearing, they also abide in him, living dependent on the one from whom their life and fruitfulness flow. The two types of abiding speak of the same reality: radical grace between new birth and departure from this life.

35. Bultmann, *The Gospel of John,* 321n.1.
36. Bultmann, *The Gospel of John,* 535-36.
37. Hermas, *Mand.* 12.3, says those who "have the Lord in their heart" are able to keep God's commandments; *Sim.* 5.4.3 says those who "have the Lord in their heart" will "receive" understanding from God.
38. Irenaeus, *Haer.* 4.20.5, says those who see God are "in God" and "receive" of God's splendor which vivifies them, i.e., they "receive life."

Fitting John 15:1-17's Indwelling into Its Larger Covenant Context

A key to understanding John 13–17's varieties of indwelling within a covenant context is supplied by 2 Kgs 11:17 (where MT and LXX agree in their readings). The NRSV translates: "Jehoiada made a covenant between the Lord and the king and people, that they should be the Lord's people; also between the king and the people." Two separate covenants are mentioned. The first is like that mentioned in 2 Kgs 23:3. "The king (Josiah) stood by the pillar and made a covenant before the Lord, to follow the Lord, keeping his commandments, his decrees, and his statutes, with all his heart and all his soul, to perform the words of this covenant that were written in this book. All the people joined in the covenant." Here the Lord is the suzerain, the king is his vassal, and the people participate in the king's vassalship. The second is like that mentioned in 2 Sam 5:1-3.

> Then all the tribes of Israel came to David at Hebron, and said, "Look, we are your bone and flesh. For some time, while Saul was king over us, it was you who led out Israel and brought it in. The Lord said to you: It is you who shall be shepherd of my people Israel, you who shall be ruler over Israel." So all the elders of Israel came to the king at Hebron; and King David made a covenant with them at Hebron before the Lord, and they anointed David king over Israel.

Here the vassal king (David) makes a separate covenant with the people he is to rule. In the first covenant the king and people are bound to Yahweh; in the second, the king and people are bound to each other.[39]

In the Fourth Gospel, the Father (= the suzerain) is in Jesus (enabling him) and Jesus (= the vassal king) is in the Father (dependent on the Father) (10:38; 14:10, 11; 17:21).[40] This is one covenant. A second covenant is linked to Jesus (= the vassal king) who is in the disciples (enabling them) and the disciples are in Jesus (dependent on Jesus) (6:56; 14:20; 15:4, 5). In such a context, how are John 17:21 and 14:23 to be understood? Jesus prays to the Father

---

39. Roland de Vaux, "The King of Israel, Vassal of Yahweh," in *The Bible and the Ancient Near East* (Garden City, NY: Doubleday, 1971), 152-62.

40. This fits with Jesus' words in 7:16 (My teaching is not mine but his who sent me), 8:28 (I do nothing on my own authority but speak thus as the Father taught me), 14:24 (The words that you hear are not mine but the Father's who sent me), 17:14 (I have given them your word). Jesus' being "in" the Father means he is dependent on the Father. The Father's being "in" the Son enables Jesus (14:10-11, The Father who dwells in me does his works).

in 17:21, asking that "as you, Father, are in me and I am in you, may they also be in *us*." In the first type of covenant mentioned above, the people under the vassal king are related not only to him but also through him to the suzerain. In that sense, the people are "in" both (dependent on both). In 14:23 Jesus says to the disciples, "Those who love me will keep my word (those who are in covenant with me will observe the stipulations of the covenant), and my Father will love them (be in covenant relation with them), and we will come to them and make our home (μονὴν, abiding place) 'with' them" (enabling them by the divine presence). In the first type of covenant mentioned above, the suzerain relates to the people under the vassal king together with the vassal king only because the people relate properly to the suzerain's vassal (= the broker). In John 15:1-17, the focus is on the second type of covenant (between the vassal king and the people). This focus is incomplete, however, until it is viewed within the larger covenantal structures of Johannine thought in chapters 13–17.

One loose end remains to be tied up. What about the Spirit? How is the Spirit's presence in/with the disciples (e.g., 14:17) to be understood?[41] The Spirit is sent by the Father in Jesus' name (14:26) or is sent by Jesus from the Father (15:26). These different ways of speaking about the Spirit's source of origin and sending could be seen as relating the Spirit to both covenant types mentioned above. The Spirit comes from the Father (the suzerain) but is mediated through Jesus (the vassal king). The Spirit's functions relate both to the Father (the Father gives the Spirit to be with and in the disciples [14:16-17], enabling them to worship the Father in Spirit, i.e., dependent on the Spirit [4:23-24]) and to Jesus (Jesus sends the Spirit who will bear witness to him [15:26] and who will teach the disciples all things and bring to their remembrance all that he said to them [14:26]; he will take what is Jesus' and declare it to the disciples [16:13-14]). That is, the Spirit functions, in the period after Jesus' departure from this world, to enable disciples to relate properly both to the vassal king and to the suzerain. He does this as the enabler of the disciples by being in them (14:17) and by their being in him

---

41. Tricia Gates Brown, *Spirit in the Writings of John: Johannine Pneumatology in Social-Scientific Perspective* (JSNTSup 253; London: T. & T. Clark, 2003), argues that in the Fourth Gospel the Spirit is a sub-broker of Jesus. Eskil Franck, *Revelation Taught: The Paraclete in the Gospel of John* (New Testament Series 14; Lund: Gleerup, 1985), 132-44, argues that the model for the Paraclete in the Fourth Gospel is the Meturgeman (= the individual in the synagogue service who translated the scriptural readings into a targum, as well as mediated the synagogal preaching). The latter is too specific, the former too general, to be helpful soteriologically.

(4:23-24).[42] Once again, it is divine grace that enables the covenants to function appropriately in the period between disciples' new birth and their departure from this life. In so doing the prophecy of Ezek 36:26-28 is fulfilled (LXX — πνεῦμα καινὸν ἐν ὑμῖν; τὸ πνεῦμα μου δώσω ἐν ὑμῖν . . . ἵνα ἐν τοῖς δικαιώμασίν μου πορεύησθε).[43]

42. Benny Thettayil, *In Spirit and Truth: An Exegetical Study of John 4:19-26* (CBET 46; Leuven: Peeters, 2007), 229, says "worship in Spirit and truth means to worship the Father in the person of Jesus." In his reading, Jesus is the new place of worship (398). One may respond, Yes. In the Fourth Gospel, Jesus is the locus of the divine presence. One must also respond, But. This is because to worship the divine presence in Jesus can only be done if worshipers are dependent upon the Spirit (= in Spirit of truth/God's faithfulness).

43. The thought of 1 John does not exhibit the discipline of the Fourth Gospel when it comes to its use of the language of indwelling and abiding (Lieu, *I, II, & III John,* 73). The concept of the mutual indwelling of Father and Son, for example, is absent from 1 John. Also, sometimes it is difficult to determine who is meant, Son or Father. The following summarizes 1 John's usage insofar as I can determine it. (1) Jesus abides in disciples (3:24); disciples abide in Jesus (2:28; 3:6, 24; 5:20). (2) God abides in disciples (4:12, 15); disciples abide in God (4:15; 5:20). (3) Disciples abide in the Son and in the Father (2:24); there is no reference to Father and Son abiding in believers. (4) The Spirit is in disciples (if 2:27's the anointing abides in you, 4:4b's he who is in you is greater than he who is in the world, and 5:10's the believer has the testimony in himself are referring to the Holy Spirit); there is no mention of disciples being in the Spirit. The keys to the meaning of such usage are the same as in the Fourth Gospel. For the deity's dwelling in believers, the background is the presence of Yahweh in the covenant people. For believers' being/abiding in the deity, the Greek classical idiom "in God," meaning "in God's hands," "dependent on God," seems as fitting for 1 John as for the Fourth Gospel.

PART III

Catholic Epistles

Ἔμφυτος Λόγος: A New Covenant Motif in the Letter of James

Jason A. Whitlark

Understanding the significance of the implanted word in James 1:21 has divided between two lines of interpretation: (1) those that invest it with cosmological significance and understand it as something akin to human reason, and (2) those who invest it with soteriological significance and relate it to Christian conversion. The argument in this article supports the soteriological line of reasoning and attempts to demonstrate through an examination of pagan, Jewish, and Christian sources that the implanted word in James conveys the notion of divine enablement, a notion that was especially suited for articulating the hope of divine enablement for faithfulness promised in the new covenant of Jeremiah.

•   •

Studies in the Letter of James have taken two tracks concerning the meaning of ἔμφυτος λόγος in 1:21. One track understands the term soteriologically while the other understands it cosmologically.[1] The soteriological track represents a majority of scholars who correlate the ἔμφυτος λόγος with what is understood as a reference to the audience's conversion through the proclamation of the gospel mentioned in Jas 1:18.[2] Matthias Konradt is a recent

---

1. Martin Dibelius, *James* (rev. Heinrich Greeven; trans. Michael Williams; Hermeneia; Philadelphia: Fortress Press, 1976), 103-4.

2. By calling this track soteriological, I am not dismissing the presence of cosmologi-

representative of this position.[3] Konradt argues that λόγῳ ἀληθείας in 1:18 should be understood within the framework of conversion and as a reference to the Christian message of salvation.[4] Konradt goes on to show from Jewish writings such as those of Philo and *Joseph and Aseneth* that the "word of truth" was often associated with conversion in early Judaism.[5] Within the early Christian tradition it could function as a quasi-technical term for the gospel.[6] According to Konradt, the ἔμφυτος λόγος in Jas 1:21 is then the power of the gospel message that brings ongoing life to Christians and thus enables the Christian life as it is set forth in James.[7]

The cosmological track correlates ἔμφυτος λόγος with the Stoic conception of human reason.[8] By doing so, proponents of this view remove ἔμφυτος λόγος and the preceding discussion in James from the particularistic context of conversion and place it within the larger context of creation. Matt Jackson-McCabe is a recent proponent of this more nuanced view. For Jackson-McCabe the ἔμφυτος λόγος is human reason, which is given to all humanity. This reason conforms to natural law, which from a Jewish perspective is embodied in the Torah.[9] Jackson-McCabe is emphatic

---

cal terminology. Within a soteriological framework, cosmological terminology is associated with the hope for a new creation (e.g., Rom 8:18-25; 2 Cor 5:17; Rev. 21:1). Cf. Peter Davids, *The Epistle of James* (NIGTC; Grand Rapids: Eerdmans, 1982), 89-90, and Franz Mussner, *Der Jakobusbrief: Auslegung* (HTKNT 13; Freiburg: Herder, 1964), 96.

3. See also Davids, *James*, 89, 95; Dibelius, *James*, 103-7, 113-14; Ralph Martin, *James* (WBC 48; Nashville: Thomas Nelson, 1988), 39-40.

4. Matthias Konradt, *Christliche Existenz nach dem Jakobusbrief: Eine Studie zu seiner soteriologischen und ethischen Konzeption* (SUNT 22; Göttingen: Vandenhoeck & Ruprecht, 1998), 71-72. Cf. Eph 1:13; Col 1:5; 2 Tim 2:15.

5. Konradt, *Chrisliche Existenz*, 73.

6. Cf. Eph 1:13; Col 1:5; 2 Tim 2:15.

7. Konradt, *Christliche Existenz*, 79-85. Konradt correlates this with the possible reference to the indwelling Spirit in Jas 4:5 (81-84).

8. Stoics did not talk about the ἔμφυτος λόγος but ἔμφυτοι προλήψεις/ἔννοιαι. Cf. Matt Jackson-McCabe, *The Logos and Law in the Letter of James: The Law of Nature, the Law of Moses, and the Law of Freedom* (SupNovT 100; Leiden: Brill, 2000), 43-86. Stoics also spoke of "seminal reason" (λόγος σπερματικός, 124-25). Interestingly, Jackson-McCabe has to speculate about a hypothetical Greek source behind Cicero's term *ratio insita* in *Leg.* 1.18-19 to derive his only instance of λόγος ἔμφυτος in Stoic parlance prior to the Letter of James (81-83).

9. Jackson-McCabe, *The Logos and Law*, 5, 242-43. Cf. Arnold Meyer, *Das Rätsel des Jacobusbriefes* (BZNW 10; Giessen: Töpelmann, 1930); Leonard Elliott-Binns, "James 1:18: Creation or Redemption?" *NTS* 3 (1957): 148-61; M. E. Boismard, "Une liturgie baptismale dans la Prima Petri: II. — Son Influence sur l'Epître de Jacques," *RB* 64 (1957): 161-83; John S.

that the λόγος in James is not the gospel but the common possession of every human. Further, there is no redemptive, soteriological significance in the notion that God gave the addressees in James birth through the λόγος or that he implanted it in them.[10]

Both of these perspectives, however, agree that the ἔμφυτος λόγος is an enablement motif in James. The ἔμφυτος λόγος makes the imperatives of James possible. Without it, the ethical life of James's audience is impossible. Both, however, radically differ on the means by which and the scope for whom this life is possible. The first perspective restricts the experience of living this radically new life to those who have been converted as a result of hearing the gospel. Also, the power for this new life is only found in the gospel. The second perspective understands that the ability to aspire to the life advocated in James is intrinsic to all humans and only requires the guidance of the Law. Jackson-McCabe concludes his thesis by stating that the λόγος which God has implanted in humanity implies innate universal ability to live according to the Torah, which is an expression of natural law.[11]

Another important difference between these perspectives is their radically different anthropological assumptions. Each interpretive track assumes either an optimistic or pessimistic view of human volition as it respects living in relationship with God. In what follows, I will first argue that James's anthropological perspective is antagonistic to the Stoic-cosmological interpretation of the ἔμφυτος λόγος. Second, I will examine the notion of "implanting" from pagan, Jewish, and Christian sources as an enablement motif that is distinct from abilities naturally or inherently possessed. I will focus on two Christian documents, the *Epistle of Barnabas* and Irenaeus's *Against Heresies*. Finally, we will see what this analysis contributes to how the Letter of James fits into the soteriology of the early Christian movement. Thus, the thesis of this study will be to demonstrate that the ἔμφυτος λόγος in Jas 1:21 is a motif of enablement grounded in inward transformation experienced through the gospel proclamation. Furthermore, such a conception embodies the fulfillment of the hopes of renewed faithfulness to God expressed by Jeremiah, who looked forward to a new covenant written on the hearts of God's restored people. What we will see is that, in the Greco-Roman world among

Kloppenborg, "Diaspora Discourse: The Construction of Ethos in James," *NTS* 53 (2007): 247-48.

10. Jackson-McCabe, *The Logos and Law*, 196, 214, 216.

11. Jackson-McCabe, *The Logos and Law*, 243.

both pagans and Jews, ἔμφυτος could refer to divine enablement distinct from inherent or inchoate human ability. Christians, like the author of the Letter of James, also adopted this usage of ἔμφυτος to communicate their experience of divine enablement through their new covenant relationship with God. In an effort to demonstrate this thesis, let us first turn to the anthropological perspective in James.

Anthropological Perspective in James

One of the major problems with the Stoic interpretation of the ἔμφυτος λόγος is its assumed optimistic anthropology, that is, the belief in intrinsic human ability to live in accordance with the divine will.[12] Seneca is representative of this perspective. He writes, "It is easy to rouse a listener so that he will crave righteousness, for nature has given the foundations and seeds of virtue to us all. And we are all born to these general privileges; hence, when the stimulus is added, the good spirit is stirred as if it were freed from bonds" (*Ep.* 108.8 [Gummere, LCL]). The perspective is also common to Cicero, who writes, "In fact no human being of any race, if he finds a guide, cannot attain to virtue" (*Leg.* 1.30 [Keyes, LCL]).[13] Again, human ability towards virtue is grounded in creation.

On the other hand, the Letter of James embodies a pessimistic anthropological assumption. Intrinsic human ability is not adequate for living the Christian life as it is envisioned in the letter. Nor does living the Christian life only lack the application of proper instruction to stir one up to perform his or her duties outlined in the letter. The Letter of James expresses this pessimism in two distinct ways. First, James makes this explicit in his invective against the tongue. The author writes, "The tongue is a fire. The tongue is a world of unrighteousness among our members. It stains the whole body and sets on fire the whole course of life and is set on fire by hell. For all species of beasts and birds and reptiles and sea creatures are tamed and have been tamed by humanity. But no one is able to tame the tongue, a restless evil, full of death-dealing poison" (3:6-8).[14] Interestingly, Stoics were fond of point-

12. The terminology, optimistic and pessimistic anthropology, is taken from Timo Laato, *Paul and Judaism: An Anthropological Approach* (trans. T. McElwain; SFSHJ 115; Atlanta: Scholars Press, 1995).

13. Cicero believes people are naturally good but that society is the corruptor of native goodness (cf. *Tusc.* 3.2-3; *Fin.* 5.59).

14. See Davids, *James*, 143, for a discussion of the translation given here.

ing to the superior reason of humanity illustrated by the fact of its mastery over the animal world.[15] James turns this type of reasoning on its head by affirming humans' superior position to the animal world while affirming their ineptitude to master their own tongue, which is a representation of the world of evil in which humanity itself is enmeshed.[16]

Second, the Letter of James demonstrates its pessimistic anthropological assumption by its explicit declaration concerning what its auditors require in order to successfully overcome trials and defeat death-dealing desires. The author of James is concerned that his audience master their passions and desires. According to Jas 1:14-15, a person's own desires (ἐπιθυμία) draw him or her into sin when tempted, which inevitably leads to death. Later in the letter, the author states that community disputes and conflicts arise from the desire for worldly pleasures (ἡδοναί) and that their unanswered prayers are informed by them (cf. Jas 4:1-3).[17] Thus, to lead a life that leads to eschatological salvation and community peace, one must master one's passions and desire for worldly pleasures.

The importance of self-mastery is not a concern peculiar to James. James represents a concern common to the larger ancient Mediterranean milieu. Going all the way back to Plato, pleasures (ἡδοναί) shackle the soul to the world of sense-perception and prevent the soul from ascending into the real, ideal world from which it came.[18] Self-mastery is also the exclusive concern of the Jewish document 4 Maccabees. One must master all desires and pleasures (πασῶν τῶν ἡδονῶν καὶ ἐπιθυμιῶν) by reason, which is instructed by the Law in order to remain faithful to God.[19] For Philo, desire (ἐπιθυμία) is a treacherous passion, the cause of all evil (*Virt.* 100).[20] Furthermore, reason that has been trained by the Law can lead to self-mastery over desires (*Dec.* 173-74) or the "bettering of the soul and the governing part, the mind" (*Spec. leg.* 2.60-62).[21] Stanley Stowers has shown that, within the Roman imperial milieu, a key aspect of the Augustan propaganda re-

---

15. Cf. Dibelius, *James*, 201.

16. Κόσμος in James refers to the corrupt, God-opposing world system (1:27; 4:4 [2x]). Cf. Dibelius, *James*, 193-94.

17. James 4:1-3 links ἐπιθυμία and ἡδονή. Titus 3:3 links them together in a description of its audience's preconversion life. See also 4 Macc 5:23.

18. Cf. *Rep.* 519B.

19. 4 Macc 5:16-38.

20. Cf. *Dec.* 142, 151-53; *Spec.* 4.95.

21. Cf. *Spec.* 2.162-63. As we will see below, for Philo, more than instruction is needed for the virtuous life.

volved around self-mastery over the passions.[22] Those who are able to master their passions are fit to rule. This propaganda is picked up in Plutarch's *Antonius,* where he writes that Octavian's justification for going to war against Antony was that Antony was no longer master of himself, given over to luxury and pleasure, and thus not fit to rule (cf. 60).[23] Earlier, Xenophon had written, "I want a ruler . . . someone who will master his passions" (*Mem.* 1.5.1-6). Thus Stowers concludes that under Roman rule the ancient Mediterranean value of self-restraint intensified.[24]

Again, when we return to the Letter of James, this self-mastery over the passions and pleasures of this life is vital for its addressees' realization of their eschatological hope.[25] The problem according to James is that humans lack the resources to master their desires and suffer joyfully in the face of trials. Something additional is needed from God beyond the natural abilities with which humans are born. This is indicated by two motifs in James, the gift of wisdom and the implanted word. Concerning the gift of wisdom, the author states that the recipients of his letter need wisdom in order to successfully navigate the various trials of their faith so that they will receive eschatological salvation (cf. 1:2-5).[26] Within the Jewish apocalyptic context that James assumes, wisdom is a gift of God associated with life in the age-to-come. First Enoch 5:8-10 reads:

> And then wisdom shall be given to the elect. And they shall all live and not turn again to sin, either by being wicked or through pride; but those who have wisdom shall be humble and not return again to sin. And they shall not be judged all the days of their lives; nor die through plague or wrath, but they shall complete the (designated) number of days of their life. And peace shall increase their lives and the years of

22. Stanley Stowers, *A Rereading of Romans: Justice, Jews, and Gentiles* (New Haven: Yale University Press, 1994), 52-57.

23. Cited in Stowers, *A Rereading of Romans,* 53. See also Dio Chrysostom, *Alex.* 60-72.

24. Stowers, *A Rereading of Romans,* 55-56.

25. Particularly harmful, according to James, is the lure of wealth and siding with the wealthy elite. For a discussion of the eschatological orientation for the instructions given in the Letter of James, see Todd Penner, *The Epistle of James and Eschatology: Rereading an Ancient Christian Letter* (JSNTSup 121; Sheffield: Sheffield Academic, 1996).

26. The joy mentioned in the preceding verse (1:2) is the eschatologically anticipated joy of the Christian, whose authenticity has been proven by his or her trials. Cf. Johannes Thomas, "Anfechtung und Vorfreude, ein biblisches Thema nach Jak, 1,2-18 im Zusammenhang mit Ps 126, Röm 5,3-5 und 1 Pet 1,5-7," *KD* 14 (1968): 183-85.

their happiness shall be multiplied forever in gladness and peace all the days of their life.[27]

Again, for James, this wisdom is not intrinsic to the human condition as reason is for the Stoic. It must be asked for from God and given by God for the Christian to become "perfect, not lacking anything," that is, for the Christian to realize his or her eschatological hopes.[28] In the body of the letter the author returns to this theme. In Jas 3:13, the good works of the Christian are born out of the gentleness that comes from wisdom (ἐν πραΰτητι σοφίας), the same wisdom that God bestows upon the Christian. Moreover, this God-given wisdom opposes the pleasures that war within the Christian and precipitate community conflict.

Before examining the implanted word motif, we need to consider Walter Wilson's recent elucidation of the significance of the sexual trope in Jas 1:12-15 as it relates to the author's anthropology. The use of the implanted word in Jas 1:21 belongs to a larger unit in the opening introductory periods of James. In 1:12-15, there is a comparison between the "man" who endures temptation and thus receives the crown of life, and the "man" who succumbs to desire when tempted and thus brings forth death.[29] Birth into God's new creation by the word of truth in verse 18 parallels the birth of death by collusion with desire in verse 15. The author continues this dichotomy by opposing the implanted word to community-disrupting wrath and avarice in verses 19-21. Desire, in verse 14, is represented as feminine seduction that "both deludes the self, making external opportunities for sin seem inviting,

---

27. The translation follows E. Isaac in *The Old Testament Pseudepigrapha: Apocalyptic Literature and Testaments* (vol. 1; ed. James H. Charlesworth; New York: Doubleday, 1983). See Davids, *The Epistle of James*, 71-72, for a discussion and list of other references from Jewish sources that reflect a similar perspective. Richard Bauckham (*James: Wisdom of James, Disciple of Jesus the Sage* [New Testament Readings; London: Routledge, 1999], 33-34) also points out the apocalyptic-eschatological character of Jewish wisdom teaching in Middle Judaism. Grant Macaskill (*Revealed Wisdom and Inaugurated Eschatology in Ancient Judaism and Early Christianity* [JSJSup 115; Leiden: Brill, 2007], 76-89) shows that, in 4QInstruction, revealed wisdom enables the elect to fulfill "the design plan of creation." The entire project of Macaskill's monograph is to demonstrate the presence and function of sapiential traditions within an apocalyptic framework. Though he does not examine James, James appears to be a clear representative of the integration of sapiential and apocalyptic. See Penner, *Eschatology*, 279-81.

28. For a similar understanding of this notion of perfection, see Heb 2:10 and 11:40.

29. Cf. Walter Wilson, "Sin as Sex and Sex with Sin: The Anthropology of James 1:12-15," *HTR* 95 (2002): 159.

and entices the self to act on the false perceptions of reality it has created."[30] So then, how does one acquire the "manly" virtue of endurance (ὑπομονή) and overcome the "feminine" seduction of desire? Ironically, one must take the female role of reception and receive from God the divine gift, i.e., a divine birth by the word of truth and the implanted word that has the power to save.[31] Thus for the author, within the psychic self, there is a tension, a struggle, with desire that would derail his audience from achieving the eschatological gift of the crown of life. What is needed is something extrinsic to a person's natural capacities. There needs to be a divine birth and a divine implanting from God through the gospel. To the understanding of implanting we now turn.

Ἔμφυτος Λόγος

The ἔμφυτος λόγος has a connection with the λόγος ἀληθείας in 1:18.[32] As stated above, the λόγος ἀληθείας is taken by many commentators as a circumlocution for the gospel. That same deposit of truth that brought the community life also continues to reside in the members of the community to sustain them in their journey to eschatological joy. In what follows, we will briefly examine the use of ἔμφυτος as an enablement motif distinct from innate, even inchoate, ability in the larger pagan, Jewish, and Christian contexts with an extensive examination of its use in the *Epistle of Barnabas* and Irenaeus. These observations will provide a context in which to understand the use of the term in James.

While a common usage of ἔμφυτος in the larger pagan context typically means innate or inherent or natural, the term is used by some authors to denote a sense of divine enablement of particular skills. Herodotus tells the story of Evenius who, after being unjustly blinded by his fellow citizens of Apollonia, was recompensed by the gods who implanted divination (ἔμφυτον

---

30. Wilson, "Sin as Sex," 160.

31. Wilson, "Sin as Sex," 167.

32. The λόγος in 1:18 and 1:21 also has a connection with the λόγος in 1:22-23. I understand the λόγος in 1:22-23 to serve as link words connecting 1:21 with what follows. The λόγος in 1:22-23 is then more closely identified with the νόμος in 1:25. As Matthias Konradt ("The Historical Context of the Letter of James in Light of Its Traditio-Historical Relations with First Peter," in *The Catholic Epistles and Apostolic Tradition: A New Perspective on James to Jude* [ed. Karl-Wilhelm Niebuhr and Robert W. Wall; Waco, TX: Baylor University Press, 2009], 108) argues, νόμος is the imperative side of the saving λόγος in 1:18 and 1:21.

μαντικήν) within him, thus enabling him to prophesy (*Hist.* 9.94). In Homer's *Odyssey*, Terpes declares that "the god has implanted (ἐνέφυσεν) in [his] heart songs of all sorts" thus enabling his skill as a singer (22.347-48).[33]

As we turn to the Jewish context, within a matrix of understanding similar to Jas 1:12-18, Philo explains that in order for a person to bring forth the fruit of virtue and immortality, that person must first receive the divine seeds from God.[34] If, however, the intellect of that person mates with desire, then that person brings forth vice or stillborn children.[35] Philo sometimes expresses this divine activity of enabling virtue as implanting. In *Plant.* 37, Philo writes that God implants (ἐμφυτύειν) in the soul a "paradise of virtues" that lead to "life and immortality."[36] "Implanting" is a metaphor that Philo draws upon to indicate that the immortal life, a life of virtue, is empowered by God. Moreover, the soul's attainment of virtue and thereby immortality is solely the initiative of God.[37]

Of particular interest is the use of ἔμφυτος in the *Epistle of Barnabas*. Before we examine its use in the *Epistle of Barnabas*, we should note that James has some peculiar similarities with certain texts from the corpus of the Apostolic Fathers to which *The Epistle of Barnabas* belongs.[38] For in-

---

33. Pindar in *Ol.* 1.86 and *Pyth.* 1.441 speaks about wisdom as an implanted gift of the gods.

34. *QG* 4.99.

35. *Abr.* 101-2; *Migr.* 33. Cited in Wilson, "Sin as Sex," 156.

36. Cf. *Agr.* 168. Philo also often uses ἔμφυτος as a descriptor of faithlessness (*Deus* 101), misanthropy (*Spec.* 3.138), moral weakness (*Praem.* 5), and effeminacy (*Vir.* 23) in the sense of that which is natural or innate to the human condition. For a similar association of ἔμφυτος with vices, see Plutarch, *Pomp.* 30.6; *Flam.* 21.5; *Frat. amor.* 486B; *Mor.* 1026D; Polybius 2.45.1; 3.87.1; 4.3.1; 6.46.9; 9.11.2; 12.14.7; Dionysius of Halicarnassus, *Ant. rom.* 7.34.2; 10.9.2; Diodorus Siculus 19.1.3; 21.21.10. Clearly context determines whether the meaning of this word refers to something innate to the human condition or to the divine activity that empowers virtue among humans.

37. Cf. *Her.* 58-60; *Plant.* 90; *Congr.* 38. Philo emphasizes the above point throughout *De Cherubim*. For a concise discussion of this point in *De Cherubim* see Fred W. Burnett, "Philo on Immortality: A Thematic Study of Philo's Concept of παλιγγενεσία," *CBQ* 46 (1984): 450-53.

38. Because of these peculiar connections, especially with Hermas, Sophie Laws has argued that James is the product of a Roman Christian community (*A Commentary on the Epistle of James* [San Francisco: Harper & Row, 1980], 22-23). Luke Timothy Johnson (*The Letter of James: A New Translation with Introduction and Commentary* [AB 37A; New York: Doubleday, 1995], 68) points out six writings from the period of the Apostolic Fathers that are most closely related to James. Of those six writings he comments that the resemblance with Hermas is most remarkable (75-79). The relationship is so remarkable that Johnson ar-

stance, the *Didache* is structured around ethical instruction and instruction for community practices (1-15) that concludes with an eschatological exhortation (16). The body of James, likewise, is taken up with instruction concerning community behavior and attitudes and concludes with an eschatological exhortation (5:7-11). More importantly, James shares some common concerns with various documents from the Apostolic Fathers. James is supremely concerned that his auditors are not δίψυχος (Jas 1:8; 4:8) in the face of trials and the temptations of wealth. In the New Testament corpus and even in the Septuagint texts, James accounts for the only two instances of this word. When one, however, turns to such documents as the *Shepherd of Hermas* in the Apostolic Fathers, the occurrence of this term is ubiquitous.[39] We also find the term in *1 Clem.* 11:2 and 23:3, *2 Clem.* 11:2 as well as *Barn.* 19:5.

More importantly, Hermas uses the term in the context of warning his audience against getting enmeshed in business affairs (*Sim.* 5.1.5; 8.8.1) and that the pursuit of wealth leads to apostasy from the Christian faith (*Sim.* 1.3-5; 6.2.1; 8.9.1-3). James likewise is concerned with the temptations of wealth and with getting enmeshed in business affairs that can lead to apostasy and community strife. James warns against trusting in wealth (1:10-12) and against the injustices of the wealthy, who will be judged by God (5:1-6).[40] The author even questions the legitimacy of his auditors' faith in Jesus for showing favoritism to the wealthy (2:1).[41] Thus getting enmeshed in business affairs (4:13-17) can be understood as a way in which the lure of wealth

---

gues that Hermas is influenced by, even dependent upon, the Letter of James (67, 79). Dibelius (*James*, 31-32) argues that there is no literary dependence between the two documents. Their similarities can be explained by the supposition that both are drawing upon "a relatively large store of paraenetic material" (32). Oscar J. F. Seitz ("The Relationship of the Shepherd of Hermas to the Epistle of James," *JBL* 63 [1944]: 131-40) has argued that a common tradition does not underlie the similarities, especially the use and understanding of δίψυχος, but a common unknown apocryphal text shared by James, 1 and 2 *Clement,* and the *Shepherd* of Hermas. Recently, however, Konradt ("The Historical Context of the Letter of James," 111-17) has argued that James is the product of Syrian-Antiochian Christianity.

39. *Vis.* 2.2.4, 2.3.2, 3.2.2, 3.3.4, 3.4.3, 3.7.1, 3.10.9, 4.1.4, 4.2.4, 6; *Man.* 2.1, 6, 5.2.1, 9.1; *Sim.* 1.3, 8.7.1; 8.11.3.

40. The snare of wealth or its pursuit is not unique to Apostolic Fathers or James. We find similar concerns in the New Testament where wealth is seen as a competitor to one's loyalty to Jesus Christ and the Christian faith. E.g., Luke 16:13; 18:18-30; 1 Tim 6:9-10.

41. Ἀδελφοί μου, μὴ ἐν προσωπολημψίαις ἔχετε τὴν πίστιν τοῦ κυρίου ἡμῶν Ἰησοῦ Χριστοῦ τῆς δόξης ("My brothers, do you have faith in our glorious Lord Jesus Christ by showing favoritism?").

drags away a person from his or her Christian confession that ultimately ends in the failure to achieve eschatological salvation (1:14-16).

We also find other interesting terms that cluster around the admonition not to be δίψυχος. For instance, a related term for restlessness or insurrection, ἀκαταστασία, occurs in Jas 1:8, 3:8, and 3:16.[42] It is used to describe the δίψυχος in 1:8 and characterizes demonic wisdom in the community in 3:16. In the *Shepherd of Hermas*, the verb form of ἀκαταστασία is used to describe the vacillating of the δίψυχοι (*Man*. 5.2.7), who are contrasted with those who clothe themselves in μακροθυμία (*Man*. 5.4.8; cf. Jas 5:7). Ἀκατάστατον is also associated with the demonic (*Man*. 2.3). Another term we see used commonly among the Apostolic Fathers is the opposite of δίψυχος, namely ἁπλοῦς and its cognates. In the *Shepherd*, the term often means enduring faithfulness (*Vis*. 2.3.2; 3.1.9). It is also associated with how one gives (*Man*. 2.4-7; *Sim*. 9.24.2-3). In *1 Clem*. 23:1-2, ἁπλῇ διανοίᾳ is contrasted with the admonition that we should not be double-minded (μή διψυχῶμεν). In *Barn*. 19:2, the exhortation to be ἁπλοῦς heads a list of admonitions among which is the emphatic prohibition, οὐ μὴ διψυχήσῃς. The Letter of James uses ἁπλῶς once as a description of the way God gives, that is, without reproach (1:5). In other words, God's gifts do not come with strings attached. They instead represent his ongoing generosity in which the addressees can trust.

When we take together the clustering of terms and similarity of concerns between the Letter of James and some of the documents of the Apostolic Fathers, an analysis of the use of ἔμφυτος in the *Epistle of Barnabas* proves both warranted and relevant for understanding its use in the Letter of James. Ἔμφυτος, while only occurring once in James and nowhere else in the New Testament, appears in *Barn*. 1:2 as a modifier of χάρις and in 9:9 modifying δωρεά.[43] The parallels are commonly cited by commentators but never explored through a comprehensive analysis of their function in the *Epistle of Barnabas*.[44] What will be argued here is that the use of this term in the *Epistle of Barnabas* is shaped by new covenant thinking in which God will write his law or covenant on the hearts of the people (cf. Jer 31:33). Moreover, the author understands this language to refer to the enabling of the faithfulness of God's people to the covenant grounded in Jesus Christ.

---

42. In the NT corpus this term only occurs seven times: three times in James listed above, three times in Paul (1 Cor 14:33; 2 Cor 6:5; 12:20), and once in Luke 21:9.

43. See also Ps. Ignatius, *Eph*. 17.2, ἔμφυτον τὸ περὶ θεοῦ παρὰ Χριστοῦ λαβόντες κριτήριον. Here we have the "implanted standard concerning God from Christ."

44. Dibelius (*James*, 113) cites these references from *Barnabas* only to demonstrate that ἔμφυτον has passed into Christian usage.

First, there needs to be some justification for talking about new covenant thinking in the *Epistle of Barnabas*. Recent discussions of this letter have strongly argued that the author of the *Epistle of Barnabas* does not think in terms of two covenants, old and new, but of one covenant.[45] For the author of *Barnabas,* God offered the covenant that he confirmed to the patriarchs (cf. 5:7; 14:1) and to Israel through his servant Moses at Sinai. This offer was ultimately rejected by Israel when they turned to idolatry to worship the golden calf (4:7-8; 14:1-4).[46] From the discussion of this episode, Reidar Hvalvik concludes:

> That means that they never got the status as the "people of inheritance." From Sinai onwards Israel was nothing but a "people of disobedience"; they never lived in accordance with God's commandments, they never understood the meaning of his ordinances. They are a people in opposition to God, a fact which becomes explicit in the killing of the prophets. The history of Israel is thus not salvation history, but rather "damnation history": it shows the Jews are increasing their sins, until sin reaches its peak in the rejection of Christ.[47]

James Rhodes offers a helpful corrective to such a reading of the *Epistle of Barnabas.* He writes:

> If Barnabas's assertion that Israel lost the covenant at Sinai is accepted as rhetorical hyperbole, references to an occasional post-Sinaitic event, to

---

45. Cf. James Carleton Paget, *The Epistle of Barnabas: Outlook and Background* (WUNT 2.64; Tübingen: Mohr, 1994), 52, 209, 220; Reidar Hvalvik, *The Struggle for Scripture and Covenant: The Purpose of the Epistle of Barnabas and Jewish-Christian Competition in the Second Century* (WUNT 2.82; Tübingen: Mohr, 1996), 91. Hvalvik even denies that the new covenant in Jer 31 has any influence in the theology of the *Epistle of Barnabas* (150). He sees closer associations in the language of the epistle and that found in Ezek 36:25-26. Earlier scholars tended to impose two-covenant theology on the *Epistle to Barnabas*. See James N. Rhodes, *The Epistle of Barnabas and the Deuteronomic Tradition: Polemics, Paraenesis, and the Legacy of the Golden-Calf Incident* (WUNT 2.188; Tübingen: Mohr, 2004), 176n.2.

46. The Exodus account seems to understand the incident in this way as well, since when Moses comes down the mountain he breaks the stone tablets which are a representation of the covenant and then must go and plead with God to forgive the people so that God does not wipe them out. This at least is how the author of the *Letter of Barnabas* reads it (cf. 14:3). Fourth Ezra 4:23 also reflects the perspective that the written covenants are no longer in effect because of Israel's disobedience.

47. Hvalvik, *Struggle,* 146.

the prophetic corpus, to David, and to the ministry of Jesus make more sense. God continues to admonish the nation, but Israel fails to heed; he reveals his future salvific intentions, but the nation fails to perceive. The rejection of Jesus finally brings the sins of Israel to full measure. The golden-calf incident is the defining moment of a history of infidelity, of which the rejection of Jesus is the culminating event.[48]

In fact, Rhodes believes that the "one covenant" theme should not be pressed too strongly, as though the author of the *Epistle of Barnabas* was actively opposing two-covenant theology among Christians. For the author, covenant refers to the relationship between God and his people, which with the coming of Jesus has been given to the church.[49]

According to Rhodes, there is then one covenant but two peoples, where the church has superseded Israel as God's people.[50] We might go further and say, for the author of the *Epistle of Barnabas,* that the church, the new people of God, has always been the divinely intended recipient of the covenant. They are a people who have been foreseen (cf. 6:14; 13:6; 14:4) and prepared (cf. 3:6; 5:7; 19:7).[51] Jesus, through his suffering, thus gives the covenant to a new people (cf. 5:7; cf. 19:7). They therefore receive the promise and covenant of the patriarchs (cf. 5:7; 14:1) and become "people of the inheritance" (14:4). Though the author does not conceive of two distinct covenants, he perceives that the second giving of the covenant to this new people is superior to the first giving since the first was mediated by Moses, a servant, and the second was done directly by the Lord himself through his suffering on the people's behalf (cf. 14:4).[52] Thus, he refers to the covenant given a second time as the "covenant of his beloved, Jesus" (4:8) and the "Lord's covenant" (6:19). The agency through which the covenant is given seems to determine its effectiveness. With the suffering and resurrection of Jesus,

48. Rhodes, *Barnabas and the Deuteronomic Tradition,* 18.

49. Rhodes, *Barnabas and the Deuteronomic Tradition,* 180.

50. Rhodes, *Barnabas and the Deuteronomic Tradition,* 110, 179.

51. If we take the ἵνα clauses in 4:8 and 9:6 as purpose clauses, then there might be a divine necessity in Israel's disobedience so that the church becomes the recipients of the promise. This is similar to Paul's argument in Rom 9–11 that God has hardened Israel in order that the gospel might go to the Gentiles. Of course for Paul, this hardening is only temporary in the scheme of salvation history.

52. Hebrews 3:1-6 has very similar dichotomy. Jesus, the son, is compared to Moses, the servant, as the superior leader of God's people. Like the author of *Epistle of Barnabas* Moses is a part of the true people of God. He belongs to God's house, the eschatological temple, as opposed to the apostate wilderness generation.

forgiveness of sins and transformation and knowledge are given to the new people of God who had been prepared and foreseen.[53] This distinction contributes to what appears to be a two-covenant dichotomy in certain places in the *Epistle of Barnabas*. Thus in 4:8 we read, "their covenant was smashed so that/in order that the covenant of his beloved, Jesus, might be sealed in our hearts."[54] What I suggest is that new covenant thinking in Jer 31 along with other exilic streams of thought reflected in Ezekiel and Deuteronomy has shaped the way the author of the *Epistle of Barnabas* conceptualizes the Lord's covenant given to Christians, who were foreseen and prepared for it.

Though he never refers to the Christians' covenant as the new covenant, he does call it "the new law of our Lord Jesus Christ" (2:6).[55] Here the author contrasts the "new law" with the ineffectual sacrificial system of Israel.[56] This system was not in accordance with true reverential awe (2:2). This "new law," however, is "without the yoke of compulsion (ἄνευ ζυγοῦ ἀνάγκης)." Ἀνάγκη often referred to distressing circumstances a person came under that necessitated a particular choice to avoid or escape those circumstances. For instance, Jewish martyrs came under compulsion when faced with torture to force them to abandon their Jewish convictions.[57] The new law of the Lord Jesus is without this compulsion. The Lord is freely submitted to and reverenced, not through compulsory sacrifices but through the God-intended sacrifice of a broken heart (cf. 2:10). Here we have new covenant thinking, namely, God's new law brings about a people who willingly fear him and freely submit to him.[58]

---

53. Cf. *Barn.* 5:1; 5:7; 6:10; 6:11; 13:5-6. Hvalvik (*Struggle*, 151) is too reductionistic when he concludes that the content of the covenant given by Jesus is nothing but forgiveness of sins.

54. Cf. *Barn.* 9:6, where the author, speaking of the Jews, refers to "their covenant." "Their covenant" might also reflect the vastly different hermeneutical approaches used to interpret the covenant between Jews as represented in the epistle and Christians as represented by the author. In fact the author demonizes the Jews' hermeneutic by asserting that their practice of circumcision came about by the inspiration of an evil angel (cf. 9:4).

55. Hvalvik (*Struggle*, 152) too quickly dismisses this as a significant reference, stating that it is an accretion of traditional Christian terminology and plays no role in the author's theology. Hvalvik also asserts that the whole content of the covenant given by Christ is nothing but the forgiveness of sins (151).

56. Ferdinand R. Prostmeier, *Der Barnabasbrief: Übersetzt und Erklärt* (Kommentar zu den Apostlischen Vätern; Göttingen: Vandenhoeck & Ruprecht, 1999), 174-76.

57. This is a typical usage in 1-4 Maccabees. Cf. 1 Macc 2:25; 2 Macc 6:1, 7; 7:1; 15:2; 3 Macc 5:7; 4 Macc 3:17; 5:2, 13, 16, 27; 6:9; 8:2, 8, 14, 22; 9:6; 18:5.

58. In *Barn.* 11:11, baptism removes sin and instills fear of the Lord in the heart along with hope in Jesus through the Spirit.

This new covenant thinking is evidenced elsewhere in the *Epistle of Barnabas*. First, in 4:8, God seals the covenant of his beloved in the hearts of believers.[59] To be sealed by God often denotes a sense of divine preservation of the one God seals.[60] Second, in 6:10, the Lord places the wisdom and knowledge of his secrets within his chosen people.[61] In the context of this passage, this is likely a reference to the God-given ability to read and interpret scriptures in reference to God's plan of redemption in Jesus Christ. Thus, from 6:1-9, the author has been interpreting select passages from scripture with reference to Jesus. This God-given ability is vital if the addressees are to avoid the deceptive error of the evil one and thereby persevere in their Christian confession (cf. 2:10; 4:10; 9:4). Third, further on in chapter 6, the author refers to God forming the people anew by removing their heart of stone, i.e., faithlessness, and giving them hearts of flesh (v. 14).[62] Fourth, in chapter 9, the author focuses on the need to have the heart and hearing circumcised.[63] This is the mark of the true people of God, not the circumcision of the flesh, which is practiced by pagans as well as avowed enemies of God (cf. 9:6).[64] The author understands the need for circumcised hearts to be a reference to the need for circumcised hearing (v. 1). He goes on to state that God's circumcision of the hearing enables a person to hear the gospel *and* believe (v. 3). Later, the author emphasizes again that through the circumcision of the heart and hearing by God, a person is able to understand the scriptures properly. Fifth, in 14:5-7, God sends Jesus to be a covenant for a people God has prepared. The result of this covenant entails "redeeming [their] hearts from darkness, hearts that were already paid out to death and given over to the lawlessness of deceit." Sixth, in 16:7, the author describes the preconversion condition of his auditors as having "corrupt and weak" hearts that were "full of idolatry" and were a "house of demons, because [they] did everything in opposition to God."[65] God delivered them because

59. Cf. Paget (*Barnabas*, 115, 219), who understands this language to have been shaped by the promise of a new covenant in Jer 31. Hvalvik (*Struggle*, 155) believes this is a reference to baptism. While the sealing of the heart might occur for the community at the moment of baptism (so Hvalvik), the language appears to be shaped by new covenant promises (so Paget).

60. Cf. Eph 1:13; Rev 7:1-17; Ezek 9:1-11.

61. Cf. *Barn.* 10:11 where the Lord's teaching is received in the heart.

62. Cf. Ezek 36:26-27.

63. Cf. Deut 30:6.

64. This is how I understand the reference to "even the Egyptians."

65. When Jesus called his first disciples they were "lawless and beyond all sin" in order to demonstrate that he had come to call sinners and not the righteous (*Barn.* 5:9 [LCL, Ehrman]).

he himself indwelt them and gave them repentance. With God dwelling in the believer, there also dwells his word of faith, promises, demands, and prophecies (vv. 8-9). Finally, *Barn.* 21:6 exhorts the addressees to become Θεοδίδακτοι.[66] This term is used in one place in the New Testament, 1 Thess 4:9. Here, Paul describes the Thessalonian Christians as those who have been θεοδίδακτοι, thus, no one had to teach them to love one another. This is an apt term within the framework of new covenant thinking. We know that new covenant fulfillment shaped and influenced Paul's own conception of how God and Christians related within the inauguration of a new creation in Jesus Christ.[67] Furthermore, Jeremiah prophesied that in the new covenant the restored people of God would not teach one another to know God and his ways but that God himself would impart this knowledge to each of them. He would write his law on their hearts. In summary, the author of the *Epistle of Barnabas* draws upon all the variegated ways the exilic prophets and historians expressed God's redemptive enablement of the people's faithfulness. I would suggest, however, because of the centrality of the covenant in the epistle that new covenant thinking provides the umbrella under which these other motifs operate.

All the examples demonstrate how entrenched is new covenant thinking in the *Epistle of Barnabas*. With such an emphasis upon the need of an inward work by God in his people, ἔμφυτος is an appropriate term to describe God's salvific enabling activity within the believer. In 1:2, the author rejoices in the "implanted grace of the spiritual gift (ἔμφυτον τῆς δωρεᾶς πνευματικῆς χάριν)" received by his addressees. The likely referent to this phrase is the poured-out Spirit in 1:3. In the *Epistle of Barnabas*, the Spirit

---

66. Θεοδίδακτος seems to be a Christian adaptation of the more common αὐτοδίδακτος in pagan and Jewish literature. In *Od.* 22.347, the term indicates that one's abilities were not learned from humans but given directly from the gods. See also Philo, *Fug.* 166; *Sacr.* 79; *Congr.* 36. In *Mut.* 88 and *Somn.* 1.160, however, the term can carry the sense of ability/knowledge naturally possessed. Θεοδίδακτος eliminates any confusion that the knowledge/ability attained is inchoate or obtained by a person's own effort but is derived from God.

67. Cf. Petrus J. Gräbe, *Der neue Bund in der frühchristlichen Literatur* (Forschung zur Bibel; Würzburg: Echter Verlag, 2001), 202. John S. Kloppenborg ("Philadelphia, Theodidaktos and the Dioscuri: Rhetorical Engagement in 1 Thessalonians 4:9-12," *NTS* 39 [1993]: 265-89) has attempted to argue that Paul coins this unique term with reference to the brotherly love exemplified by the deified Dioscuri. While Kloppenborg's argument merits consideration, that Paul would allude to pagan deities as an example worthy to imitate is hard to believe. It seems more likely that this term is an adaptation of the more common αὐτοδίδακτος for the reasons cited in n. 66 above.

prepares the people for Jesus and his covenant (19:7), prophesies (6:14; 9:2, 7; 10:2; 14:4), instructs God's people (10:9), and instills fear and hope (11:11). Within the overall context of the letter, this phrase (ἔμφυτον τῆς δωρεᾶς πνευματικῆς χάριν) contributes to the understanding of God's enabling work through the covenant that he has initiated in Jesus. Notice here, the notion of ἔμφυτος is not something natural or innate to the believer, but an indwelling gift given by God to the addressees in order to overcome a "corrupt and weak" heart given over to opposition to God. The second occurrence of ἔμφυτος comes in 9:9. Here the author refers to the "implanted gift of the covenant (τὴν ἔμφυτον δωρεὰν διαθήκης)."[68] Here again, ἔμφυτος does not carry the idea of innate or natural but seems to be a reference to the new covenant that God will put within his people (cf. Jer 31:33). This passage concludes a discussion of the true sign of the covenant, the circumcision of the heart and hearing of the addressees, so that they might believe and obey. Both of these uses of ἔμφυτος in the *Epistle of Barnabas* serve as a soteriological enabling motif associated with the covenant inaugurated by Jesus Christ.

Also noteworthy is Irenaeus's use of ἔμφυτος, because Irenaeus employs the language of implanting within the context of new covenant enablement. First, for Irenaeus, the advent of Christ has brought forth the new covenant, which he refers to as the law that gives life (*Haer.* 4.34.4). Irenaeus elsewhere explains that this new covenant/law did not abrogate the precepts of the old covenant but extended them while also providing the liberating power to fulfill this heightened interpretation of the Mosaic Law. With the new covenant, God gives a new heart and a new spirit, thereby announcing freedom so that God's chosen people might bring forth his praises (*Haer.* 4.33.14). More importantly, for our purposes, Irenaeus uses the language of implanting to speak of this new covenant enabling. Irenaeus states, "These things [referring to Christ's extension of the commandments in the Sermon on the Mount] he did not teach in order to oppose the law but fulfill the law and implant (ἐμφύων) the righteous requirements of the law within us" (*Haer.* 4.13.1).[69] Irenaeus goes on to contrast the bondage of the old covenant with the "Word that set free the soul" (*Haer.* 4.13.2). Moreover, these teachings of freedom increase subjection and thus service to God.[70] For

68. Some manuscripts have διδαχῆς instead of διαθήκης.

69. Unless otherwise indicated the translations are my own. The Greek text consulted was Irénée de Lyon, *Contre les hérèses* 4, part 2 (SC 100; Paris: Éditions du Cerf, 1965).

70. Δὲ δόγματα τῆς ἐλευθερίας καὶ αὐξηθῆναι τὴν πρὸς τὸν Βασιλέα ὑποταγήν.

Irenaeus, the extension of the commandments by Jesus implies there is a greater freedom because "a greater subjection and piety has been implanted (ἐμπεφυκυῖαν) in us towards our liberator" (*Haer.* 4.13.3). This close association of implantation, freedom, and the new covenant will be important when we return to James.

All these examples from pagan, Jewish, and Christian texts associate ἔμφυτος and its cognates with divine enablement. This enablement is not an innate or inherent ability of humanity, but something that is additional to and goes beyond inherent, created abilities. Within the Christian context, ἔμφυτος and its cognates are adapted to new covenant thinking by the author of the *Epistle of Barnabas* and Irenaeus.

῎Εμφυτος Λόγος and James

When we read James in light of the previous analysis, Konradt's conclusion about ἔμφυτος λόγος is apt. The implanted word is not just the cause of the Christian life but also its ongoing power. It brings one to eschatological salvation, sets one free from death to life in the present, and makes the imperatives of the author's exhortations and admonitions possible.[71] The implanted word frees the Christian from death-dealing desire and creates the possibility of doing the good defined by the author's interpretation of the Law. Moreover, the language of implantation is how new covenant thinking finds expression in the Letter of James. Other scholars have instinctively noted this connection.[72] The *Epistle of Barnabas* and Irenaeus provide warrant for associating the language of ἔμφυτος with new covenant thinking within a Christian context.

Thus, Richard Bauckham's line of reasoning about the "perfect law that brings freedom" in Jas 1:25 and its relationship to the "implanted word" is fitting, especially if we invest τέλειος with eschatological significance.[73] Bauckham writes:

71. Konradt, *Christliche Existenz*, 85. Konradt prefers "inborn" instead of "implanted" as the translation of ἔμφυτος in view of the birthing metaphor used in 1:18 (77).

72. Cf. Konradt, *Christliche Existenz*, 78-79; Rinaldo Fabris, *Legge della Libertà in Giacomo* (Supplementi alla RivistB 8; Brescia: Paideia, 1977); Luke Cheung, *The Genre, Composition and Hermeneutics of the Epistle of James* (Paternoster Biblical Monograph Series; Milton Keynes: Paternoster Press, 2003), 90-91.

73. Cf. Mussner, *Jakobusbrief*, 108-9; also cited in Martin, *James*, 51. Konradt, *Christliche Existenz*, 95-97, notes that freedom is not a quality of the law but of the Christian

It is difficult to be sure what James means by the unparalleled term "law of freedom" (1:25; 2:12), but in a context of Jewish thought the reference is presumably to the freedom to serve God, freedom from sin, freedom from the evil inclination which otherwise succumbs to temptation, and produces sin and death (1:14-15). In that case, it should probably be related to "birth by the word of truth" (1:18; cf. Ezek. 11:19; 36:26; Ps. 51[50]:10?) and "the implanted word" (1:21; cf. Jer. 31:27?), which give the ability to overcome the evil inclination and set one free to serve God in obedience to his law. Behind these ideas would seem to lie Jeremiah's prophecy of the new covenant (31[LXX 38]:31-34; cf. Ezek. 11:19-20; 36:26-27).[74]

Finally, Davids has noted that the call to receive the word that has already been implanted sounds contradictory.[75] To "receive the implanted word which has the power to save your soul,"[76] however, has an interesting parallel with a Pauline enablement motif that can possibly elucidate this paradox.[77] In Gal 3:27, Paul states, "as many of you as were baptized in Christ have put on Christ."[78] In Rom 13:14, he exhorts the Roman Christians "to put

---

who, empowered by the implanted word, follows the law. According to Philo, the surest freedom is service to the only God (cf. *Conf.* 94). The whole of Philo's *Quod omnis probus liber sit* was written to demonstrate that "every virtuous person is free" while every worthless or bad person is a slave (1:1). Luke Cheung (*Epistle of James,* 94-95) also sees this language grounded in the Exodus typology. Israel is freed from slavery in Egypt in order to love and serve God within a covenant relationship. Philo in *Her.* 58-60 (cf. *Conf.* 94) likewise uses the Exodus motif to talk about the deliverance of the soul from vice to virtue.

74. Bauckham, *James,* 146. See also, Martin, *James,* 50-51.

75. Davids, *James,* 95. Jackson-McCabe's Stoic interpretation runs into thorny problems with this language. He admits that Stoics never talked about hearing, receiving, or doing the λόγος (*The Logos and Law,* 135). He ends up equating the implanted logos not with Stoic reason, as he proposed, but with the Torah as the external expression of natural law (137).

76. Konradt, *Christliche Existenz,* 80. Konradt also prefers "has the power to save" over "is able to save" as the translation of δυνάμενον σῶσαι in Jas 1:21. That preference is followed here.

77. Margaret M. Mitchell, "The Letter of James as a Document of Paulinism," in *Reading James with New Eyes: Methodological Reassessments and the Letter of James* (ed. Robert L. Webb and John S. Kloppenborg; LNTS 342; London: T. & T. Clark, 2007), 87, has also recognized that James shares the forms and paradoxes of paranesis similar to Paul. She writes, "the recipients [of James] . . . are admonished and encouraged not just to be hearers (ἀκροαταί) of the law, but doers (ποιηταί) (Jas 1.22-23; Rom 2.13), even as the ethical impulse to do the good is theoretically already said to be within them (Jas 1.21; Gal 5.18)."

78. Cf. Eph 6:11; Col 3:12.

on the Lord Jesus Christ." Moreover, both the exhortation in Romans and that in James follow upon the exhortation to "take off" (ἀποτίθημι) certain vices unbecoming one's Christian confession. Charles Talbert has demonstrated that the language of clothing or putting on is a way that divine enablement of the Christian life would have been understood. He writes, "To be clothed by Christ means to be transformed by Christ and to be enabled by Christ with Christ's own power."[79] Thus, both in James and in Galatians and Romans, we have an exhortation to embrace and receive the ongoing, post-conversion power from God in order to live as a faithful follower of Jesus Christ. While both Paul and the author of James acknowledge that the Christian's life is from God from beginning to end, they also both acknowledge that their addressees are not passive recipients of this power. They must continue to recognize their ongoing need to appropriate God's power to withstand temptation and inherit life in the age-to-come.

So then, what do these observations have to say about James's place in the broader early Christian mission? Margaret Mitchell has argued that James is a letter written within Paulinism and attempts to show that Paul and the "pillar apostles" are on the same page.[80] If this is the case, I would argue that an element of the script from that page is a shared soteriological pattern.[81] James is not a fringe element of early Christianity that represents "a form of the Christian movement where soteriology centered not on rebirth through 'the gospel,' but on observance of the Torah."[82] James does not attempt to give balance to Paul's radical view of grace *by* minimizing the role

---

79. Charles Talbert, "Paul, Judaism, and the Revisionists," *CBQ* 63 (2001): 21. The baptismal context in Paul's exhortation is noteworthy in light of the argument made by Franz Mussner (*Jakobusbrief*, 95-96, and "Die Tauflehre des Jakobusbriefes," in *Ziechen des Glauben* [ed. Hansjörg Auf der Maur and Bruno Kleinheyer; Freiburg: Herder, 1972], 61-67), that the instruction in the Letter of James assumes a baptismal context.

80. Mitchell, "The Letter of James," 87. See also David Nienhuis, "The Letter of James as a Canon-Conscious Pseudepigraph," in Niebuhr and Wall, eds., *The Catholic Epistles and Apostolic Tradition*, 189, who agrees with Mitchell's assessment.

81. Robert Wall ("A Unifying Theology of the Catholic Epistles," in Niebuhr and Wall, eds., *The Catholic Epistles and Apostolic Tradition*, 27-28, 35) seems to suggest that while the Pauline corpus emphasizes the grace of initiation into the community, James and the other Catholic Epistles focus on the necessity of ongoing obedience to participate in the final triumph. While I agree that perseverance is necessary to experience the final triumph, James like Paul understands that perseverance to be divinely enabled by God.

82. Jackson-McCabe, *Logos and Law*, 253; cf. 243. Observance of the Torah as filtered through the Jesus tradition was important for James, but not to the exclusion of the rebirthing and enabling power of the implanted word of truth.

and power of the gospel to live righteously before God. James participates in Paul's full-orbed understanding of grace and uniquely articulates the necessity of a gospel-empowered life from beginning to end for the realization of eschatological salvation.[83]

83. The enabling power of the λόγος in James can also be seen in 1 Peter. Postulating that 1 Pet 1:22–2:2 and Jas 1:18-21 are dependent upon a shared tradition, Konradt ("The Historical Context of the Letter of James," 109) writes, "In 1 Peter therefore the tradition is tailored to provide the indicative foundation for 1:22b, or more exactly, for the perpetuance and steadfastness of love. The call for permanent brotherly love results consequently from the fact that the effective word, to which Christians owe their conversion, is not transitory, but remains eternally. It does not merely give one single impulse, but works permanently, continuously providing the necessary vital elements for the new life."

Milk to Grow On: The Example of Christ in 1 Peter

Clifford A. Barbarick

In 1 Peter, the Christian community lives between two revelations of Jesus (1:7, 13, 20); and while they are tested in the time between the revelations, the power of God protects them (1:5-7). The metaphor of rebirth describes the work of God in all these moments of Christian life. He gave them new birth through his living and enduring word (1:22-23), and now he nourishes the newly born with his word-milk in order to grow them into eschatological salvation (2:2-3). The example of Christ (2:4-10, 18-25) functions as the word-milk that nourishes the Christian community in the time between the revelations, a function that fits within the ancient understanding of *exempla*.

•   •

The call to imitate the pattern of Christ stands at the heart of 1 Peter (2:21-25), but how should we understand the function of that pattern in the post-conversion lives of the Petrine community? What is the soteriological value of the example of Christ? Morna Hooker finds the language of imitation soteriologically inadequate. Commenting on Paul, she claims, "Appeals to imitate the example of others are all very well, but do not in the long run provide the power which is necessary to put the appeal into effect."[1] In his recent monograph on 1 Peter, J. de Waal Dryden offers a more hopeful analysis of the value of Christ's example, stating, "Christ is not only an exemplar,

---

1. Morna D. Hooker, *Pauline Pieces* (London: Epworth Press, 1979), 78.

but also a savior. He not only provides a model, but also the *means* for the moral life."[2] He affirms that Christ as exemplar can simultaneously be both the pattern for life and the power that enables imitation. He does not adequately explain how this is so in 1 Peter, however. The present study will demonstrate how the example of Christ functions soteriologically within the conceptual framework of 1 Peter. In short, the author of 1 Peter portrays the example of Christ as the "milk" that nourishes the Christian community after their conversion and grows them into eschatological salvation. After establishing the situation of the Petrine audience, we will outline the metaphor of rebirth that the author uses to describe both the conversion and post-conversion experiences of his audience. We will conclude by reviewing the function of *exempla* in ancient paranesis and showing how the example of Christ functions as part of the metaphor of rebirth.

Living between the Revelations

In 1 Peter, the Christian community lives between two revelations of Jesus. He *was revealed* (φανερωθέντος) at the end of the ages (1:20), and he *will be revealed* in the future (ἐν ἀποκαλύψει Ἰησοῦ Χριστοῦ, 1:7, 13; φανερωθέντος τοῦ ἀρχιποίμενος, 5:4). The first revelation was Jesus' advent within human history, and in particular it connotes the suffering and resurrection of Jesus. The prophets, filled with the Spirit of Christ, testified in advance to this first revelation (1:10-11); and although the Petrine community did not personally witness the suffering and glorification of Jesus, it is made present to them through the proclamation of the good news. For them, in other words, the first revelation is the initial proclamation of the suffering and glorification of Jesus Christ that precipitated their conversion.

The second revelation will be the eschatological advent of Jesus. When God reveals Jesus again in the last time, he will also reveal the salvation he has prepared and kept ready for his children (1:5). Jesus will bring them grace when he is revealed (1:13), consummating the goal of their faith, the salvation of their souls (1:9). Hope for the future revelation thus marks the present experience of the Christian community (1:3, 13). First Peter 1:8-9 positions the audience between these two revelations and might be paraphrased as follows: "Although you did not witness Jesus during his first revelation, you

---

2. J. de Waal Dryden, *Theology and Ethics in 1 Peter: Paraenetic Strategies for Christian Character Formation* (WUNT 209; Tübingen: Mohr-Siebeck, 2006), 173.

love him; and even though you do not see him now because you are waiting for him to be revealed in the future, you have utmost confidence in his coming revelation and the salvation it will bring, and thus you can rejoice with an indescribable joy."

For the audience of 1 Peter, "various trials" fill the time between the revelations. Because of the exclusive monotheism of the Christian community, they have withdrawn from participation in the Roman religious cult and have suffered religious, political, and social repercussions. Glimpses of their plight abound in 1 Peter, but 4:3-4 states it most succinctly. They once joined with their associates (co-workers, neighbors, friends, family members) in Gentile-like living. Now that they abstain from idolatry and licentiousness, their associates are surprised, "and so they blaspheme." The author describes their change in lifestyle as a movement from darkness into light, from having no identity to being part of God's own people (2:9-10). From the author's viewpoint, they have been ransomed from the futile ways of their ancestors, but the audience's former associates would have described the change in behavior differently.

The withdrawal from all forms of honoring the Roman gods would have led to various accusations. From a religious perspective, their refusal to honor the gods would have been considered atheism. Because the Roman cult functioned to placate the gods and thus protect the city and ensure future benefaction from the gods, however, participation in the Roman cult was more than a religious duty. It was also a matter of civic duty. Therefore, abstention would have been considered unpatriotic and possibly treasonous. Also, a Christian convert who refused to worship the household gods threatened the stability of the οἶκος, the basic building block of ancient society. As a result, "the Christian mission was necessarily understood as an attack on the social foundations."[3] Christian slaves and wives who converted apart from the rest of the household would have been labeled insubordinate "home-wreckers," and the community as a whole would have been labeled anti-social "haters of humanity" for the perceived threat they posed to society. The family and neighbors of the converted Christians would have responded by applying social pressure — through verbal abuse, economic restrictions, or other forms of ostracizing — in order to correct the social deviancy.

First Peter shows evidence of the verbal abuse the community is suffering. As mentioned above, their neighbors blaspheme (βλασφημοῦντες)

---

3. Reinhard Feldmeier, *The First Letter of Peter: A Commentary on the Greek Text* (trans. Peter H. Davids; Waco, TX: Baylor University Press, 2008), 8.

on account of their changed behavior (4:4). The author states elsewhere that they are unjustly accused of evildoing (καταλαλοῦσιν ὑμῶν ὡς κακοποιῶν; 2:12; cf. 3:16) and therefore will potentially suffer for doing good (2:20; 3:14, 17). Jesus, the living stone, was rejected by mortals (ὑπὸ ἀνθρώπων ἀποδεδοκιμασμένον) despite being chosen by God, and the author calls his audience to be like living stones who, though rejected by mortals because of their election by God, will not be put to shame (καταισχυνθῇ) if they trust Jesus, the rejected cornerstone (2:4-6). Jesus also refused to return abuse for the abuse he suffered (2:23), an attitude the author calls his audience to emulate when they receive abuse (3:9).

Joel Green nicely summarizes the situation of the Petrine community: "These are people whose commitments to the lordship of Christ have led to transformed dispositions and behaviors that place them on the margins of respectable society. Their allegiance to Christ has won for them animosity, scorn, and vilification."[4] They were once "insiders" in society, but they have defected from cultural norms by joining the Christian community, becoming in the process "foreigners."[5] Thus, the author addresses them as "aliens and exiles" (παροίκους καὶ παρεπιδήμους, 2:11). They are experiencing the "flipside of election."[6] Belonging to God and his family results in an otherness that places them on the margins of society and exposes them to forms of social control that include shaming through "name-calling or public ostracism or malice."[7]

During this period of trials in the time between the revelations of Jesus, God sustains and protects the Christian community. The author of 1 Peter affirms that their present suffering is neither meaningless nor outside of God's control. He describes their "fiery ordeal" as a period of testing that he likens to a refining fire that purifies precious (though perishable) metals (1:7). Their sufferings are one means of preparing them for the second revelation of Christ. Second, the author affirms that the arc of their lives matches Jesus'. He moved through shame and suffering into vindication and glory, and their narrative will mirror his. He is their pattern; they should neither fear nor be surprised by their present suffering (2:21; 4:1). Third, the author regularly employs language that reveals God as the enabling power that will

4. Joel B. Green, *1 Peter* (THNTC; Grand Rapids: Eerdmans, 2007), 196.

5. Miroslav Volf, "Soft Difference: Reflections on the Relation Between Church and Culture in 1 Peter," *ExAud* 10 (1994): 18-19.

6. Feldmeier, *The First Letter of Peter*, 14-15. See also Lutz Doering, "First Peter as Early Christian Diaspora Letter," in *The Catholic Epistles and Apostolic Tradition* (ed. Karl-Wilhelm Niebuhr and Robert W. Wall; Waco, TX: Baylor University Press, 2009), 231.

7. Green, *1 Peter*, 194.

sustain the community during their time of testing. They are "protected by the power of God" while they await the salvation prepared for them (1:5); God supplies the words and strength they need to live out the ethical demands of the present time (4:11); after a short time of suffering, God will "restore, support, strengthen, and establish" them (5:10).

For the author of 1 Peter, all three moments of the Christian life outlined above — the moment of conversion associated with the first revelation of Christ, the Christian life marked by hope in the midst of various trials, and the eschatological salvation that awaits the community and grounds their present hope — have soteriological significance. In other words, "for Peter, salvation is past, present, and future."[8] And in all three moments, the Christian community relies ultimately on the enabling power of their gracious Father. To communicate the community's dependence on divine enablement in every part of the "soteriological journey," the author employs the metaphor of new birth and growth to maturation.

New Birth through the Living and Enduring Word

In the opening verses of 1 Peter, the author characterizes his community as those to whom God has given "new birth (ἀναγεννήσας) into a living hope through the resurrection of Jesus Christ" (1:3). He returns to the vivid image in 1:23 when he asserts, "You have been born anew (ἀναγεγεννημένοι), not of perishable but of imperishable seed, through the living and enduring word of God." Green notes that in 1 Peter the "existential beginning point of this [soteriological] journey is entry into the new reality to which Peter refers as God's having 'given us new birth' (1:3)."[9] The provision of God at this beginning point is clear: he is the subject of the indicative verb in 1:3 and the implied subject of the passive verb in 1:23. He regenerates through his enduring word, and they are the recipients of his gracious action. Eugene Boring notes that the rebirth metaphor aptly describes God's role in conversion: "Just as God's act in raising Jesus was the divine overturning of all human possibilities, so begetting and birth is an apt metaphor for the conversion process: none of us decides to be born, the initiative is prior and apart from us, we simply find ourselves having been given life."[10]

---

8. Green, *1 Peter*, 274.
9. Green, *1 Peter*, 276.
10. M. Eugene Boring, *1 Peter* (ANTC; Nashville: Abingdon, 1999), 62.

Along with depicting the moment of conversion, the rebirth metaphor also describes the present situation of the Christian community. Rebirth results in new kinship relationships. The community now relates to God as Father (1:17), and they should act as his obedient children. As God's children, they are now heirs (1:4), an image that captures the "in-between-ness" of their life between the revelations of Jesus. They are guaranteed to receive the imperishable inheritance that will be revealed at the eschaton, but they have not received it yet. The assurance of the coming inheritance, however, allows them to live with hope during their present crisis.

Following their new birth, the community's members also relate to one another as siblings, and they are called to love one another in accordance with this new relationship (1:22). The metaphor of rebirth affirms that "they are not called to be heroic individuals but members of a family that cares for and supports them."[11] Conversion and relationship with God, therefore, should never be misunderstood as a purely individual experience. As the metaphor of rebirth affirms, conversion involves incorporation into the family of God.

As with their conversion, the post-conversion lives of the community members depend on the gracious providence of God. The author of 1 Peter affirms that the brotherly and sisterly love (φιλαδελφίαν) that they steadfastly give to one another is founded on the sustaining work of God. The spiritual energy to fulfill the love command comes from the "living and enduring word of God" (1:23), which he later defines as the good news that was pronounced to the community (1:25).[12] Matthias Konradt paraphrases the meaning of the 1:22-23: "The call for permanent brotherly love results consequently from the fact that the effective word, to which Christians owe their conversion, is not transitory, but remains eternally. It does not merely give one single impulse, but works permanently, continuously providing the necessary vital elements for the new life."[13]

The author of 1 Peter explains how the word continuously provides the

---

11. Boring, *1 Peter*, 87.

12. In 1:3, new birth is attributed to the resurrection of Jesus, but we need not posit two distinct sources for regeneration. As Boring explains (*1 Peter*, 88): "In 1:3 the new birth was by the resurrection of Jesus Christ; here it is through the word that is inseparably bound to the event and mediates it to the believer."

13. Matthias Konradt, "The Historical Context of the Letter of James in Light of Its Traditio-Historical Relations with First Peter," in Niebuhr and Wall, eds., *The Catholic Epistles and Apostolic Tradition*, 109. Konradt notes the similarity between the imagery of Jas 1:18-21 and 1 Pet 1:22-23, concluding that they share traditions from their common Antiochene provenance.

vital elements necessary for the new life by extending the metaphor in 2:1-3 to describe not only birth but also the nourishment and growth of the newly born. Because the primary concern of the present study is the post-conversion lives of the Petrine community, we will give more attention to the milk metaphor that describes divine sustenance in the time between the revelations of Jesus Christ.

Milk That Nourishes unto Salvation

In 1 Pet 2:2, we encounter an "unquestionably difficult"[14] phrase: τὸ λογικὸν ἄδολον γάλα. The phrase is usually translated as "pure, spiritual milk" (NRSV, NIV) or "pure milk of the word" (NASB, NKJV), though it is variously glossed by commentators.[15] While interpreters debate the referent of the metaphorical milk and the meaning of the odd adjective λογικὸν (issues we will address presently), they generally agree about the function of the milk. As newborn babies crave the nourishing milk they need for growth, so the Petrine community is exhorted to long for that which will "nourish" them and grow them into salvation. The milk, whatever it might be, is the means (ἐν αὐτῷ)[16] for growth into eschatological salvation. Thus, scholars who define the milk differently can still affirm its basic function. For example, Eugene Boring, who argues that the milk "must be the divine word that brought their new life into being," concludes that the metaphor reminds the readers that "just as their entrance into the household of faith was a matter of divine begetting and birth, so their continued growth is not something they can generate themselves, but depends on life-giving nourishment."[17] Karen Jobes, who argues passionately that the milk cannot be the word of God, likewise concludes that Peter "is saying that God in Christ alone both conceives and sustains the life of the new birth."[18] The metaphor clearly communicates, therefore, that the Christian life lived between the revela-

14. F. J. A. Hort, *The First Epistle of St. Peter I.1–II.17: The Greek Text with Introductory Lecture, Commentary, and Additional Notes* (London: Macmillan, 1898), 100.

15. For example: "guileless milk of the word" (John H. Elliott, *1 Peter: A New Translation with Introduction and Commentary* [AB 37B; New Haven: Yale University Press, 2000], 394) and "unadulterated milk of God's word" (Paul J. Achtemeier, *1 Peter: A Commentary on 1 Peter* [Hermeneia; Minneapolis: Fortress, 1996], 143).

16. Both Achtemeier (*1 Peter*, 147) and Elliott (*1 Peter*, 401) note that ἐν αὐτῷ functions as a dative of instrument, indicating that the milk is the means for further growth.

17. Boring, *1 Peter*, 92.

18. Karen H. Jobes, *1 Peter* (BECNT; Grand Rapids: Baker, 2005), 140.

tions of Christ is divinely nourished. Just as the Christian community depended wholly on God for their rebirth through his enduring word, they now depend wholly on his sustenance for growth to salvation.

Commentators also generally agree on two further important points. First, even though the author metaphorically describes his audience as "newly born newborns" (ἀρτιγέννητα βρέφη), we should not assume that they are freshly baptized new converts.[19] The author describes his whole audience as newborn children of God (1:3, 23), and a general audience that includes Christians from across Asia Minor cannot all be newly baptized. The metaphor is not intended to describe the newness of their conversion but rather to "instruct them to crave the things of God even as newborn babies crave milk — instinctively, eagerly, incessantly."[20]

Second, craving for "spiritual milk" is not a sign of spiritual immaturity. In other NT texts, milk has pejorative connotations. In Heb 5:12-13, for example, the preacher chides his audience for still needing infantile milk, which he defines as the basic elements of the "oracles of God" (τῶν λογίων τοῦ θεοῦ). He hopes they can advance to eating solid food; that is, he hopes they will mature into being teachers skilled in the "word of righteousness" (λόγου δικαιοσύνης). Peter, on the other hand, does not expect his community to outgrow their craving for spiritual milk. Again, the focus of the metaphor is not the spiritual youth of the readers but the intensity of their desire. And their desire for the sustenance that nurtures their new life should never wane.

While commentators largely agree on the basic function of the imagery in 2:1-3 (the Christian life is sustained by divine nourishment), the metaphor raises what Karen Jobes calls "two puzzling questions." Namely, how should λογικόν be understood and translated, and what is the referent of the metaphorical milk? We turn now to analyze these questions, and as Jobes notes, "The answer to either question informs the other."[21]

In the most common interpretation, the meaning of λογικόν actually helps define the milk's referent. As mentioned above, many modern interpreters translate λογικὸν γάλα as "milk of the word,"[22] and even those who translate the phrase as "spiritual milk" will often relate the milk to the word

19. Contra F. W. Beare, who argues that the expression is fitting for those who have just been received into the church through baptism. *The First Epistle of Peter: The Greek Text with Introduction and Notes* (3d ed.; Oxford: Blackwell, 1970), 114.

20. Jobes, *1 Peter*, 132.

21. Jobes, *1 Peter*, 132.

22. See n. 15 above for Elliott's and Achtemeier's translations. See also Green, *1 Peter*, 47.

of God, "either through the cognate relationship between λόγος (*logos*, word) and *logikos* or by proximity with the immediately preceding context in 1:23-25."[23] Paul Achtemeier appeals to both lines of reasoning. He assumes the meaning of the adjective λογικόν is determined by its etymological root, λόγος. "If the root λόγος is to be understood in the sense of 'word,' then λογικός would express the relationship of γάλα ('milk') to the word of God as the proper nourishment for Christians."[24] He also draws on evidence from the immediate context:

> Since, therefore, in this context the word of God (λογὸς θεοῦ) was the agency by which the readers were rebegotten as Christians (1:23), and since the word of the Lord (ῥῆμα κυρίου) was the good news that has been communicated to them (1:25b), some relationship between the divine word and the adjective λογικός seems most likely.[25]

Achtemeier's analysis is typical, though it still leaves room for considerable variation. Even if it is established that 2:2 refers to "milk of the word," what exactly *is* the divine word? Few follow Grudem in identifying the milk-word as the Bible itself.[26] Many more assume the word refers to the proclaimed gospel mentioned most immediately in 1:25.[27] Often, however, this question is not adequately addressed. After surveying two significant challenges to the common interpretation of λογικὸν γάλα, we will return to this question in our own interpretation.

Karen Jobes cites a few dissenters to the "widespread consensus among modern interpreters that the pure spiritual milk of 2:2 is the word of God" that have "seen in the metaphor a wider view of God's life-sustaining grace in Christ."[28] She considers herself among the number of dissenters that have roots going back at least as far as Calvin. Also cited as a dissenter is J. Ramsey Michaels. We will address his challenge to the mainstream interpretation before surveying Jobes's more substantial critique.

---

23. Jobes, *1 Peter*, 132.

24. Achtemeier, *1 Peter*, 147.

25. Achtemeier, *1 Peter*, 147.

26. W. A. Grudem, *The First Epistle of Peter* (TNTC; Grand Rapids: Eerdmans, 1988), 95. Grudem sees in the description of the milk as "pure" or "guileless" (ἄδολον) evidence for the inerrancy of scripture.

27. E.g., Green notes that the word in 1:23–2:3 is not "the 'word of Scripture' *per se*, but the word as good news, the gospel concerning Jesus Christ" (*1 Peter*, 53).

28. Jobes, *1 Peter*, 141.

Michaels admits that the author of 1 Peter may be using milk as a metaphor for the proclaimed message of the gospel, as 1:25 indicates, but he argues that the translation "milk of the word" misses the point of the metaphor. "It shifts the emphasis from 'milk,' where it belongs, to 'word,' where it does not belong."[29] When interpreters too quickly identify the milk as word, they ignore the rich imagery of the milk metaphor in its own right. In fact, he argues, λογικòν is best understood as "metaphorical." It does not interpret the milk as much as indicate that it is spiritual milk. If λογικòν does not define the milk, then one must look elsewhere to explicate the meaning of the "pure spiritual milk." Michaels turns to nursing imagery in the *Odes of Solomon* for insight.

In the *Odes of Solomon* the image of milk from the breasts of the Lord most often relates to God's life-giving mercy or kindness. Thus, Christ says of his followers, "my own breasts I prepared for them, that they might drink my holy milk and live by it" (8.14). Elsewhere the narrator sings, "A cup of milk was offered me, and I drank in the sweetness of the Lord's kindness. The Son is the cup, and the Father is he who was milked; and the Holy Spirit she who milked him" (19.2). In this fascinating example, the milk is clearly the kindness that comes from God through the work of the Spirit and the mediation of the Son. Thus, Michaels concludes that in 1 Peter the milk probably represents both divine mercy and divine life. While the proclaimed message of the gospel might be the medium by which the milk is received, "the milk itself is more appropriately interpreted as the sustaining life of God given in mercy to his children."[30]

Michaels's interpretation admirably returns the focus of the metaphor to the life-sustaining power of the milk, but his conclusion proposes a false dichotomy. He makes an unnecessary distinction between the medium and the power. The cup is different from the milk, of course, and logically one can make a distinction between the message (or medium) and the power the message communicates. Such logical distinctions are complicated, however, when speaking of the word of God, which is often portrayed as both message and active power.

In the creation account of Gen 1, for example, the commanding word of God, "Let there be light," has both content and power. It communicates the command and actualizes it. Likewise in the writings of Isaiah, which Peter appeals to in 1:24-25, God announces that his word (τò ῥῆμά μου) will ac-

---

29. J. Ramsey Michaels, *1 Peter* (WBC 49; Nashville: Thomas Nelson, 1988), 87.
30. Michaels, *1 Peter*, 89.

complish his will (55:11). His word not only announces his will; like the rain and snow that fall and cause seeds to sprout, his word has effective power to accomplish his life-giving will.[31] In the NT, Paul uses the term "gospel" to refer not only to the message about Jesus but also to the effective power of God. In Rom 1:16, for example, Paul describes the gospel as "the power of God for salvation" (δύναμις θεοῦ εἰς σωτηρίαν). We should be careful not to truncate the meaning of "word," therefore, when the author of 1 Peter defines it as the proclaimed gospel. Michaels does well to remind us of the life-giving power of the milk, but that does not mean the milk needs to be distinguished from the announcement of the good news. The gospel can be both medium and power.

Karen Jobes offers a sustained critique of the prevailing interpretation of the λογικὸν ἄδολον γάλα in her commentary on 1 Peter.[32] She notes several problems with relating the milk to the word of God. First, interpreters must avoid the etymological fallacy of assuming λογικός derives its meaning from its root λόγος. A word means what it means in context, and frequently in extra-biblical contexts λογικός has the sense of "rational" or "reasonable."[33] The Stoics, for example, used λογικός to mean reasonable "in the sense of being true to the ultimate reality, which in Stoic thought was ordered by the divine rationality of the *Logos*."[34] Jobes concludes, therefore, that Peter (and Paul as well in Rom 12:1) might also use λογικός to describe what is true to the ultimate reality, only their ultimate reality is not defined by the Stoic *Logos* but the new creation established with the resurrection of Jesus.

Most commentators avoid the etymological fallacy by appealing to the immediate context of 1 Pet 2:2. The term λογικός is related to the word of God not because of its etymology, but rather because of its proximity to the references to the divine word (1:23, 25). In this case, even if one chooses to

---

31. It should not be missed that in the imagery of Isa 55 the word is compared to rain that nourishes plant growth (and even provides more seeds for further planting). The image may be agricultural rather than neonatal, but the function of the word closely resembles what Peter describes in 2:2-3.

32. Jobes, *1 Peter*, 130-41. See also her earlier article: "Got Milk? Septuagint Psalm 33 and the Interpretation of 1 Peter 2:1-3," *WTJ* 63 (2002): 1-14.

33. See Dan G. McCartney ("'λογικός' in 1 Peter 2,2," *ZNW* 82 [1991]: 128-32), who nonetheless concludes that λογικός should be understood as "having to do with verbal communication," since rationality and verbal communication were closely related in the ancient world.

34. Jobes, *1 Peter*, 136.

translate λογικός as "rational" or "spiritual," the context still indicates that the term would have been associated with the similar-sounding λόγος. Jobes counters that one's understanding of the milk in 2:2 should be determined by the context, but the immediate context is 2:1-3, not 1:23-25. In fact, the author's use of ῥῆμα rather than λόγος in 1:24-25 indicates that those verses do not provide the best context for understanding the λογικός as milk. Instead, she argues, one must find an interpretation that accounts for 2:1 and 2:3.

In 1 Pet 2:3, the author alludes to LXX Ps 33, an acrostic psalm of thanksgiving that envisions David's deliverance from afflictions while he is "sojourning" away from home.[35] The author of 1 Peter, who slightly changes LXX Ps 33:9 (34:8) in order to make it fit his context,[36] clarifies the referent of the metaphorical milk with the biblical allusion. The milk that the newborns have tasted and now crave is their experience of the Lord himself.[37] Any interpretation of the milk metaphor, Jobes contends, must take this into account.

For Jobes, the milk metaphor must also fit with 2:1. The vice list in 2:1 begins with a participle (ἀποθέμενοι) that depends on the imperative in 2:2 (ἐπιποθήσατε), linking the two verses syntactically. Jobes argues that the participle in 2:1 is "the mode in which craving for the pure milk is expressed."[38] Her reading has much to commend it, so we will quote her explanation at length before noting some potential difficulties:

> The word preached to Peter's readers mediated their experiences of God (1:25) and gave them their initial taste of the Lord. But when Peter exhorts them to crave spiritual milk, he is not telling them to crave the

35. The LXX translator highlights the theme of "sojourning" by translating the Hebrew וּמִכָּל־מְגוּרוֹתַי הִצִּילָנִי ("from all my fears he delivered me") as ἐκ πασῶν τῶν παροικιῶν μου ἐρρύσατό με ("from all my sojourning he delivered me"). The reading might reflect the translator's own experience of exile, and it certainly fits the exile motif in 1 Peter.

36. First, he changes the tense of the main verb "to taste" from the imperative mood (γεύσασθε) to the indicative (ἐγεύσασθε). He is not imploring his audience to experience the Lord; rather, he is reminding them of their past experience (possibly their conversion when they first tasted the goodness of God's mercy). Second, he omits the second verb from LXX Ps 33:9, which reads "taste *and see* (καὶ ἴδετε) that the Lord is good." He probably omits the second verb in order to maintain the coherence of the milk metaphor. One craves the taste of milk, not the sight of it. The omission might also reflect his understanding of the Christian life as being lived between the two revelations of Christ. In the present, they do not *see* Jesus (1:8).

37. Jobes, "Got Milk?" 10.

38. Jobes, *1 Peter*, 140. See also Marietjie du Toit ("The Expression λογικόν ἄδολον γάλα as the Key to 1 Peter 2.1-3," *HvTSt* 63 [2007]: 221-29), who closely follows Jobes's interpretation.

word of God, as if commanding them to listen to more sermons or to read more Scripture, as good and even necessary as those activities may be. He is saying that God in Christ alone both conceives and sustains the life of the new birth. They are to crave the Lord God for spiritual nourishment. They have tasted the goodness of the Lord in their conversion, but there is more to be had. The more-of-the-Lord-to-be-had by Peter's readers involves putting off all evil and all deceit and hypocrisies and jealousies, and all backbiting (2:1). Refusal to do so would stunt their growth in the new life.[39]

Jobes's emphasis on moral transformation needs to be appreciated. First Peter 1:22 and 2:1 demonstrate the author's overarching purpose in this section: to encourage the brotherly love that builds community (1:22) and to discourage the attitudes that destroy it (2:1). The nourishing milk is part of that transformation process.

A recent article by Philip Tite[40] supports Jobes's intuition that the milk is tied to moral transformation. He studies the Greco-Roman context in order to articulate the role of wet nurses and breast-feeding in moral development. Romans typically used a wet nurse, who might be either a "free mercenary nurse" (from outside the household) or a slave nurse (from within the household). Slave nurses would often accompany the child into young adulthood as a nanny or chaperone, while the mercenary nurse would care for the child for a set period of time (usually about two years) before returning the child to the parents.

Ancient medical theorists offer advice on choosing the wet nurse. The quality of the milk and the quality of the wet nurse were both important considerations because, as Tite notes, "the character and lifestyle of the nurse affected the quality of the milk, the proper care of the nursling, and the development of habits in the child."[41] Thus, Soranus (*Gyn.* 2.19)[42] recommends that parents choose a wet nurse who is self-controlled and Greek because a self-controlled person will refrain from drinking (which would spoil the milk and possibly lead to the nurse neglecting the child) and a

---

39. Jobes, *1 Peter*, 140.

40. Philip L. Tite, "Nurslings, Milk and Moral Development in the Greco-Roman Context: A Reappraisal of the Paraenetic Utilization of Metaphor in 1 Peter 2.1-3," *JSNT* 31 (2009): 371-400.

41. Tite, "Nurslings," 379.

42. For a translation of Soranus see O. Temkin, *Soranus' Gynecology* (Baltimore: Johns Hopkins University Press, 1991).

Greek-speaking person will expose the child to the best speech. Likewise, Quintilian says that a child's nurse must speak correctly and should ideally be a philosopher, because the child will try to imitate his nurse (*Inst.* 1.1.5). Because children are so impressionable, parents should take great care in choosing who will make those first impressions on their newborn.

In a striking example, Aulus Gellius tells the story of a certain philosopher Favorinus, who advises a senator to have the mother instead of a slave nurse the baby. In building his case, he notes that children adopt the moral qualities of those who birth and nurse them: "Just as the power and nature of the seed are able to form likeness of body and mind, so the qualities and properties of the milk have the same effect" (*Attic Nights* 12.1.15 [Rolfe, LCL]). Plutarch also praises the benefits of a mother nursing her own children. In the story of Cato the Elder's wife, he recalls that she nobly nursed her own child but "gave suck also to the infants of her slaves, so that they might come to cherish a brotherly affection for her son" (*Cat. Mai.* 20.2-3 [Perrin, LCL]). As Tite notes, the mother thus "enables a mutual affection between the son and his playmates (and later his servants). The milk becomes a bonding."[43]

Tite firmly establishes the importance of breast-feeding in the moral development of children. Milk not only sustains life, it shapes it. Ancient thinkers took care in choosing wet nurses for their children because they knew the milk and the wet nurse would not only support the life of their child; they would also shape their moral development. Also noteworthy, considering what immediately precedes and follows 1 Pet 2:1-3, the milk builds familial relations. According to Plutarch, children who share milk from the same source, even if they are not biologically related, build brotherly affection. Tite's survey supports Jobes's interpretation by affirming the importance of moral transformation in the milk metaphor. The milk builds the community and develops it morally.

Despite all that commends Jobes's interpretation, she overstates her case in two ways. First, like Michaels, she assumes a truncated definition of the "word of God" that she rightly rejects as an insufficient interpretation of the milk. In 2:1, she argues, Peter is not urging his readers to listen to more sermons or to read more scripture; therefore, it would be incorrect to assume that he wants them to crave the "word of God." The word in 1 Pet 1:22–2:3, however, cannot be simply identified with preaching or scripture. The word is the good news (1:25), which can be proclaimed, but which is also the

---

43. Tite, "Nurslings," 386.

generating power of the Christian life. It is the message about Jesus, the imagination-shaping story of his death and resurrection, which one can encounter in the apostolic preaching and the prophetic writings, to be sure, but which one can also encounter in the memory, prayer, and worship. The story of Jesus' suffering and glorification can be an object of praise and proclamation in the gathering of the Christian community, and it can be a pattern recalled in the memory that shapes the imagination, enabling new ways of living in the world.

Second, Jobes overstates her case by implying that the moral transformation itself *is* the nourishment. In the section quoted above, she explains, "The more-of-the-Lord-to-be-had by Peter's readers involves putting off all evil and all deceit and hypocrisies and jealousies, and all backbiting (2:1)." And in the next paragraph she reiterates, "Peter's readers are to crave the Lord by adopting the attitudes and behaviors that will sustain the new life they have begun by faith in Christ."[44] Certainly, actions shape identity and generate moral development.[45] But by equating the milk with the putting off of vice, Jobes threatens to contradict her own affirmation that "God in Christ alone . . . sustains the life of the new birth." The milk enables the moral transformation; it is not the moral transformation itself. Also, such an understanding of the milk is incoherent with 2:3. Peter says explicitly that his audience has tasted the Lord. Jesus, and the story of his death and resurrection, is the milk they have tasted, affirmed as good, and now crave. Jobes's contribution ensures that we remember the milk has moral implications, but the milk need not be equated with right living.

Is there a way that we can incorporate Michaels's and Jobes's insights into an interpretation of 1 Pet 2:1-3 and still maintain the milk's relation to the word? A careful definition of the word as the gospel, the story of Jesus Christ's death and resurrection that acts as both pattern and power for Christian living, fits the context of 1 Pet 1:23–2:3 (and beyond). As pattern, the gospel gives shape to the moral life Peter expects of his audience. As power, the gospel enables the moral transformation for which it calls. With this interpretation, the milk, associated with the word of God mentioned in 1:23-25, is both the sustaining life of God and the way of life consistent with new birth.

44. Jobes, *1 Peter*, 140.

45. As Joel Green rightly notes, "because 'being' and 'doing' are inseparable and because human identity grows out of the interrelations of imagination, dispositions, and practices, we should not imagine that practices are *only* the outward manifestation of 'who we are.' The reverse is also true. Practices effect character development" (*1 Peter*, 279).

A survey of Greco-Roman moral philosophers will demonstrate that Peter's description of the story of Jesus as both pattern and power fits within the ancient understanding of the function of *exempla* in moral transformation. Then, two examples from 1 Peter (2:4-10, 18-25) will illustrate how Peter offers the nourishing milk of the word to his audience in order to sustain their life in the time between the revelations of Jesus.

Exempla in Moral Philosophy

Abraham Malherbe notes in his survey of Hellenistic moralists that the use of *exempla* is widespread. He explains, "To be a true follower one must imitate (μιμεῖσθαι) his model, be his μιμητής or ζηλωτής. The moralist therefore reminds (ὑπομιμνήσκειν) his hearers of outstanding figures, taking care to describe the qualities of the virtuous men. This call to remembrance is in fact a call to conduct oneself as a μιμητής of the model."[46] Examples were particularly effective because "they were regarded as more persuasive than words and as providing concrete models to imitate."[47]

Exempla, unlike other forms of precepts, can be pictured or placed before the eyes, and this is part of their power. The ancients believed that moral transformation could occur as the result of attention to a given object, a process sometimes called "transformation by vision."[48] By seeing their teacher, therefore, students of a philosopher were transformed and enabled to live like him (Xenophon, *Mem.* 4.1.1). In a similar way, devotees of the gods were also changed by their attention to the gods during worship (Seneca, *Ep.* 94.42). This pervasive cultural assumption undergirds the importance of *exempla* in moral training.

The cultural assumption is rooted in Plato's metaphysics. In the creation of the cosmos, Plato imagines an Architect (τεκταινόμενος) or Constructor (δημιουργός) who keeps his gaze fixed on a model, the Eternal,

46. Abraham J. Malherbe, "Hellenistic Moralists and the New Testament," *ANRW* 26.1:282.

47. Abraham J. Malherbe, *Moral Exhortation: A Greco-Roman Sourcebook* (LEC 4; Philadelphia: Westminster, 1986), 135.

48. Charles Talbert outlines the concept in his recent work on Matthean ethics and soteriology: "Indicative and Imperative in Matthean Soteriology," *Bib* 82 (2001): 515-38; *Reading the Sermon on the Mount: Character Formation and Decision Making in Matthew 5-7* (Columbia: University of South Carolina Press, 2004). See also his contributions to the present volume on the Pastoral Epistles and the Gospel of Matthew.

while forming the cosmos (*Tim.* 28C-29C). The beauty of the cosmos stands as proof that the architect maintained his gaze on the Eternal, the pattern only apprehensible by reason, while forming the cosmos. Plato explains that "when the artificer of any object, in forming its shape and quality, keeps his gaze fixed on that which is uniform, using a model of this kind, that object, executed in this way, must of necessity be beautiful" (*Tim.* 28A-B [Bury, LCL]). Contrariwise, if his gaze were to stray from the perfect model, the object would not be beautiful. Thus, the model or pattern, and one's focused attention on it, determines the quality of the object.[49]

Middle Platonists like Plutarch and Philo applied Plato's metaphysics more explicitly to the field of ethics. Philo uses the language of "imprinting" to describe the transformative power of patterns or examples. Like Plato, he imagines that a demiurge created the visible world by attending to the intelligible, incorporeal patterns (*Opif.* 17-20). He uses the analogy of an architect who receives the patterns of a city in his soul, "as it were in wax." "Then," Philo continues, "by his innate power of memory, he recalls the images of the various parts of this city, and imprints their types yet more distinctly in it: and like a good craftsman begins to build the city of stones and timber, keeping his eye upon his pattern" (Whitaker, LCL). The architect's work results from imprinting the pattern on his soul, reinforcing it through memory, and keeping his gaze on it while building.

In other contexts, Philo explicitly states that vision of human exemplars imprints their pattern on the soul. Israel, for example, will be a blessing to the nations by living virtuously. A virtuous nation stands above all other nations, seen from every side, "not for its own glory but rather for the benefit of the beholders. For to gaze continuously upon noble models imprints their likenesses in souls which are not entirely hardened and stony" (*Praem.* 114 [Colson, LCL]). Therefore those who would imitate these examples, Philo continues, need not despair of changing for the better. Their souls are altered by the vision of the virtuous. They are imprinted with the pattern and thereby shaped into its image.

Plutarch prefers the language of "implanting." Attention to the pat-

---

49. Also interesting is Plato's description of human sight. A fire-stream issuing from the eyes meets a fire-stream coming from the object of vision, and "distributes the motions of every object it touches, or whereby it is touched, through all the body even unto the Soul, and brings about the sensation which we now term 'seeing'" (*Tim.* 45C-D [Bury, LCL]). Sight resonates in the soul, changing its vibrations. Thus, attending to the ordered revolutions on display in the heavens stabilizes the revolutions of the soul according to the same ordered beauty (*Tim.* 47B-C [Bury, LCL]).

terns of virtuous exemplars implants an impulse toward virtue in the observer. Plutarch explains, in very Platonic terms, "The Good creates a stir of activity towards itself, and implants at once in the spectator an active impulse." The Good acts with almost magnetic pull and draws the observer toward itself. Therefore, Plutarch concludes, "our intellectual vision must be applied to such objects as, by their very charm, invite it onward to its own proper good" (*Per.* 1-2 [Perrin, LCL]). He records the lives of virtuous exemplars in order to implant in his readers the impulse that will accomplish moral transformation.

In the work of Stoic moral philosophers, like Seneca, the pervasive cultural assumption of "transformation by vision" undergirds the importance of *exempla*. Seneca may not use the language of implanting or imprinting, but he still assumes that "seeing"[50] exemplars has transformative effects. In his letters to his student Lucilius, Seneca not only employs copious *exempla;* he also discusses the importance of good examples in moral transformation. He disagrees with philosophers who find no place for precepts, or practical advice and instruction, in their teaching. Some want only to teach dogmas and define the Supreme Good, but Seneca emphasizes the importance of practical advice. Practical advice "engages the attention and rouses us, and concentrates the memory, and keeps it from losing grip," and it stirs to growth that which is honorable (*Ep.* 94.25, 29 [Gummere, LCL]). And the most effective form of practical advice, Seneca notes, comes in the form of good examples: "Nothing is more successful in bringing honorable influence to bear upon the mind, or in straightening out the wavering spirit that is prone to evil, than association with good men. For the frequent seeing, the frequent hearing of them little by little sinks into the heart and acquires the force of precepts" (94.40 [Gummere, LCL]).

The path to virtue is long, however, and the soul needs guidance along the way, just as a student needs letters to trace in order to perfect his writing (94.51). Good examples, living or dead (*Ep.* 52.7-9), act as guides for the student. Seneca exhorts Lucilius to choose a master whose life he admires and "picture him always to yourself as your protector and your pattern. For we must indeed have someone according to whom we may regulate our characters; you can never straighten that which is crooked unless you use a ruler"

50. I add scare quotes here because the philosophers do not necessarily assume that transformation by vision requires literal sight. Plutarch speaks of "intellectual vision" (*Per.* 1-2, quoted above) and Philo describes Moses contemplating incorporeal patterns in his soul (*Mos.* 2.74). Comprehension, contemplation, and memory are all part of "seeing" in this sense.

(*Ep.* 11.10 [Gummere, LCL]). Seneca quotes Epicurus to the same effect in *Ep.* 25: "'Do everything as if Epicurus is watching you.' There is no real doubt that it is good for one to have appointed a guardian over oneself, and to have someone whom you may look up to, someone whom you may regard as a witness to your thoughts" (25.5 [Gummere, LCL]). If he keeps before his eyes this person (whom Seneca variously calls guardian, attendant, and pattern), Lucilius will have both an example to follow and a witness, a good man at his side to protect him from the things that prompt him to evil.

The Example of Christ in 1 Peter

With the understanding of the function of *exempla* in ancient moral philosophy in mind, we turn now to the example of Christ in 1 Peter. The author does not call his audience to imitate specific details of Jesus' teachings or works but rather the general arc of his life, specifically his suffering and death. In his survey of the narrative of 1 Peter, Boring notes, "Scenes from the life of Jesus play a minimal role in this story. It is important to the author that Jesus lived, that his life was righteous, and that he suffered unjustly for the sake of others without threatening retaliation. . . . [T]he saving act of God in Jesus is concentrated in his suffering, death, and resurrection, not in his life."[51] Thus, the gospel that was proclaimed to the Christian community — Jesus' death and resurrection — is also the pattern or example that remains with them.

The pattern of Christ is broadly defined in 1 Peter, and it lacks the specificity that concrete stories from his life might provide. This does not detract from the effectiveness of his example, however. In ancient paranesis, the teacher provided examples to inculcate the emulation of a particular character trait, not necessarily the mimicry of particular actions. Paul's exhortation to the Philippians illustrates the point. He calls them to have the same "mind" or "attitude" of Christ Jesus (which, not unlike the author of 1 Peter, he defines as a self-sacrificing obedience to God that leads through suffering to glorification) rather than to ape specific actions. In Phil 2:1-13 the community's participation in the pattern of Christ "is guided by analogy rather than isomorphic imitation."[52] The many examples provided in the

---

51. Boring, *1 Peter*, 201. In the first appendix of his commentary, Boring offers a detailed narrative outline of 1 Peter, plotting the events mentioned in the letter in chronological order.

52. Stephen E. Fowl, *Philippians* (THNTC; Grand Rapids: Eerdmans, 2005), 107.

letter to the Philippians shape the imagination of the audience so that they can learn to draw analogies and formulate how the pattern might take shape in their unique context.

The example of Christ in 1 Peter functions in similar ways. The author highlights the continuity between the situation of his audience and the life of Christ, so that some members — slaves and wives in particular — can imitate him almost exactly. They too suffer unjustly; and they too should respond without retaliation. As Joel Green notes, however, "'imitation' has a more expansive sense of 'performance' or 'putting into play' the *character* of the person or thing imitated" (italics mine).[53] Imitation of Christ's example calls for "creative fidelity" to the "score" of Christ's character. Like a Jazz musician improvising according to the chord progressions of a song, the imitator of Christ submits to the pattern while freely expressing it in her own particular context. Green summarizes: "the imitation of Christ might take different forms — not because the pattern of Christ's life has changed, but because the social contexts within which that pattern is imitated vary. What is crucial here, then, is Peter's concern that we internalize or come to embody the pattern of Christ, that our dispositions be conformed to his."[54] The whole Christian community, therefore, can follow the example of Christ even if their life circumstances do not match his.

The basic pattern of Christ, as mentioned above, includes his fidelity to God that leads through suffering to resurrection and glorification. Thus, the basic content of the gospel has become the pattern for the lives of the Christian community. The proclaimed word through which they were reborn is now the word that sustains in the time between the revelations of Jesus. The author appeals to this pattern multiple times, but two illustrations will demonstrate how the example of Christ functions as the sustaining word.

First, immediately following Peter's exhortation to crave the nourishing milk of the word, he appeals to the example of Christ to encourage the growth of the Christian community. He calls his audience to come to the living stone, which he defines according to the pattern of Christ outlined above. It is the stone rejected by mortals but chosen by God. He then calls his audience to imitation of Christ's example. They too are living stones, implying that they too have been rejected by humans because of divine election. Their imitation leads not to shame, however, but to incorporation into

53. Green, *1 Peter,* 278.
54. Green, *1 Peter,* 278.

God's family. They are built into a spiritual house founded on the rejected cornerstone.

In this case, the imitation of the example of Christ carries an indicative force more than an imperative one. Green explains that when the author develops the identity of his audience in terms of the imitation of Christ, "he does so not in terms of what his audience must become but in terms of what they already are."[55] The author highlights what we might call the "typological imitation" of Christ: the situation of his audience mirrors the situation of Jesus.[56] They imitate him because they are experiencing the shame of God's election. The world maligns and rejects what God finds precious. The imperative force of the image is more implied: "You share in Jesus' identity, so respond to your antagonists as he did (knowing that it is only God's evaluation that matters)."[57]

First Peter 2:4-10 affirms that the imitation of Christ depends on Christ himself. The passive tense hints at what the imagery makes explicit. They are "being built" (οἰκοδομεῖσθε) into a temple founded on the living cornerstone. The verb implies that God, who must be the architect since he is choosing the cornerstone, is responsible for the building of the spiritual house, just as he was responsible for generating the new birth. The imagery of the living cornerstone indicates that they depend on Christ for their existence as the people of God. Just as their rebirth came through the living word, now their new life depends on the enduring word. Christ the example is Christ the foundation that undergirds the new community.

The second illustration of the function of the example of Christ in 1 Peter closely follows the first. In 2:18-25, the author addresses the slaves in his audience and places the example of Christ before them in order to encourage their endurance through unjust suffering. He instructs the slaves to defer to their masters, both gentle and harsh, continuing to do good despite suffering. He then invokes the example of Christ: Christ left a pattern of suffering without retaliation that they must follow in their present circumstances. He faithfully followed God and was abused because of it; but the abuse did not alter his faithfulness. He endured by entrusting himself to

---

55. Green, *1 Peter*, 60.

56. Victor A. Copan labels this form of unintentional imitation "paralleling reality" (*Saint Paul as Spiritual Director: An Analysis of the Imitation of Paul with Implications and Applications to the Practice of Spiritual Direction* [Paternoster Biblical Monographs; Eugene, OR: Wipf & Stock, 2007], 53).

57. Green, *1 Peter*, 60.

God, the only judge that matters. The slaves are called to similarly endure and thereby enjoy the approval of the ultimate judge.

The instruction in 2:18-25 specifically addresses the slaves in the author's audience, but the call to imitation applies more broadly to the audience as a whole. Slaves who have joined the Christian community without the rest of their household are likely suffering abuse for their conversion. As mentioned earlier, they are likely being maligned as "home-wreckers" whose refusal to worship the household gods destabilizes the οἶκος and thereby threatens the stability of the society at large. The author encourages them to continue doing right in the midst of suffering in order to silence and shame the slanderers. If they live as model slaves in every possible way, they will undercut the accusation that they are destroying the household by embracing this strange new religion. In fact, they might even earn the Christian community a positive reputation. Such instruction applies by analogy to the whole community (2:12; 3:16), and so the call to follow Christ's example also applies by analogy to the whole community.

As in 2:4-10, the gospel provides both the example and the means of imitation.[58] The word initially proclaimed to the Christian community doubtlessly included the story of the unjust suffering that Jesus resolutely endured, maintaining faithfulness to God through death and ultimately into his glorification. They are called to imitate that example, continuing to do good in the midst of unjust suffering and clinging to the hope of future glorification. The story of Jesus' suffering, death, and resurrection also provides the means for the Christian life. Christ's suffering brought the community to God initially (3:18) and now continues to sustain the community. The author adopts the language of Isa 53 to explain how Christ and his exemplary suffering function in the community. He takes the burden of sins from the community and heals them with his wounds. As free and healed people, they now can live for righteousness; but Christ's act was not a one-time occurrence. He now remains with those who have come to him as shepherd and guardian or overseer (ἐπίσκοπον).

The language of 2:25 shares affinities with Seneca's descriptions of ex-

---

58. My conclusions cohere with scholars such as John Elliott, who affirms "Jesus Christ the model is Jesus Christ the means" and "Christ the enabler is Christ the example" ("Backward and Forward 'In His Steps': Following Jesus from Rome to Raymond and Beyond. The Tradition, Redaction, and Reception of 1 Peter 2:18-25," in *Discipleship in the New Testament* [ed. Fernando F. Segovia; Philadelphia: Fortress, 1985], 202), and Dryden, quoted above, who also asserts "Christ is not only an exemplar, but also a savior. He not only provides a model, but also the *means* for the moral life" (*Theology and Ethics in 1 Peter*, 173).

emplars. Seneca exhorts Lucilius to find a man of high character, living or dead, and "keep him ever before your eyes, living as if he were watching you, and ordering all your actions as if he beheld them" (*Ep.* 11.8, quoting Epicurus [Gummere, LCL]). Seneca calls this exemplar a *custodem* (guardian or protector), *paedagogum* (attendant), or *exemplum* (pattern or example). He continues his advice to Lucilius:

> We can get rid of most sins, if we have a witness who stands near us when we are likely to go wrong. The soul should have someone whom it can respect — one by whose authority it may make even its inner shrine more hallowed. Happy is the man who can make others better, not merely when he is in their company, but even when he is in their thoughts! And happy also is he who can so revere a man as to calm and regulate himself by calling him to mind! One who can so revere another, will soon be himself worthy of reverence. Choose therefore a Cato; or, if Cato seems too severe a model, choose some Laelius, a gentler spirit. Choose a master whose life, conversation, and soul-expressing face have satisfied you; picture him always to yourself as your *protector* and *pattern*. For we must indeed have someone according to whom we may regulate our characters; you can never straighten that which is crooked unless you use a ruler. (*Ep.* 11.9-10 [Gummere, LCL], italics mine)

Seneca calls Lucilius to find a witness whose authority will make his soul into a hallowed place, an image of the soul as a holy temple that calls to mind 1 Pet 1:16 and 2:5. Lucilius's attention to that exemplar will regulate his actions and shape him into a person worthy of reverence. Seneca therefore exhorts Lucilius to choose an exemplar and picture him always, and in that way he will function as both the pattern and protector for Lucilius's moral transformation.

Likewise, the author of 1 Peter pictures Jesus as the pattern and guardian[59] for his community. And additionally, Jesus acts as the foundation for the community's new life. His suffering, death, and resurrection — the event the gospel proclaims — heals the community and frees them from sins, bringing them to God and giving them birth into a new life. The same

---

59. Obviously, a direct linguistic connection cannot be made between Seneca, who writes in Latin, and the author of 1 Peter, who writes in Greek. The conceptual framework is the same, however. Both Seneca and Peter appeal to an exemplar who acts as an overseer or protector for those who seek to imitate him.

gospel provides the pattern of life — faithful endurance through suffering into glorification — that the community is called to emulate by analogy in their own circumstances of unjust suffering. The author of 1 Peter places the pattern before the eyes of the slaves (and the whole community) in order to encourage their continued endurance. By keeping the gospel before their eyes, the community has both a pattern and a protector. Jesus acts as their guardian or overseer, regulating their characters by his example, and he will continue to do so until he appears again.

Conclusion

The author of 1 Peter depicts the Christian community living between two revelations of Christ. His suffering, death, and resurrection mark his first appearance, and his revelation at the eschaton marks the second. Between these two appearances, the community is protected by the power of God during their various trials. The author describes the three moments of the Christian life — conversion, post-conversion life, and eschatological salvation — with the metaphor of rebirth, which can be summarized as follows.

The community was given new birth through the resurrection of Jesus (1:3), an event they experienced first through the proclamation of the gospel, the word of God (1:25). Thus, the author of Peter can say both that they were given new birth by the resurrection of Jesus and by the word of God (1:23). That word, the gospel as event and proclamation, endures forever. It was not a one-time event experienced only at conversion. It is an event that endures with them in their post-conversion lives, nourishing them to salvation during the trials they experience in the time between the revelations of Christ. The word endures with them specifically in the pattern of Christ, which both describes and compels the moral transformation expected of the community. In this way, Christ himself — experienced by the community through the proclamation of the gospel, the story of his death and resurrection — is the word that provides new birth and the milk that grows the Christian community into salvation.

The (Un)Conditionality of Salvation:
The Theological Logic of 2 Peter 1:8-10a

Scott J. Hafemann

Through a close reading of the theological logic of 2 Pet 1:8-10a, this essay raises the central question of the relationship between divine agency ("indicatives") and human agency ("imperatives") in NT soteriology. The argument demonstrates that obedience to God's commands is not conceived of as the believer's distinct "response" to God's prior work in his or her life. Rather, increasing virtue is the inherent character of an ongoing, holistic, covenant relationship with God. Hence, the unconditional, determining character of God's grace does not diminish but underscores the necessary and determining character of the believer's zeal for God's commands.

•   •

Nowhere else in the New Testament do we find a more carefully argued presentation of the contours of salvation than in 2 Peter 1:3-11. In a striking manner, this passage brings together the provisions of God's saving actions in the past (vv. 3-4), their implications for the life of faith in the present (vv. 5-7), and the resultant promises of God's redemption (and implied judgment) in the future (vv. 8-11). As I have argued elsewhere, the interpretive key to understanding the theological logic of this text is to recognize that it thus follows the threefold covenant structure known to us from the ancient Near East, which runs throughout the OT and early Jewish literature, and which became the basis for a standard homiletic pattern in early Jewish and

Christian literature.[1] Read against this backdrop, the argument of 2 Peter outlines as follows:

1. The Historical Prologue (vv. 3-4)[2]
2. The Covenant Stipulations (vv. 5-7, 10a)[3]
3. The Covenant Promises and Curses (vv. 8-9; 10bc-11).[4]

Second Peter 1:3-11 therefore provides an extended example of the "covenantal nomism" now recognized to form the theological backbone not only of the OT, but also of much of post-biblical Judaism and, in my view, of the NT as well. In so doing, its stress on the necessity of keeping God's commands (vv. 5-7, 10a) in view of God's electing, saving grace (vv. 3-4; cf. 1:1-2), and in anticipation of the certainty of his coming judgment (vv. 8-11; cf. 1:16-21; 3:1-12), raises the central question of the relationship between the "indicative" (divine agency) and the "imperative" (human agency) in NT soteriology.

This question is consequently also at the heart of understanding covenantal nomism. The "new perspective on Paul" has rightly taken up covenantal nomism in order to challenge the view that Paul's polemic regarding the Law was a response to a Jewish theology of preconversion works-righteousness or legalism, in which God was seen as responding

---

1. Unless otherwise noted, all citations are to 2 Peter. See my "Salvation in Jude 5 and the Argument of 2 Peter 1:3-11," in *The Catholic Epistles and Apostolic Tradition* (ed. Karl-Wilhelm Niebuhr and Robert W. Wall; Waco, TX: Baylor University Press, 2009), 331-42, 475-82, and cf. Richard Bauckham, *2 Peter and Jude* (WBC 50; Waco, TX: Word, 1983), 173, who recognizes that verses 3-11 "appear to follow" this pattern; he points to the work of K. Baltzer as support for its OT backdrop and to that of K. P. Donfried for its development in the early church and application to the whole of 2 Peter.

2. The prologue recounts the *gracious,* one-sided provisions of the king on behalf of his vassal that have led to and support the covenant relationship. Cf., e.g., Exod 19:1–20:2; Josh 24:1-13, 17-18. These acts in the past provide the *foundation* for the expected obedience on the part of the vassal.

3. The stipulations outline the necessary responses of the vassal if the covenant relationship is to be maintained. Cf., e.g., Exod 20:3-17; 21–24; Josh 24:14-15. These are the *conditions* that must be kept by the vassal in order to inherit the promises that the king has made upon entering into the covenant relationship.

4. This section states the promises themselves, often implied in the historical prologue (e.g., future deliverance for the vassal based on the past deliverance already experienced), which will be fulfilled if the covenant stipulations are kept, as well as the corresponding curses or judgment that will befall the vassal if the covenant is not maintained. Cf., e.g., Deut 28; Josh 24:20. These promises and curses are the *focus* of the covenant stipulations.

salvifically to the "meritorious" obedience of those seeking him. However, Campbell has recently argued that this "covenantal nomism" has simply shifted the location of "legalism" from "getting in" the covenant to "staying in," since, as 2 Peter emphasizes, those within the covenant must now maintain a life of sustained obedience in order to inherit its promises, at the heart of which is entrance into the eternal kingdom itself (see again 1:8-11)! In view of such an emphasis, eschatological salvation is now contingent on "staying in," which is conceived to be a second-step, synergistic "response" or human "partnership" with God's initial saving work. Hence, covenantal nomism is just as legalistic as the traditional reading of Judaism before it.[5]

Granted that such a second-stage legalism may indeed be part of the covenant-conceptuality of various strands of post-biblical Judaism, is such a "legalism" also at the heart of the covenantal nomism incorporated within the soteriology of the NT?[6] The way forward in this important debate will be through a close reading of those texts that delineate the nature of the (covenant) relationship between God and his people. To that end, the purpose of this essay is to pose this question in the light of the theological logic of 2 Pet 1:8-10a.

---

5. Douglas A. Campbell, *The Deliverance of God: An Apocalyptic Rereading of Justification in Paul* (Grand Rapids: Eerdmans, 2009), 104: "In short, it seems that the essential theoretical differences between covenantal nomism and legalism have effectively collapsed," since both are contractual or conditional (cf. too 101-3, 446-48, 463, 473, 1054n.87). As Campbell himself seems to recognize, the only way out of this legalism is to posit a thoroughgoing monergism, in which all of salvation, including the response of faith/obedience, is attributed to the apocalyptic work of God by means of his Spirit, as seen, e.g., in the Qumran texts (108, 116, 118, 569-70).

6. Campbell's own revision of Sanders's work is highly ambiguous in this regard, since he rejects the idea that Paul's apocalyptic, participatory, liberative soteriology is conditional or contractual, and hence covenantal (eliminating "faith" as a condition of salvation and the concept of a judgment by works as non-Pauline), while at the same time dismissing the "Calvinist" view of the human will and the Spirit, since he posits the possibility of the rejection of God's decisive work based on human freedom (cf. *Deliverance*, 59-60, 113, 160-64, 705-7, 712-13, 817-20, 903, 957n.33). In contrast, for the essential parallel between the soteriology of Paul (and now I would add, 2 Peter!) and the monergistic, covenantal nomism of Qumran, see my "The Spirit of the New Covenant, the Law, and the Temple of God's Presence: Five Theses on Qumran Self-Understanding and the Contours of Paul's Thought," in *Evangelium, Schriftauslegung, Kirche* (ed. Jostein Ådna, Scott J. Hafemann, and Otfried Hofius; Göttingen: Vandenhoeck & Ruprecht, 1997), 172-89.

The Argument of 2 Pet 1:3-11

To set the context of our study, a discourse analysis of the argument of 2 Pet 1:3-11 may be presented as follows, with the logical relationship between each of its propositions italicized.

3a *Because* (ὡς) his divine power has bestowed to us all things pertaining to life and godliness

3b *by means of* (διὰ + gen.) the knowledge of the one having called us by his own glory and virtue

4a *and* by means of this same glory and virtue (δι' ὧν) he has bestowed to us the precious and very great promises

4b *in order that* (ἵνα + subj.) through them you might become fellow participants of the divine nature

4c *as a result of* (adv. ptcp.) having fled the corruption in the world (that comes about) through desire,

5a *i.e.* (δέ), *indeed for this very reason* (καὶ αὐτὸ τοῦτο), *in that* (adv. ptcp.) you bring in alongside all zeal,

5b supply in(to) your faith, virtue,

5c *and supply* (δὲ) in(to) virtue, knowledge,

6a *and supply* (δὲ) in(to) knowledge, self-control,

6b *and supply* (δὲ) in(to) self-control, endurance,

6c *and supply* (δὲ) in(to) endurance, godliness,

7a *and supply* (δὲ) in(to) godliness, love for the brothers,

7b *and supply* (δὲ) in(to) love for the brothers, love (for all).

8a *For* (γάρ), *if* (adv. ptcp.) these things are yours

8b *and* (καὶ) *if* (adv. ptcp.) they are increasing,

8c *then* they make (you) neither useless nor unfruitful with regard to the knowledge of our Lord, Jesus Christ.

9a *For* (γάρ) the one who may not have these things is blind,

9b *though* (adv. ptcp.) he is nearsighted,

9c *because* (adv. ptcp.) he has "received forgetfulness" of the cleansing of his old sins.

10a *Therefore* (διὸ) (to restate the main point of vv. 5a-7b),

all the more, brothers, be zealous to make firm your calling
and election.

10b   *For* (γὰρ), *if* (adv. ptcp.) you are doing these things

10c   *then* you will never ever stumble.

11   *For* (γὰρ) in this way the entrance will be richly provided for
you into the eternal kingdom of our Lord and savior, Jesus
Christ.

The main point of 1:3-11 is stated twice, first in the chain of virtues found in
5a-7b, and then in summary form in proposition 10a. In both cases the main
point is an imperative that is drawn by way of inference from the surrounding indicative arguments. Verses 3a-4c function together to ground 5a-7b,
which are then further grounded by 8a-8c. Propositions 8a-c are in turn
grounded by 9a-c, which functions bilaterally to ground both 8a-c and 10a.
Verses 10b-11 then complete the argument by adding still further support to
10a. Following the common covenant pattern, in which indicatives logically
ground imperatives, everything in this passage points forward and backward
to the two imperative statements found in 5a-7b and 10a.

The Promise of Redemption (Covenant Blessing)

Verses 8-11 support the imperatives of verses 5-7, summarized in verse 10a, by
setting forth the covenant promises and curses linked to the covenant stipulations (see the γὰρ ["for"] of v. 8a and the threefold use of ταῦτα ["these
things"] in vv. 8-10, each of which refers back to the virtues of vv. 5-7). Verse
8 grounds the need to pursue "these things" (ταῦτα) with all zeal by pointing
to the *positive* consequences of such growth in virtue, i.e., to the covenant
blessings that are linked to obedience. Verse 9a then outlines the corresponding *negative* consequences of not persevering in "these things"
(ταῦτα), i.e., the covenant curses that are linked to disobedience, while verse
10b will return to the positive implication of doing "these things" (ταῦτα).

The necessity of progressing in the virtues in order to participate in
the fulfillment of God's promises in the age-to-come is made explicit by
the two adverbial, present tense participles of verse 8, both of which are to
be construed as continuous and conditional in force: "if [these things] are
yours and if they are increasing" (ὑμῖν ὑπάρχοντα καὶ πλεονάζοντα).[7] The

---

7. So too already Johann Huther (*Kritisch-exegetisches Handbuch über den 1. Brief des*

use of the dative of possession with the equative verb (ὑμῖν ὑπάρχω = "to be yours"), rather than using the simple genitive, further underscores the necessity of pursuing the virtues by emphasizing that which is possessed, not the one who possesses it: "if *these things* are yours and if *these things* are increasing. . . ."[8]

The doublet ὑμῖν ὑπάρχοντα καὶ πλεονάζοντα ("existing to you and increasing") is another of the twenty-nine uses of a hendiadys in 2 Peter, one of the five made up of participles (cf. 1:12; 2:10; 3:3-4, 12).[9] As such, the second element interprets the first by defining what is meant by the existence of these virtues in the life of the believer: they only belong to someone *in that* they are increasing. If the virtues, represented as a whole, are not increasing, they do not exist. The hendiadys of verse 8 reflects the fact that the ethical virtues of verses 5-7 are not static qualities to be possessed by the believer in a stair-step progression of spiritual attainments. Rather, they are a dynamic, growing, organic expression of the transforming power of God's presence (vv. 3-4). The prayer for this increasing *grace* in 1:2 is therefore matched by the expectation of an increasing *virtue* among recipients of that grace in verse 8b: increasing grace brings increasing virtue. Far from being a series of separate, moral accomplishments as a result of the believer's distinct "re-

---

Petrus, den Brief Judas und den 2. Brief des Petrus [4th ed.; KEK; Göttingen: Vandenhoeck & Ruprecht, 1887], 354), and now Thomas J. Kraus (*Sprache, Stil und historischer Ort des zweiten Petrusbriefes* [WUNT 2. Reihe 136; Tübingen: Mohr-Siebeck, 2001], 270), who takes both ὑπάρχοντα καὶ πλεονάζοντα as adverbial and conditional; see James M. Starr, *Sharers in Divine Nature: 2 Peter 1:4 in Its Hellenistic Context* (Coniectanea Biblica, New Testament Series 33; Stockholm: Almqvist & Wiksell, 2000), 45, for the implication of this reading: only as one shows signs of Christ's moral nature in one's own behavior is knowledge effective (1:8), one's call confirmed (1:10), and participation in Christ's eternity and incorruptibility assured (1:11).

8. Following Daniel B. Wallace (*Greek Grammar Beyond the Basics* [Grand Rapids: Zondervan, 1996], 150) and the examples of ὑπάρχω with the genitive and dative he lists. Although Huther (*Petrus*, 354) already argued that πλεονάζω in this context meant "to be abundant," the consensus has rightly followed Friedrich Spitta (*Der zweite Brief des Petrus und der Brief des Judas* [Halle a. S.: Waisenhause, 1885], 70) in taking it to mean "to increase"; see now the arguments of, e.g., Gene Green (*Jude & 2 Peter* [Baker Exegetical Commentary on the New Testament; Grand Rapids: Baker, 2008], 196). For the opposing view, see now Thomas Schreiner, *1, 2 Peter, Jude* (NAC 37; Nashville: Broadman & Holman, 2003), 302.

9. On this "striking" characteristic of 2 Peter, see Kraus (*Sprache*, 162, 164), who lists the noun doublets in 1:2, 3 (2x), 4, 10, 16, 17; 2:8, 11, 12, 13, 17, 22; 3:2, 5, 7 (2x), 10, 11, 12, 13, 14, 16, 18. Contra Schreiner (*2 Peter*, 302), who does not recognize this hendiadys, so that he wrongly argues that the NIV obscures the meaning by merging the two participles into the one assertion, "if you possess these qualities in increasing measure."

sponse" to God's prior work in his or her life, increasing virtue is the inherent character of an ongoing, holistic, covenant relationship with God.

The link between God's grace and the moral transformation of his people explains the logic of verse 8. If the protasis is fulfilled, i.e., if these things are yours in that they are increasing, then the apodosis is true: "[then] these things make you (καθίστησιν) neither *useless nor unfruitful* with regard to the knowledge of our Lord, Jesus Christ."

We must be careful here. The meaning of καθίστημι ("to make") in this context is not to establish or appoint one in a *subsequent* position or state of being due to one's prior actions or qualifications. The point is not that one's virtues *qualify* one to be useful and fruitful in some other way, thereby reflecting a judicial context or evaluation (cf. Exod 2:14; Deut 28:13; Pss 2:6; 8:6; Matt 24:45, 47; Luke 12:14, 42, 44; Titus 1:5; Heb 5:1; etc.).[10] Rather, here the verb refers to the act of *making* or *causing* someone or something *to be or experience* something, since in this context the virtues *are* the useful and fruitful things themselves (cf. Josh 8:2; Ps 96:1; Job 16:12; Jer 23:3 [!]; 2 Macc 15:9; Wis 10:7; Rom 5:19, and especially Jas 3:6; 4:4).[11] Moreover, the front-loaded litotes (λιτότης, i.e., making an affirmation by denying its opposite: these things make one useful and fruitful!) calls attention to the character of the virtues themselves as the determining quality of one's life. The existence of the virtues of verses 5-7 is the very *definition* of the godly life by which one will participate in the final establishment of the eternal kingdom of Jesus Christ (cf. vv. 3-4, 10-11). As Kraftchick puts it, verse 8 "clarifies the eschatological status of those who display the virtues just listed."[12]

---

10. Contra, e.g., G. Green (2 *Peter*, 197), who argues that having and growing in virtue will make one useful and productive as a συνεργός ("one who helps") or εὐεργέτης ("benefactor"; following Spicq). In the context, however, the result of such virtue is the person's own entrance into the kingdom of Christ, not an ability to provide for others. Although the virtues include meeting the needs of others, God, in Christ, remains the only benefactor or helper (vv. 3, 8).

11. See BDAG, 492, and Charles Bigg, *A Critical and Exegetical Commentary on the Epistles of St. Peter and St. Jude* (ICC; Edinburgh: T. & T. Clark, 1901), 259. Carl Friedrich Keil (*Commentar über die Briefe des Petrus und Judas* [Leipzig: Dörffling & Franke, 1883], 221, 222) emphasized that the verb expresses what something/someone really is, not simply what they might appear to be or are presented to be. Contra F. W. Danker, "2 Peter 1: A Solemn Decree," *CBQ* 40 (1978): 64-82, 74-75, who takes καθίστημι in the legal sense of "to establish" on the basis of a judicial scrutiny, so that ἐπίγνωσις is taken to mean a "decision" or recognition or approval rendered by Jesus Christ (subj. gen.) rather than a reference to one's knowledge of Jesus Christ (see below).

12. Steven J. Kraftchick, *Jude, 2 Peter* (ANTC; Nashville: Abingdon, 2002), 99. Cf. the

The most difficult decision to make concerning verse 8 is the meaning of the adverbial prepositional phrase, εἰς τὴν τοῦ κυρίου ἡμῶν Ἰησοῦ Χριστοῦ ἐπίγνωσιν (to be rendered, "with regard to the knowledge of our Lord, Jesus Christ"). Though εἰς + accusative in non-literal contexts most often refers to a result or purpose of some action, the distinction in meaning between εἰς and ἐν in the Koine period is blurred, so that εἰς, like ἐν, can also refer to the means by which, or the cause/source of which, something takes place.[13] Commentators are therefore divided over whether here the virtues bring about the knowledge of our Lord, Jesus Christ (with εἰς + acc. rendered as result or purpose), or whether the knowledge of Christ brings about the virtues (with εἰς + acc. rendered as origin, cause, or even instrumentality).[14]

In support of taking εἰς + accusative to refer to gaining a knowledge of Christ as the purpose or result of growing in the virtues is the fact that the other uses of ἐπίγνωσις ("knowledge") in 2 Peter occur with the preposition ἐν + dative (1:2; 2:20) or διά + genitive (1:3), both of which are clearly instrumental or causal ("by means of knowledge"). This suggests that the use of εἰς in verse 8, in contrast to ἐν and διά elsewhere, is intended to refer to the idea of purpose or result.

Against this view, however, is the meaning of ἐπίγνωσις itself, which

---

common NT use of "fruit" as a metaphor for the present realization of the life of the age to come, embodied in the good works of the righteous that are brought about by the presence of God/Christ/the Spirit or the reality of the kingdom. Conversely, ἄκαρπος connotes having a life that is eschatologically, i.e., morally, "unproductive" (cf. BDAG, 35; and Jude 12; Jer 2:6; 4 Macc 16:7; Wis 15:4; *Sib. Or.* 5:453; *Jub.* 2:7; *4 Bar.* 9:16; *Liv. Pro.* 1:9; 1 Cor 14:14; *Herm.* 51.3; 53.4; 96.2).

13. BDAG, 291: εἰς as a "marker of instrumentality, *by, with*" (meaning 9) and esp. 1 Sam 1:17; Mark 5:34; Acts 7:53. See Peter H. Davids, *The Letters of 2 Peter and Jude* (PNTC; Grand Rapids: Eerdmans, 2006), 185n.50, who points out that eight of the eleven uses of εἰς in 2 Peter point forward in time or forward to results, the exceptions being 1:8, 1:17 (cf. the parallel use of ἐν in the Gospel narratives), and 3:9.

14. For the two views in Spitta's day, see his list (*Petrus,* 70-71); Spitta himself supported the idea of origin or cause, arguing that elsewhere in 2 Peter ἐπίγνωσις is always the ground, never the goal. In favor of "goal" or "result" today, see Bauckham's list (*2 Peter,* 189), and now, e.g., Anton Vögtle, *Der Judasbrief/Der Zweite Petrusbrief* (EKK 22; Solothurn and Düsseldorf: Benziger; Neukirchen-Vluyn: Neukirchener, 1994), 152 (based on 3:18, without distinguishing ἐπίγνωσις from γνῶσις), and Starr, *Divine Nature,* 96. In favor of cause or instrumentality, see now Edna Johnson, *A Semantic Structure Analysis of 2 Peter* (Dallas: Summer Institute of Linguistics, 1988), 42-43; Bauckham, *2 Peter,* 188-89, following Spitta, Bigg, and Kelly; Ben Witherington, *A Socio-Rhetorical Commentary on 1-2 Peter* (Letters and Homilies for Hellenized Christians 11; Downers Grove, IL: IVP Academic, 2007), 312; Kraftchick, *2 Peter,* 99; Schreiner, *2 Peter,* 303n.63; and Davids, *2 Peter,* 185.

refers throughout 2 Peter to the "knowledge" of God and Christ gained at conversion, by which one is given grace and peace (v. 2), which brings the power needed for the life of godliness (v. 3), and which entails God's precious and great promises (v. 4; cf. 2:20 and the corresponding use of the verb in 2:21).[15] As such, this "conversion-knowledge" is to be distinguished from the increasing "knowledge" (γνῶσις) of God's continuing faithfulness (cf. 2:9; 3:8-9, 13), which is part of the virtues themselves (vv. 5-6; cf. 3:18). This distinction is confirmed by verse 9, where the content of the "knowledge" in view in verse 8 is unpacked as the cleansing of one's old sins, which is gained at one's conversion, not attained later through one's virtues.

The positive point of verse 8 is that the increasing existence of the virtues means that one is neither useless nor unfruitful *in regard to* conversion-knowledge of Christ as Lord, inasmuch as they are brought about *by means of* this knowledge. *Not* to increase in "these things," therefore, would mean not that one had failed to "respond" to God's grace in order to know Christ (more deeply?), but that one had not, in fact, encountered the divine glory, here identified explicitly with Christ, that brings about this conversion-knowledge in the first place (v. 3). For as verse 3 declares, the knowledge of the divine glory, which is also expressed in (God's) virtue (!), grants all things necessary for a life defined as godliness (v. 3).

This link between knowledge and virtue is underscored by the front-loaded emphasis in verse 8 on knowing Jesus Christ as *Lord* (κύριος). For as Starr has pointed out, to speak of Christ as "Lord" highlights his sovereignty in history to bring about God's promised salvation and to execute judgment (vv. 4, 11), as well as his sovereignty over the conduct of individuals to bring about moral changes in their lives, since submission to sovereignty is manifested in corresponding moral changes in behavior.[16] The reality of the redemption to come in the new heavens and new earth, "in which righteous-

---

15. So too Bigg, *St. Peter*, 259; Douglas J. Moo, *2 Peter and Jude* (NIV Application Commentary; Grand Rapids: Zondervan, 1996), 42; Bauckham, *2 Peter*, 178, 189; and Starr, *Divine Nature*, 36-38. Many of those who argue for "knowledge" as the goal of the virtues simply posit either a tension or inconsistency with verse 3, or that ἐπίγνωσις can be both the source and goal of the virtues, thereby not limiting its meaning in 2 Peter to conversion-knowledge.

16. Cf. Starr (*Divine Nature*, 29, 76, 228-29), though his insight (228) that in 2 Peter "knowledge" is the "prerequisite to the Christian life and makes possible the subsequent escape from sinful desire and entry into a life of moral fruitfulness and effectiveness, in other words, one is given the ability to live virtuously," is difficult to square with Starr's own preference for εἰς as result in verse 8.

ness dwells" (3:13), has decisively invaded the present evil age in the righteousness of God's people, so that the citizens of the eternal kingdom are already being marked by its character (cf. 2:5-9; 3:13).

This interpretation of verse 8 as a statement of the inevitable progress in virtue of those who know (ἐπίγνωσις) Christ seems to be contradicted, however, by the subsequent warning in 2:21 concerning the very real danger of having known (ἐπιγινώσκω) the way of righteousness, only to turn back "from the holy commandment that was handed down to them [with this knowledge]" (cf. 1 Pet 1:13-17). The answer to this tension is found in the argument of 1:9.

The Promise of Judgment (Covenant Curse)

Verse 9a indicates the basis for the assertion of verse 8: the increasing virtues of verses 5-7 make one neither useless nor unfruitful with regard to the knowledge of our Lord, Jesus Christ, "*for* (γάρ) the one who may not have these things (literally: 'to whom these things may not be present') is blind." Rhetorically, the switch from the direct address of verse 8 to the impersonal use of the third person in verse 9a supports verse 8 by basing it on a universally applicable principle: everyone to whom the virtues are not present is blind (therefore, by implication, where the virtues pertaining to the divine character do exist, v. 3, a person is "seeing," in the sense of having a knowledge of Jesus Christ, v. 8).

Again we must be careful in tracing out the logic of the text. In the same way that the knowledge of Christ brings about the virtues in verse 8, in verse 9 it is not the lack of virtues that makes one blind, but it is being spiritually blind that results in a failure to progress in virtue.[17] Hence, if a person should be lacking these virtues,[18] this indicates that one *is* (ἐστιν) blind. The former *defines* the latter. The link in verse 9a between the state of being blind and the lack of virtues corresponds to the biblical association of spiritual "blindness" with a lack of obedience in, e.g., Isa 59:10 (cf.

---

17. Contra Bauckham, *2 Peter*, 189.

18. The use of μή with the indicative πάρεστιν indicates a hypothetical situation, since it is not assumed that the readers fall into this category. So already Huther, *Petrus*, 355; R. C. H. Lenski, *The Interpretation of the Epistles of St. Peter, St. John, and St. Jude* (Columbus, OH: Wartburg, 1945), 272; and G. Green (*2 Peter*, 199), who therefore rightly critiques the TNIV's use of the second person plural in the attempt to make the text generic; Johnson, *Structure*, 43; Kraus, *Sprache*, 203, 203n.703.

59:2-3, 12-13); Matt 15:14 (cf. 15:3); 23:16-24; Luke 6:39; Rom 2:19; 1 John 2:11; Rev 3:17.[19]

Like the tension between 1:8 and 2:21, however, this reading of verse 9a appears to be contradicted by 9bc, which modifies the main assertion ("he is blind") with two adverbial participles: μυωπάζων and λαβών. The former qualification, μυωπάζων, refers to "being nearsighted," not blind, thereby rendering the combination "curious" or "somewhat odd."[20] Faced with this mixed metaphor, commentators, like the translations, have often sought to relieve the tension by treating the participle as a distinct, finite verb (RSV: "For whoever lacks these things is blind and shortsighted"), even reversing the order to create a sense of progression from one to the other (TNIV: "But if any of you do not have them, you are nearsighted and blind"; so too NRSV, NIV).[21] But the present tense participle is clearly subordinate to the indicative, main verb, indicating a contemporaneous action.[22] Others have therefore taken μυωπάζων to refer to the condition of being nearsighted or to the action of shutting one's eyes as the cause of

---

19. For the idea of being made "blind" by one's actions, attitudes, Satan, or even God, expressed by the verb τυφλόω, which in turn determines one's actions, cf. John 12:40; 2 Cor 4:4; *T. Dan.* 2:4; *T. Gad* 3:3; *T. Sim.* 2:7; *T. Jud.* 11:1; 18:3, 6; 19:4. Cf. CD I, 9; XVI, 2-4; 1QS IV, 11. For the contrasting concept of being given light or enlightened (φωτίζω), see e.g., John 1:9; Eph 1:18; 3:9; Heb 6:4; 10:32. For the link between "seeing poorly (ἀμβλυωπῆσαι) with respect to faith" and not walking according to God's commandments or one's duty toward Christ, see *1 Clem.* 3:4.

20. So J. N. D. Kelly (*A Commentary on the Epistles of Peter and Jude* [BNTC; Peabody, MA: Hendrickson, 1969], 308): "especially as the former is a stronger term than the latter"; cf. e.g., Bauckham (*2 Peter,* 189): the combination is "odd, since it ought to refer to a less severe condition than blindness"; Kraftchick (*2 Peter,* 100): "The combined phrase cannot be taken literally because near-sightedness is superfluous if one is blind"; Moo (*2 Peter,* 48): the combination of words "seems rather strange: If a person is 'blind,' how can he or she be 'near-sighted'?"

21. So Bauckham (*2 Peter,* 172), who thus takes the two verbs as virtually synonymous, as does Kraftchick, *2 Peter,* 100, Schreiner, *2 Peter,* 303; similarly Joseph B. Mayor, *The Epistle of St. Jude and the Second Epistle of St. Peter* (London: Macmillan, 1907), 193, and the meaning suggested by BDAG, 663, in which the nearsighted condition is assumed to be so severe as to be blindness, i.e., "he is so near-sighted that he is blind." Anders Gerdmar (*Rethinking the Judaism-Hellenism Dichotomy: A Historiographical Case Study of Second Peter and Jude* [Coniectanea Biblica, New Testament Series 36; Stockholm: Almqvist & Wiksell, 2001], 315) rightly rejects Fornberg's attempt to take μυωπάζω to be an allusion to the Eleusinian mysteries (cf. their use of μύστης and ἐπόπτης [see 1:16] for the two classes of initiates) as too subtle to be convincing.

22. So, too, Davids (*2 Peter,* 186), who rejects the attempt to take the two assertions as parallel because it ignores the grammar.

being blind.[23] Recently, Gene Green has supported this view by offering a new solution to the problem, arguing that μυωπάζων did not refer to myopia, but to a much more serious eye disease, equivalent to ophthalmia, "which could indeed close it."[24] Thus, "the squinting that the term describes is the experience of a person going blind," so that μυωπάζων is the cause and blindness is the effect.[25] Construed in these ways, the point of the metaphor seems to be that such people do not experience Christ and consequently do not exhibit the virtues (or vice versa) because they have intentionally or unintentionally shut their eyes to the knowledge they had, so that their "blindness" is the consequence of their own actions.

The use of μυωπάζων is extremely rare in ancient literature, with only one attested use prior to 2 Peter (in the fragments of Dorotheus [first c. B.C.E.–first c. C.E.]), where it is also used metaphorically to describe one's moral character in association with one's "spiritual" identity.[26] The later lexical evidence also does not support taking it to refer in the first century, if at all, either to the act of squinting or to the shutting of the eye due to disease.[27]

---

23. See in various ways, Spitta, *Petrus,* 73-75; Moo, *2 Peter,* 48; Kelly, *Commentary,* 308 (following Spicq); Vögtle, *Petrusbrief,* 153; and J. Daryl Charles, *Virtue amidst Vice: The Catalog of Virtues in 2 Peter 1* (JSNTSupp 150; Sheffield: Sheffield Academic, 1997), 149-50.

24. G. Green, *2 Peter,* 198; he thus renders the text, "But the one who does not possess these things is blind, diseased of the eye." On the basis of the thirteenth-century-C.E. lexicon of Ps-Zonaras, Green describes this disease as producing a discharge from the eyes that could be caused by carrion flies.

25. G. Green, *2 Peter,* 198.

26. TLG lists sixty examples of μυωπάζω, all the rest dating from the fourth century on. In Dorotheus (*Fragmenta Graeca* [ed. Pingree, 1976], 412, line 9), μυωπάζων is associated with being "dark" (μέλας) and "small-eyed" (μικρόφθαλμος, due to the squinting associated with nearsightedness?), in contrast to being "wide/large-eyed" (μεγαλόφθαλμος, 412, line 7). Here μυωπάζω is also associated with the moral qualities of being a liar (ψεύστης) and one who dissembles or hides his thoughts (κρυψίνους), in contrast to the positive morality (εὐέκτης) of the one who is "wide-eyed" and revealed by Zeus. The use of the quality of one's eyes to represent one's character and identity with the gods continues throughout the passage.

27. See LSJ, 1157: "*blink* the eyes, as shortsighted people do; hence, *to be shortsighted,* metaph." (referring to 2 Pet 1:9 as this metaphorical use of the verb; cf. μυωπίας: "*shortsighted person*"), thus relating the verb to the noun, μύωψ *("closing* or *contracting the eyes,* as shortsighted people do, and so, *shortsighted");* and BDAG, 663: "be nearsighted" (related to the noun, μύωψ: "'closing or contracting the eyes' = squinting, as nearsighted [myopic] people do"). The early, available lexical evidence confirms this virtually uniform meaning of the verb. Cf. Hesychius (fifth/sixth century) (*Lexicon* [vol. 2; ed. Latte; 1966], entry 1874), who associates μυωπάζων with παρακαμμύων ("to give a side wink at"), reflecting the squinting associated with being nearsighted; so too Photius (ninth century), *Lexicon* [vol. 1; ed. Theo-

Rather, μυωπάζων refers to the stative condition of "being nearsighted."[28] Moreover, the action of "squinting" associated with being nearsighted was not an unintentional result of a disease or an intentional attempt to keep oneself from seeing but rather a natural attempt to see more clearly.[29] Finally, the cause for the blindness is not given with the present, contemporaneous participle, μυωπάζων, but with the aorist, antecedent participle,

doridis; 1998), entry 639, line 1; cf. his reference as well to ἄκροις τοῖς ὀφθαλμοῖς προσέχων ("observing with the edge of his eyes"), which is also found in Suda (tenth century), *Lexicon* (ed. Adler, 1928-1935), entry 1429, line 1; entry 1065, line 1. The latter adds, τὸ τύπτω ("to close the eyes"). As entry 1430, Suda (*Lexicon*) also lists μύωψ as the gadfly or insect that infests cattle, which is a second, distinct meaning of the noun (cf. *LSJ*, 1157). For the early literary evidence, see, e.g., Epiphanius (fourth century) (*Panarion* [= *Adv. haereses*] [ed. K. Holl, 1922], 2:376, line 9), where it is also used together with being blind to describe heresy: "every heresy from the truth, having run aground in darkness, is being blind and short-sighted (τυφλώτει καὶ μυωπάζει)." Later, in 3:196, line 18, μυωπάζω is paired with the human propensity to dream (ὀνειροπολέω) instead of facing the reality of the truth of God's word. Similarly, Basilius (fourth century) (*Sermo de contubernalibus*, MPG 30, p. 825, line 28) refers to the lack of sense perception (metaphorically: the mental obtuseness) of those who are being shortsighted (τὴν ἀναισθησίαν τῶν μυωπαζόντων).

28. Hence, contra Green (n. 24), Ps-Zonaras (*Lexicon* [ed. Tittmann, 1808/1967], 1380, line 2) deviates from the norm by defining μυωπάζω with ὀφθαλμιῶ ("to suffer from ophthalmia," a disease of the eyes). Green seems to assume that μυωπάζω is then related to or defined by the next entry, μυωπίζω, which Zonaras says derives from μύωπος, which can refer to a "goad," or "spur" (cf. *LSJ*, 1157, μύωψ [= μύωπος] II.2), though he takes it to refer to "horsefly/gadfly" (cf. *LSJ*, μύωψ II.1). The two verbs, however, corresponding to the different meanings of μύωψ (as an adj: "shortsighted," as a subst.: "horse-fly," or "goad"), are distinct. Though Ps-Zonaras does take μυωπάζω to refer to a medical disease of the eye characterized by discharges, this does not mean that the source of this disease was necessarily the flies in view in the distinct verb, μυωπίζω, nor that the consequence of this disease was complete blindness. Thus, on 711, line 11, Ps-Zonaras, like Photius and Suda, lists ἐμυωπίασεν with the meaning ἄκροις τοῖς ὀφθαλμοῖς προέσχε ("you observe with the edge of his eyes"), which he supports by equating μυωπάζω with τὸ καμμύω ("to close the eyes"), so that this shutting need not be permanent or complete. The precise cause or consequences of ὀφθαλμιῶ are not clear. Thus, even if this late evidence could apply to the first century, it would not necessarily alter the meaning of the text of 2 Pet 1:9 unless one assumed, as Green does, that this disease shut the eyes completely.

29. A point forcibly made by Mayor (*Second Epistle*, 96), now emphasized by Bigg (*St. Peter*, 260); Bauckham, *2 Peter*, 189; Henning Paulsen, *Der Zweite Petrusbriefe und der Judasbrief* (KEK 12/2; Göttingen: Vandenhoeck & Ruprecht, 1992), 111; see already Huther (*Petrus*, 355-56), pointing out against the older commentaries that μυωπάζω is therefore not an equivalent to τυφλώττω ("to be blind"), which would render the text a tautology (contra too later, Spitta, *Petrus*, 73-74). As he points out, the Vulgate's rendering, *manu tentans* ("feeling with the hand"), which informs Luther's interpretation, seems based on the gloss, ψηλαφῶν ("feeling about like a blind man"; cf. LXX Deut 28:29; Isa 59:10).

λαβών (see below). The tension within the text consequently remains: those who are blind are described as being, at the same time, "nearsighted."

For this reason, those who correctly maintain the imagery of "being nearsighted" have often interpreted the metaphor as a reference to being able to "see" what is "up close" (e.g., earthly realities or desires, or one's present identity as a believer), but being "blind" to what is "far away" (e.g., heavenly realities, who Christ is, how one became a Christian, or the coming eschatological judgment).[30] Though conceptually accurate within 2 Peter as a whole, these explanations do not do justice to the tension between the two images: nearsighted people are not considered blind, since they are able to see well up close, while also being able to see, albeit in a blurred way, in the distance (and hence the need to squint to see more clearly). Conversely, to be blind is not simply to be nearsighted.

Rather than seeking to mitigate the discord between the two metaphors by explaining one in terms of the other or by assigning them to different realities, the key to the argument is actually to be found in the very tension caused by combining the two images as they stand.[31] In view of their conflicting content, the adverbial participle is not intended to unpack the nature of the blindness (serving a modal or synonymous function, so Mayor, Bauckham, Kraftchick, Davids, Schreiner, Gerdmar, et al.), or to indicate the source of the blindness (taking on a causal function, so Spitta, G. Green, Charles, Moo, Kelly, Vögtle, et al.). Rather, the point of declaring those who are "nearsighted" to be, in fact, "blind," is to call attention to the *true* nature of the partial vision of those who are only able to "see" what is "near." Although they have some knowledge of the glory of God in Christ (1:3, 8), their lack of the virtues of verses 5-7 reveals that they are, in reality, not converted at all.[32] A knowledge of Christ without covenant-keeping is

30. E.g., Huther, *Petrus,* 356 (heavenly vs. earthly realities); Keil, *Petrus,* 222 (Jesus Christ vs. earthly realities); Hofmann [reported by Keil] (being a Christian vs. not knowing how one became one); Davids, *2 Peter,* 186 (focused on present desires so they cannot see the past or future judgment).

31. The linking of μυωπάζω with τυφλός/τυφλώττω continues on in Ephraem (fourth century), who explicitly follows 2 Peter (see below, n. 35), Chrysostom (fourth-fifth century), quoting 2 Peter (see below, n. 35), in the *Anonymous Dialogues with the Jews* (fifth-tenth century), Maximum the Confessor (seventh century), and Theodorus (eighth-ninth century), who also quotes 2 Pet 1:9, and Ps-Gregentios (tenth century).

32. Cf. Ps-Dionysius Areopagita (fifth-sixth century), *De ecclesiastica hierarchia,* PTS 36, p. 74, line 18, where, contra Spitta's reading, "being short-sighted" (μυωπάζω) is used to describe the consequence of the will that has turned away from the light available to it as a result of its love for evil, much like those who do not increase in virtue are said to be near-

actually no knowledge of Christ at all in regard to the consummation of the kingdom (v. 11; cf. 3:13).[33] Read in this way, the point expressed metaphorically in verse 9 parallels the deception pictured in Jas 1:26; 2:14-17; Rom 2:13, 17-24; 6:2; 1 Cor 6:9-11; Gal 6:3-7; 1 John 2:6; etc., and warned against in Matt 7:15-23.

Μυωπάζων ("being short- or nearsighted") is therefore best rendered as a concessive or adversative participle, contemporaneous to the main verb: "For the one to whom these things are not present is blind, *though* [at the same time] being nearsighted." Although such people have some knowledge of "the way of righteousness" (2:21), they are in fact blind — no matter what they claim about their knowledge or experience of the truth. Indeed, although such people can in fact "see" aspects of the truth, being spiritually "nearsighted" now takes on a negative spiritual, and hence eschatological connotation.[34] This imagery closes the door on any attempt to excuse those who are claiming to know the Lord (1:8), but are not progressing in the virtues, by suggesting that they are merely "shortsighted" when it comes to the implications of their faith.

The adversative relationship in 1:9b anticipates the adversative relationships that characterize the false teachers, who in their own lack of the virtues represent the epitome of this "blindness," despite a presumed, "nearsighted" knowledge of the truth: though bought by the Lord, they deny him (2:1); though promising freedom, they are slaves of corruption (2:19); though having escaped the defilements of the world by the knowledge (ἐπίγνωσις) of our Lord and Savior, Jesus Christ, they are again overcome by them (2:20); and though having known (ἐπιγινώσκω) the way of righteous-

sighted in 1:9. Interestingly, as in 2 Peter, the description of those who are shortsighted as "intellectuals" may reflect their purported knowledge of what they in fact do not know.

33. So Lenski (*St. Peter,* 272), who stresses the proper use of the image of myopia here, "for this is not a pagan who never heard the Word and is therefore blind; this is a person who knows about the Word but has only a useless glimmer left in his heart."

34. For the metaphorical association of being nearsighted with a negative moral or spiritual state, see in addition to *Fragmenta Graeca,* 412, line 9 (cf. n. 26 above), the TLG references to Epiphanius (fourth century), who uses it to describe heresy, since heretics do not know the proper function of what they teach; Basilius (fourth century), who uses it to refer to mental obtuseness; Ps-Dionysius (fifth-sixth century), who associates being nearsighted with being far off from the light of morality; the *Anonymous Dialogues with the Jews,* which links it to not coming to the light of the knowledge of Christ as seen in the Law and the Prophets (cf. 2 Pet 1:8! so too Neophytus, twelfth-thirteenth century); and Theodorus (eighth-ninth century) speaks of the one who is shortsighted to his or her own passionate attachment to the world.

ness, they turn back from the holy commandment (2:21).[35] Here too, their apostasy is ultimately not the result of their own efforts or lack thereof, but the consequence of their "nature" (cf. the comparison in 2:12 and the description in 2:14, 17).

The ground for the evaluation that the person who is not progressing in virtue is, by nature, "blind" is given in the second adverbial participle clause in verse 9c: such a person is blind "*because* he has forgotten (λήθην λαβών, literally: 'having received forgetfulness of') the cleansing of his old sins." Both its content and its antecedent action in relation to the main verb support this causal reading.[36] Since "forgetfulness" (λήθη), like being blind, is considered a state of being or condition, it can be "received" (λαμβάνω), or "possessed" (ἔχω), as well as "taking place," "happening" (γίνομαι), or "accomplished/done" (ποιέω); one can also be given over to it (παραδίδωμι).[37] As such, "to receive forgetfulness" (λήθην λαμβάνειν), as an

35. That 2:19-22 is an interpretive key to 1:9b is confirmed by Ephraem's commentaries on the text (fourth century) (*De patientia et consummatione* [ed. Phrantzoles, 1992], 4:178, line 15, to 179, lines 1-5; and *Adhortatio de silentio et quiete* [ed. Phrantzoles, 1996], 6:45, lines 5-15, to 46, lines 1-2), in which he interprets 1:9 by glossing it with direct quotations from 2 Pet 2:20-22. In the former context, as a parallel to 2 Pet 1:9, he grounds his quote of 2 Pet 1:8 with the assertion, "For the individual (μοναχός), who does not acquire these things, but is forgetting his own salvation" (ἀλλὰ ἀμελεῖ τῆς ἑαυτοῦ σωτηρίας), "is blind, being short-sighted (τυφλός ἐστι μυωπάζων), having received forgetfulness of his old sins." Conversely, Ephraem (*Sermo compunctorius* [ed. Phrantzoles, 1988], 103, line 2) also uses the mixed metaphors of 2 Pet 1:8-9 to describe the one who, as in 1 John 1:6, 8, falsely claims not to sin, showing that he is "blind, being shortsighted and miserable above all men" (τυφλός ἐστι μυωπάζων καὶ ἄθλιος παρὰ πάντας ἀνθρώπους). The interpretation of 1:9 in view of 2:20-22 is also found in Chrysostom, *De patientia et de consummatione huius saeculi*, MPG 63, p. 942, lines 23-41 (cf. line 31 for τυφλός ἐστι, μυωπάζων). Chrysostom further interprets the return to the defilement of the world in 2:20, 22 to be a rejection of the things associated with the "holy bath" (ταῦτα ἐν τῷ ἁγίῳ λουτρῷ ἀπαρνησάμενοι), thus explicitly associating the forgetting of 1:9 with what has been learned at baptism as alluded to in 2:20-22 (line 36).

36. So already Huther (*Petrus*, 356), and now Kraus (*Sprache*, 270), contra those who, like Keil (*Petrus*, 223), take it to support μυωπάζων, and Spitta (*Petrus*, 76), who takes it to refer not to forgiveness by God but to one's own action of fleeing sin in his life, as in Sir 51:20; 2 Cor 7:1; Jas 4:8; 1 John 3:3, and thus construes the participle as the result of being blind, not its cause.

37. This emphasis on the state of being blind as manifest by forgetfulness seems to be reflected in the fact that "the notion of willfulness does not seem to lie in the phrase" (Bigg, *St. Peter*, 260). Λήθη occurs only here in the NT; never in the Apostolic Fathers, but 11x in the LXX. It is used absolutely to mean "forgetfulness" in 3 Macc 5:28; 4 Macc 1:5; 2:24; Wis 17:3; cf. too Aristob. 5:7 (5:15 OTP). For its use with λαμβάνω, see 3 Macc 6:20; Josephus, *A.J.* 2.163 (as the equivalent to "not remembering," οὐδὲ . . . μνημονεύω, cf. 2.162); *B.J.* 2.202; 4.304;

idiomatic expression for the act of forgetting, is the opposite of "being re-minded" or "remembering," or "receiving remembrance" (cf. 2 Tim 1:5: ὑπόμνησιν λαβών). In this way it anticipates the purpose of 2 Peter as ex-pressed in 1:12-15 and 3:1-2, and is part of the same semantic field as λανθάνω ("to escape one's notice," "to overlook"), which will be picked up in 3:5 and 8.[38] The churches are being reminded of God's faithfulness in Christ in order to keep them from the moral forgetfulness that characterizes spiritual blind-ness. Indeed, as Mayor pointed out, "This forgetfulness is itself an example of failure in the knowledge of Christ."[39]

The specific content of what has been forgotten is "the cleansing of his old sins." As the converse of verse 8, this forgotten reality further unpacks "the knowledge of our Lord, Jesus Christ" that brings about a life of increas-ing virtue. Accordingly, the knowledge in view is described in terms of the cultic imagery of ritual cleansing associated with the sacrificial practices of the tabernacle/temple, which functioned to purify both the place of God's presence and the life of the covenant member or community.[40] This "cleans-ing" (LXX: καθαρισμός) is usually associated with the forgiveness of sins, which is no doubt implied here.[41] This association is confirmed by the fact

---

10.242; 14.448; and esp. 5.107, where he expresses incredulity that those who had been in-structed in God's will, had heard the Law, and had received their heritage of land by God's grace, "could have straightway forgotten Him." Cf. Wis 16:11 for the construction ἐμπίπτω εἰς βαθεῖαν λήθην ("to fall into deep forgetfulness"); Sir 14:7 for ποιέω ἐν λήθῃ (to act in forget-fulness/unintentionally); Job 7:21 for ποιέω λήθην ("to make/perform forgiveness" of law-lessness, used as a parallel to the cleansing [καθαρισμός] of sin!); cf. T. Job 47:8 (λήθην ἔχω).

38. Cf. too ἐπιλανθάνομαι (8x in NT; 11x in LXX); and see Lev 5:15; Num 5:27: λήθη is used together with λανθάνω to intensify the action of escaping notice; Deut 8:19: λήθη is used with ἐπιλανθάνομαι ("to forget") to intensify the action of forgetting (ἐὰν λήθῃ ἐπιλάθῃ: lit: "if you should forget with/by forgetfulness").

39. Mayor, *Second Epistle*, 96.

40. See John Dennis ("The Function of the חטאת Sacrifice in the Priestly Literature: An Evaluation of the View of Jacob Milgrom," *ETL* 78 [2002]: 108-29), who argues, contra Milgrom, that although the primary function of the חטאת sacrifice is to purify the sanctu-ary from the sins/impurities of the people, the act also "directly results in the forgiveness/purification of the people" (125-26, 129).

41. For καθαρισμός as ritual cleansing, see Mark 1:44; Luke 2:22; 5:14; John 2:6; 3:25; for ritual cleansing or purification: Lev 14:32; 15:13; 1 Chron 23:28; 2 Macc 1:18; 2:19, including the purification of the altar (Heb 1:3; cf. Exod 29:36; 30:10). For the ritual use of the corre-sponding verb, καθαρίζω, see Matt 8:2-3 par. Mark 1:40-42; Matt 10:8; 11:5 par. Luke 7:22; Luke 4:27; 5:12-13; 17:14, 17 (cf. LXX Lev 13:6-7, 13-35, 59; 14:2-8, 57); Mark 7:19; Acts 10:15; 11:9; 15:9; Heb 9:22-23. For the LXX backdrop of the verb, referring both to ritual cleansing and to forgiveness, see Gen 35:2; Exod 20:7; Exod 29:36-37; 30:10; 34:7; Lev 8:15; 12:7-8; 14:8-31; 16:19-

that the foundational promise of the "new covenant" is the forgiveness of sins (Jer 31:34), which parallels the cleansing from all uncleanness (Ezek 36:25: cf. ὕδωρ καθαρὸν . . . καθαρισθήσεσθε). Moreover, the result of this cleansing/forgiveness is obedience to God's laws (Jer 31:33; Ezek 36:27), just as in verse 9 the cleansing from one's old sins leads to a growing life of the virtues (1:5-7, 8). Conversely, forgetting the cleansing of one's past sins indicates that one has not come to know the grace of God's transforming presence now being revealed in the new covenant, i.e., that one is "blind" to the knowledge of the Messiah as the new covenant revelation of the knowledge of God (Jer 31:34; for the covenant context of the danger of forgetting, see, e.g., Deut 4:9, 23; 6:12; 8:11; 2 Kgs 17:38; Ps 9:17; 103:2; Isa 17:10).[42]

At the same time, although the forgiveness of sins is clearly in view in 1:9, this is not its sole referent. In the context of the promises of verses 3-4, with their emphasis on God's provisions for the life of godliness that is already escaping the corruption of this world, and in view of the virtue list of verses 5-7 picked up in 8-11, the "cleansing" must also refer to the removal of former sins through the moral transformation brought about by the knowledge of the glory of God in Christ (vv. 2, 3, 8). So, too, the probable allusion to baptism contained in the cultic image of "being cleansed"[43] must not be constrained to the forgiveness of sins.[44] To be washed in baptism is to be cleansed *from* one's old sins in order to be cleansed *for* a new life of virtue represented by verses 5-7, which is "the way of truth" or "righteousness" (2:2,

---

20, 30; Num 14:18; Deut 5:11; 2 Kgs 5:10-14; Ps 18:13-14 (= 19:12-13); 50:4, 9 (= 51:2, 7); Jer 40:8 (= 33:8); Ezek 36:25, 33; Sir 38:10, etc.

42. I owe these OT references to J. Blake Arnoult, who pointed them out in regard to 1:12-15 (unpublished paper, Gordon-Conwell Theological Seminary, February 2009), and Mayor, *Second Epistle,* 193.

43. So virtually all commentators since Huther (*Petrus,* 356) and Mayor (*Second Epistle,* 96-97); for the exceptions, see Spitta, *Petrus,* 76, and Moo, *2 Peter,* 48. The primary support for such an allusion is 1 Pet 3:21 (cf. too John 3:25-26; Heb 6:4-6; 10:32 (which Mayor sees as conclusive). For secondary references, see 1 Cor 6:11; Titus 3:5; Col 1:13-14; Acts 22:16; Heb 1:3: Christ made purification of sins (καθαρισμὸν τῶν ἁμαρτιῶν ποιησάμενος) at the cross; *Barn.* 11:11; 2 *Clem.* 6:9.

44. Contra Walter Grundmann (*Der Brief des Judas und der zweite Brief des Petrus* [THKNT 15; 3d ed.; Berlin: Evangelische Verlagsanstalt, 1986], 74-75), who views 1:9 as orientated only to the past and hence views 2 Peter's view as inadequate in regard to the early Christian understanding of baptism, which included not only the cleansing of the past, but also an orientation to the foundation of the believer's future (Rom 6:1-11; 7:4, 6; 1 Cor 6:11; Gal 3:25-28; Titus 3:5). Rather than reflecting an early Catholicism, as Grundmann posits, 1:9 actually emphasizes the very thing Grundmann argues it omits.

21), a life "in holiness and godliness" (3:11).[45] For from the perspective of the covenant structure of 1:3-11, remembering such progress in regard to one's *past* sins strengthens one's trust in God for his deliverance in the *future*, which results in continuing to grow in the virtues of faith in the *present* (cf. 3:11, 14). Those who are not increasing in the virtues of verses 5-7 show themselves to have "forgotten" the initial progress they have made in obedience, falling back again into the old attitudes and ways of behavior that characterize life apart from Christ. Those who are "blind" to the glory of God in Christ, "forget"; those who "see," do not. Those who do not forget, persevere in virtue.

Here too our passage anticipates the discussion in 2:18-22 of the danger posed to young believers by the false teachers, who embody what it means to "forget the cleansing of one's old sins."[46] In short, the false teachers are like the dogs and pigs pictured in the aphorisms of 2:22. As a result, the corresponding cultic language of being "spotted and blemished" (σπίλοι καὶ μῶμοι) can be used in 2:13-14 to describe the "cursed children" who have forgotten that they have been cleansed of their sins. Conversely, the "beloved," who do not "forget" this reality (cf. Ps 103:2-5!), are pictured in 3:14 as "without spot or blemish" (ἄσπιλοι καὶ ἀμώμητοι). The "cultic cleanness" in view throughout 2 Peter is the life of obedience grounded in forgiveness and characterized by the increasing virtues of verses 5-7.[47]

---

45. For the act of ritual cleansing used metaphorically to refer to the removal of immoral behavior that "defiles" holiness, cf. e.g., Num 14:18; Job 7:21; Matt 23:25-26 (the *blind* [τυφλέ] Pharisee is called to cleanse the inside [καθάρισον], that the outside may be clean [καθαρός]); Luke 11:39; 2 Cor 7:1; Titus 2:14; Heb 9:14; 10:2; Jas 4:8; 1 John 1:7, 9.

46. For 2:20-22 as an interpretive key to 1:9c, see Spitta, *Petrus*, 76 (albeit with a different application, see above); Bigg, *St. Peter*, 260; Vögtle, *Petrusbrief*, 153; Bauckham, *2 Peter*, 189-90; Moo, *2 Peter*, 48; Charles, *Virtue amidst Vice*, 150.

47. Cf. John Calvin (*The Epistle of Paul the Apostle to the Hebrews and the First and Second Epistles of St. Peter* [Calvin's Commentaries; trans. W. B. Johnston; Grand Rapids: Eerdmans, 1963], 332), who uses the imagery of 2:22 (and Jas 2:17) in interpreting 1:9, which he takes to be written against those who plead that they have "faith by itself," showing they lack "true understanding." They wander in darkness like blind men, "because they do not keep to the way shown to us by the light of the gospel" (332). Thus, since the gospel shows the way of obedience, "those who have no concern for a pure and holy life do not even keep the elementary rules of faith" (333). "The blood of Christ has not made us clean simply to be stained by our dirt again," since cleansing does not consist "simply of pardon alone" (333).

The (Un)Conditionality of the Covenant Stipulations

Verse 10a brings the main point of verses 8-9 to a conclusion: (since) pursuing the virtues makes (you) neither useless nor unfruitful with regard to the knowledge of our Lord, Jesus Christ (v. 8c), "*therefore* (διὸ), all the more, brothers, be zealous. . . ." In so doing, the command of verse 10a (σπουδάσατε) restates the command of verse 5b (cf. σπουδὴν πᾶσαν), which was the main point of verses 5-7, and hence of 1:3-11 as a whole. Verses 8-9 thus function as a bilateral support both for the commands of verses 5-7 and for the command of verse 10: supply *with zeal* the virtues *because* of verses 8-9; *because* of 8-9, *be zealous* to make firm your calling and election.

In keeping with the legal, covenant imagery of our passage,[48] this call to be zealous (σπουδάσατε) is a summons to be "especially conscientious in discharging an obligation."[49] Specifically, they are to "make firm" or "confirm" (but not to initiate or sustain!) their "calling and election" as a continuing fulfillment of Israel's identity as God's "chosen," covenant people (cf. 1 Pet 1:14-16; 2:9; 2:21; 3:9; 5:10).

The argument of 10b-11, restating 8-9, again affirms that God's people establish the certainty of their calling and election by zealously persevering in the virtues of verses 5-7. The secondary, but early and well-attested variant inserted after the command, "be zealous," sought to remove all doubt concerning this point: ἵνα διὰ τῶν καλῶν ἔργων (ὑμῶν) . . . ποιῆσθε (be zealous "in order that through [your] good works you might make" firm your calling and election).[50] If "getting in" the covenant is a matter of God's *uncondi-*

---

48. So G. Adolf Deissmann, *Bible Studies* (Edinburgh: T. & T. Clark, 1923 [1901]), 104-9, on the Attic βεβαίωσις, which he construes as the legal "confirmation" from the seller of a transaction, a guarantee that a sale had indeed taken place if someone should question it (pointing to its use in papyri, Lev 25:23LXX, Wis 6:19; 2 Cor 1:21-22). Hence, as in 2 Cor 1:6 and Rom 4:16, in 2 Pet 1:10, 19, we should take βέβαιος to mean "confirm" and "sure," "in the sense of legally guaranteed security" (109).

49. *BDAG*, 939. Cf. Gal 2:10 (also with ποιέω); Eph 4:3; 1 Thess 2:17; 2 Tim 2:15; Heb 4:11; G. Green (*2 Peter*, 200) and *BDAG* (939) suggest that σπουδάζω can also indicate swift action, pointing to 2 Tim 4:9, 21; Titus 3:12; but in all three cases the temporal nuance is conveyed by adverbial modifiers, not by the verb itself.

50. As a later commentary on the text, it is of interest that the thirteenth-century (Category 3) ms. 2718 substitutes πίστιν for κλῆσιν, while the Sahidic Coptic tradition (fourth/fifth century) reads πίστιν καὶ κλῆσιν. The inextricable link between faith and good works is here made explicit, albeit in a way that may miss the text's own emphasis. Good works do not confirm one's faith, but faith, expressed in good works, confirms one's calling.

tional grace, "staying in" is clearly *conditional*, being based on keeping the covenant stipulations (v. 10).

Once again we must be careful in delineating the theological logic between "getting in" and "staying in" within the argument of 2 Pet 1:3-11. According to verses 8-9, whether one exhibits such zeal reveals whether one still is, *by nature*, "useless," "fruitless," and "blind," being without the cleansing of sin that opens the way into the eternal kingdom of the Christ. The emphasis in 8-9 on the state of being or condition of those who obey or disobey reflects the fact that within the covenant *relationship* divine calling and election, which determine one's covenant *status*, are not separated statically or abstractly from the life of faith-filled obedience that characterizes and hence maintains this relationship.[51] God's unconditional, increasing, life-changing grace (cf. 1:2!) is *equally* expressed *not only* in their divine call and election, *but also* in the believers' ongoing obedience to God's ensuing commands. Covenantally, there is no conflict between the indicatives of God's past calling (and future consummation!) and the present imperatives that correspond to them, since in "moving" from the indicatives to the imperatives, one never moves away from God. Hence, although the reality of God's grace as the effective cause of both "getting in" and "staying in" establishes an ethical tension between divine sovereignty and human moral agency, it must not be resolved by the common move of positing gratitude, not God's presence and promises, to be the motivational cause for obedience. To do so would make the believer, in effect, ultimately responsible for contributing this attitude, so that "the burden clearly rests on the shoulders of the readers to hold up their side of the covenant agreement."[52] Rather, the reality of the divine calling (vv. 3-4) and consummation (vv. 10b-11) is worked out in the creating and sustaining of God's people in a life of progressive obedience (vv. 5-10a).

This is why perseverance in obedience confirms the believer's election and calling, since it is God's grace (1:1-2, 3-4) that brings about the very increase in virtues necessary to enter the kingdom (v. 11).[53] Specifically, the

51. Cf. Kevin J. Vanhoozer, *The Drama of Doctrine* (Louisville: Westminster/John Knox, 2005), 391 (emphasis his): "Jesus' death saves because it achieves *covenantal* (not mere legal) *rightness* and *covenantal* (not mere interpersonal) *relationship*. It is crucial not to exaggerate the disjunction between the 'legal' and the 'relational.'"

52. So, representatively, Charles (*Virtue amidst Vice*, 151), who downsizes God's sovereignty in this way.

53. Contra Grundmann (*Petrus*, 75), who ignores the context of verses 3-4 and thus finds it striking that 1:10 speaks only of human effort, without making it clear that all human effort is God's work through his Spirit (as in Phil 2:12-13; 1:6; Gal 5:22; Rom 8:5-11; 9:16).

zealous pursuit of the virtues called for in verse 10 is derived from the two-fold cleansing of sins made possible by Christ referred to in verses 8-9. Moreover, verses 10b-11 assert that the "indicative" of God's provisions in the past (vv. 3, 9c) is inextricably linked to his "indicative" promises for the future (v. 4), so that together they bring about the keeping of the "imperative" stipulations in the present (1:5-7, 8, 10a). The power for growing in virtue is found in God's provisions; its motivation, in God's promises.

Nevertheless, though based on God's eternal election and sure promises, the command to make one's calling and election firm cannot be downsized to an exercise in subjective assurance, by which believers are simply confirming to themselves the truth of their redemption. There is no support contextually for such a reading: the promises of eschatological deliverance *in the future* are conditioned on increasing obedience in the *present* (vv. 8ab, 10b, 11).[54] The gravity of God's commands derives from the sober realization that there is a "nearsighted" apprehension of God, which must also be a matter of God's activity (!), but which stops short of being salvific, since it is void of the continuing virtue of verses 5-7 (cf. 2:20-22; Matt 10:22; Mark 4:16-19; Rom 11:22; 1 Cor 10:1-13; 15:1-2; 2 Cor 6:1; Gal 5:4; Col 1:23; 2 Tim 4:10; Heb 3:14; 6:1-8; 10:26-31; 12:15-17, etc.). In contrast, God's saving work is demonstrated in the believers' continuing zeal to confirm their election. The determining character of God's grace does not diminish but underscores the determining character of the believers' covenant-keeping. The one reality necessitates the other. Given humanity's "blind" nature, God must grant what he commands. But God therefore also commands what he grants.

The impetus behind the commands for zeal in 1:5 and 10a is the fact that entrance into the eternal kingdom of Christ is at stake in the believer's continuing obedience, a truth being called into question by the false teachers (2:17-22). The inheritance of God's promises, which is granted unconditionally, is conditional on persevering in the obedient life of faith that God's provision and promises themselves create. On the other hand, life within the covenant relationship must not be dissected by downsizing God's grace to the act of "getting in," thereby denying that "his divine power has bestowed to us all things pertaining to life and godliness" (v. 3a).[55] Nor should we di-

---

54. Contra too Charles (*Virtue amidst Vice*, 151n.115), who says the middle voice of ποιέω in verse 10a suggests "that the evidence is to oneself," which is to confuse the middle with the reflexive.

55. See Otto Knoch, *Der Erste und Zweite Petrusbrief. Der Judasbrief* (RNT; Regensburg: Pustet, 1990), 240-41 (emphasis and translation mine): "The writer thus assumes that

minish what it means to live in God's presence by upsizing covenant-keeping to a synergistic human "response," "contribution," "partnership," or "nomism," thereby denying that God's power and promises are, by definition, determinative.

---

the state of salvation that has been granted contains *in itself* the ability and the drive to live as a Christian according to the will of God and Christ. The indicative of the grace of salvation includes *within itself* the imperative of the ethical life of faith (cf. Phil 2:12f; 1 Pet 1:3-21; Jude 3)."

PART IV

Revelation

Divine Assistance and Enablement of Human Faithfulness in the Revelation of John Viewed within Its Apocalyptic Context

Charles H. Talbert

In Revelation, enablement of Christian faithfulness between the beginning of discipleship and its consummation is grounded in both a knowledge of the certainty of history's outcome and in special grace spoken of in terms of sealing, measuring, one's name being written in the Book of Life, being clothed, and the descent of the new Jerusalem from God.

•   •

It is an opinion widely held by NT scholars that most NT writers "shared a more or less explicit awareness that the Christian 'ought' now flowed from a specifically Christian indicative" (i.e., the new action of God in Christ and the continuing action of the Holy Spirit).[1] The linkage between the indicative (God's gift) and the imperative (the divine demand) is, nevertheless, less apparent in some NT writers than in others. It has been claimed, for example, that "in Revelation salvation sometimes seems to be on the basis of one's own deeds rather than on the grace of God."[2] Is this a fair assessment of the Apocalypse of John?

The purpose of this essay is to survey selected apocalypses, both Jewish

1. Tom Deidun, "The Bible and Christian Ethics," in *Christian Ethics: An Introduction* (ed. B. Hoose; Collegeville, MN: Liturgical Press, 1998), 36.

2. Eugene M. Boring, *Revelation* (IBC; Louisville: Westminster/John Knox, 1989), 5. As will become evident later in the essay, Boring does not think this judgment is an accurate one for all of Revelation.

and Christian,[3] and certain other writings that, although not apocalypses, reflect apocalyptic eschatology in an attempt to answer two questions. First, what is the virtue or behavior advocated by the authors as desirable of embodiment by the readers? That is, how is the divine *demand* understood? Second, what divine *assistance* and/or *enablement,* if any, is available to those who would pursue the desired virtue or behavior? That is, how is the divine *gift* perceived? Of the two, it is the latter question that holds the more interest in this project. The quest will focus first on Jewish and Christian writings that reflect the apocalyptic worldview of John's Apocalypse. Then attention will be directed to the Revelation to John in an attempt to determine where this canonical apocalypse fits within the currents of ancient apocalyptic eschatology. The primary concern is: If an ancient auditor, familiar with the apocalyptic eschatology characteristic of John's milieu, heard Revelation read, what would he/she have understood John to be saying about divine enablement of human faithfulness?[4] That is, how did this prophet perceive the relation between God's gift and the divine demand in the period between a Christian's conversion and resurrection?[5]

Apocalyptic Eschatology Apart from John's Apocalypse

Desired Behavior or Virtue

The first question to be addressed is: What is the desired virtue or behavior espoused by these ancient writings? An answer for the non-Christian Jewish sources involves two trajectories; for Christian sources yet another.

3. The Jewish apocalypses can be found in J. H. Charlesworth, ed., *The Old Testament Pseudepigrapha* (Garden City, NY: Doubleday, 1983); the Christian apocalypses can be located in W. Schneemelcher, ed., *New Testament Apocrypha* (Louisville: Westminster/John Knox, 1992). A helpful selection of both Jewish and Christian apocalypses and selected related materials may be found in M. G. Reddish, ed., *Apocalyptic Literature: A Reader* (Peabody, MA: Hendrickson, 1995).

4. This is called "reading with the authorial audience," following Peter J. Rabinowitz, *Before Reading: Narrative Conventions and the Politics of Interpretation* (Ithaca, NY: Cornell University Press, 1987); "Truth in Fiction: A Reexamination of Audiences," *Critical Inquiry* 4 (1977): 121-41; "Whirl without End: Audience Oriented Criticism," in *Contemporary Literary Theory* (ed. G. Douglas Atkins; Amherst: University of Massachusetts Press, 1989), 81-100. Cf. also Hans R. Jauss, "Literary History as a Challenge to Literary Theory," *New Literary History* 2, no. 1 (1970): 7-37.

5. The survey that follows makes no attempt to be exhaustive. It does claim to be representative.

Non-Christian Jewish Sources

The overarching norm for the main trajectory within Jewish sources for the period *after* Moses is keeping the covenant (*4 Ezra* 7:46), with covenant understood as synonymous with the Mosaic law. This is sometimes expressed in terms of loyalty to God, standing firm, persevering in loyalty to the Jewish God (Dan 11:32 — as opposed to violating the covenant; 12:12). At other times it is spoken of as keeping the law (*4 Ezra* 7:89 — keep the Law of the Lawgiver perfectly; *2 Bar.* 46:5 — obey the Law; 48:22 — keep your [God's] statutes; 51:7 — saved because of their works [of the Law]; 1QS IV, 4). *Testament of Moses* 9 holds up Taxo and his sons as the ideal. In verses 6-7 Taxo advocates their dying rather than transgressing the commandments. If they do so, he says, this will bring God's intervention and judgment. Some sources refer to a store of works laid up with God (*4 Ezra* 7:77; 8:36; *2 Bar.* 14:12; 24:1; 1QS IV, 15-17). In addition, in 1QS IV, 2-6, there is a virtue list giving the paths of the righteous in the world:

> to enlighten the heart of man, straighten out in front of him all the paths of justice and truth, establish in his heart respect for the precepts of God; it is a spirit of meekness, patience, generous compassion, eternal goodness, intelligence, understanding, potent wisdom which trusts in all the deeds of God and depends on his abundant mercy; a spirit of knowledge in all the plans of action, of enthusiasm for the decrees of justice, of holy plans with firm purpose, of generous compassion with all the sons of truth, of magnificent purity which detests all unclean idols, of unpretentious behavior with moderation in everything, of prudence in respect of the truth concerning the mysteries of knowledge. These are the counsels of the spirit for the sons of truth in the world.[6]

This would have been understood by the covenanters as an explication of the Mosaic laws. It is representative of this first trajectory generally.

Another trajectory reflects the hypothetical setting of a time *before* Moses. In *1 Enoch*, the ways of righteousness are set over-against the ways of wickedness (91:18; 93:10). In the *Testament of Abraham* 17:7, righteous deeds (12:12; 13:9) and hospitality are highlighted. Righteous deeds are classified as being merciful, hospitable (1:3-4; 2:4), righteous, truthful, God-fearing, re-

---

6. F. García-Martínez, *The Dead Sea Scrolls Translated* (Grand Rapids: Eerdmans, 1996), 6.

fraining from every evil deed (4:6). Abraham sees the judgment of souls and is told that one's destiny depends on whether or not one has at least one more good deed than bad on record in heaven (14:2-4). Although not reflected upon in an explicit way by either author, *1 Enoch* and the *Testament of Abraham* must assume some sort of natural law (= Noachic commandments?) prior to the Mosaic code for which humans before Moses are held accountable (cf. *2 Bar.* 57:2's reference to the unwritten law in the time of Abraham). Its contents represent the ideal for behavior.

Christian Sources

Christian sources, of course, involve Christology in the mix of what is expected (*Mart. Ascen. Isa.* 9:26; Herm. *Vis.*, 4.2.4 — "salvation can be found through nothing save through the great and glorious name"; *Apoc. Paul* 41 — the most severe punishment in eternity is reserved for those who "have not confessed that Christ came in the flesh and that the Virgin Mary bore him, and who say that the bread of the Eucharist and the cup of blessing are not the body and blood of Christ"). The righteous also are involved in good works, which are spelled out mainly in contrast with wrong behavior that is punished (*Apoc. Pet.* 6, 13; *Apoc. Paul* 14).

Divine Assistance

The second question is: What kind of divine assistance is offered to those who would live as the authors advocate? Any answer to this question must take account of the great diversity of answers given in these sources. Nevertheless, there is one overriding answer given, whatever the additional responses. We will, therefore, take first the dominant answer and only thereafter survey the additional responses to our query.

Widespread Perspective

In Mediterranean antiquity there was widespread agreement about an ethical theism in terms of which history was the scene of divine reward and retribution.[7] Dionysius of Halicarnassus, *Ant. Rom.*, 6.6.2 puts the pagan case well.

7. F. Gerald Downing, "Common Ground with Paganism in Luke and Josephus," *NTS* 28 (1982): 546-59.

The gods by omens, sacrifices and other auguries promise to grant to
our commonwealth liberty and a happy victory, both by the way of re-
warding us for the piety we have shown toward them and the justice we
have practiced during the whole course of our lives, and also from re-
sentment, we may reasonably suppose, against our (forsworn) enemies.
(Cary, LCL)

A similar representative refrain may be heard in Josephus, *Ant.*, 1.14-15.

The main lesson to be learned from this history by any who cares to pe-
ruse it is that men who conform to the will of God, and do not venture
to transgress laws excellently laid down, prosper in all things beyond belief and are rewarded by God with felicity; whereas, in proportion as
they depart from the strict observance of these laws, things else practica-
ble become impracticable, and whatever imaginary good they strive to
do ends in irretrievable disasters. (Marcus, LCL)

The overall pattern of such thinking, whether pagan or Jewish, can be
reduced to a broad outline: A — God is powerful; B — We must therefore be
virtuous, keeping the ancient rules; C — We shall then enjoy the good life; D
— And escape the unpleasant alternatives.[8] Sometimes in Jewish and early
Christian sources, the bad consequences/judgments by God were removed
from the historical process to the end of history. So in Josephus, *J.W.* 3.374,
the focus of the retribution is the last judgment and the focus of the reward
is resurrection. Also in Acts 17:30-31, at the end of a speech to pagan philosophers, Paul says:

While God has overlooked the times of human ignorance, now he commands all people everywhere to repent, because he has fixed a day on
which he will have the world judged in righteousness by a man whom he
has appointed, and of this he has given assurance to all by raising him
from the dead. (NRSV)

This conviction of a common ethical theism that good would be rewarded and evil punished, which in some Jewish and Christian sources was
transferred to the end of history, is precisely that which apocalyptic eschatology asserts.

---

8. F. Gerald Downing, "Ethical Pagan Theism and the Speeches in Acts," *NTS* 27
(1981): 548.

Virtually all, if not all, sources with an apocalyptic eschatology, Jewish and Christian, believe that *understanding* God's plan and purposes for the creation will cause proper behavior. The resources for ethical living are found in the *knowledge* that there will be a judgment resulting in rewards and punishments.[9] This understanding is given by revelation to certain individuals (e.g., *1 En.* 93:1-10 + 91:11-17 — history is divided into periods of ten weeks during which God's plan is worked out;[10] *4 Ezra* 11:1–12:51 — a reinterpretation of the fourth beast of Dan 7 is given to make it apply to Rome; *1 En.* 61; 69 — judgment is certain; *2 Bar.* 26-27 — the period of suffering is divided into twelve separate periods; 82 — God will certainly take care of his people's enemies and do it soon; 83 — what has been promised will come soon; 85:10 — the end is very near; *T. Ab.* 12-13 — every soul will be judged by three witnesses: Abel, the twelve tribes of Israel, and God himself; *T. Mos.* 12 — God has foreseen everything to the end and will carry it out; *Sib. Or.* 2 — history divides into ten days; *Mart. Ascen. Isa.* 6-11 — knowledge is provided to Isaiah of what is involved in the coming of Christ to earth and his return to heaven; *Apoc. Pet.* — a striking vision of hell and of paradise; *5 Ezra* 2:42-48 — vision of the saints on Mount Zion receiving their crowns from the Son of God; *6 Ezra* 16:63-67 — the end will be soon; *Apoc. Paul* — a vision of where the wicked and righteous go after death and before the judgment; the millennium, followed by judgment; *Apoc. Thom.* — eight days of signs of the end of the world).

The purpose of such revelation is sometimes made explicit. The recipient of the revelation will himself understand and then pass it on to the larger community. In the Book of Watchers (*1 En.* 1–36), chapter 5 says explicitly that such wisdom is given to the chosen so that they will not again do wrong, either through forgetfulness or pride. As a consequence, they will

---

9. Note the later Ps-Clementine, *Epistula Clementis* 4.1 ("But I know myself, O Clement, that I am bestowing on you sorrows and discouragement, dangers and reproaches from uneducated multitudes, which you will be able to bear nobly if you look to the great reward for endurance that is given you by God") and 10:4 ("But this and all that is similar you will continue to do to the end, if you are unceasingly mindful in your hearts of the judgment which comes from God"). Translations come from Schneemelcher, *New Testament Apocrypha*, 2:498, 500. *T. Levi* 3-4 reflects an earlier Jewish version of the same beliefs. In 3:10 Levi is told, after his visions of the heavens, "Yet men do not perceive these things, and they sin and provoke the Most High." In 4:5 Levi is told, "This is why wisdom is given to you, that you may instruct your sons."

10. David S. Russell, *The Method and Message of Jewish Apocalyptic* (Philadelphia: Westminster, 1964), 224, treats the division of history into epochs as a way apocalyptic authors attempted to show the certainty of judgment (cf. *4 Ezra* 14:11, 13; Herm., *Vis.*, 4:2.5).

not die of divine wrath. In Daniel the visions and their interpretation in chapters 7–12 impart understanding of God's purposes and plans for creation and creatures (11:33; 12:10). This allows the wise to understand (12:10) and to persevere (12:12) in righteousness (12:3). This also enables the wise to give this understanding to many (11:33) and to lead many to righteousness (12:3). This revealed understanding, moreover, allows the wise to accept their sufferings as a means of purification, cleansing, and refinement (12:10; 11:35; cf. *4 Ezra* 7:14; *6 Ezra* 16:19, 74-75 — famine and plague, tribulation and anguish are sent as scourges for the correction of humans; knowledge of this fact allows God to deliver the elect from the tribulation). Knowing the certainty of reward and punishment at the end of life or at the end of history will, it is believed, cause proper behavior in the here and now (*T. Mos.* 12; *6 Ezra* 16:63-67). This seems to be the dominant view in apocalyptic eschatology of how God motivates the righteous in their achievement of the desired behavior.

Divine Role

In addition to this overriding perspective there is occasionally a divine enablement mentioned. This enablement goes beyond any motivation that knowledge provides. It may involve things done outside the person or done to or within the person. Some examples are found in only Jewish or only Christian sources; others are found in both. (1) God *protects* those with works and faith (*4 Ezra* 13:23; cf. 2 Thess 2:6-7). (2) God will *speed up* his times (*2 Bar.* 83:22; cf. Mark 13:20). (3) God himself (or through his Son) will *guide* them/*keep* them (*Apoc. Paul* 9). (4) Each saint has his/her own angel to *help* (*Apoc. Paul* 19). (5) There is an angel that *intercedes* for the nation of Israel (*T. Levi* 5:7). Righteous saints also *intercede* for people (e.g., Moses — *T. Mos.* 11:17; Abraham — *T. Ab.* 14:10; the holy virgin — *Sib. Or.* 2:312). (6) Angels *measure* the righteous so they may remain faithful (*1 En.* 61). (7) A *book* with the names of the righteous written in it guarantees the right outcome for them in the Last Day (Dan 12:1; cf. Luke 10:20; Phil 4:3). (8) A heavenly *city* Zion (God's true people? cf. 4QpIs^d), not made with human hands and kept by God in heaven, will appear at the Last Day (*4 Ezra* 7:26; 8:52; 10:26-27, 44, 54; 13:36; *4 Bar.* 4:2-6). In both some Jewish and some early Christian materials, then, there is an extra measure of aid over and beyond a certain knowledge of the future given to the people of God to enable them to persevere.

Charles H. Talbert

Apocalyptic Eschatology in the Apocalypse of John

The same two questions will be asked of the Christian Revelation to John that have been asked of other apocalypses and documents with an apocalyptic eschatology. Even though Revelation's primary concern is "not with individual conversions but with the defeat of the Satanic trinity — the powers behind human resistance — which can only be carried out finally by God,"[11] the seer still gives attention to the divine assistance to and enablement of individual Christians who live in the midst of a world dominated by illusion. It is this subplot on which this essay focuses.

Desired Behavior

What type of behavior is regarded by Revelation as desirable for John's readers?[12]

Chapters 2–3, which contain the seven letters to the seven churches, supply explicit evidence of what the prophet John regards as constituting proper behavior: enduring patiently and bearing up for the sake of Jesus' name (2:3; 2:19 — patient endurance; 3:10 — patient endurance; holding fast to Jesus' name, not denying one's faith in him; 3:8 — not denying Jesus' name); to conquer (2:7; 2:11; 2:17; 2:26; 3:5; 3:12; 3:21), which is under-

---

11. J. M. P. Sweet, "Maintaining the Testimony of Jesus: The Suffering of Christians in the Revelation of John," in *Suffering and Martyrdom in the New Testament* (ed. W. Horbury and B. McNeil; Cambridge: Cambridge University Press, 1981), 116.

12. Phil A. Harland, "Honouring the Emperor or Assailing the Beast: Participation in Civic Life among Associations (Jewish, Christian, and Other) in Asia Minor and the Apocalypse of John," *JSNT* 77 (2000): 99-121, distinguishes two types of imperial related activities: (1) involvement in ascribing honors to emperors and their representatives, and (2) cultic activities/honors for emperors that often included a communal meal involving consumption of some of the foods offered to the gods. The former found some Jews (e.g., Josephus, *C. Ap.* 2.68-78; *A.J.* 16.165) and some early Christians (e.g., 1 Pet 2:11-17) as participants. The latter were not considered proper by most Jews and early Christians. Revelation does not recognize the distinction between (1) and (2). John attempts to convince his readers that what at first appears to be a normal practice is in fact an utterly unacceptable compromise with evil. Those addressed, however, apparently viewed their behavior not as idolatry but as a necessary part of living and working with the *polis*. So, as Giancarlo Biguzzi, "Ephesus, Its Artemision, Its Temple to the Flavian Emperors, and Its Idolatry in Revelation," *NT* 40 (1998): 276-90, esp. 289, says: "Revelation is a book of resistance to the ideology of the Roman empire which provided 'the lure of well-being that softened the spirit of the believers.'"

stood as being faithful unto death (2:10), continuing to do Jesus' works to the end (2:26); holding fast to what one has (2:25; 3:11); keeping Jesus' word (3:8).[13]

Chapters 4–22, which contain the seven visions of the shift of the ages, continue the emphases of chapters 2–3. Patient endurance is the chief virtue.[14] A number of images are used to convey the same message. (1) Christians are expected to conquer (12:11; 15:2; 21:7). Here also to conquer/overcome means "to persevere while suffering."[15] Believers are followers of the Lamb wherever he goes (14:4). If the Lamb who has conquered is the one who has been slain (5:6), then his people will also conquer by the blood of the Lamb (12:11). They do not cling to life in the face of death (12:11). If they are taken captive, into captivity they go. They do not respond by killing with the sword (13:9-10). Resisting the impulse to violence and trusting God's vindication, they thereby conquer.[16] G. B. Caird's interpretation is on target.

> If God allows the monster to wage war on his people and conquer them, what must God's people do? They must allow themselves to be conquered as their Lord had done, so that like their Lord they may win a victory not of this world. . . . [T]he church must submit without resistance to the conquering attack of the monster, since only in this way can the monster be halted in its track. Evil is self-propagating. Like the Hydra, the many-headed monster can grow another head when one has been cut off. When one man wrongs another, the other may retaliate, bear a grudge, or take his injury out on a third person. Whichever he does, there are now two evils where before there was one; and a chain reaction is started, like the spreading of a contagion. Only if the victim

---

13. All of these expressions are to be regarded as synonyms for faithfulness to God. Jürgen Kerner, *Die Ethik der Johannes-Apokalypse im Vergleich mit der des 4. Esra* (BZNW 94; Berlin: De Gruyter, 1998), 39-51.

14. Rudolf Schnackenburg, *The Moral Teaching of the New Testament* (New York: Seabury, 1979), 378.

15. Gregory K. Beale, *The Book of Revelation* (NIGTC; Grand Rapids: Eerdmans, 1999), 312.

16. This is a part of the larger reinterpretation of military imagery by the book of Revelation. Cf. Richard B. Hays, *The Moral Vision of the New Testament* (San Francisco: HarperCollins, 1996), 174-79; Thomas B. Slater, *Christ and Community: A SocioHistorical Study of the Christology of Revelation* (JSNTSS 178; Sheffield: Sheffield Academic, 1999), 169, 181, speaks of the reversal of expectations. Cf. also Loren L. Johns, *The Lamb Christology of the Apocalypse of John* (WUNT 2/167; Tübingen: Mohr-Siebeck, 2003).

absorbs the wrong and so puts it out of currency, can it be prevented from going any further. And this is why the great ordeal is also the great victory.[17]

(2) When 21:8 (and 22:15) list the vices that exclude people from the heavenly city,

> [e]ach transgression can be balanced antithetically by a positive trait that is to characterize members of the heavenly city. For example, in contrast to the "cowardly" are believers who respond positively to the exhortation to be fearless (2:10).[18]

Fearlessness for Christians in Revelation is, of course, fearlessness to persevere even in the face of death. (3) Faithful believers are not to worship the beast (13:8; 14:9; 20:4) or to receive the mark of the beast on forehead or hand (13:17; 14:9; 20:4). This requires "the endurance and faith of the saints" (13:10b; cf. 12:17 — keeping the commandments of God and holding the testimony of Jesus;[19] 14:12 — endurance + keeping God's commandments and the faith of Jesus). This, of course, refers to the struggle of the church with Roman imperial power and the worship of the emperor in the emperor cult. Worship of any man, including the emperor, was unthinkable for the prophet John. Not to do so, even if it cost one economically or resulted in martyrdom (16:6; 20:4), was the desired behavior. To endure unto death was the meaning of "to conquer." (4) In 18:4, the voice from heaven cries: "Come out of her, my people" (cf. Jer 51:45). The summons is a call to Jesus' followers to separate themselves from the idolatry, oppression, and greed of the larger Roman society.[20] It is not a call to geographical relocation but rather an exhortation to inner reorientation.[21] It is another way of saying: do not assimilate into Roman imperial culture. (5) Another image is that of being clothed with fine linen, bright and pure

---

17. G. B. Caird, *A Commentary on the Revelation of St. John the Divine* (BNTC; New York: Oxford University Press, 1966), 169-10.

18. Beale, *The Book of Revelation*, 1059.

19. Sweet, "Maintaining the Testimony of Jesus," 106, says: "It is not only the verbal witness to the true God and his will . . . but also the obedience to his commands that goes with it."

20. Mitchell G. Reddish, *Revelation* (Smyth & Helwys Bible Commentary; Macon, GA: Smyth & Helwys, 2001), 354.

21. Boring, *Revelation*, 189.

(19:8a), which refers to "the righteous deeds of the saints" (cf. 3:4-5), in contrast to the harlot's unrighteous deeds (17:4-6). Being clothed with such fine deeds, of course, is to reflect in one's behavior the desired faithfulness to Jesus. So stay awake and remain clothed (16:15). The related image of "washing one's robes" (22:14; 7:14) in the blood of the Lamb carries a similar meaning: salvific perseverance.[22]

Divine Assistance

The Dominant Assistance

In Revelation, as in the other apocalypses and writings with apocalyptic eschatology, the conventional dominant assistance is employed for the people of God to embody the behavior deemed desirable. Why endure? It is the certainty of God's ultimate victory, involving judgment with its accompanying rewards and punishments.[23] In chapters 2–3 the language of eschatological rewards is prominent. To the one who conquers, the risen Jesus will give the tree of life to eat (2:7) and some of the hidden manna (2:17). Such a person will not be hurt by the second death (2:11). Rather Jesus will confess this person's name before the Father (3:5). Such a one will be given power over nations (2:26), will be made into a pillar in the temple of God (3:12), and will sit with Jesus on his throne (3:21).

Chapters 4–22 have repeated presentations of final judgment (6:12-17; 11:17-18; 14:9-11; 14:17-20; 20:11-15; 22:12), just as there are repeated presentations of the glorious state of affairs after the judgment (11:15-16; 14:1-5; 15:2-4; 21:1–22:5; 22:14). There are also repeated reassurances of God's ultimate victory, judgment with rewards and punishments (chs. 4–5; 7:9-17; 8:2-6; 11:19; 19:1-10; 22:12). Like apocalyptic eschatology in general, that of the Revelation to John assumes that if humans know the certain outcome of history, they will act properly. One clear example comes in chapter 14. In verse 12 there is a call for Christians' endurance. On either side of this exhortation motivating factors are given. Before it, in verses 9-11, there is a warning that those who worship the beast and receive the mark of the beast will share the judgment sent on Roman imperial power. After it, in verse 13, there are two voices from

22. Beale, *The Book of Revelation*, 1138.

23. C. Freeman Sleeper, *The Bible and the Moral Life* (Louisville: Westminster/John Knox, 1992), 80-81.

heaven promising blessedness to those who remain faithful even unto death. It is the certainty of final judgment with its punishments and rewards that is designed to motivate believers to remain faithful. A second example comes in 18:4 when the voice calls, "Come out of her, my people." The spiritual exodus required is from demonic values, the pride of power (18:3, 9-10), and greed (18:3, 11-19) that marked Rome. Such an exodus "could be undertaken only in the assurance of the victory of the Lamb . . . who judges justly" and of the certainty of the new world to come.[24] Yet another example is found in the glorious picture of the new Jerusalem that is offered in 21:9–22:5. The new Jerusalem is not so much a place as it is a people — the people of God who are the bride of Christ.[25] This grand picture is offered as an incentive for first-commandment faithfulness in the present.[26] This is the type of motivation that predominates in all of the other apocalypses and in other writings with apocalyptic eschatology. The Revelation to John participates in this thought world. The apocalypse was revealed so believers would gain a heavenly perspective on redemptive history and from their immersion in John's symbolic universe would consequently obey the commands of the Lord of history.[27] If they know, they will do.

Additional Aids

There is, however, another dimension — that of divine enablement, which produces the desired behavior to be found in Revelation. Two images are primary in the earlier visions of the Apocalypse.[28] The first main metaphor comes in the interlude (7:1-17) of cycle one (4:1–8:1): the *sealing* of the servants of God (7:1-8). The four winds are commanded not to do harm on the earth until "we have sealed the servants of God upon their foreheads" (v. 3). The sealed number is 144,000 (v. 4). The sealing, in context,

---

24. A. Verhey, *The Great Reversal* (Grand Rapids: Eerdmans, 1984), 151.

25. Robert H. Gundry, "The New Jerusalem: People as Place, Not Place for People," *NT* 29 (1987): 254-64. Cf. 4QpIs^d from Qumran, which gives an allegorical interpretation of Isa 54:11-17 in which the new Jerusalem is the community itself.

26. Charles H. Talbert, *The Apocalypse* (Louisville: Westminster/John Knox, 1984), 103.

27. Beale, *The Book of Revelation*, 184.

28. Adela Y. Collins, *The Combat Myth in the Book of Revelation* (HDR 9; Atlanta: Scholars, 1976), 8, says: "In current research on the book of Revelation, there is very little consensus on the overall structure of the work and how that structure should be interpreted. There are almost as many outlines of the book as there are interpreters." This essay's argument does not depend on any given structure.

conveys ownership and protection (cf. Ezek 9:1-11).[29] The 144,000 are, according to verses 13-14, those who have come out of the great tribulation. They are the same group found in 14:1-4 (cf. 5:9b). If so, then the reference is to the whole people of God.[30] What is the function in Rev 7 of this sealing of the people of God? It depicts God's spiritual protection of believers during the great period of suffering so that they do not commit apostasy.[31] The divine seal empowers "the saints to remain loyal to Christ and not to compromise in the midst of pressures to do so."[32] Boring reminds us that "with the mark of God on their foreheads, faithful Christians are preserved through (not from!) the great persecution."[33] That the saints in heaven (7:9-17) have endured because they were sealed by divine order (7:3), makes a clear point. Christian faithfulness, while a human act, is enabled by divine grace.[34]

The second main metaphor for divine enablement of believers in the earlier visions of Revelation comes in the interlude (10:1–11:2) of cycle two (8:2–11:18). After the recommissioning of the prophet in chapter 10, in 11:1-2 we meet the *measuring* of the inner courts of the Temple. The act of measuring is linked with protection (cf. *1 Enoch* 61);[35] the inner courts with the faithful people of God; and the outer courts with either unfaithful Christians[36] or the unbelieving world.[37] Either way, the measuring of the temple in cycle two serves the same function as the sealing of the servants of God in cycle one. It is another way to speak of the preservation of the church from spiritual danger during the apocalyptic tribulations.[38] The measuring connotes God's presence, which upholds his people's faith so "no aberrant

---

29. Reddish, *Revelation*, 143. This judgment is that of virtually all commentators.

30. Beale, *The Book of Revelation*, 412-13. This is the judgment of most commentators.

31. Reddish, *Revelation*, 145, 152, 155. Again, Reddish's judgment is representative.

32. Beale, *The Book of Revelation*, 414.

33. Boring, *Revelation*, 128.

34. Talbert, *The Apocalypse*, 37.

35. Isbon T. Beckwith, *The Apocalypse of John* (New York: Macmillan, 1919), 597, contends that the imagery is suggested by Ezek 40–43 but not the meaning. "The meaning is shown by the contrast in v. 2 to be the symbol of preservation; the measurement marks off the sphere whose bounds the devastation or profanation of the enemy may not cross."

36. Contra Marko Jauhiainen, "The Measuring of the Sanctuary Reconsidered (Rev. 11,1-2)," *Bib* 83 (2002): 507-26. Context is determinative for meaning. Talbert, *The Apocalypse*, 45, appealing to 3:19.

37. Reddish, *Revelation*, 209.

38. Gerhard Krodel, *Revelation* (ACNT; Minneapolis: Augsburg, 1989), 219; Robert H. Mounce, *The Book of Revelation* (NICNT; Grand Rapids: Zondervan, 1977), 219.

Charles H. Talbert

. . . influences will be able to spoil or contaminate their true faith and worship."[39] The following segment of text, 11:3-13, which depicts the church as
two end-time witnesses who suffer, die, and are then vindicated, shows that
for the prophet John "Christians go to the presence of God through tribulation and martyrdom, not instead of it."[40] The *measuring*, just as the *sealing*,
speaks of God's enablement of Christian faithfulness, an enablement that is
something more than the provision of a certain knowledge. It involves the
empowering of persons.

A minor way of referring to divine enablement of believers' faithfulness is also found in a later section of Revelation. It runs: God provides a
place of nourishment (12:6), a means of escape (12:14), and the aid of the
natural order (12:16) to defend and protect the people of God from Satan's
attacks. Time is controlled, moreover, so that Satan's attacks are allowed only
in specified periods (12:14). Here the enablement comes by divine manipulation of the circumstances of the saints' experience.

In the later visions of the Apocalypse one finds additional references to
God's enablement of believers' faithfulness. (1) One way is reflected in the
image of the *Book of Life*. God, before the foundation of the world, has written the names of the faithful in the Lamb's book of life (13:8; 17:8b; 20:12; cf.
3:5). In 20:11-15, the Last Judgment scene, judgment is conducted on the basis
of two books: the Book of Life and the Book of Accounts.

> These two sets of books symbolize a paradox. The names in the book of
> life have been written from before the foundation of the world (= divine
> election, 13,8); but only those who endure are written in the book of rec-
> ords (= human responsibility). All judgment scenes regard human re-
> sponsibility as crucial (= judged by what they had done, 22,12b), but the
> book of life says that the ones who endured do so only because of God's
> grace.[41]

In these two books is portrayed the paradox of works and grace.
"John's pictorial language makes both statements in one picture."[42] If, how-

39. Beale, *The Book of Revelation*, 559.
40. Talbert, *The Apocalypse*, 148.
41. Talbert, *The Apocalypse*, 98. David E. Aune, *Revelation 17–22* (WBC 52C; Nashville:
Thomas Nelson, 1998), 1102, devoid of theological sensitivity, can say only that the reference
to the book of life (20:12) appears to be an insertion into the basic judgment scene!
42. Boring, *Revelation*, 212. Revelation has been characterized as a "picture book" by
Jorg Frey, "Die Bildersprache der Johannesapokalypse," *ZTK* 98 (2001): 161-85.

278

ever, one's record in the Book of Accounts is acceptable,[43] it is because one's name had already been written in the Book of Life. Divine enablement is critical.

(2) In 19:8, within the context of the praise of heaven (vv. 6b-8), we hear a great multitude crying:

> the marriage of the Lamb has come,
>   and his Bride has made herself ready;
> to her it *has been granted* to be clothed with fine linen,
>   bright and pure —
>   for the fine linen is the righteous deeds of the saints.
>
> (NRSV)

The bride of Christ is, of course, the church (cf. 2 Cor 11:2; Eph 5:25-33).[44] Her fine attire is her righteous deeds (= deeds that reflect faithfulness to Christ). This fine attire, her righteous behavior, "was given to her so that she might clothe herself" (my literal translation designed to bring out the point that the church's faithfulness is the result of divine enablement).[45] "Given to her" must not be minimized.[46] The gift is God's "unconditional, sovereign provision."[47]

In the second half of the Apocalypse of John there is also a minor technique used to speak about divine enablement of God's people. In Revelation 21:2, 10 we hear that the new Jerusalem "comes down out of (ἐκ) heaven from (ἀπό) God." The former preposition refers to the place of origin, the

43. Grant R. Osborne, *Revelation* (ECNT; Grand Rapids: Baker Academic, 2002), 722, emphasizes that the theme of judgment on the basis of works in Revelation is applied to believers (2:23; 11:18b; 14:13; 22:12) and unbelievers (11:18b; 18:6; 20:13) alike.

44. J. Ramsey Michaels, *Revelation* (The IVP New Testament commentary series; Downers Grove, IL: InterVarsity, 1997), 212.

45. Robert H. Charles, *A Critical and Exegetical Commentary on the Revelation of St. John* (vol. 2; ICC; Edinburgh: T. & T. Clark, 1920), 127, says that in this text "we have presented God's part and man's part in the work of redemption."

46. Fritz Grünzweig, *Johannes-Offenbarung* (vol. 2; Neuhausen/Stuttgart: Hänssler, 1983), 178, says that it is not what the bride does for or gives to the bridegroom; it is rather what her Lord does for and gives to her. Mounce, *The Book of Revelation*, 340, sees a soteriological similarity between 19:8 and Eph 2:10. Beckwith, *The Apocalypse*, 727, says the word *give* is significant. "Only by the gift of God can the church attire herself fittingly for the Lamb." Cf. also Eduard Schick, *Die Apokalypse* (GS 23; Düsseldorf: Patmos-Verlag, 1971), 201.

47. Beale, *The Book of Revelation*, 942; Beckwith, *The Apocalypse*, 727; E. Schick, *Die Apokalypse*, 201.

latter to the divine originator.[48] This is a way to say that the redeemed community, God's people, are perfected by God. Their location (heaven) and their source (God) speak to their redemption by the Creator who now makes all things new. Boring puts it well. The Bride-City

> is not a human achievement. . . . Without in the least minimizing human responsibility . . . , he pictures the new Jerusalem as "coming down from heaven from God" (21:2). As important as "works" are for John, participation in the heavenly city is finally a matter of grace freely given (21:6).[49]

So the city's descent to earth on the Last Day connotes its establishment by God rather than by human effort. If any saints make it to the new world, it is God's doing! In all of these examples, God's enablement of the saints goes beyond assistance provided through certain knowledge.

Conclusion

What has this survey revealed? We have seen that the Revelation to John belongs, in its soteriology, to the world of apocalyptic eschatology generally.

1. The *knowledge* of the certainty of judgment with its rewards and punishments functions in both the Revelation to John and its apocalyptic context as the conventional means of divine assistance to produce human faithfulness. How should this means be regarded theologically? If E. P. Sanders views "staying in" in ancient Judaism as motivated by gratitude for past grace, "staying in" in the apocalypses surveyed is motivated by revealed knowledge of an assured future.

2. Additional means of enablement of human faithfulness by divine means are also found in both the Revelation to John and its apocalyptic eschatological milieu.

> a. In both, God *protects* the people of God.
>
> | | |
> |---|---|
> | *1 Enoch* 61 | Revelation 7:2-3 — the sealing |
> | 2 Thessalonians 2:6-7 | Revelation 11:1-2 — the measuring |
> | *4 Ezra* 13:23 | Revelation 3:10b — I will keep you from the hour of trial (cf. John 17:15) |

---

48. Beckwith, *The Apocalypse*, 751.
49. Boring, *Revelation*, 221.

b. In both, God's control of time is an aid.
Mark 13:20   Revelation 12:14
2 Baruch 83:22

c. In both, there is angelic assistance.
Testament of Levi 5:7   Revelation 7:2-3; 8:3-4
Apocalypse of Paul 19

d. In both, there is a heavenly city, not built with hands, that comes from God.
4 Ezra 7:26; 8:52;   Revelation 21:2, 10
10:26-27, 44, 54
2 Baruch 4:2-6

e. In both, there is a heavenly book in which the names of the faithful are written.
Daniel 12:1   Revelation 13:8; 17:8b; 20:12; 21:27; cf. 3:5
Luke 10:20
Philippians 4:3

Sometimes, moreover, Revelation speaks of God's enablement of the people of God in a way that seems to have roots in the prophetic and wisdom parts of the biblical tradition more so than in apocalyptic specifically. For example, take "to the bride it was given (ἐδόθη) to clothe herself (περιβάληται) in her righteous deeds" (19:8). Isaiah 61:10 MT is especially close conceptually and linguistically to Rev 19:8. "I will greatly rejoice in the Lord . . . for he has *clothed* me with the garments of salvation, he has covered me with the robe of *righteousness,* as a bridegroom decks himself with a garland, and as a *bride adorns herself* with her jewels." Baruch 5:2 LXX reflects conceptual and linguistic similarities also. "*Clothe yourself* (περιβάλου) with a double garment of *righteousness from God.*" For our purposes one may say that Revelation uses the image of clothing, of a bride, with righteousness, which comes from God, to express divine enablement, images whose roots seem to be in Isaiah and Baruch.

In at least some of these ways of speaking of divine enablement of human faithfulness there is something done not only outside the persons involved but also to or in them. The heavenly book, the heavenly city, the sealing and measuring, and the clothing with righteousness all push beyond acting rightly because of what one knows about the future. In these images a divine enablement supplies the resources to enable people to act out of gratitude and/or in line with the certainty of future judgment and rewards.

Reflecting on the line of thought pursued so far, if ancient auditors immersed in the biblical and apocalyptic traditions heard the Revelation to John read aloud, what would have been communicated to them? It is certain that the ancient auditor would have understood almost everything in John's apocalypse, because it was part of the conventional world of biblical and apocalyptic thought. If there was any sense of John's individuality, it was probably that the Revelation to John has arguably a greater degree of emphasis on divine enablement of the faithfulness of God's people than the other apocalypses, even the other Christian ones. This is especially true of what God does to and in the persons involved. If there is any distinctiveness to the soteriology of Revelation, it is here: where the emphasis lies. The Revelation to John, then, clearly participates in the new covenant piety[50] reflected in other NT documents by making explicit that the Christian life between conversion and resurrection is lived not only with divine assistance but also by divine enablement, however that enablement is envisioned.

Summary

Like the Jewish and Christian apocalypses generally and other genres that reflect apocalyptic eschatology, the Revelation to John believes the major motivation for religious faithfulness is certain knowledge of future judgment with its rewards and punishments. By revealing this knowledge to a seer who then imparts it to others, God provides *assistance* to human faithfulness. Revelation, even more than other apocalypses, also speaks of divine *enablement* of human faithfulness through manipulation of circumstances and especially through God's actions on and in people to empower them for faithfulness in difficult times.

50. J. A. Du Rand, "The Ethos of the Book of Revelation," *Verbum et Ecclesia* 24 (2003): 374-95.

Bibliography of Modern Authors

Abegg, Martin G. "4QMMT C 27,31 and 'Works Righteousness.'" *Dead Sea Discoveries* 6 (1999): 139-47.

Achtemeier, Paul J. *1 Peter: A Commentary on 1 Peter.* Hermeneia. Minneapolis: Fortress, 1996.

Anderson, Bernhard W. "Exodus Typology in Second Isaiah." Pages 177-95 in *Israel's Prophetic Heritage.* Edited by Bernhard W. Anderson and Walter Harrelson. New York: Harper, 1962.

Austin, J. L. *How to Do Things with Words.* Cambridge, MA: Harvard University Press, 1962.

Attridge, Harold W. *The Epistle to the Hebrews.* Philadelphia: Fortress, 1989.

Aune, David E. *Revelation 17–22.* Word Biblical Commentary 52C. Nashville: Thomas Nelson, 1998.

Avemarie, Friedrich. "Erwählung und Vergeltung zur optionalen Struktur Rabbinischer Soteriologie." *New Testament Studies* 45 (1999): 108-26.

———. *Tora und Leben: Untersuchungen zur Heilsbedeutung der Tora in der frühen rabbinischen Literatur.* Text und Studien zum antiken Judentum 55. Tübingen: Mohr-Siebeck, 1996.

Bacon, Benjamin Wisner. "Jesus and the Law: A Study of the First 'Book' of Matthew (Mt 3–7)." *Journal of Biblical Literature* 47 (1928): 203-31.

Barclay, John, and Simon Gathercole, eds. *Divine and Human Agency in Paul and His Cultural Environment.* Library of New Testament Studies 335. London: T. & T. Clark, 2006.

Barrett, C. K. *The Holy Spirit and the Gospel Tradition.* London: SPCK, 1970.

———. *The Pastoral Epistles.* Oxford: Clarendon, 1963.

———. *Paul: An Introduction to His Thought.* Louisville: Westminster/John Knox, 1994.

Barth, Markus. *Ephesians: Introduction, Translation, and Commentary.* The Anchor Bible 34-34A. Garden City, NY: Doubleday, 1974.

Bauckham, Richard. *James: Wisdom of James, Disciple of Jesus the Sage.* New Testament Readings. London and New York: Routledge, 1999.

———. *2 Peter and Jude.* WBC 50. Waco, TX: Word, 1983.

Beale, Gregory K. *The Book of Revelation: A Commentary on the Greek Text.* The New International Greek Testament Commentary. Grand Rapids: Eerdmans, 1999.

———. "Exodus vi 9-13: A Retributive Taunt Against Idolatry." *Vetus Testamentum* 41 (1991): 257-78.

Beardslee, William A. "Parable Interpretation and the World Disclosed by the Parable." *Perspectives in Religious Studies* 3 (1976): 123-39.

———. "Uses of the Proverb in the Synoptic Gospels." *Interpretation* 24 (1970): 61-73.

Beare, F. W. *The First Epistle of Peter: The Greek Text with Introduction and Notes.* 3d ed. Oxford: Blackwell, 1970.

Beckwith, Isbon T. *The Apocalypse of John.* New York: Macmillan, 1919.

Beker, Johan Christiaan. *The Triumph of God: The Essence of Paul's Thought.* Minneapolis: Fortress Press, 1990.

Best, Ernest. *The Temptation and the Passion: The Markan Soteriology.* 2d ed. Cambridge: Cambridge University Press, 1990.

Bigg, Charles. *A Critical and Exegetical Commentary on the Epistles of St. Peter and St. Jude.* ICC. Edinburgh: T. & T. Clark, 1901.

Biguzzi, Giancarlo. "Ephesus, Its Artemision, Its Temple to the Flavian Emperors, and Its Idolatry in Revelation." *Novum Testamentum* 40 (1998): 276-90.

Boccaccini, Gabriele. *Middle Judaism: Jewish Thought, 300 B.C.E.–200 C.E.* Minneapolis: Fortress Press, 1991.

Bock, Darrell L. *Luke 9:51–24:53.* Baker Exegetical Commentary of the New Testament. Grand Rapids: Baker Academic, 1996.

Boismard, M. E. "Une liturgie baptismale dans la Prima Petri: II. Son Influence sur l'Epître de Jacques." *Revue biblique* 64 (1957): 161-83.

Bonnard, Pierre. *L'évangile selon Saint Matthieu.* 2d ed. Commentaire du Nouveau Testament. Neuchâtel: Delachaux & Niestlé, 1970.

Boring, M. Eugene. *1 Peter.* Abingdon New Testament Commentaries. Nashville: Abingdon, 1999.

———. *Revelation.* Interpretation: A Bible Commentary for Teaching and Preaching. Louisville: Westminster/John Knox, 1989.

Braumann, Georg. "Mit euch, Matth 26:29." *Theologische Zeitschrift* 21 (1965): 161-69.

Bréhier, Émile. *Les idées philosophiques et religieuses de Philon d'Alexandrie.* Etudes de philosophie médiévale 8. Paris: Librairie philosophique J. Vrin, 1925.

Brown, Raymond Edward. *The Gospel According to John: Introduction, Translation, and Notes.* The Anchor Bible 29-29A. 1st ed. Garden City, NY: Doubleday, 1966.

Brown, Schuyler. *Apostasy and Perseverance in the Theology of Luke.* Analecta Biblica 36. Rome: Pontifical Biblical Institute, 1969.

Brown, Tricia Gates. *Spirit in the Writings of John: Johannine Pneumatology in Social-Scientific Perspective.* Journal for the Study of the New Testament Supplement Series 253. London: T. & T. Clark, 2003.

Bultmann, Rudolf Karl. *The Gospel of John: A Commentary.* Philadelphia: Westminster, 1971.

———. *Theology of the New Testament.* 2 vols. Translated by Kendrick Grobel. New York: Scribner's, 1951-1955.

Burnett, Fred W. "Philo on Immortality: A Thematic Study of Philo's Concept of Παλιγγενεσία." *Catholic Biblical Quarterly* 46 (1984): 450-53.

Byrne, Brendan. *Reckoning with Romans: A Contemporary Reading of Paul's Gospel.* Good News Studies 18. Wilmington, DE: M. Glazier, 1986.

———. *Sons of God, Seed of Abraham: A Study of the Idea of the Sonship of God of All Christians in Paul against the Jewish Background.* Analecta Biblica 83. Rome: Biblical Institute, 1979.

Byrskog, Samuel. *Jesus the Only Teacher: Didactic Authority and Transmission in Ancient Israel, Ancient Judaism and the Matthean Community.* Coniectanea Biblica: New Testament Series 24. Stockholm: Almqvist & Wiksell International, 1994.

Caird, G. B. *A Commentary on the Revelation of St. John the Divine.* Black's New Testament Commentaries. New York: Oxford University Press, 1966.

———. *Saint Luke.* Westminster Pelican Commentaries. Philadelphia: Westminster, 1963.

Calvin, John. *The Epistle of Paul the Apostle to the Hebrews and the First and Second Epistles of St. Peter.* Calvin's Commentaries. Translated by W. B. Johnston. Grand Rapids: Eerdmans, 1963.

Calvin, John, and William Pringle. *Commentaries on the Epistles of Paul to the Galatians and Ephesians.* Grand Rapids: Eerdmans, 1957.

Campbell, Douglas A. *The Deliverance of God: An Apocalyptic Rereading of Justification in Paul.* Grand Rapids: Eerdmans, 2009.

Carson, D. A. *Divine Sovereignty and Human Responsibility: Some Aspects of Johannine Theology against a Jewish Background.* New Foundations Theological Library. Atlanta: John Knox, 1981.

Carson, D. A., Peter T. O'Brien, and Mark A. Seifrid, eds. *Justification and Variegated Nomism: Volume 1, The Complexities of Second Temple Judaism.* Wissenschaftliche Untersuchungen zum Neuen Testament 2.140. Tübingen: Mohr-Siebeck, 2001.

Charette, Blaine. *Restoring Presence: The Spirit in Matthew's Gospel.* Journal of Pentecostal Theology Supplement Series 18. Sheffield: Sheffield Academic, 2000.

Charles, J. Daryl. *Virtue amidst Vice: The Catalog of Virtues in 2 Peter 1.* JSNTSup 150. Sheffield: Sheffield Academic, 1997.

Charles, R. H. *A Critical and Exegetical Commentary on the Revelation of St. John: With Introduction, Notes, and Indices, also the Greek Text and English Translation.* The International Critical Commentary 44. Edinburgh: T. & T. Clark, 1920.

Charlesworth, James H., ed. *The Old Testament Pseudepigrapha.* 2 vols. 1st ed. Garden City, NY: Doubleday, 1983.

Chennattu, Rekha M. *Johannine Discipleship as a Covenant Relationship.* Peabody, MA: Hendrickson, 2006.

Cheung, Luke L., and Richard Bauckham. *The Genre, Composition and Hermeneutics of* the Epistle of James. Paternoster Biblical and Theological Monographs. Waynesboro, GA: Paternoster, 2003.

Chilton, B. D. "The Transfiguration." *New Testament Studies* 27 (1980): 114-25.

Christiansen, Ellen Juhl. *The Covenant in Judaism and Paul: A Study of Ritual Boundaries as Identity Markers.* Arbeiten zur Geschichte des antiken Judentums und des Urchristentums 27. Leiden: Brill, 1995.

Collins, Adela Y. *The Combat Myth in the Book of Revelation.* Harvard Dissertations in Religion 9. Atlanta: Scholars, 1976.

Collins, Raymond F. *1 & 2 Timothy and Titus: A Commentary.* New Testament Library. Louisville: Westminster/John Knox, 2002.

Coloe, Mary L. *Dwelling in the Household of God: Johannine Ecclesiology and Spirituality.* Collegeville, MN: Liturgical Press, 2007.

Copan, Victor A. *Saint Paul as Spiritual Director: An Analysis of the Imitation of Paul with Implications and Applications to the Practice of Spiritual Direction.* Paternoster Biblical Monographs. Eugene, OR: Wipf & Stock, 2007.

Copenhaver, Brian P. *Hermetica: The Greek Corpus Hermeticum and the Latin Asclepius in a New English Translation, with Notes and Introduction.* Cambridge: Cambridge University Press, 1992.

Craghan, John F. "The Gerasene Demoniac." *Catholic Biblical Quarterly* (1968): 522-36.

Cranfield, C. E. B. "The Works of the Law in the Epistle to the Romans." Pages 1-14 in *On Romans and Other New Testament Essays.* Edinburgh: T. & T. Clark, 1998.

Crates. *Epistle 12.* Translated by Ronald F. Hock. Page 63 in *The Cynic Epistles: A Study Edition.* Edited by A. J. Malherbe. SBLSBS 12. Atlanta: Scholars Press, 1977.

Crook, Zeba. *Reconceptualizing Conversion: Patronage, Loyalty, and Conversion in the Religions of the Ancient Mediterranean.* Beihefte zur Zeitschrift für die neutestamentliche Wissenschaft 130. New York: De Gruyter, 2004.

Crump, David Michael. *Jesus the Intercessor: Prayer and Christology in Luke-Acts.* Wissenschaftliche Untersuchungen zum Neuen Testament 2/49. Tübingen: Mohr-Siebeck, 1992.

Danker, Frederick W. *Benefactor: Epigraphic Study of a Graeco-Roman and New Testament Semantic Field.* St. Louis: Clayton, 1982.

―――. "2 Peter 1: A Solemn Decree." *CBQ* 40 (1978): 64-82.

Davids, Peter H. *The Epistle of James: A Commentary on the Greek Text.* New International Greek Testament Commentary. Grand Rapids: Eerdmans, 1982.

―――. *The Letters of 2 Peter and Jude.* Pillar New Testament Commentary. Grand Rapids: Eerdmans, 2006.

Davies, Margaret. *The Pastoral Epistles.* Sheffield: Sheffield Academic Press, 1996.

Davies, W. D. "Knowledge in the DSS and Matthew 11:25-30." *Harvard Theological Review* 46 (1953): 113-39.

Davies, W. D., and D. C. Allison. *The Gospel according to Saint Matthew 1.* International Critical Commentary. Edinburgh: T. & T. Clark, 1988.

Deidun, Tom. "The Bible and Christian Ethics." Pages 3-46 in *Christian Ethics: An Introduction.* Edited by Bernard Hoose. Collegeville, MN: Liturgical Press, 1998.

Deissmann, G. Adolf. *Bible Studies: Contributions, Chiefly from the Papyri and Inscriptions, to the History of Language.* Edinburgh: T. & T. Clark, 1923.

Dennis, John. "The Function of the חטאת Sacrifice in the Priestly Literature: An Evaluation of the View of Jacob Milgrom." *ETL* 78 (2002): 108-29.

Derrett, J. Duncan M. "Contributions to the Study of the Gerasene Demoniac." *Journal for the Study of the New Testament* 3 (1974): 2-17.

———. "'Where Two or Three Are Convened in My Name' . . . : A Sad Misunderstanding." *Expository Times* 91 (1979): 83-86.

DeSilva, David Arthur. *Despising Shame: Honor Discourse and Community Maintenance in the Epistle to the Hebrews*. Society of Biblical Literature Dissertation Series 152. Atlanta: Scholars Press, 1995.

———. *Honor, Patronage, Kinship, and Purity: Unlocking New Testament Culture*. Downers Grove, IL: InterVarsity, 2000.

———. *Perseverance in Gratitude: A Socio-Rhetorical Commentary on the Epistle "to the Hebrews."* Grand Rapids: Eerdmans, 2000.

Deutsch, Celia. *Hidden Wisdom and the Easy Yoke: Wisdom, Torah and Discipleship in Matthew 11:25-30*. Journal for the Study of the New Testament Supplement Series 18. Sheffield: JSOT, 1987.

Dibelius, Martin. *James: A Commentary on the Epistle of James*. Revised by Heinrich Greeven. Translated by Michael Williams. Hermeneia. Philadelphia: Fortress, 1976.

Dillon, John. *The Middle Platonists: 80 B.C. to A.D. 220*. Ithaca, NY: Cornell University Press, 1977.

———, and Jackson Hershbell, eds. *On the Pythagorean Way of Life by Iamblichus*. Atlanta: Scholars, 1991.

Dodd, C. H. *The Interpretation of the Fourth Gospel*. Cambridge: Cambridge University Press, 1953.

Doering, Lutz. "First Peter as Early Christian Diaspora Letter." Pages 215-36 in *The Catholic Epistles and Apostolic Tradition*. Edited by Karl-Wilhelm Niebuhr and Robert W. Wall. Waco, TX: Baylor University Press, 2009.

Donaldson, Terence L. *Paul and the Gentiles: Remapping the Apostle's Convictional World*. Minneapolis: Fortress, 1997.

Donelson, Lewis R. *Pseudepigraphy and Ethical Argument in the Pastoral Epistles*. Hermeneutische Untersuchungen zur Theologie 22. Tübingen: Mohr-Siebeck, 1986.

Dowd, Sharyn. *Reading Mark: A Literary and Theological Commentary on the Second Gospel*. Macon, GA: Smyth & Helwys, 2000.

Downing, F. Gerald. "Common Ground with Paganism in Luke and Josephus." *New Testament Studies* 28 (1982): 546-59.

———. "Ethical Pagan Theism and the Speeches in Acts." *New Testament Studies* 27 (1981): 544-63.

Dryden, J. de Waal. *Theology and Ethics in 1 Peter: Paraenetic Strategies for Christian Character Formation*. Wissenschaftliche Untersuchungen zum Neuen Testament 209. Tübingen: Mohr-Siebeck, 2006.

Du Plessis, Paul Johannes. *TELEIOS: The Idea of Perfection in the New Testament*. Kampen: J. H. Kok, 1959.

Dunn, James D. G. "4QMMT and Galatians." *New Testament Studies* 43 (1997): 147-53.

————. "The New Perspective on Paul." *Bulletin of John Rylands University Library of Manchester* 65 (1982-1983): 95-122.

————. *Romans.* Analecta Biblica 38A. Dallas: Word Books, 1988.

————. *The Theology of Paul the Apostle.* Grand Rapids: Eerdmans, 1998.

————. "Works of the Law and the Curse of the Law (Gal 3:10-14)." *New Testament Studies* 31 (1985): 523-42.

Du Rand, J. A. "The Ethos of the Book of Revelation." *Verbum et Ecclesia* 24 (2003): 374-95.

Dvornik, Francis. *Early Christian and Byzantine Political Philosophy: Origins and Background* 1. Dumbarton Oaks Studies 9. Washington, DC: Dumbarton Oaks Center for Byzantine Studies, 1966.

Ellingworth, Paul. *The Epistle to the Hebrews: A Commentary on the Greek Text.* Grand Rapids: Eerdmans, 1993.

Elliott, John H. "Backward and Forward 'In His Steps.'" Pages 184-209 in *Discipleship in the New Testament.* Edited by Fernando Segovia. Philadelphia: Fortress, 1985.

————. *1 Peter: A New Translation with Introduction and Commentary.* Anchor Bible 37B. New Haven: Yale University Press, 2000.

————. Review of J. de Wahl Dryden's *Theology and Ethics in 1 Peter. Review of Biblical Literature.* December 2009. Online: http://www.bookreviews.org/bookdetail.asp?TitleId=7248&CodePage=7248.

Elliott-Binns, Leonard. "James 1:18: Creation or Redemption?" *New Testament Studies* 3 (1957): 148-61.

Ellis, E. Earle. *The Gospel of Luke.* Grand Rapids: Eerdmans, 1983. Repr., Eugene, OR: Wipf & Stock, 2003.

Eskola, Timo. "Paul, Predestination and Covenantal Nomism — Re-assessing Paul and Palestinian Judaism." *Journal for the Study of Judaism in the Persian, Hellenistic, and Roman Periods* 28 (1997): 390-412.

Farrer, Austin M. *A Study in St. Mark.* Westminster: Dacre, 1951.

————. *Theodicy and Predestination in Pauline Soteriology.* Wissenschaftliche Untersuchungen zum Neuen Testament 2/100. Tübingen: Mohr-Siebeck, 1998.

Fears, J. Rufus. "Theology of Victory at Rome: Approaches and Problems." *ANRW* 17.2:736-826. Part 2, *Principat,* 17.2. Edited by H. Temporini and W. Haase. New York: De Gruyter, 1989.

Feldmeier, Reinhard. *The First Letter of Peter: A Commentary on the Greek Text.* Translated by Peter H. Davids. Waco, TX: Baylor University Press, 2008.

Fiore, Benjamin. *The Function of Personal Example in the Socratic and Pastoral Epistles.* Analecta Biblica 105. Rome: Biblical Institute Press, 1986.

Fitzmyer, Joseph A., S.J. *The Gospel According to Luke (X–XXIV).* The Anchor Bible 28a. New York: Doubleday, 1985.

————. *Paul and His Theology: A Brief Sketch.* 2d ed. Englewood Cliffs, NJ: Prentice Hall, 1989.

————. *Romans.* Analecta Biblica 33. New York: Doubleday, 1993.

Foerster, Werner. "Lukas 22,31f." *Zeitschrift für die neutestamentliche Wissenschaft und die Kunde der älteren Kirche* 46 (1955): 129-33.

Fowl, Stephen E. *Philippians*. The Two Horizons New Testament Commentary. Grand Rapids: Eerdmans, 2005.

France, R. T. *The Gospel of Mark: A Commentary on the Greek Text*. Grand Rapids: Eerdmans, 2002.

Franck, Eskil. *Revelation Taught: The Paraclete in the Gospel of John*. New Testament Series 14. Lund: Gleerup, 1985.

Frankemölle, Hubert. *Matthäus Kommentar 2*. Düsseldorf: Patmos Verlag, 1997.

———. *Yahwebund und Kirche Christi*. Neutestamentliche Abhandlungen 10. Münster: Verlag Aschendorff, 1974.

Fuhrmann, Sebastian. "Failures Forgotten: The Soteriology in Hebrews Revisited in the Light of Its Quotation of Jeremiah 38:31-34 [LXX]." *Neotestamentica* 41 (2007): 295-316.

García Martínez, Florentino, ed. *The Dead Sea Scrolls Translated: The Qumran Texts in English*. 2d ed. Leiden: Brill, and Grand Rapids: Eerdmans, 1996.

Garland, David E. *Luke*. Zondervan Exegetical Commentary. Grand Rapids: Zondervan, forthcoming.

Gench, Frances Taylor. *Wisdom in the Christology of Matthew*. Lanham, MD: University Press of America, 1997.

Georgi, Dieter. *Theocracy in Paul's Praxis and Theology*. Minneapolis: Fortress, 1991.

———. "Who Is the True Prophet?" *Harvard Theological Review* 79 (1986): 100-126.

Gerber, Daniel. "1 Tm 1:15b: L'indice d'une sotériologie pensée prioritairement en lien avec la venue de Jésus?" *Revue d'histoire et de philosophie religieuses* 80, no. 4 (2000): 463-77.

Gerdmar, Anders. *Rethinking the Judaism-Hellenism Dichotomy: A Historiographical Case Study of Second Peter and Jude*. Coniectanea Biblica: New Testament Series 36. Stockholm: Almqvist & Wiksell, 2001.

Glasson, T. F. *Moses in the Fourth Gospel*. Studies in Biblical Theology. Naperville, IL: Allenson, 1963.

Gnilka, Joachim. *Das Evangelium nach Markus*. Evangelisch-Lutherische Kirchenzeitung 2. 2 vols. Zurich: Benziger Verlag, 1978, 1979.

Goodenough, E. R. "The Political Philosophy of Hellenistic Kingship." *Yale Classical Studies* 1 (1928): 55-102.

Görg, Manfred. "Ich bin mit Dir: Gewicht und Anspruch einer Redeform im Alten Testament." *Theologie und Glaube* 70 (1980): 214-40.

Gräbe, Petrus J. *Der neue Bund in der frühchristlichen Literatur: Unter Berücksichtigung der alttestamentlich-jüdischen Voraussetzungen*. Forschung zur Bibel 96. Würzburg: Echter Verlag, 2001.

Grässer, Erich. *An die Hebräer: Hb 7,1–10,18 2*. Evangelische-katholischer Kommentar zum Neuen Testament 17. Zurich: Benziger, 1993.

Grasso, Santi. *Il Vangelo di Matteo*. Roma: Edizioni Dehoniane, 1995.

Gray, Sherman W. *The Least of My Brothers: Matthew 25:31-46: A History of Interpretation*. Dissertation Series Society of Biblical Literature. Atlanta: Scholars, 1989.

Green, Gene L. *Jude & 2 Peter*. Baker Exegetical Commentary on the New Testament. Grand Rapids: Baker, 2008.

Green, Joel B. *1 Peter*. The Two Horizons New Testament Commentary. Grand Rapids: Eerdmans, 2007.

Greenberg, Martin S., and Solomon P. Shapiro. "Indebtedness: An Adverse Aspect of Asking For and Receiving Help." *Sociometry* 34 (1971): 290-301.

Grudem, W. A. *The First Epistle of Peter*. Tyndale New Testament Commentaries. Grand Rapids: Eerdmans, 1988.

Grundmann, Walter. *Der Brief des Judas und der zweite Brief des Petrus*. Theologischer Handkommentar zum Neuen Testament 15. 3d ed. Berlin: Evangelische Verlagsanstalt, 1986.

Grünzweig, Fritz. *Johannes-Offenbarung*. Edition C-bibelkommentar 24-25. Neuhausen/Stuttgart: Hänssler, 1983.

Guelich, Robert A. "'The Beginning of the Gospel': Mark 1:1-15." *Biblical Research* 27 (1982): 5-15.

Gundry, Robert H. "Grace, Works, and Staying Saved in Paul." *Biblica* 66 (1985): 1-38.

———. *Mark: A Commentary on His Apology for the Cross*. Grand Rapids: Eerdmans, 1993.

———. "The New Jerusalem: People as Place, Not Place for People." *Novum Testamentum* 29 (1987): 254-64.

Hafemann, Scott J. "Salvation in Jude 5 and the Argument of 2 Peter 1:3-11." Pages 331-42, 475-82 in *The Catholic Epistles and Apostolic Tradition*. Edited by Karl-Wilhelm Niebuhr and Robert W. Wall. Waco, TX: Baylor University Press, 2009.

———. "The Spirit of the New Covenant, the Law, and the Temple of God's Presence: Five Theses on Qumran Self-Understanding and the Contours of Paul's Thought." Pages 172-89 in *Evangelium, Schriftauslegung, Kirche*. Edited by Jostein Ådna, Scott J. Hafemann, and Otfried Hofius. Göttingen: Vandenhoeck & Ruprecht, 1997.

Hahn, Scott W. "A Broken Covenant and the Curse of Death: A Study of Hebrews 9:15-22." *Catholic Biblical Quarterly* 66 (2004): 416-36.

Hammer, Reuven, trans. *Sifre: A Tannaitic Commentary on the Book of Deuteronomy*. Yale Judaica Series 24. New Haven: Yale University Press, 1986.

Harding, Mark. *Tradition and Rhetoric in the Pastoral Epistles*. New York: Peter Lang, 1998.

Harland, Phil A. "Honouring the Emperor or Assailing the Beast: Participation in Civic Life among Associations (Jewish, Christian, and Other) in Asia Minor and the Apocalypse of John." *Journal for the Study of the New Testament* 77 (2000): 99-121.

Harrison, James R. *Paul's Language of Grace in Its Graeco-Roman Context*. Wissenschaftliche Untersuchungen zum Neuen Testament 2. Tübingen: Mohr-Siebeck, 2003.

Hartman, Lars. *'Into the Name of the Lord Jesus': Baptism in the Early Church*. Studies of the New Testament and Its World. Edinburgh: T. & T. Clark, 1997.

Hawthorne, Nathaniel. *Hawthorne's Short Stories*. Edited, and with an Introduction by Newton Arvin. New York: Alfred A. Knopf, 1975.

Hays, Richard B. *The Moral Vision of the New Testament: Community, Cross, New Cre-*

ation: A Contemporary Introduction to New Testament Ethics. 1st ed. San Francisco: HarperSanFrancisco, 1996.

Heen, Erik M., and Philip D. W. Krey, eds. *Hebrews.* Ancient Christian Commentary Series, New Testament 10. Downers Grove, IL: InterVarsity, 2005.

Heise, Jürgen. *Bleiben: Menein in den Johanneischen Schriften.* Hermeneutische Untersuchungen zur Theologie 8. Tübingen: Mohr, 1967.

Heising, A. "Exegese und Theologie der alt- und neutestamentlichen Speisewunder." *Zeitschrift für Theologie und Kirche* 86 (1964): 80-96.

Heitmüller, Wilhelm. *'Im Namen Jesu': eine sprach- und religionsgeschichtliche Untersuchung zum Neuen Testament, speziell zur altchristlichen Taufe.* Forschungen zur Religion und Literatur des Alten und Neuen Testaments 1. Part 2. Göttingen: Vandenhoeck & Ruprecht, 1903.

Hobbs, E. C. "The Gospel of Mark and the Exodus." Ph.D. diss., University of Chicago, 1958.

Holtzmann, Heinrich Julius. *Der Synoptiker.* Handkommentar zum Neuen Testament 1.1. Tübingen: Mohr, 1901.

Hooker, Morna D. *Pauline Pieces.* London: Epworth Press, 1979.

———. "What Doest Thou Here Elijah?" Pages 59-70 in *The Glory of Christ in the New Testament: Studies in Christology in Memory of George Bradford Caird.* Edited by L. D. Hurst and N. T. Wright. Oxford: Clarendon, 1987.

Hort, F. J. A. *The First Epistle of St. Peter I.1–II.17: The Greek Text with Introductory Lecture, Commentary, and Additional Notes.* London: Macmillan, 1898.

Hoskyns, Edwyn Clement. *The Fourth Gospel.* Edited by Francis Noel Davey. London: Faber & Faber, 1947.

Huther, Johann. *Kritisch-exegetisches Handbuch über den 1. Brief des Petrus, den Brief Judas und den 2. Brief des Petrus.* KEK. 4th ed. Göttingen: Vandenhoeck & Ruprecht, 1887.

Hvalvik, Reidar. *The Struggle for Scripture and Covenant: The Purpose of the Epistle of Barnabas and Jewish-Christian Competition in the Second Century.* Wissenschaftliche Untersuchungen zum Neuen Testament 2. Tübingen: Mohr-Siebeck, 1996.

Inwood, Brad. *Seneca: Selected Philosophical Letters.* Oxford: Oxford University Press, 2007.

Isaac, Edward. *The Old Testament Pseudepigrapha: Apocalyptic Literature and Testaments 1.* Edited by James H. Charlesworth. New York: Doubleday, 1983.

Isaacs, Marie E. *Sacred Space: An Approach to the Theology of the Epistle to the Hebrews.* Journal for the Study of the New Testament Supplement Series 73. Sheffield: JSOT, 1992.

Jackson-McCabe, Matt A. *Logos and Law in the Letter of James: The Law of Nature, the Law of Moses, and the Law of Freedom.* Supplements to Novum Testamentum 100. Leiden: Brill, 2000.

Jauhiainen, Marko. "The Measuring of the Sanctuary Reconsidered (Rev. 11,1-2)." *Biblica* 83 (2002): 507-26.

Jauss, Hans Robert. "Literary History as a Challenge to Literary Theory." *New Literary History* 2, no. 1 (1970): 7-37.

Jeremias, Joachim. *Jesus' Promise to the Nations.* Studies in Biblical Theology. 1st English ed. Naperville, IL: Allenson, 1958.

Jobes, Karen H. *1 Peter.* Baker Exegetical Commentary on the New Testament. Grand Rapids: Baker, 2005.

———. "Got Milk? Septuagint Psalm 33 and the Interpretation of 1 Peter 2:1-3." *Westminster Theological Journal* 63 (2002): 1-14.

Johns, Loren L. *The Lamb Christology of the Apocalypse of John.* Wissenschaftliche Untersuchungen zum Neuen Testament 2/167. Tübingen: Mohr-Siebeck, 2003.

Johnson, Edna. *A Semantic Structure Analysis of 2 Peter.* Dallas: Summer Institute of Linguistics, 1988.

Johnson, Luke Timothy. *The Acts of the Apostles.* Sacra Pagina 5. Collegeville, MN: Liturgical Press, 1992.

———. "First Timothy 1:1-20." Pages 19-39 in *1 Timothy Reconsidered.* Colloquium Oecumenicum Paulinum 18. Leuven: Peeters, 2008.

———. *The Gospel of Luke.* Sacra Pagina 3. Collegeville, MN: Liturgical Press, 1991.

———. *The Letter of James: A New Translation with Introduction and Commentary.* The Anchor Bible 37A. 1st ed. New York: Doubleday, 1995.

———. "2 Timothy and the Polemic against False Teachers: A Re-examination." *Ohio Journal of Religious Studies* 6, no. 7 (1978/79): 1-26.

Joubert, Stephan. "ΧΑΡΙΣ in Paul: An Investigation into the Apostle's 'Performative' Application of the Language of *Grace* within the Framework of His Theological Reflection on the Event/Process of Salvation." Pages 187-212 in *Salvation in the New Testament.* Edited by Jan G. van der Watt. Novum Testamentum Supplements 121. Atlanta: SBL, 2005.

———. *Paul as Benefactor: Reciprocity, Strategy and Theological Reflection in Paul's Collection.* Wissenschaftliche Untersuchungen zum Neuen Testament 2. Tübingen: Mohr-Siebeck, 2000.

Kanagaraj, Jey J. *Mysticism in the Gospel of John.* Journal for the Study of the New Testament Supplements 158. Sheffield: Sheffield Academic, 1998.

Käsemann, Ernst. "Das Formular einer neutestamentlichen Ordinationsparänese." Pages 101-8 in *Exegetische Versuche und Besinnungen.* Vol. 1. Göttingen: Vandenhoeck & Ruprecht, 1960.

———. "Paul and Israel." Pages 183-87 in *New Testament Questions of Today.* Philadelphia: Fortress, 1969.

Käsemann, Ernst, and Geoffrey William Bromiley. *Commentary on Romans.* Grand Rapids: Eerdmans, 1980.

Keck, Leander E., ed. The New Interpreter's Bible. 12 vols. Nashville: Abingdon, 2003.

Kee, Howard Clark. *Community of the New Age: Studies in Mark's Gospel.* Philadelphia: Westminster, 1977.

Keil, Carl Friedrich. *Commentar über die Briefe des Petrus und Judas.* Leipzig: Dörffling & Franke, 1883.

Kelly, J. N. D. *A Commentary on the Epistles of Peter and Jude.* BNTC. Peabody, MA: Hendrickson, 1969.

Kennedy, George A. *Progymnasmata: Greek Textbooks of Prose Composition and Rheto-*

ric. Writings from the Greco-Roman World 10. Atlanta: Society of Biblical Literature, 2003.

Kerner, Jürgen. *Die Ethik der Johannes-Apokalypse im Vergleich mit der des 4. Esra: Ein Beitrag zum Verhältnis von Apokalyptik und Ethik.* Beihefte zur Zeitschrift für die neutestamentliche Wissenschaft und die Kunde der Älteren Kirche 94. Berlin/ New York: De Gruyter, 1998.

Kittel, G., and G. Friedrich, eds. *Theological Dictionary of the New Testament.* Translated by G. W. Bromiley. 10 vols. Grand Rapids: Eerdmans, 1964-1976.

Kloppenborg, John S. "Diaspora Discourse: The Construction of Ethos in James." *New Testament Studies* 53 (2007): 247-48.

————. "Philadelphia, Theodidaktos and the Dioscuri: Rhetorical Engagement in 1 Thessalonians 4:9-12." *New Testament Studies* 39 (1993): 265-89.

Klöpper, A. "Zur Soteriologie der Pastoralbriefe." *Zeitschrift für wissenschaftliche Theologie* 47 (1904): 57-88.

Knoch, Otto. *Der Erste und Zweite Petrusbrief. Der Judasbrief.* RNT. Regensburg: Pustet, 1990.

Koester, Craig R. *Hebrews.* New York: Doubleday, 2001.

Konradt, Matthias. *Christliche Existenz nach dem Jakobusbrief: Eine Studie zu seiner soteriologischen und ethischen Konzeption.* Studien zur Umwelt des Neuen Testaments 22. Göttingen: Vandenhoeck & Ruprecht, 1998.

————. "The Historical Context of the Letter of James in Light of Its Traditio-Historical Relations with First Peter." Pages 101-26 in *The Catholic Epistles and Apostolic Tradition: A New Perspective on James to Jude.* Edited by Karl-Wilhelm Niebuhr and Robert W. Wall. Waco, TX: Baylor University Press, 2009.

Kraftchick, Steven J. *Jude, 2 Peter.* ANTC. Nashville: Abingdon, 2002.

Kraus, Thomas J. *Sprache, Stil und historischer Ort des zweiten Petrusbriefes.* WUNT 2. Reihe 136. Tübingen: Mohr-Siebeck, 2001.

Krodel, Gerhard. *Revelation.* ACNT. Minneapolis: Augsburg, 1989.

Kruse, Colin G. *Paul, the Law, and Justification.* Peabody, MA: Hendrickson, 1997.

Kupp, David D. *Matthew's Emmanuel: Divine Presence and God's People in the First Gospel.* Monograph Series Society for New Testament Studies 90. Cambridge: Cambridge University Press, 1996.

Kvalbein, Hans. "The Kingdom of God in the Ethics of Jesus." *Studia Theologica* 51 (1997): 60-84.

Laato, Timo. *Paul and Judaism: An Anthropological Approach.* South Florida Studies in the History of Judaism. Atlanta: Scholars, 1995.

Läger, Karoline. *Die Christologie der Pastoralbriefe.* Harvard Theological Studies 12. Münster: LIT, 1996.

Lambrecht, Jan, and Richard W. Thompson. *Justification by Faith: The Implications of Romans 3:27-31.* Zacchaeus Studies New Testament. Wilmington, DE: M. Glazier, 1989.

Lane, William L. *Hebrews 1–8.* Word Biblical Commentary 47a. Dallas: Thomas Nelson, 1991.

————. *Hebrews 9–13.* Word Biblical Commentary 47b. Dallas: Thomas Nelson, 1991.

Laporte, Jean. *Eucharistia in Philo*. Studies in the Bible and Early Christianity 3. Lewiston, NY: E. Mellen, 1983.

Laws, Sophie. *A Commentary on the Epistle of James*. Harper's New Testament Commentaries. San Francisco: Harper & Row, 1980.

Lehne, Susanne. *The New Covenant in Hebrews*. Journal for the Study of the New Testament Supplement Series 44. Sheffield: JSOT, 1990.

Lenski, R. C. H. *The Interpretation of the Epistles of St. Peter, St. John, and St. Jude*. Columbus, OH: Wartburg, 1945.

Lieu, Judith. *I, II & III John: A Commentary*. The New Testament Library. 1st ed. Louisville: Westminster/John Knox, 2008.

Lincoln, A. T. *Ephesians*. Word Biblical Commentary 42. Waco, TX: Word Books, 1990.

Lindars, Barnabas. *The Gospel of John*. New Century Bible. Greenwood, SC: Attic, 1972.

―――. "The Rhetorical Structure of Hebrews." *New Testament Studies* 35 (1989): 382-406.

Luomanen, Petri. *Entering the Kingdom of Heaven: A Study on the Structure of Matthew's View of Salvation*. Wissenschaftliche Untersuchungen zum Neuen Testament 101. Tübingen: Mohr-Siebeck, 1998.

Luz, Ulrich. "The Disciples in the Gospel according to Matthew." Pages 115-48 in *The Interpretation of Matthew*. 2d ed. Edited by Graham Stanton. Edinburgh: T. & T. Clark, 1995.

Macaskill, Grant. *Revealed Wisdom and Inaugurated Eschatology in Ancient Judaism and Early Christianity*. Supplements to the Journal for the Study of Judaism 115. Leiden: Brill, 2007.

Malatesta, Edward. *Interiority and Covenant: A Study of and in the First Letter of Saint John*. Analecta Biblica 69. Rome: Biblical Institute, 1978.

Malherbe, Abraham J. "Hellenistic Moralists and the New Testament." *ANRW* 26.1:267-333. Part 2, *Principat*, 26.1. Edited by Wolfgang Haase and Hildegard Temporini. New York: De Gruyter, 1992.

―――. *Moral Exhortation, A Greco-Roman Sourcebook*. Library of Early Christianity 4. Philadelphia: Westminster, 1986.

Malina, Bruce J. *The Social World of Jesus and the Gospels*. London: Routledge, 1996.

Malina, Bruce J., and Richard L. Rohrbaugh. *Social-Science Commentary on the Gospel of John*. Minneapolis: Fortress, 1998.

Marcus, Joel. *The Mystery of the Kingdom*. Society of Biblical Literature Dissertation Series 90. Atlanta: Scholars, 1986.

―――. *The Way of the Lord: Christological Exegesis of the Old Testament*. Louisville: Westminster/John Knox, 1992.

Marshall, I. Howard. *The Gospel of Luke: A Commentary on the Greek Text*. The New International Greek Testament Commentary. Grand Rapids: Eerdmans, 1978.

―――. "Salvation." Pages 719-24 in *Dictionary of Jesus and the Gospels*. Edited by Joel B. Green and Scot McKnight. Downers Grove, IL: InterVarsity, 1992.

―――. "Salvation, Grace and Works in the Later Writings in the Pauline Corpus." *New Testament Studies* 42 (1996): 339-58.

―――. "Salvation in the Pastoral Epistles." Pages 449-69 in *Geschichte — Tradition —*

Reflexion: Festschrift für Martin Hengel, vol. 3. *Frühes Christentum*. Edited by Hubert Cancik et al. Tübingen: Mohr-Siebeck, 1996.

―――. "Universal Grace and Atonement in the Pastoral Epistles." Pages 51-69 in *The Grace of God, the Will of Man*. Edited by Clark Pinnock. Grand Rapids: Zondervan, 1989.

Martin, Ralph. *James*. Word Biblical Commentary 48. Nashville: Thomas Nelson, 1988.

Martin, Sean Charles. *Pauli Testamentum: 2 Timothy and the Last Words of Moses*. Tesi Gregoriana, Serie Teologia 18. Rome: Pontificia Universita Gregoriana, 1997.

Martyn, J. Louis. *Galatians: A New Translation with Introduction and Commentary*. 1st ed. The Anchor Bible 33A. New York: Doubleday, 1997.

―――. "A Law-Observant Mission to Gentiles." Pages 7-25 in *Theological Issues in the Letters of Paul*. Nashville: Abingdon, 1997.

Marxsen, Willi. *New Testament Foundations for Christian Ethics*. Minneapolis: Fortress, 1993.

Matera, Frank J. "Galatians in Perspective: Cutting a New Path through Old Territory." *Interpretation* 54 (2000): 233-45.

Matthews, Victor H. "The Unwanted Gift: Implications of Obligatory Gift Giving in Ancient Israel." *Semeia* 87 (1999): 91.

Mauser, Ulrich W. *Christ in the Wilderness: The Wilderness Theme in the Second Gospel and Its Basis in the Biblical Tradition*. Studies in Biblical Theology 39. Naperville, IL: Allenson, 1963.

Mayer, Roland G. "Roman Historical *Exempla* in Seneca." Pages 299-315 in *Seneca*. Edited by John G. Fitch. Oxford: Oxford University Press, 2008.

Mayor, Joseph B. *The Epistle of St. Jude and the Second Epistle of St. Peter*. London: Macmillan, 1907.

McCartney, Dan G. "'λογικός' in 1 Peter 2,2." *Zeitschrift für die neutestamentliche Wissenschaft und die Kunde der älteren Kirche* 82 (1991): 128-32.

McEleny, N. J. "Conversion, Circumcision and the Law." *New Testament Studies* 20 (1974): 319-41.

Mealand, David L. "The Language of Mystical Union in the Johannine Writings." *Downside Review* 95 (1977): 19-34.

Meranda-Feliciano, Evelyn. *Filipino Values and Our Christian Faith*. Manila: OMF Literature, 1990.

Meyer, Arnold, and Universität Zürich. *Das Rätsel des Jacobusbriefes: Herausgegeben mit Unterstützung durch die Stiftung für wissenschaftliche Forschung an der Universität Zürich*. Beihefte zur Zeitschrift für die neutestamentliche Wissenschaft und die Kunde der Älteren Kirche 10. Giessen: A. Töpelmann, 1930.

Meyer, Ben F. *Five Speeches That Changed the World*. Collegeville, MN: Liturgical Press, 1994.

Michaels, J. Ramsey. *1 Peter*. Word Biblical Commentary 49. Nashville: Thomas Nelson, 1988.

―――. *Revelation*. The IVP New Testament Commentary Series 20. Downers Grove, IL: InterVarsity, 1997.

Michel, O. "Der Abschluss des Matthäus-Evangeliums." *Evangelische Theologie* 10 (1950-1951): 16-26.

Mitchell, Margaret M. "Corrective Composition, Corrective Exegesis." Pages 41-62 in *1 Timothy Reconsidered*. Colloquium Oecumenicum Paulinum 18. Leuven: Peeters, 2008.

———. "The Letter of James as a Document of Paulinism." Pages 75-98 in *Reading James with New Eyes: Methodological Reassessments and the Letter of James*. Edited by Robert L. Webb and John S. Kloppenborg. Library of New Testament Studies 342. London: T. & T. Clark, 2007.

Moffatt, James. *A Critical and Exegetical Commentary on the Epistle to the Hebrews*. Edinburgh: T. & T. Clark, 1924.

Mohrlang, Roger. *Matthew and Paul: A Comparison of Ethical Perspectives*. Monograph Series Society for New Testament Studies 48. Cambridge: Cambridge University Press, 1984.

Moloney, Francis J. *Glory Not Dishonor: Reading John 13–21*. Minneapolis: Augsburg Fortress, 1998.

Montefiore, C. G. *Judaism and St. Paul: Two Essays*. New York: Dutton, 1915.

Moo, Douglas J. *2 Peter and Jude*. NIV Application Commentary. Grand Rapids: Zondervan, 1996.

Moore, George F. *Judaism in the First Three Centuries*. 3 vols. Cambridge, MA: Harvard University Press, 1927-1930.

Mott, Stephen C. "Greek Ethics and Christian Conversion: The Philonic Background of Titus 2:10-14 and 3:3-7." *Novum Testamentum* 20 (1978): 22-48.

———. "The Power of Giving and Receiving: Reciprocity in Hellenistic Benevolence." Pages 60-72 in *Current Issues in Biblical and Patristic Interpretation*. Edited by Gerald F. Hawthorne. Grand Rapids: Eerdmans, 1975.

Mounce, Robert H. *The Book of Revelation*. New International Commentary on the New Testament. Grand Rapids: Zondervan, 1977.

Mussner, Franz. *Der Jakobusbrief: Auslegung*. Herders theologischer Kommentar zum Neuen Testament 13. Part 1. Freiburg: Herder, 1964.

———. "Die Tauflehre des Jakobusbriefes." Pages 61-67 in *Ziechen des Glauben*. Edited by Hansjörg Auf der Maur and Bruno Kleinheyer. Freiburg: Herder, 1972.

Nauck, Wolfgang. "Zum Aufbau des Hebräerbriefes." Pages 199-206 in *Judentum, Urchristentum, Kirche: Festschrift für Joachim Jeremias*. Edited by Walther Eltester. Berlin: Alfred Töpelmann, 1960.

Neusner, Jacob. *Judaic Law from Jesus to the Mishnah: A Systematic Reply to Professor E. P. Sanders*. South Florida Studies in the History of Judaism. Atlanta: Scholars, 1993.

———. "Was Rabbinic Judaism Really 'Ethnic'?" *Catholic Biblical Quarterly* 57 (1995): 281-305.

Newman, Barclay Moon, and Eugene Albert Nida. *A Translator's Handbook on the Gospel of John*. London: United Bible Societies, 1980.

Neyrey, Jerome H. *The Gospel of John*. New Century Bible. New York: Cambridge University Press, 2007.

Nienhuis, David. "The Letter of James as a Canon-Conscious Pseudepigraph." Pages 183-200 in *The Catholic Epistles and Apostolic Tradition: A New Perspective on*

James to Jude. Edited by Karl-Wilhelm Niebuhr and Robert W. Wall. Waco, TX: Baylor University Press, 2009.

Nock, A. D., and A. J. Festugière. *Corpus Hermeticum.* 2 vols. Paris: Société édition 'Les belles lettres.' 1954-1960.

Nolland, John. *Luke.* 3 vols. Word Biblical Commentary 35A-C. Dallas: Word Books, 1989-1993.

Nützel, J. M. *Die Verklärungserzählung im Markusevangelium.* Forschung zur Bibel 6. Würzburg: Echter Verlag, 1973.

O'Brien, Peter Thomas. *The Letter to the Ephesians.* The Pillar New Testament Commentary. Grand Rapids and Cambridge: Eerdmans, 1999.

———. "Prayer in Luke-Acts." *Tyndale Bulletin* 24 (1973): 111-27.

O'Day, Gail. *The Interpreter's Bible,* vol. 9. Nashville: Abingdon, 1995

Odeberg, Hugo. *Pharisaism and Christianity.* St. Louis: Concordia, 1964.

Osborne, Grant R. *Revelation.* Baker Exegetical Commentary on the New Testament. Grand Rapids: Baker Academic, 2002.

———. "Soteriology in the Epistle to the Hebrews." Pages 144-66 in *Grace Unlimited.* Edited by Clark H. Pinnock. Minneapolis: Bethany House, 1975.

Ott, Wilhelm. *Gebet und Heil: Die Bedeutung der Gebetsparänese in der lukanischen Theologie.* Munich: Kösel, 1965.

Overman, J. *Church and Community in Crisis: The Gospel according to Matthew.* The New Testament in Context. Valley Forge, PA: Trinity Press International, 1996.

Paget, James Carleton. *The Epistle of Barnabas: Outlook and Background.* Wissenschaftliche Untersuchungen zum Neuen Testament 2. Tübingen: Mohr-Siebeck, 1994.

Parker, Robert. "Pleasing Thighs: Reciprocity in Greek Religion." Pages 105-26 in *Reciprocity in Ancient Greece.* Edited by Christopher Gill, Norman Postlethwaite, and Richard Seaford. New York: Oxford University Press, 1998.

Parsenios, George L. *Departure and Consolation: The Johannine Farewell Discourses in Light of Greco-Roman Literature.* Supplements to Novum Testamentum 117. Leiden: Brill, 2005.

Parsons, Mikeal C. *Acts.* Paideia Commentaries on the New Testament. Grand Rapids: Baker Academic, 2008.

Parsons, Mikeal C., and Richard I. Pervo. *Rethinking the Unity of Luke and Acts.* Minneapolis: Fortress, 1993.

Paulsen, Henning. *Der Zweite Petrusbrief und der Judasbrief.* KEK 12/2. Göttingen: Vandenhoeck & Ruprecht, 1992.

Penner, Todd C. *The Epistle of James and Eschatology: Re-reading an Ancient Christian Letter.* Journal for the Study of the New Testament Supplement Series 121. Sheffield: Sheffield Academic, 1996.

Perkins, Pheme. *Jesus as Teacher.* Understanding Jesus Today. Cambridge: Cambridge University Press, 1990.

Pesch, Rudolph. *Das Markusevangelium.* 2 vols. Herders theologischer Kommentar zum Neuen Testament 2. Freiburg: Herder, 1976, 1977.

Peterson, David. *Hebrews and Perfection: An Examination of the Concept of Perfection in the "Epistle to the Hebrews."* Cambridge: Cambridge University Press, 1982.

Pickar, C. H. "The Prayer of Christ for Saint Peter." *Catholic Biblical Quarterly* 4 (1942): 133-40.

Pinnock, Clark. "From Augustine to Arminius: A Pilgrimage in Theology." Pages 15-30 in *The Grace of God, the Will of Man: A Case for Arminianism.* Edited by Clark H. Pinnock. Grand Rapids: Zondervan, 1989.

Pollard, T. E. "The Father-Son and God-Believer Relationship according to St. John: A Brief Study of John's Use of Prepositions." Pages 363-70 in *L'Evangile de Jean: Sources, redaction, théologie.* Edited by M. de Jonge. Bibliotheca ephemeridum theologicarum lovaniensium 44. Gembloux: J. Duculot, 1977.

Powell, Mark A. "Worship." Pages 28-61 in *God with Us: A Pastoral Theology of Matthew's Gospel.* Minneapolis: Fortress, 1995.

Prostmeier, Ferdinand R. *Der Barnabasbrief: Übersetzt und Erklärt.* Kommentar zu den Apostolischen Vätern. Göttingen: Vandenhoeck & Ruprecht, 1999.

Pryor, J. W. "Covenant and Community in John's Gospel." *Reformed Theological Review* 48 (1988): 44-51.

Quinn, J. D. "Jesus as Savior and Only Mediator." Pages 249-60 in *Fede e cultura alla luce della Bibbia: Atti della sessione plenaria 1979 della Pontificia Commissione Biblica.* Torino: Editrice Elle Di Ci, 1981.

Rabinowitz, Peter J. *Before Reading: Narrative Conventions and the Poetics of Interpretation.* Ithaca, NY: Cornell University Press, 1987.

———. "Truth in Fiction: A Reexamination of Audiences." *Critical Inquiry* 4 (1977): 121-41.

———. "Whirl without End: Audience Oriented Criticism." Pages 81-100 in *Contemporary Literary Theory.* Edited by G. Douglas Atkins. Amherst: University of Massachusetts Press, 1989.

von Rad, Gerhard. *Old Testament Theology* 1. Edinburgh: Oliver & Boyd, 1962.

Reddish, Mitchell Glenn, ed. *Apocalyptic Literature: A Reader.* Peabody, MA: Hendrickson, 1995.

———. *Revelation.* Smyth & Helwys Bible Commentary. Macon, GA: Smyth & Helwys, 2001.

Rhodes, James N. *The Epistle of Barnabas and the Deuteronomic Tradition: Polemics, Paraenesis, and the Legacy of the Golden-Calf Incident.* Wissenschaftliche Untersuchungen zum Neuen Testament 2. Tübingen: Mohr-Siebeck, 2004.

Ridderbos, Herman N. *The Gospel according to John: A Theological Commentary.* Grand Rapids: Eerdmans, 1997.

Robbins, Vernon K. *Jesus the Teacher: A Socio-Rhetorical Interpretation of Mark.* Philadelphia: Fortress Press, 1984.

Robinson, J. A. *St. Paul's Epistle to the Ephesians: A Translation with Exposition and Notes.* London: Macmillan, 1903.

Russell, D. S. *The Method and Message of Jewish Apocalyptic, 200 BC–AD 100.* The Old Testament Library. Philadelphia: Westminster, 1964.

Salkinson, Isaac Edward, Christian D. Ginsburg, and Trinitarian Bible Society. *Ha-Berit ha-hadashah. Ha'takah hadashah mi-leshon Yaven li-lashon 'Ivrit, me-et Yitshak Zalkinson zal. Huva'ah li-defus 'im tikunim ve-he 'arot me-et Kh. David Gintsburg.* London: The Trinitarian Bible Society, 194-.

Sanders, E. P. "Jesus, Paul and Judaism." *ANRW* 25.1:390-450. Part 2, *Principat*, 25.1. Edited by H. Temporini and W. Haase. New York: De Gruyter, 1989.

―――. *Paul*. Oxford/New York: Oxford University Press, 1991.

―――. *Paul and Palestinian Judaism: A Comparison of Patterns of Religion*. 1st American ed. Philadelphia: Fortress Press, 1977.

―――. *Paul, the Law, and the Jewish People*. Philadelphia: Fortress, 1983.

Sandmel, Samuel. *The Genius of Paul: A Study in History*. New York: Farrar, Straus & Cudahy, 1958.

Sarason, Richard S. "The Interpretation of Jeremiah 31:31-34 in Judaism." Pages 99-123 in *When Jews and Christians Meet*. Edited by Jakob J. Petuchowski. Albany: SUNY Press, 1988.

Schenck, Kenneth L. "A Celebration of the Enthroned Son: The Catena of Hebrews 1." *Journal of Biblical Literature* 120 (2001): 469-85.

―――. *Cosmology and Eschatology in Hebrews: The Settings of the Sacrifice*. Society for New Testament Studies Monograph Series 143. Cambridge: Cambridge University Press, 2007.

Schick, Eduard. *Die Apokalypse. Gesammelte Studien* 23. Düsseldorf: Patmos-Verlag, 1971.

Schlier, Heinrich. *Der Brief an die Epheser: Ein Kommentar*. Düsseldorf: Patmos-Verlag, 1963.

Schmidt, T. E. "Mark 15.16-32: The Crucifixion Narrative and the Roman Triumphal Procession." *New Testament Studies* 41 (1995): 1-18.

Schnackenburg, Rudolf. *The Moral Teaching of the New Testament*. New York: Seabury, 1979.

Schneemelcher, W., ed. *New Testament Apocrypha*. Louisville: Westminster/John Knox, 1992.

Schoeps, Hans Joachim. *Paul: The Theology of the Apostle in the Light of Jewish Religious History*. Philadelphia: Westminster, 1961.

Scholem, Gershom Gerhard, and George Lichtheim. *Major Trends in Jewish Mysticism*. Rev. ed. New York: Schocken Books, 1946.

Scholtissek, Klaus. *In ihm sein und bleiben: Die Sprache der Immanenz in den Johanneischen Schriften*. Herders biblische Studien 21. Freiburg: Herder, 2000.

Schreiner, R. "Works of Law in Paul." *Novum Testamentum* 33 (1991): 217-44.

Schreiner, Thomas. *1, 2 Peter, Jude*. NAC 37. Nashville: Broadman & Holman, 2003.

Schulz, Thomas N. *The Meaning of* Charis *in the New Testament*. Genoa: Editrice lanterna, 1971.

Seaford, Richard. "Introduction." Pages 1-11 in *Reciprocity in Ancient Greece*. Edited by Christopher Gill, Norman Postlethwaite, and Richard Seaford. New York: Oxford University Press, 1998.

Seeley, David. "Deconstructing Matthew." Pages 21-52 in *Deconstructing the New Testament*. Biblical Interpretation Series 5. Leiden: Brill, 1994.

Segal, Alan F. *Paul the Convert: The Apostolate and Apostasy of Saul the Pharisee*. New Haven: Yale University Press, 1990.

―――. *Rebecca's Children: Judaism and Christianity in the Roman World*. Cambridge, MA: Harvard University Press, 1986.

Seifrid, Mark A. "The 'New Perspective on Paul' and Its Problems." *Themelios* 25 (2000): 4-18.

Seitz, Oscar J. F. "The Relationship of the Shepherd of Hermas to the Epistle of James." *Journal of Biblical Literature* 63 (1944): 131-40.

Sievers, Joseph. "Where Two or Three . . . : The Rabbinic Concept of Shekhinah and Matthew 18:20." Pages 171-82 in *Standing Before God*. Edited by Asher Finkel and L. Frizzell. New York: Ktav, 1981.

Slater, Thomas B. *Christ and Community: A Socio-Historical Study of the Christology of Revelation*. Journal for the Study of the New Testament Supplement Series 178. Sheffield: Sheffield Academic, 1999.

Sleeper, C. *The Bible and the Moral Life*. 1st ed. Louisville: Westminster/John Knox, 1992.

Smalley, Stephen S. "Spirit, Kingdom, and Prayer in Luke-Acts." *Novum Testamentum* 15 (1973): 59-71.

Smith, Craig A. *Timothy's Task, Paul's Prospect: A New Reading of 2 Timothy*. New Testament Monographs 12. Sheffield: Sheffield Phoenix Press, 2006.

Snodgrass, Klyne. "Spheres of Influence: A Possible Solution to the Problem of Paul and the Law." *Journal for the Study of the New Testament* 32 (1988): 93-113.

Spicq, Ceslas. *L'Épître aux Hébreux*. Paris: Librairie Lecoffre, 1977.

Spitta, Friedrich. *Der zweite Brief des Petrus und der Brief des Judas*. Halle a. S.: Waisenhause, 1885.

Starr, James M. *Sharers in Divine Nature: 2 Peter 1:4 in Its Hellenistic Context*. Coniectanea Biblica: New Testament Series 33. Stockholm: Almqvist & Wiksell, 2000.

Stauffer, Ethelbert. *Christ and the Caesars: Historical Sketches*. Philadelphia: Westminster, 1955.

Stendahl, Krister. *Paul among Jews and Gentiles, and Other Essays*. Philadelphia: Fortress, 1976.

Sternberg, Meir. *The Poetics of Biblical Narrative: Ideological Literature and the Drama of Reading*. Indiana Literary Biblical Series. Bloomington: Indiana University Press, 1985.

Stowers, Stanley Kent. *A Rereading of Romans: Justice, Jews, and Gentiles*. New Haven: Yale University Press, 1994.

Stuhlmacher, Peter. "Theologische Probleme des Römerbriefpräscripts." *Evangelische Theologie* 27 (1967): 374-89.

Sweet, J. M. P. "Maintaining the Testimony of Jesus: The Suffering of Christians in the Revelation of John." Pages 101-17 in *Suffering and Martyrdom in the New Testament*. Edited by W. Horbury and B. McNeil. Cambridge: Cambridge University Press, 1981.

Syreeni, Kari. *The Making of the Sermon on the Mount*. Annales Academiae Scientiarum Fennicae Dissertationes Humanarum Litterarum 44. Helsinki: Suomalainen Tiedeakatemia, 1987.

Talbert, Charles H. *The Apocalypse: A Reading of the Revelation of John*. 1st ed. Louisville: Westminster/John Knox, 1994.

———. "Discipleship in Luke-Acts." Pages 62-75 in *Discipleship in the New Testament*. Edited by Fernando F. Segovia. Philadelphia: Fortress, 1985.

―――. "The Fourth Gospel's Soteriology between New Birth and Resurrection." *Perspectives in Religious Studies* 37 (Summer 2010): 133-45.

―――. "Freedom and Law in Galatians." *Ex Auditu* 11 (1995): 17-28.

―――. "Indicative and Imperative in Matthean Soteriology." *Biblica* 82 (2001): 515-38.

―――. "Matthew and Character Formation." *Expository Times* 121 (2009): 53-59.

―――. "Paul, Judaism, and the Revisionists." *Catholic Biblical Quarterly* 63 (2001): 20-21.

―――. "Paul on the Covenant." *Review and Expositor* 84 (1987): 299-313.

―――. *Reading Acts: A Literary and Theological Commentary on the Acts of the Apostles.* New York: Crossroad, 1997.

―――. *Reading John: A Literary and Theological Commentary on the Fourth Gospel and the Johannine Epistles.* Reading the New Testament. Rev. ed. Macon, GA: Smyth & Helwys, 2005.

―――. *Reading Luke: A Literary and Theological Commentary on the Third Gospel.* Rev. ed. Macon, GA: Smyth & Helwys, 2002.

―――. *Reading the Sermon on the Mount: Character Formation and Decision Making in Matthew 5–7.* Columbia: University of South Carolina Press, 2004.

―――. *Romans.* Macon, GA: Smyth & Helwys, 2002.

Tannehill, Robert C. *The Narrative Unity of Luke-Acts,* Volume 2: *The Acts of the Apostles.* Foundations and Facets. Philadelphia: Fortress, 1990.

―――. *The Sword of His Mouth: Forceful and Imaginative Language in Synoptic Sayings.* Semeia Supplements. Philadelphia: Fortress, 1975.

Tate, Marvin E. *Psalms 51–100.* Word Biblical Commentary 20. Dallas: Word Books, 1990.

Temkin, O. *Soranus' Gynecology.* Baltimore: Johns Hopkins University Press, 1991.

Thettayil, Benny. *In Spirit and Truth: An Exegetical Study of John 4:19-26 and a Theological Investigation of the Replacement Theme in the Fourth Gospel.* Contributions to Biblical Exegesis and Theology 46. Leuven: Peeters, 2007.

Thielman, Frank. "Paul as Jewish Christian Theologian: The Theology of Paul in the Magnum Opus of James D. G. Dunn." *Perspectives in Religious Studies* 25 (1998): 381-87.

Thomas, Johannes. "Anfechtung und Vorfreude, ein biblisches Thema nach Jak, 1,2-18 im Zusammenhang mit Ps 126, Röm 5,3-5 und 1 Pet 1,5-7." *Kerygma und Dogma* 14 (1968): 183-206.

Tiede, David L. *Luke.* Augsburg Commentary on the New Testament. Minneapolis: Augsburg, 1988.

Tite, Philip L. "Nurslings, Milk and Moral Development in the Greco-Roman Context: A Reappraisal of the Paraenetic Utilization of Metaphor in 1 Peter 2.1-3." *Journal for the Study of the New Testament* 31 (2009): 371-400.

Toit, Marietjie du. "The Expression λογικὸν ἄδολον γάλα as the Key to 1 Peter 2.1-3." *Hervormde teologiese studies* 63 (2007): 221-29.

Towner, Philip H. *The Goal of Our Instruction: The Structure of Theology and Ethics in the Pastoral Epistles.* Journal for the Study of the New Testament Supplement Series 34. Sheffield: JSOT, 1989.

Trites, Allison A. "The Prayer Motif in Luke-Acts." Pages 168-86 in *Perspectives on Luke-*

Acts. Edited by Charles H. Talbert. Danville, VA: Association of Baptist Professors of Religion, 1978.

Trummer, Peter. *Paulustradition der Pastoralbriefe.* Beiträge zur biblischen Exegese und Theologie 8. Frankfurt: Peter Lang, 1978.

Van der Watt, Jan G. *Salvation in the New Testament: Perspectives on Soteriology.* Supplements to Novum Testamentum 121. Atlanta: SBL, 2005.

Vanhoozer, Kevin J. *The Drama of Doctrine: A Canonical-Linguistic Approach to Christian Theology.* Louisville: Westminster/John Knox, 2005.

Vanhoye, Albert. "L'οἰκουμένη dans l'Épître aux Hébreux." *Biblica* 45 (1964): 248-53.

Van Unnik, W. C. "*Dominus Vobiscum:* The Background of a Liturgical Formula." Pages 270-305 in *New Testament Essays: Studies in Memory of T. W. Manson.* Edited by A. J. B. Higgins. Manchester: Manchester University Press, 1959.

Van Wees, Hans. "The Law of Gratitude: Reciprocity in Anthropological Theory." Pages 13-50 in *Reciprocity in Ancient Greece.* Edited by Christopher Gill, Norman Postlethwaite, and Richard Seaford. New York: Oxford University Press, 1998.

De Vaux, Roland. "The King of Israel, Vassal of Yahweh." Pages 152-62 in *The Bible and the Ancient Near East.* Garden City, NY: Doubleday, 1971.

Velunta, Enriquez. "*Ek Pisteōs eis Pistin* and the Filipino's Sense of Indebtedness." Pages 33-54 in volume 1 of the *SBL Seminar Papers, 1998.* 2 vols. Society of Biblical Literature Seminar Papers 37. Atlanta: Scholars, 1998.

Verhey, Allen. *The Great Reversal: Ethics and the New Testament.* Grand Rapids: Eerdmans, 1984.

Vetter, D. *Yahwes Mit-Sein — ein Ausdruck des Segens.* AT 1, no. 45. Stuttgart: Calwer Verlag, 1971.

Vögtle, Anton. *Der Judasbrief/Der Zweite Petrusbrief.* EKKNT 22. Neukirchen-Vluyn: Neukirchener Verlag, 1994.

Volf, Miroslav. "Soft Difference: Reflections on the Relation Between Church and Culture in 1 Peter." *Ex Auditu* 10 (1994): 15-30.

Wall, Robert. "A Unifying Theology of the Catholic Epistles." Pages 13-40 in *The Catholic Epistles and Apostolic Tradition: A New Perspective on James to Jude.* Edited by Karl-Wilhelm Niebuhr and Robert W. Wall. Waco, TX: Baylor University Press, 2009.

Wallace, Daniel B. *Greek Grammar Beyond the Basics: An Exegetical Syntax of the New Testament.* Grand Rapids: Zondervan, 1996.

Watson, Francis. *Paul, Judaism, and the Gentiles: A Sociological Approach.* Monograph Series Society for New Testament Studies 56. Cambridge: Cambridge University Press, 1986.

Watts, Rikki E. *Isaiah's New Exodus in Mark.* Biblical Studies Library. Grand Rapids: Baker, 1997.

Weiss, Hans Friedrich. *Der Brief an die Hebräer.* Göttingen: Vandenhoeck & Ruprecht, 1991.

Whitlark, Jason A. *Enabling Fidelity to God: Perseverance in Hebrews in Light of the Reciprocity of the Ancient Mediterranean World.* Paternoster Biblical Monographs. Milton Keynes: Paternoster, 2008.

Wieland, George M. *The Significance of Salvation: A Study of Salvation Language in the Pastoral Epistles*. Milton Keynes: Paternoster, 2006.

Wilckens, Ulrich. "Was heisst bei Paulus: 'Aus Werken des Gesetzes wird kein Mensch gerecht'?" Pages 77-109 in *Rechtfertigung als Freiheit*. Neukirchen-Vluyn: Neukirchener Verlag, 1974.

Wild, Robert. "The Image of Paul in the Pastoral Letters." *The Bible Today* 23, no. 4 (1985): 239-45.

Wilson, Marcus. "Seneca's Epistles to Lucilius: A Reevaluation." Edited by John G. Fitch. Oxford: Oxford University Press, 2008.

Wilson, Marvin R. *Our Father Abraham: Jewish Roots of the Christian Faith*. Grand Rapids: Eerdmans, 1989.

Wilson, Walter. "Sin as Sex and Sex with Sin: The Anthropology of James 1:12-15." *Harvard Theological Review* 95 (2002): 147-68.

Windisch, Hans. *Der Sinn der Bergpredigt*. Wissenschaftliche Untersuchungen zum Neuen Testament 16. Leipzig: Hinrich, 1937.

Winston, David. "Philo's Ethical Theory." *ANRW* 21.1:372-416. Part 2, *Principat*, 21.1. Edited by H. Temporini and W. Haase. New York: De Gruyter, 1989.

Witherington, Ben. *A Socio-Rhetorical Commentary on 1-2 Peter*. Letters and Homilies for Hellenized Christians 11. Downers Grove, IL: IVP Academic, 2007.

Wolter, Michael. *Die Pastoralbriefe als Paulustradition*. Forschungen zur Religion und Literatur des Alten und Neuen Testaments 146. Göttingen: Vandenhoeck & Ruprecht, 1988.

Wright, N. T. *The New Testament and the People of God*. Minneapolis: Fortress, 1992..

———. "Romans and the Theology of Paul." Pages 30-67 in *Pauline Theology*, Volume III: *Romans*. Edited by David M. Hay and E. Elizabeth Johnson. Minneapolis: Fortress, 1995

Young, Frances. *The Theology of the Pastoral Letters*. Cambridge: Cambridge University Press, 1994.

Zeller, Deter. *Charis bei Philon und Paulus*. Stuttgarter Bibelstudien 142. Stuttgart: Verlag Katholisches Bibelwerk, 1990.

———. "The Life and Death of the Soul in Philo of Alexandria: The Use and Origin of a Metaphor." *Studia Philonica* 7 (1995): 19-55.

Ziesler, J. A. "The Transfiguration Story and the Markan Soteriology." *Expository Times* 81 (1970): 263-68.

Index of Ancient Sources

304